Corrs Lane

# FLAVOURS OF MELBOURNE

## FAVOURITE RESTAURANTS AND BARS IN MELBOURNE'S LANEWAYS AND ROOFTOPS

Published in 2011 by Smudge Books
www.smudgepub.com.au

Copyright © Text Daniele Wilton
Copyright © Photographs Brad Hill
Except those credited © Other Photographers

All rights reserved. No part of this publication may be reproduced, stored in a retrieval system or transmitted in any form by any means, electronic, mechanical, photocopying, recorded or otherwise, without the prior written permission of the publishers and copyright holders.

National Library of Australia
Cataloguing in Publication Data
George, Jonette 1955 -
Wilton, Daniele 1988 -
Flavours of Melbourne - Favourite restaurants and bars in Melbourne's laneways and rooftops.
Includes Index.

ISBN 978-0-9807891-8-8

* All photos by Brad Hill unless indicated

Front Cover
'My monsters' in Hosier Lane, Street Art
by Berlin based artist Mymo - 2010

# FLAVOURS OF MELBOURNE

## FAVOURITE RESTAURANTS AND BARS IN MELBOURNE'S LANEWAYS AND ROOFTOPS

Written, edited, designed and published by

Smudge Publishing

Jonette George & Daniele Wilton

Introduction - Rita Erlich

Photography - Brad Hill

# DISCOVER MELBOURNE WINE AND SUNRISE SEEN FROM A

THE SPIRIT OF THROUGH FOOD, AN UNEXPECTED OR SUNSET, LANEWAY OR ROOFTOP.

# FOREWORD

The story about today's ever-changing food scene in Melbourne needs to be told. Upstairs, downstairs and throughout the urban jungle, new-age chefs are emerging to meet the growing, sophisticated demand.

No longer is a simple coffee acceptable. Customers want the freshest, roasted coffee beans made in a myriad of ways. Americano, Black, Café a Lait, Café Breva, Café Latte, Café Macchiato, Cappuccino, Double Shot, Dry Cappuccino, Espresso Con Panna, Frappé, Greek Coffee, Turkish Coffee, Hammerhead, Shot in the Dark, Iced coffee, Indian (Madras) filtered coffee, Irish coffee, Kopi Tubruk, Lungo, Macchiato, Melya, Mocha, Oliang/Oleng, Ristretto... the list grows daily. Customers know their coffee like a sommelier his wine. And cafés are being judged according to the coffee they produce.

Breakfast, brunch and lunch menus are being scrutinised and inner city eateries provide the choice of walking or riding a bike to local, community hubs on the weekend. Newspapers flourish and neighbours catch up. Local gossip flies as the waiters and owners banter with clients about the week's affairs.

TV shows like Masterchef have given diners a belief that they know what they want on a menu, and how they want it served on their plates. Restaurants are under the spotlight and rightfully and wrongfully, being pulled up if any shortcomings are found. This new-found knowledge is having a positive affect - with people demanding fresh, seasonal produce and demonstrating they are willing to try new ingredients.

The fusion of east and west methods of cooking and ingredients has fawned a new style of cuisine - and the sky is the limit. Chefs are using their new freedom to express their creativity.... bartenders showing flair with the concoctions they mix.

Discover what goes on behind closed doors in Melbourne's laneway and rooftop restaurants and bars. You can even try out some of the signature recipes from our best chefs.

Laneways, rooftops, shabby and chic, the best of Melbourne's restaurants and bars are showcased in this book about the spirit of Melbourne, starting with some history of our ancient ancestors, the humble beginnings of the white settlers, the influence of multi cultures during the Gold Rush and the subsequent influx of citizens from far away lands. Stirring the pot and we showcase the diversity of food being served in an eclectic mix of venues today. The story takes the reader to the predictable revelation of why Melbourne is the food capital of Australia today.

Jonette George

VOTED THE MOST LIVABLE CITY IN THE WORLD, MELBOURNE COMES ALIVE AT NIGHT WHEN OFFICE WORKERS, CITY DWELLERS AND URBAN REVELLERS EXPLORE THE NOOKS AND CRANNIES OF THIS DISTINCTIVE TERROIR CALLED HOME.

# GETTING THE SPIN ON THE RUSH AND THE HIGH LIFE OF MELBOURNE

# AN INTRODUCTION BY RITA ERLICH

Rita Erlich, who was named a legend in the 2010 Melbourne Food and Wine Festival, loves her city - and its food and wine. She writes about food in all its aspects - reviewing restaurants, writing recipes, food history, tourism and nutrition - as well as judging and advisory work in the hospitality industry.

Rita is the author of many books, including "More Than French: Recipes & Stories with leading chef, Philippe Mouchel". She is also the editor of "50 Fabulous Chocolate Cakes". When she is not cooking, eating or drinking, Rita listens to music, spends time tending the garden, and travels widely. She has hosted food and wine tours in Italy, Portugal and France.

Call it the Hoddle factor: without him, we might not have had all our laneways. The grid pattern for the city established by surveyor Robert Hoddle in 1837 set the scene for the development of Melbourne. That straightforward grid, with narrower streets providing right of way for the broader main streets, was endlessly divided up into smaller and smaller subdivisions as the city grew – and the subdivisions required access lanes and thoroughfares. And so, from the mid-1850s, Melbourne built the laneways that now give the city its character. If the main streets are the skeleton of Melbourne, the laneways are its ligaments, veins and arteries.

They've gone through some hard times, these laneways. They have been slums and scary places, some of them have been built over, others have been threatened with redevelopment. But they've come through to find a vigorous new life in the 21st century.

They're not all easy to find. The major ones are simple: Flinders Lane, which is actually a street, runs the length of the city between Flinders Street and Collins Street. At its eastern end, it used to be the centre of the rag trade, then it turned to art galleries and food. It is now an eating street. You could spend weeks just exploring the cafés and restaurants in and off Flinders Lane. Some of Melbourne's best restaurants are here: Verge, Cumulus, Cecconi's Cantina, Ezard on Flinders Lane. Move a few steps off the street and there's the richness of more choice - The Italian (inside 101 Collins Street, and accessed only from Flinders Lane at night), Coda (technically Flinders Lane, but the entrance is off Oliver Lane. Movida is in Hosier Lane. And those are only some of the options.

Further along Flinders Lane are more treats off to the side: Degraves Street, entirely filled with people at tables, and Centre Place, filled with mini-businesses. On the Lane itself are bigger places – restaurants like Bluestone and Hako.

The pattern is repeated all through the city area. Each dividing street has its own identity: Chinatown in Little Bourke Street, the hip and chic places in Little Collins Street. Every city block is dissected by lanes that yield cafes, bars, and restaurants.

The names are often confusing, it is true. Melbourne Place sounds like something major, but is a tiny laneway that is home to one of the men's clubs and St Peter's seafood restaurant. Liverpool Street is only a connecting laneway between Bourke and Little Bourke Street, with a number of good small Asian eating places. Bond

Street, which sounds very grand to anyone who knows London, turns out to be a small alley with Maha, a modern Middle Eastern restaurant.

There are lanes and alleys named for people (Oliver, Crossley), and for lost landmarks. There are lanes that give their name to a restaurant: Punch and Gills, for example. Market Lane recalls the Eastern Market that once stood on Bourke Street. But who wouldn't head into Equitable Place? Or the beautifully named Celestial Avenue? That's not an avenue at all, but an alleyway.

Nowhere is so small or so narrow that it cannot include good places for meeting, eating, and drinking.

Melburnians love hidden places, the less obvious treats. That's one of the attractions of the arcades, like Block and Howey Place, off the main streets – and their architecture is the other drawcard, of course.

But so much do we love the hidden that many newer restaurants seem to be built to be hard to find, and hard to see. Who would know that the restaurant and the bar at Seamstress on Lonsdale Street (named for a former life as a garment factory) are upstairs? The modern Japanese restaurant Izakaya Den is technically on Russell Street, but there's no indication from the street that there is a restaurant further down the stairs that lead to the clothing store. Tiny Von Haus, named for Eugene von Guerard, is identifiable only by a little sign above the Crossley Street doorway. Those with lively appetites have to keep their eyes and ears open.

It also pays to have a sense of smell. Follow the scent of coffee (one of Melbourne's favourite scents), or the rich aromas of long-cooked dishes down sidestreets, into arcades, along alleyways. There will always be a reward.

But perhaps, since they have all been discovered, laneways have become mainstream. What's next? Look up! What do you see? Nothing from the street. And that's one of the charms of rooftop spaces. Not the only charm, of course: rooftop bars and cafes are a way of making the best of a space otherwise ignored, a way of breathing fresh air in the centre of the city. Robert Hoddle couldn't have even imagined it all way back in 1837, when he laid out the plans for Melbourne.

It's a good thing we live now, not then.

# CONTENTS

| | |
|---|---|
| An Introduction | 16 |
| Our Ancestors | 28 |
| Historical Timeline | 30 |
| Today | 33 |
| The Grid | 34 |
| Laneways Story | 36 |
| Melbourne Today | 38 |
| Melbourne Map | 40 |
| Street Art | 42 |
| STREAT | 46 |
| Laneways | 54 |
| Recipes | 342 |
| Index | 388 |

Centre Place

# LANEWAYS

| | | | | | |
|---|---|---|---|---|---|
| ACDC Lane | 66 | Exhibition St | 170 | Postal Lane | 268 |
| Artemis Lane | 72 | Federation Square | 176 | Queen St | 274 |
| Bank Place | 80 | Flinders Lane | 184 | Rainbow Alley | 282 |
| Bligh Place | 88 | George Pde | 196 | Rakaia Way | 288 |
| Block Arcade | 94 | Highlander Lane | 202 | Rebecca Walk | 294 |
| Bourke St | 100 | Hosier Lane | 208 | Russell St | 300 |
| Centre Place | 122 | Little Bourke St | 214 | Scott Alley | 310 |
| Chinatown | 128 | Little Collins St | 222 | Tattersalls Lane | 316 |
| Collins St | 134 | Little Lonsdale St | 230 | Waratah Place | 322 |
| Corrs Lane | 142 | Lonsdale St | 236 | Warburton Lane | 328 |
| Croft Alley | 148 | McKillop St | 248 | Yarra Footbridge | 336 |
| Curtin House | 154 | Meyers Place | 254 | | |
| Drewery Lane | 164 | Pink Alley | 262 | | |

# RECIPES

**Entrée**

| | |
|---|---|
| Calamari with Chickpeas & Radichio – Grossi Grill | 344 |
| Galician Octopus – Portello Rosso | 346 |
| Spicy Tuna Tataki – Izakaya Den | 348 |
| Pork Belly – Red Spice Road | 350 |
| Chicken Liver Parfait – Collins Quarter | 352 |
| Cambodian Amok – Bopha Devi | 354 |
| Pork & Peanut Tapioca Dumplings – Cookie | 356 |
| Cured Ocean Trout – Syracuse Restaurant | 358 |

**Main**

| | |
|---|---|
| Risotto Venere – Grossi Florentino | 360 |
| Braised Pork Belly – Seamstress | 362 |
| Trio of Rabbit – Caterina's Cucina e Bar | 364 |
| Shake Oyako Don – Chocolate Buddha | 366 |
| Tortellini Di Zucca – Grossi Cellar | 368 |
| Roasted Rack of Lamb – Ca de Vin | 370 |
| Baccala Alla Livornese – Merchant | 372 |
| Almond Crusted Lamb Rack – Terra Rossa | 374 |

**Dessert**

| | |
|---|---|
| Rhubarb & Custard Tart – Punch Lane | 376 |
| Pavlova – Hopetoun Tea Rooms | 378 |
| Strawberry & Berry Almond Tart – Le Petit Gateau | 380 |
| Chocolate Bread & Butter Pudding – Self Preservation | 382 |

Duck Duck Goose

"THAT'S WHAT I SAY ABOUT RESTAURANTS - THE BACK PART IS MANUFACTURING, THE FRONT PART IS RETAILING, THE THEATRE IS WHAT HOLDS THE WHOLE THING TOGETHER."

TERENCE CONRAN

DOWN A MELBOURNE
LANEWAY THROUGH AN
OPEN DOOR
I SMELL A COFFEE
BREWING, AND
FOOD NOT SEEN BEFORE.

TODAY I FIND THE BEAUTY
IN GRIMY, BRICKED UP
WALLS, PAINTED OVER
WITH MURALS
UNTIL THE COUNCIL CALLS.

THESE HISTORIC ALLEYS
ONCE DIVES FOR CRIMS &
THIEVES, TODAY THEY ARE
CELEBRATED LIKE GOLDEN,
AUTUMN LEAVES.

JONETTE

Cnr Exhibition & Collins Streets

# OUR TRIBAL ANCESTORS

Our ancient ancestors, the Australian Aborigines, are the oldest living culture in the world. We know they lived here for at least 68,000 years before white man arrived. In fact, in 2005, archaeologists found the endocast of a primitive, hominid-like skull dating back 7 million years in Bega, NSW, suggesting that our Aboriginal people may have been preceded on this continent by earlier races.

Australian Aboriginal culture must be seen and protected as a national treasure. Although we have struggled to live side by side since white settlers arrived in Australia, we would have done well to learn their ways rather than obliterate them. Centuries of living on this land they revered led to a nomadic lifestyle, following the seasons for the best, food cycles and shelter from the changing climate. Each clan had a defined area to hunt and gather, allowing free reign in their territory and minimal disputes.

The Kulin nation was an alliance of five aboriginal, language groups living in Central Victoria, on land stretching from Melbourne to Port Phillip and Western Port Bays. The tribes – Wurundjeri, Boon Wurrung, Wathaurong, Taungerong and Jaara - shared a similar language, customs, traditions, burial rights and enjoyed very strong trading links.

Stories passed down through centuries of song, dance and painting tell stories of tribes walking all the way to Tasmania when sea levels were much lower and the bay was dry. In those days, the Yarra River, known as "Birrarung", passed through kilometres of grassy hunting grounds, southward to the ocean. There was a narrow, walking track, which allowed access all the way to Tasmania.

### Bunjil, the Eagle

Many customs and ancestral gods were unique to different aboriginal nations. The Kulin nation believed in "Bunjil, the Eagle" who according to their legend, created their land. And land was a core piece of aboriginal spirituality. They believe that the land is their "Mother" and should be respected as such. They believed that one should "only take away what you can give back".

One legend that is passed down tells of a time when the Kulin nations were fighting amongst themselves, and a period of chaos reigned. The land became neglected and the sea became angry and started to rise. The river flooded and started to stretch over the grassy plains until they were covered, to become what is today Port Phillip Bay.

The story tells that the various clans became frightened and asked their spiritual creator, Bunjil, to stop the sea from rising. Bunjil told them that they had to stop their fighting and change their ways if they wanted to save their land. They agreed to follow Bunjil's teachings about respect for the land, their people and his other creations, and to obey his laws. Bunjil then walked out to the sea, raised his spear and directed the sea to stop rising further.

Archaeological evidence shows that the bay was flooded somewhere around eight to ten thousand years ago, and the aboriginal story may be one of the first recorded instances of a tsunami in the world.

Water played an important role in tribal life. Not only the source for everyday drinking water, it also provided many foods for a diet which was rich and plentiful. The river and the ocean provided fish, shellfish, turtles, seals and eels. The fertile land around the river and numerous swamps provided edible native plants. There were many animals to be hunted, gathered and cooked in century-old traditional methods, including kangaroos, possums, goannas, lizards, rats, wombats, birds and their eggs, insects and snakes.

With efficient and sustainable systems for living off the land, the aboriginal people achieved a balanced diet by hunting and gathering and moving seasonally between camps, as food supplies dictated. They demonstrated a highly developed connection with the land and followed their creator, Bunjil's laws to respect and look after the earth.

### Traditional Cooking

Traditional recipes and methods for cooking food were passed down the centuries from generation to generation. Game such as kangaroo was often cooked by first singeing the fur on an open fire until the carcass started to swell. The skin would then be removed, the animal gutted, and any remains of fur scraped off with a sharp implement. By this time the fire would be a bed of hot coals and the carcass would be buried and cooked slowly until ready.

Fish and turtles would be cooked on the open coals, while shellfish was cooked briefly at the side of a fire. As soon as the shellfish contents started to froth, they were removed from the heat. This method prevented the shellfish being overcooked and tough.

Local bush and tree seeds were pounded into dough to make damper, bread and even a type of cake, and then baked in the ashes of carefully selected wood. Often damper or goanna would be placed on the hot ground beneath the ashes and covered with more ash to cook. A scooped out hollow was then made to cook yams and other small vegetables by covering them with a further layer of ash and coals.

Numerous plants such as the Bidgee Widgee, the Chocolate and Vanilla Lilies, various Banksias, native leeks, native orchids, the salt bush, sedges and tetragonia were used as foods and medicines.

### William Buckley

The first white people to be seen by the Wathaurong were most likely members of Matthew Flinder's party surveying the district in 1802. William Buckley, a convict who escaped from a penal settlement in Sorrento in 1803, made his way around Port Phillip Bay and ended up living with the Wathaurong people for 32 years.

Buckley was able to tell many stories of tribal life, history and customs when he eventually met up with white settlers again in Melbourne. In 1836 he was given the job of interpreter to the aboriginal people, and he was party to the original "treaty" signed by members of a Tasmaniana consortium, including John Batman and Joseph Gellibrand. This group met up with Wurundjeri elders and, with Buckley's help bartered for the rental of land around Port Phillip, near the present site of the city of Melbourne. The document came to be known as "Batman's Treaty" and is also considered significant as it was the first and only documented time when Europeans negotiated their presence and occupation of Aboriginal lands directly with the traditional owners. However, the Treaty was declared nul and void by the Governor of New South Wales, Richard Bourke, stating that the natives had no claim to theland and it was "owned" by the crown.

Thousands of years of tradition was set to change forever with the arrival of white settlers. The rapid decline in numbers was due to many factors, including the introduction of new diseases, loss of access to traditional foods and tribal lands, alcoholism, death in gaol and death through poisoning and murder.

*Photography - Garry Radler

Melbourne 1837: Painted by Joseph Anderson Panton 1831-1913. The painting shows Captain Lonsdale's wattle and daub residence near the present-day corner of Bourke and Spencer streets. Mrs. Lonsdale is feeding poultry in front. Governor Bourke and his aide-de-camp, Captain Westmacott, can be seen walking under the umbrella behind the house, John Batman is visible to the left of the residence standing next to Captain Hobson and a group of Aboriginal people, Mt. Macedon can be seen in the background. William Buckley and a group of aboriginal people. The tall figure standing to the far left of the group is William Buckley, the absconder from the Sorrento settlement of 1803-04, who lived with Aboriginal people for many years until identifying himself to John Batman at Indented Head in 1835. From The State Library of Victoria collection.

# MELBOURNE'S HISTORICAL TIMELINE

**1797** Surgeon and explorer, George Bass, explored the South-east coast of Victoria, leaving a glowing report about its potential.

**1803** In 1803 Melbourne was declared to be "totally unfit for the purpose of settlement" by Lt. Governor David Collins, who was sent there to check its suitability as a convict settlement. He only sails inside the heads and settles in Sorrento for 1 year. He moves to Tasmania.

**1835** John Batman, one of a group of Van Diemen's Land (Tasmanian) investors and pastoralists, visited to search for good pastoral land. He claimed to have bought 240,000 ha from the Woi wurrung people.

**1835** Melbourne is founded by two consortiums of Tasmanians, John Batman and John Pascoe Fawkner.

**1837** General Sir Richard Bourke, governor of the NSW colony, took possession of the land of Melbourne in the name the crown and sold it at public auction. Bourke sent government surveyors Robert Hoddle and Robert Russell to plan the town. Their grid model endures today as the framework on which Melbourne is based. This pattern of wide and elegant streets was named after the British kings and queens in one direction and of the key players and friends of the Governor in the other.

**1838** Melbourne is declared a legal port and administrative centre, opening the way for vastly increased immigration.

**1840** The Depression in England begins, wool prices drop.

**1847** Melbourne declared a city by Queen Victoria on 25 June.

**1850** Population grew to 23,000 with immigrants from United Kingdom.

**1850** Beginning of the Victorian gold rush with discovery of gold at Buninyong. Over the next 10 years, Victoria produced 20 million ounces of gold which was one third of the world's total.

**1850** 80 named laneways.

**1851** A period of huge population growth and prosperity as immigrants arrived from all over the world to search for gold.

**1855** William Haines became Victoria's first premier when parliament was formed.

**1857** Queen Victoria Market was founded.

**1861** First Melbourne Cup, an annual thoroughbred horse race, ran for the first time and later became one of the world's most prestigious racing events.

**1880** Melbourne was given the title 'Marvellous Melbourne', and boasted a city that rivalled the great cities of Europe and North America.

**1885** First cable tram - running from the city centre to Richmond, later to be replaced by electric tram services.

**1894** City streets first lit by electric lighting.

**1914** Myer Bourke Street was the second largest department store in the world.

**1916** Introduction of 6:00pm closing for all hotels.

**1927** Australia's capital was transferred from Melbourne to Canberra - a fully planned and purpose-built city.

**1946** Television begins in Australia.

**1956** Australia converts from pounds, shillings and pence to decimal currency.

**1967** Australian Prime Minister Harold Holt disappeared, presumed drowned, while swimming at Cheviot Beach near Portsea on Victoria's Mornington Peninsula.

**1975** 16 February - Ash Wednesday fires occur.

**1986** Rialto Towers completed and becomes the city's tallest building as well as the tallest in the southern hemisphere.

**1986** Hoddle Street Massacre, killing 7 and injuring 19.

**1987** Queen Street Massacre, killing 8 and injuring 5.

**1992** Melbourne wins right to host Australian Grand Prix at Albert Park Lake.

**1996** Bolte Bridge open for traffic.

**2006** Victorian bushfires around Melbourne - worst fires in the history of the city

**2009** Melbourne Celebrates it's 175th Birthday

**2011** Melbourne voted the World's most liveable city

Photos from the State Library of Victoria Collection

1. Bourke Street 1907
2. Flinders Lane: Charles Nettleton 1826-1902, ; Date(s): [ca. 1875]. Looks East up Flinders Lane from Elizabeth Street, towards Russell Street. Shows the business premises for Thomas Cooper, wine-merchant and Vice-Consul for Portugal, J. Schofield, soft goods broker at 3 Little Flinders Street East, Paterson, Ray, Palmer & Co., importers and warehousemen, 13-15 Little Flinders Street East, and other similar premises.
3. Collins Street circa 1912. Painted by George Hyde Pownall 1876-1932
4. Bank Place, 1974. Photo taken by K.J. Halla.

Opposite page:

In the 1870's, wine merchants, Bligh and Harbottle, started to utilise Bligh Place next to their premises in Flinders Lane. During their time in business they registered with the Victorian Patents Office at the Melbourne Town Hall for the copyright of the printed black and white wine label, showing a spotted grey hound's head and neck, with text reading: "Australian Wine / Ettamogah Red / Albury / N.S.W." From The State Library of Victoria collection.

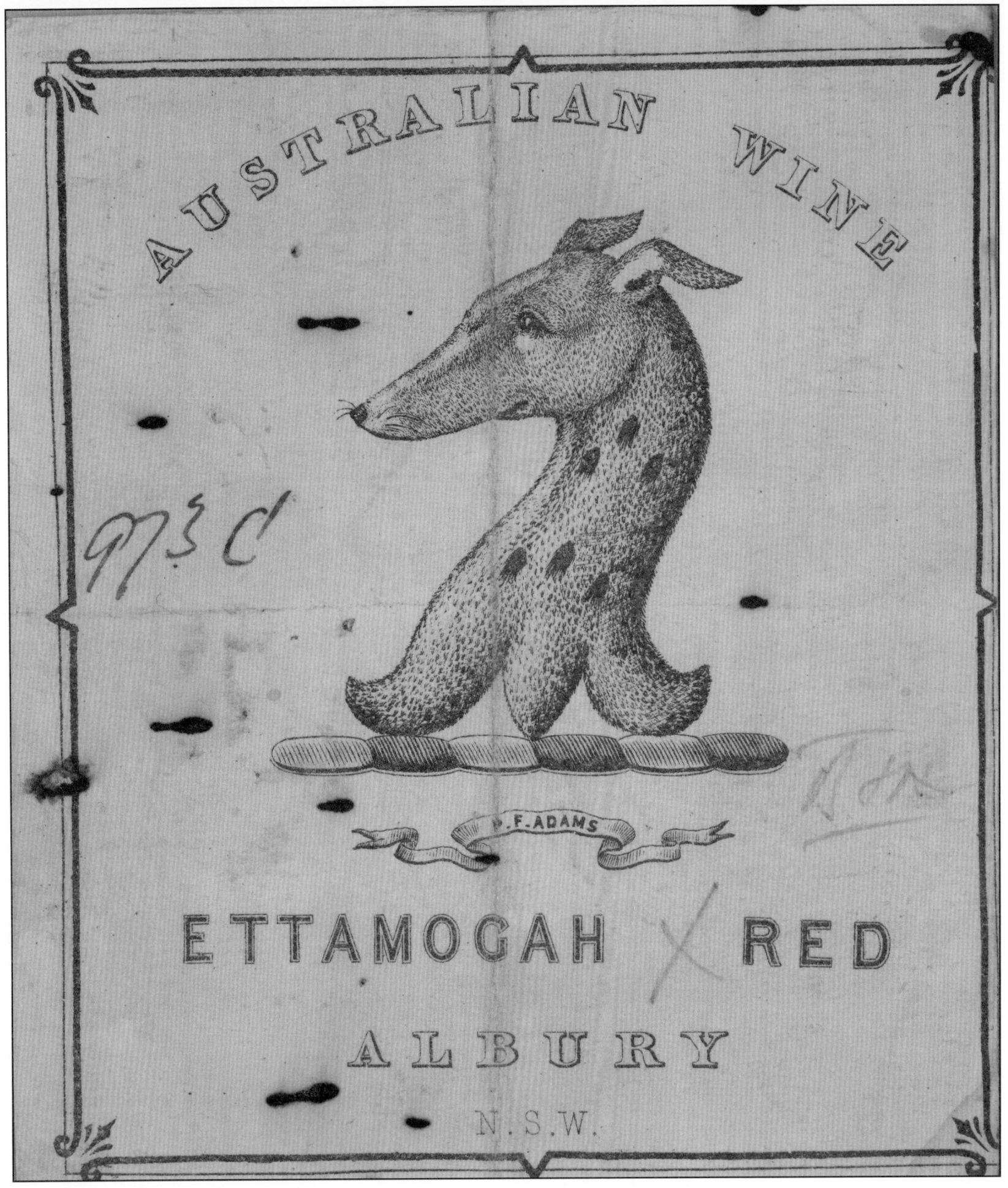

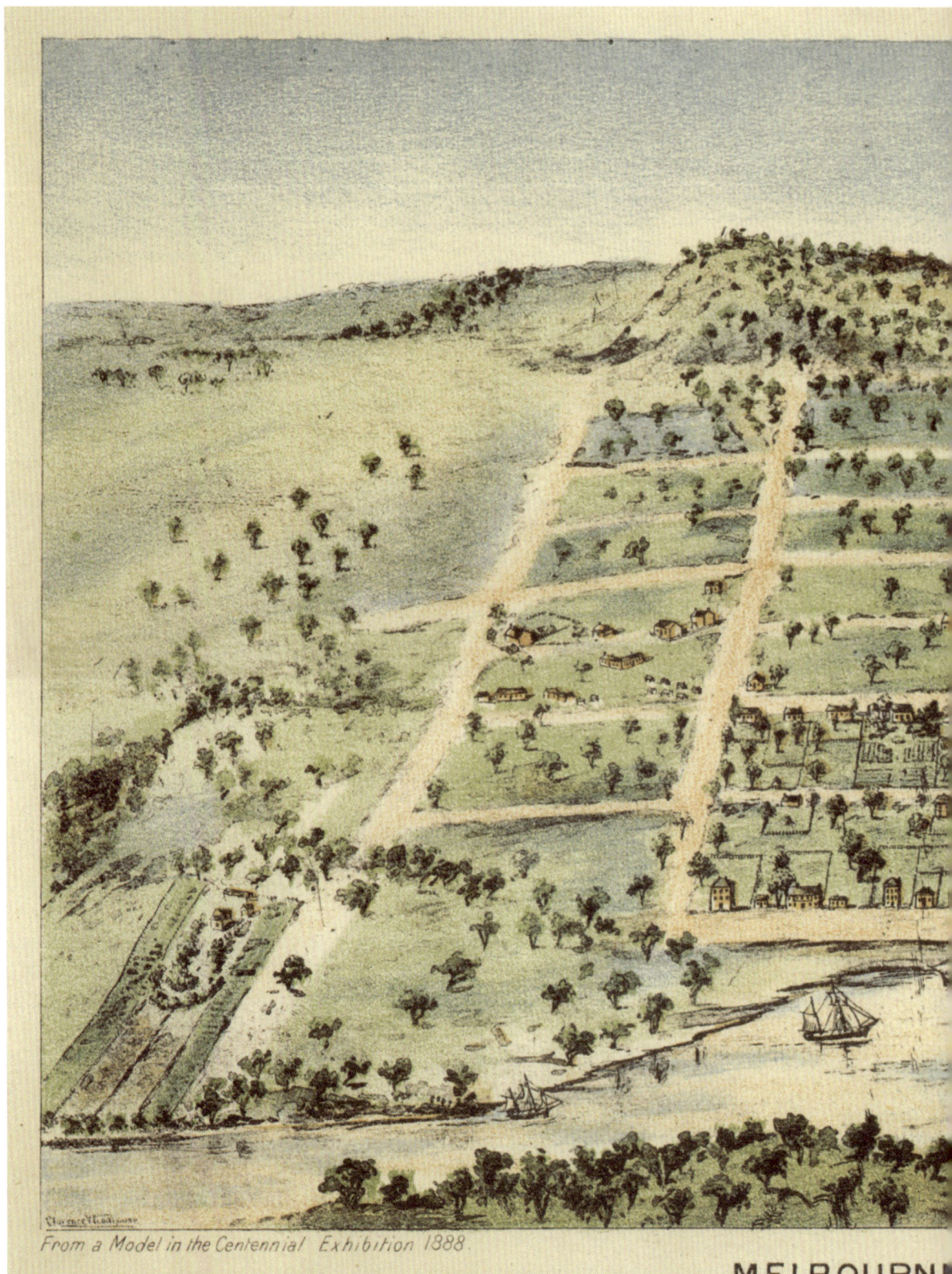

Colour lithograph signed by artist, Clarence Woodhouse (1852 - 1931). Inscribed below image: From a model in the Centennial Exhibition 1888. Also inscribed below image: Prepared for the City Council by Monsieur Drouhet. From The State Library of Victoria collection.

# 1837 HODDLE'S GRID

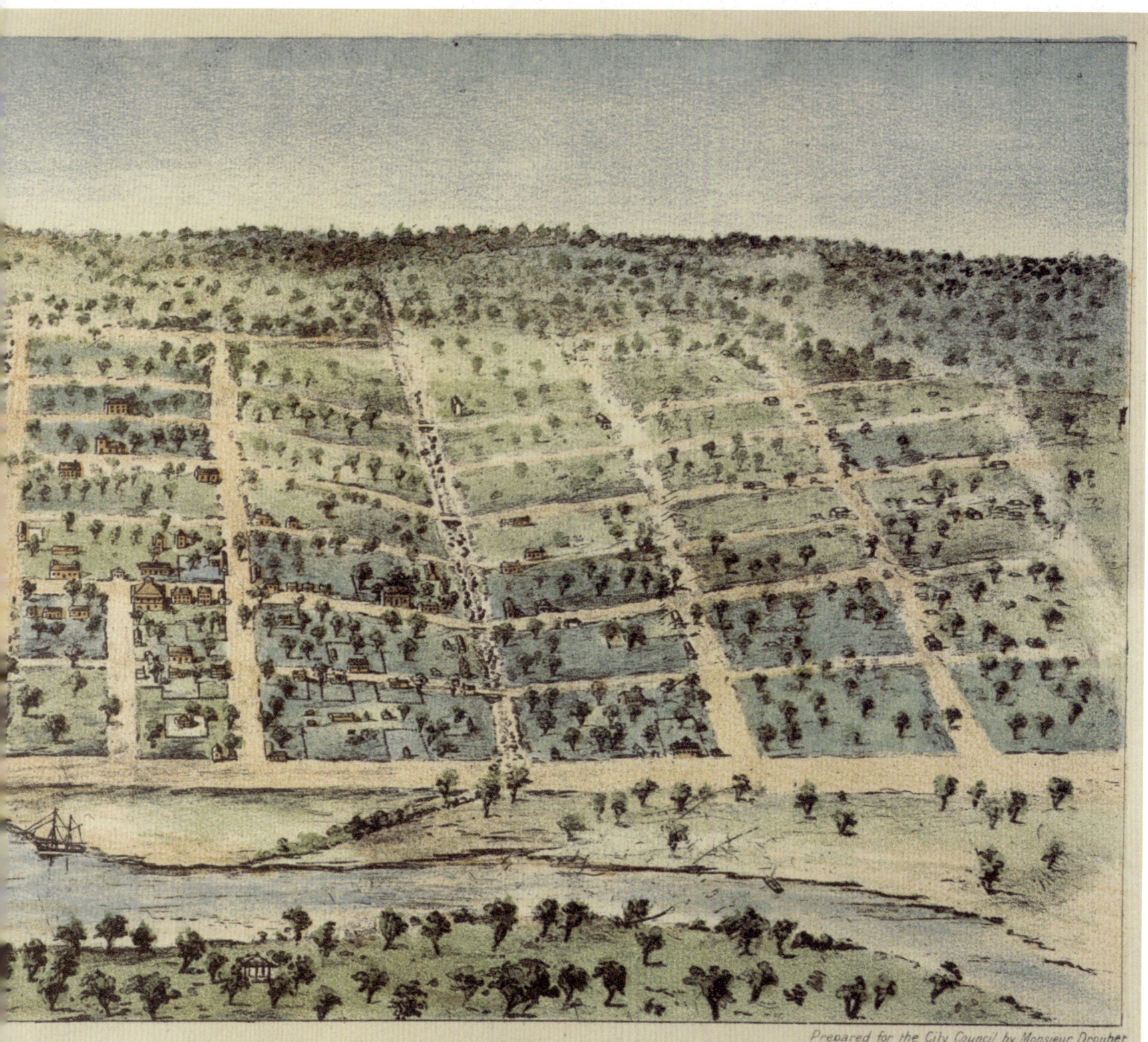

1838, FROM THE YARRA YARRA.

Prepared for the City Council by Monsieur Drouhet

# MELBOURNE'S LANEWAY STORY

When Robert Hoddle designed Melbourne in 1837, he had no idea that in 180 years the city would be named "The Most Liveable City in the World".

His foresight in creating wide, elegant streets generated a footprint that has allowed the overlay of a 21st Century, modern city to emerge from its design. His grid-pattern of 30-feet-wide, elegant streets was designed to allow horse-drawn vehicles and bullock carts to move through the city without obstructing each other. He was also an advocate of good ventilation in towns, to minimise contamination and the spread of disease.

Today the wide streets allow the usage of bicycles, cars and trams with double lanes and plenty of parking, without losing the integrity of the original infrastructure or the city's historical buildings.

Although Hoddle built "little" streets to service the major streets, he didn't take into account the need for back lanes and alleys to provide warehouses and factories with a service or rear entry.

However a proliferation of lanes and alleys grew naturally as required and by the 1850's, there were 80 named lanes and 112 right-of-ways throughout the city of Melbourne. By 1895, there were signposts on 158 lanes.

Lanes were not officially named, instead they grew their own names after the nearest business, factory, landowner or significant entity, purely to help identify and find each location. Many of those names are still in use today.

Rear entries were critical for the collection of night soil, delivery of goods and removal of rubbish. However, being poorly lit, they often became improvised toilet stops and smelt, by day, of urine. Shadowy deals were often done in these back-streets and the red-light district proliferated from back-lane addresses.

In the early 20th Century, laneways were associated with crime, and were avoided especially at night. It wasn't until the late 20th Century that the laneways were recognised for their historical significance. Melbourne City Council started an upgrade laying down bluestone paving and providing lighting and street furniture.

At the same time, street art was emerging, and laneways were being painted with what has become one of the city's major tourist attractions, its street art. The laneways became cool places to hang out and cafés, bars and other small enterprises started to spring up.

Today, Melbourne's lanes and alleys are recognised for their heritage and artistic value, and space in old warehouses, shops and pubs have been taken up by quirky bars, cafés, restaurants, galleries and boutiques.

Take an exciting adventure and get lost down Melbourne's myriad of laneways, alleys and arcades….

You may lose yourself, but discover a whole new you!

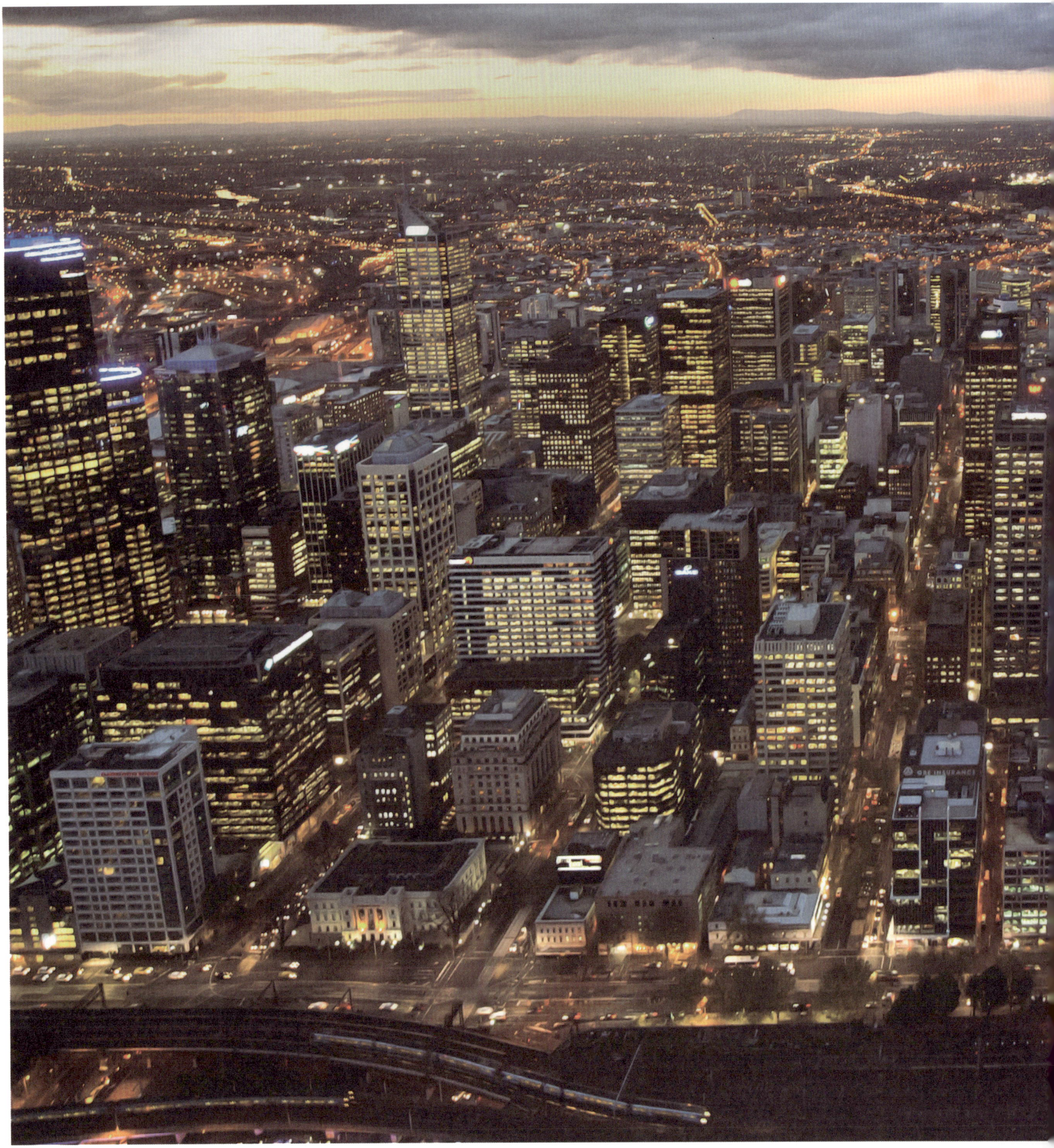

# MELBOURNE TODAY

Flagstaff Gardens
La Trobe St
Little Lonsdale
Lonsdale St
Little Bourke St
Bourke St
Little Collins St
Collins St
Flinders La
Flinde
Spencer St
Docklands Drive
Rakaia Way
Newquay Promenade
Waterfront City
Central Pier
Etihad Stadium
Victoria Harbour
Docklands Park

Refer to larger maps on each Laneway page.

# STREET ART

Melbourne is rapidly being recognised for having some of the best street art in the world. The city boasts both local and international artists "instilled" in the most unexpected places - down laneways, up stairwells, on rooftops, in pubs, basement car parks and even through pedestrian underpasses. A variety of walls, doors, nooks and crannies are canvases for a diverse range of artwork, which can all be enjoyed at our leisure. The quirky thing about street art is that today you may find it, but tomorrow it may be gone – painted over, vanished, or with a totally new work of art on display.

Navigating Melbourne's secretive art scene requires some insider knowledge of the many laneways that proudly display our most talented artists. One of the pioneers of Melbourne's street art movement is Andrew Mac, a Victorian College of the Arts graduate who turned abandoned shopfronts in Centre Place into a laneway gallery in the early 1990's. In 1996 he established the "Citylights Project", a 24 hour lightbox gallery in a dead-end alley off Centre Place. In 1998, he launched a second lightbox gallery in Hosier Lane, possibly today's most renowned laneway for street art. Each month or so, a series of printed artworks are featured in illuminated box frames and can be viewed 24/7.

For centuries, people have left their "mark" on walls, signs, trains, trees…. and today is no different. Melbourne's crew of innovative artists are spraying, pasting or stencilling on what they see as a blank canvas and many are being commissioned to decorate bare walls. Unfortunately the artistic talent of a few leaves a lot to be desired, and their work can only be seen as destructive. Of course, there will always be delinquents damaging our earth and the ugly art of "tagging" is illegal everywhere in Melbourne.

However, from newfound blank canvases, a unique style of art has emerged. Today's street artist will take his place in history as a radical who started a new movement in art. What began as mere graffiti which upset local councils and home-owners, has become public art which can be viewed indoors and out.

Historically, the beginnings of art, music or other creative movements began by upsetting tradition. The shock factor creates a lot of noise, and gives the "revolutionaries" the attention they are seeking. Classical music took a twist in the 1780's when Mozart, Haydn and Bach "revolutionised" the music of the time. The 1960's saw another revolution when "The Beatles" hit the music waves, and gave momentum to another generation of revolutionaries.

Now I see a new art movement, shifting from traditional art forms in studios and galleries to finding fresh ways to present their artistic talents. Melbourne's street art is creative, colourful and artistic. The dull brick and steel structures of yesterday's architects are being revived with vibrant artwork.

This art form has no boundaries and is open to the public for comment. Many councils have still not taken on board the fact that street art is an art form, but the City of Melbourne has embraced it. This community respect is quite unique and revolutionary in itself.

One couldn't write a piece on Melbourne's street art without mentioning the infamous English street artist, Banksy, who visited Melbourne in 2003 and painted various pieces in hidden laneway locations. There was public outcry when one of his works was vandalised and another, inadvertently "cleaned" by council workers. The ensuing publicity possibly created the necessary shift in Melbourne mainstream's view of street art. It created a lot of discussion and made locals realise what works of art were sitting in their back yard. The cultural capital of Australia has acknowledged the artists and their work, and street art is now promoted as one of the city's tourist attractions.

Melbourne City Council has introduced a permit system that gives building owners permission to display graffiti works. The council has differentiated between street art and tagging, and hence allowed this new form of art to blossom.

Meyers Place

# STREET ART

Banksy's "Little Diver", which was vandalised in 1998, has resurfaced in Cocker Alley. Street artist, Phoenix went to great lengths to bring this little girl back to life. Phoenix said, "This collage wall application restored parts of the original lost beneath the vandals' paint but preserves the other parts still visible. It was created by enlarging photos of the original work, obtained from the internet, and the vandalised one - using a photocopier. Two life-size mockups were made, which were then placed together on a light-table and a tracing made of the areas covered by paint. Cut out the tracing - and you have a pasting ready to bring the Little Diver girl back to the surface".

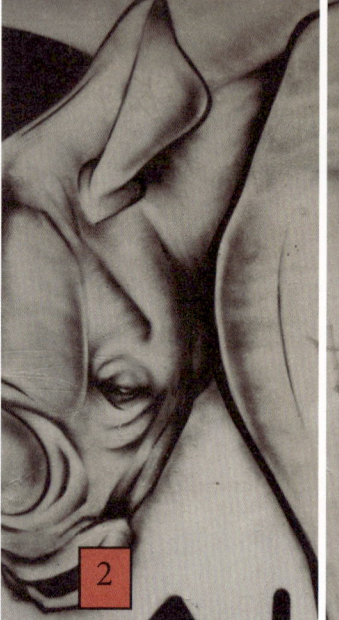

1. Zevenboom Lane

2. Finlay Lane

3. Finlay Lane

4. Caledonian Lane

5. Caledonian Lane

6. Drewery Lane

7. Croft Alley

8. Finlay Lane

STREAT

# STOP HOMELESSNESS THE DELICIOUS WAY

# STREAT

## STOP HOMELESSNESS THE DELICIOUS WAY

100 million young people live or work on the world's streets. If you find this hard to swallow, use one of your life's 80,000 meals to make this stop by eating with STREAT.

What is STREAT?

STREAT is a social enterprise providing Melbourne's homeless youth with a supported pathway to long-term careers in the hospitality industry. These days the line between public, private, and non-profit are beginning to blur.

STREAT sees social enterprise as one of the new ways that this is happening. By running street cafes in Melbourne, homeless youth get their hospitality training - by learning hygiene, kitchen etiquette, how to cook, how to follow a recipe, how to run a street stall - ultimately acquiring the skills they will need to enter the hospitality industry.

A food and coffee cart is located in Melbourne University. Their food is inspired by street hawker food from around the world. Another coffee cart is in Melbourne Central.

Take a moment to share a taco or enjoy a coffee, and give back to our homeless children of the streets. The trainees in the program haven't been living on the streets, they've been existing on them.

As a social enterprise, STREAT believes in delivering social outcomes, but be highly focused on generating profit to do this. And unlike a community enterprise where the general community owns and runs the organisation, STREAT is run by a social entrepreneur who reports to a board that has some community representation. On a spectrum of activities, STREAT is placed further towards the business end than many other community or social enterprises in the sector. They are dedicated to maximising their social footprint, while minimising their environmental one.

STREAT
RECLAIMS STREET SPACE
MAKES IT SOCIALLY INCLUSIVE.
MAKES IT DELICIOUS.
MAKES IT VIBRANT.
MAKES IT WORTH LIVING ON.
IT'S YOUR STREET TOO.
WALK IT...  WATCH IT...
PLAY IT...  CYCLE IT...  PARTY IT...
SCOOT IT...  GARDEN IT...
SKATE IT...  HOP IT...  SING IT...
DANCE IT...  CREATE IT...
DRAW IT...  EAT IT...
LIVE ON IT.

Rebecca Scott, cofounder of STREAT with Kate Farrell, says "At STREAT we see the planet as an equal partner in our programs and strive for environmental sustainability through all aspects of our operations – including our supply chain, building premises, food service operations, transport and travel, and training programs".

STREAT's training curriculum and street café menu also take an eco-gastronomic perspective. In-house chef and trainer, Rob Auger is a chef with over 10 years experience cooking in various countries around the world.

He has worked at Glaze and 312, before turning to training in hospitality and commercial cookery. He says he is excited about the challenge of combining his passion for cooking with training young homeless trainees.

Rob says he took on the role with STREAT because, "I can't reconcile proclamations such as "land of the fair go" with the fact that as a society, we're not doing enough to ensure that all of our young people have an equal starting point.

He says, "I see our food as a fusion of the best of slow food and fast food. Food that's fresh, tasty, healthy, fair, cultural but also served quickly, can be eaten on the run and great value".

"But most importantly, it's food that helps someone else!

50

"ONE OF THE VERY NICEST THINGS ABOUT LIFE, IS THE WAY WE MUST REGULARLY STOP WHATEVER IT IS WE ARE DOING, AND DEVOTE OUR ATTENTION TO EATING."
LUCIANO PAVAROTTI & WILLIAM WRIGHT, "PAVAROTTI, MY OWN STORY".

**THERE IS THIS OLD MAN SITTING NEXT TO ME, MAKING LOVE TO HIS TONIC AND GIN.**

Roulle Galette

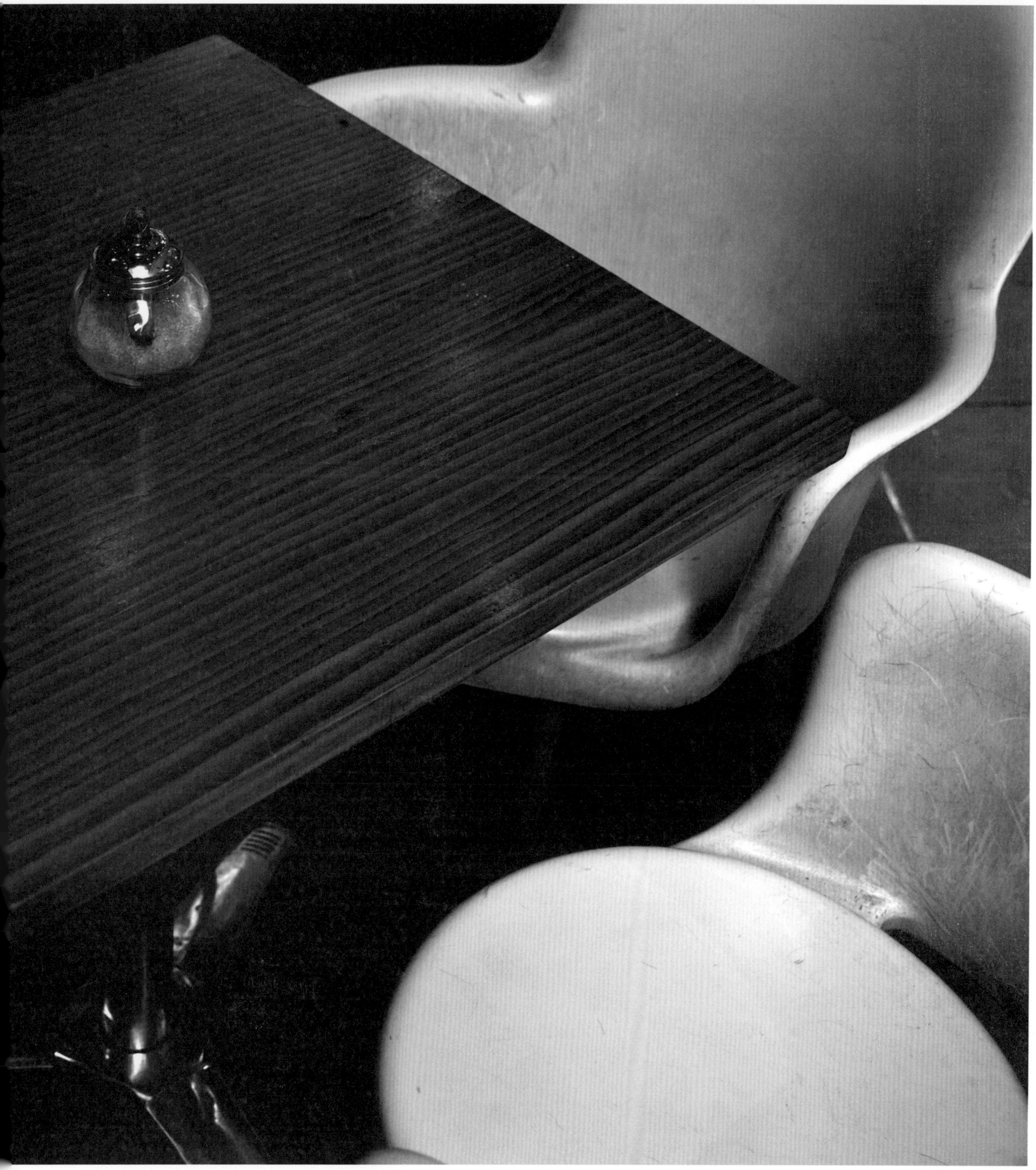

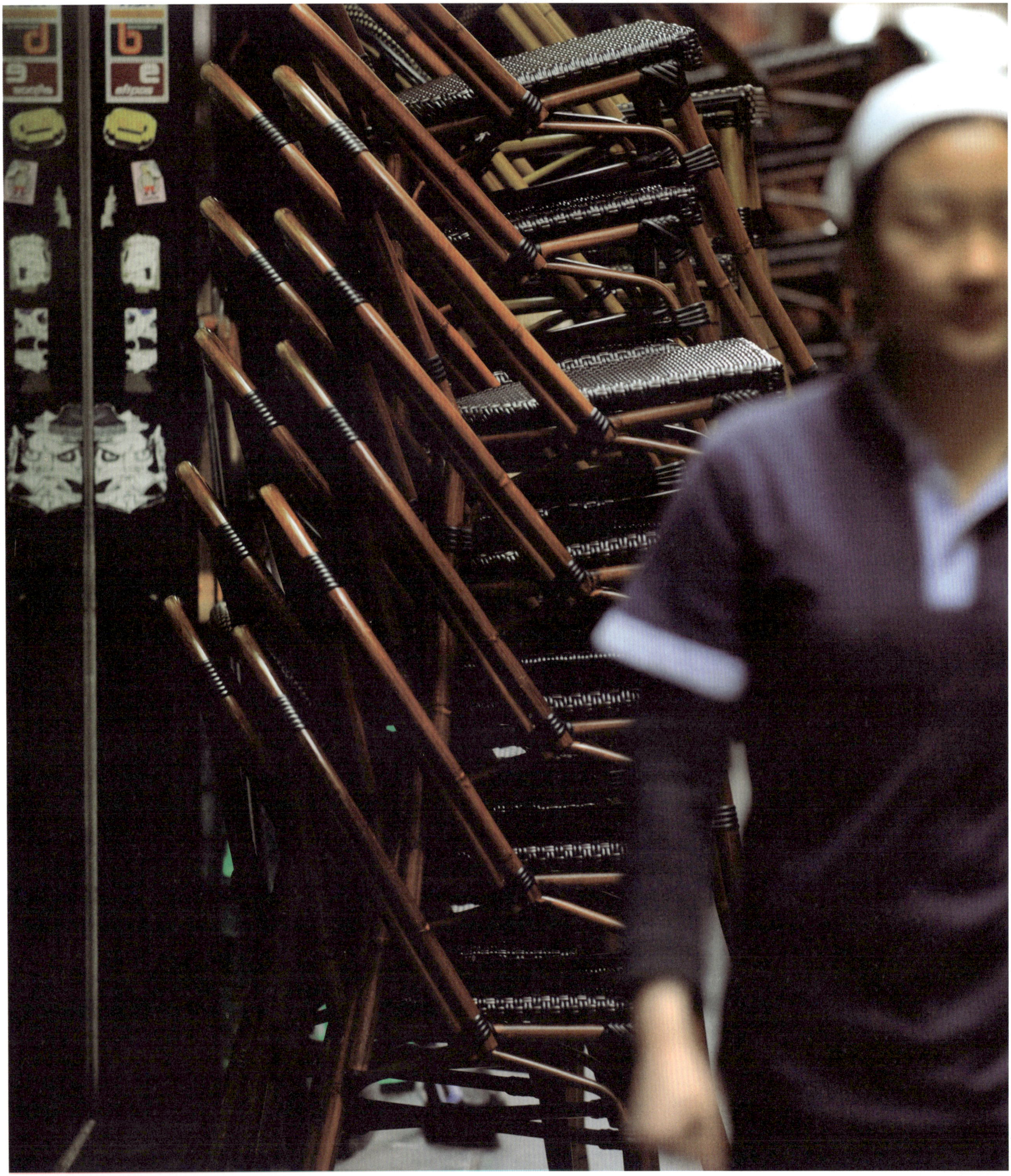

# LANEWAYS

| | | | | | |
|---|---|---|---|---|---|
| ACDC Lane | 66 | Exhibition St | 170 | Postal Lane | 268 |
| Artemis Lane | 72 | Federation Square | 176 | Queen St | 274 |
| Bank Place | 80 | Flinders Lane | 184 | Rainbow Alley | 282 |
| Bligh Place | 88 | George Pde | 196 | Rakaia Way | 288 |
| Block Arcade | 94 | Highlander Lane | 202 | Rebecca Walk | 294 |
| Bourke St | 100 | Hosier Lane | 208 | Russell St | 300 |
| Centre Place | 122 | Little Bourke St | 214 | Scott Alley | 310 |
| Chinatown | 128 | Little Collins St | 222 | Tattersalls Lane | 316 |
| Collins St | 134 | Little Lonsdale St | 230 | Waratah Place | 322 |
| Corrs Lane | 142 | Lonsdale St | 236 | Warburton Lane | 328 |
| Croft Alley | 148 | McKillop St | 248 | Yarra Footbridge | 336 |
| Curtin House | 154 | Meyers Place | 254 | | |
| Drewery Lane | 164 | Pink Alley | 262 | | |

Tattersalls Lane

Tattersalls Lane

Manchester Lane

58

Southgate Footbridge

Federation Square

Flinders Lane

Drewery Lane

Federation Square

Drewery Lane

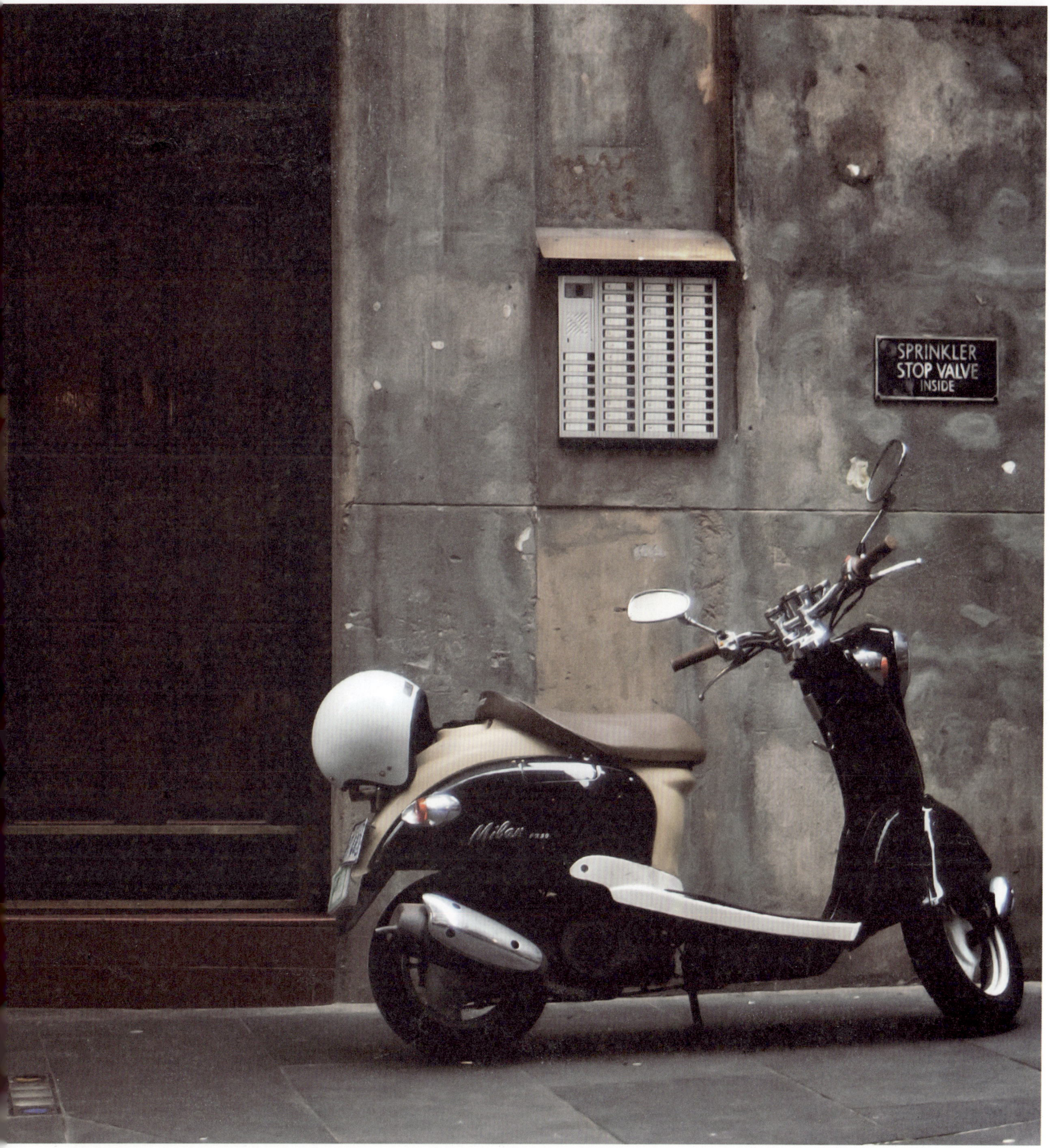
SPRINKLER
STOP VALVE
INSIDE
Milan

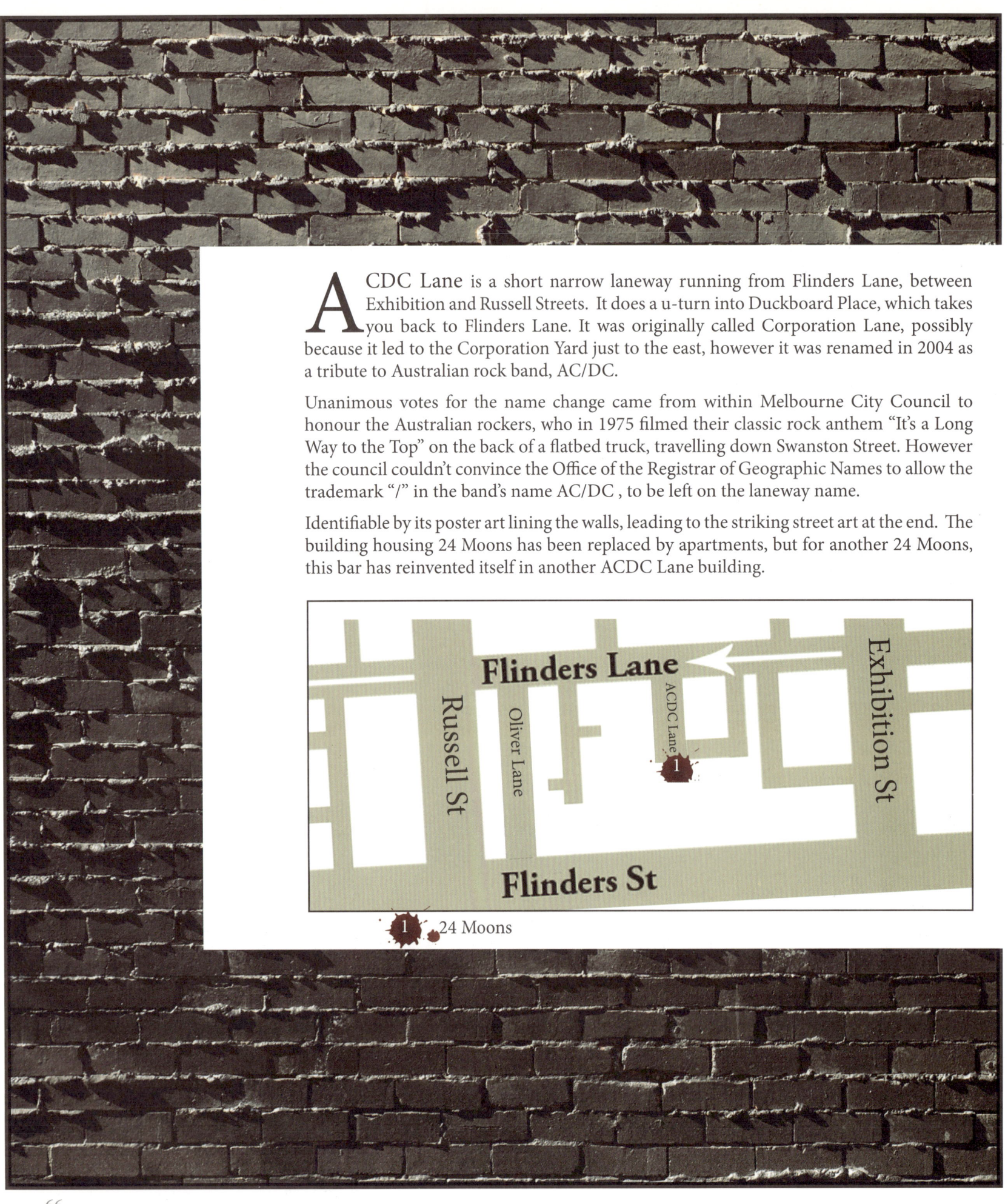

ACDC Lane is a short narrow laneway running from Flinders Lane, between Exhibition and Russell Streets. It does a u-turn into Duckboard Place, which takes you back to Flinders Lane. It was originally called Corporation Lane, possibly because it led to the Corporation Yard just to the east, however it was renamed in 2004 as a tribute to Australian rock band, AC/DC.

Unanimous votes for the name change came from within Melbourne City Council to honour the Australian rockers, who in 1975 filmed their classic rock anthem "It's a Long Way to the Top" on the back of a flatbed truck, travelling down Swanston Street. However the council couldn't convince the Office of the Registrar of Geographic Names to allow the trademark "/" in the band's name AC/DC , to be left on the laneway name.

Identifiable by its poster art lining the walls, leading to the striking street art at the end. The building housing 24 Moons has been replaced by apartments, but for another 24 Moons, this bar has reinvented itself in another ACDC Lane building.

1. 24 Moons

# ACDC LANE

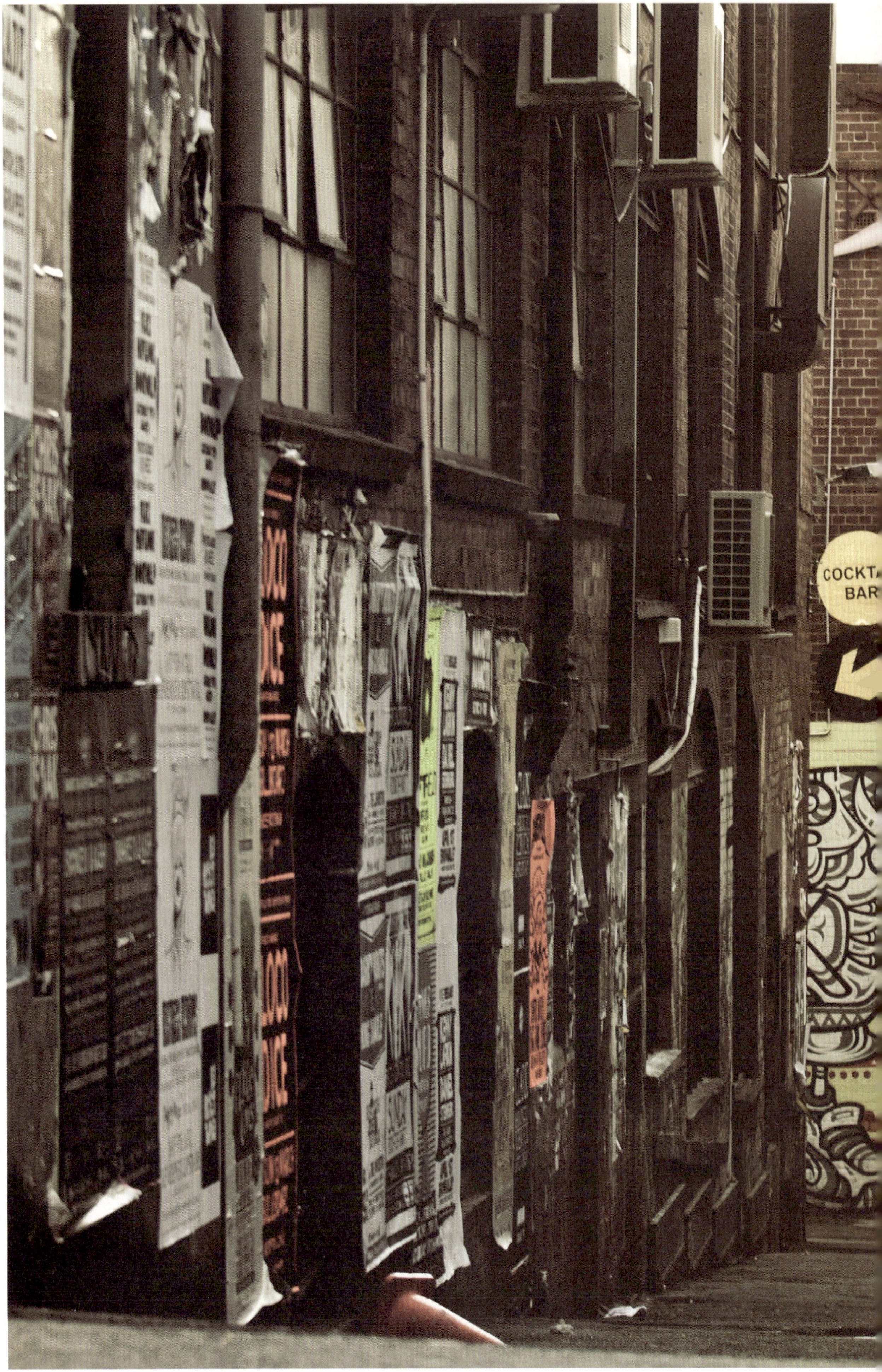
COCKTA
BAR

ACDC Lane

# 24 MOONS

ACDC Lane
03 9650 0035
www.24moons.com.au

The life-span of 24 Moons was set at 24 months, and this modern-day "speakeasy" bar popped up in ACDC Lane in late 2009. Given a limited life-span (or lease) of 24 months, creators of this visionary bar moulded this underground space in ACDC Lane into a contemporary cocktail bar environment. Given a new lease of life, another 24 moons in another ACDC Lane space, this bar has similarities to the illegal bars that popped up and disappeared just as quickly during the prohibition years.

You will find 24 Moons discreetly hidden down the infamous street-art and graffiti splattered ACDC laneway. You could cut the dark, almost smokey air with a knife, as your eyes adjust to the "moonlit forest-at-night" design of one of Melbourne's trendiest and sophisticated bars.

The blend of textures, the use of digital urban elements and forest motifs on the walls, create an opulent and rich atmosphere to enjoy one of the bar's signature cocktails, spirit degustation, cocktail table service and platters of assorted dumplings.

Creators of this unique cocktail bar include "Mr Creative", Boris von Rechenberg (Ellis Street/Swan Lake Studios) who came up with the concept and design; "Mr Delicious", Marcus Motteram (F4/New Guernica), who is in charge of food and drink; "Mr Hospitality", Michael Christodoulou (Pharmacy) who is in charge of service and venue; and "Mr Music", Simon Digby (Alumbra) who is in charge of groove and vibe.

With such a strong and creative force behind this bar, its place in Melbourne's history will remain. It has evolved from speakeasy origins of the 1920's, where Jazz, striptease and light entertainment were staged. Today it is a vibrant hub of night-people, visionaries and thinkers coming together in this mystical, blue-moon ambience.

What better way to enjoy with an evening than with a blend of passionate cocktails, an adventurous blend of creative events and music, and a selective menu.

The signature cocktail, Lady Yvette, is a mixture of Belvedere black raspberry, lemon juice, French violet liqueur and sugar syrup, decorated with a beautiful orchid. The "Lite Bites" menu includes favourites like prawn and scallop, spinach and pinenut, duck and shitake, and chicken and chive dumplings.

Your time at 24 Moons may be a "once in a blue moon" experience, but you can be sure that the creative foursome behind this bar, and their passionate team, will be popping in and out of Melbourne's food and wine scene for many years to come.

24 MOONS

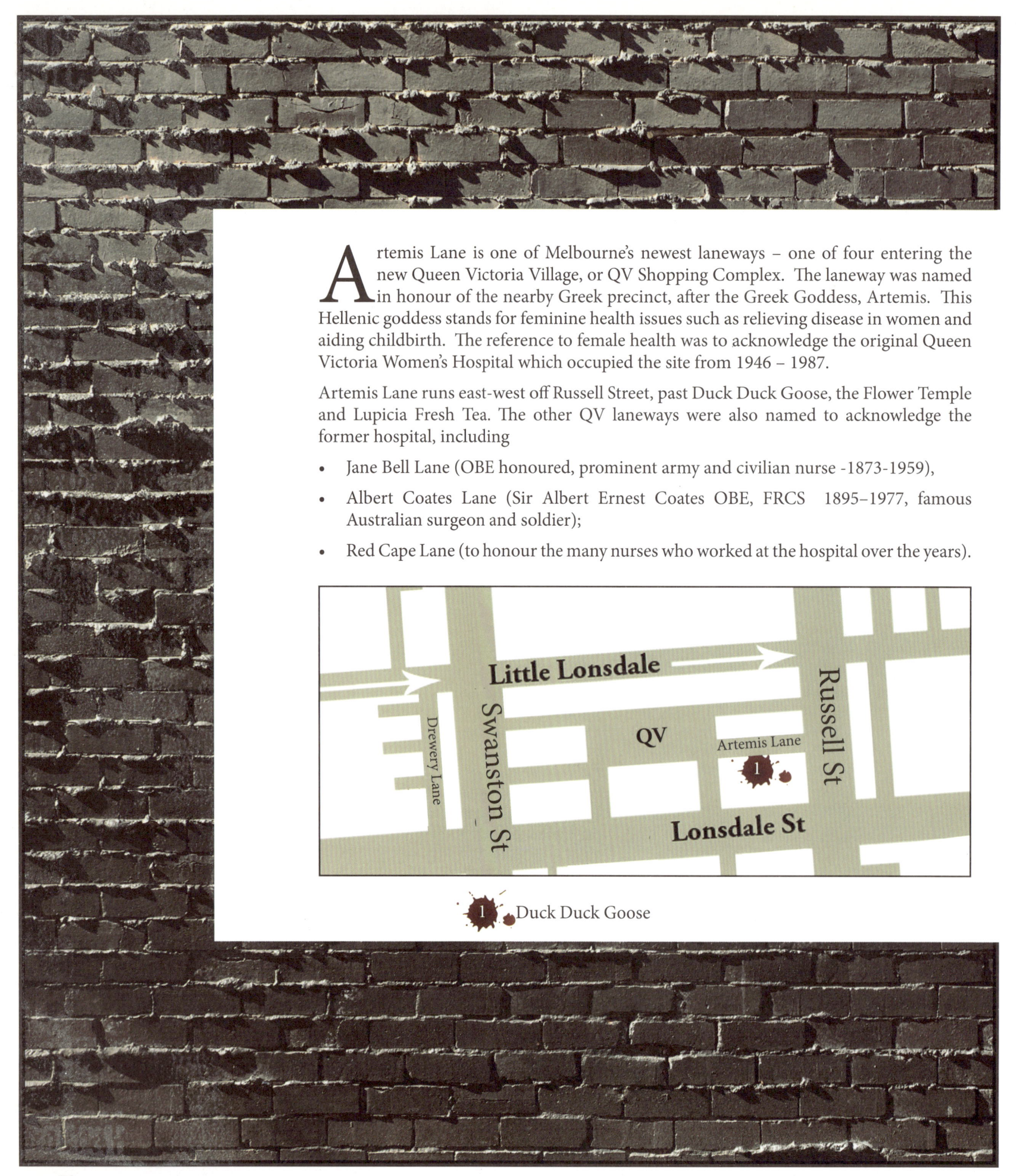

Artemis Lane is one of Melbourne's newest laneways – one of four entering the new Queen Victoria Village, or QV Shopping Complex. The laneway was named in honour of the nearby Greek precinct, after the Greek Goddess, Artemis. This Hellenic goddess stands for feminine health issues such as relieving disease in women and aiding childbirth. The reference to female health was to acknowledge the original Queen Victoria Women's Hospital which occupied the site from 1946 – 1987.

Artemis Lane runs east-west off Russell Street, past Duck Duck Goose, the Flower Temple and Lupicia Fresh Tea. The other QV laneways were also named to acknowledge the former hospital, including

- Jane Bell Lane (OBE honoured, prominent army and civilian nurse -1873-1959),
- Albert Coates Lane (Sir Albert Ernest Coates OBE, FRCS 1895–1977, famous Australian surgeon and soldier);
- Red Cape Lane (to honour the many nurses who worked at the hospital over the years).

1. Duck Duck Goose

# ARTEMIS LANE

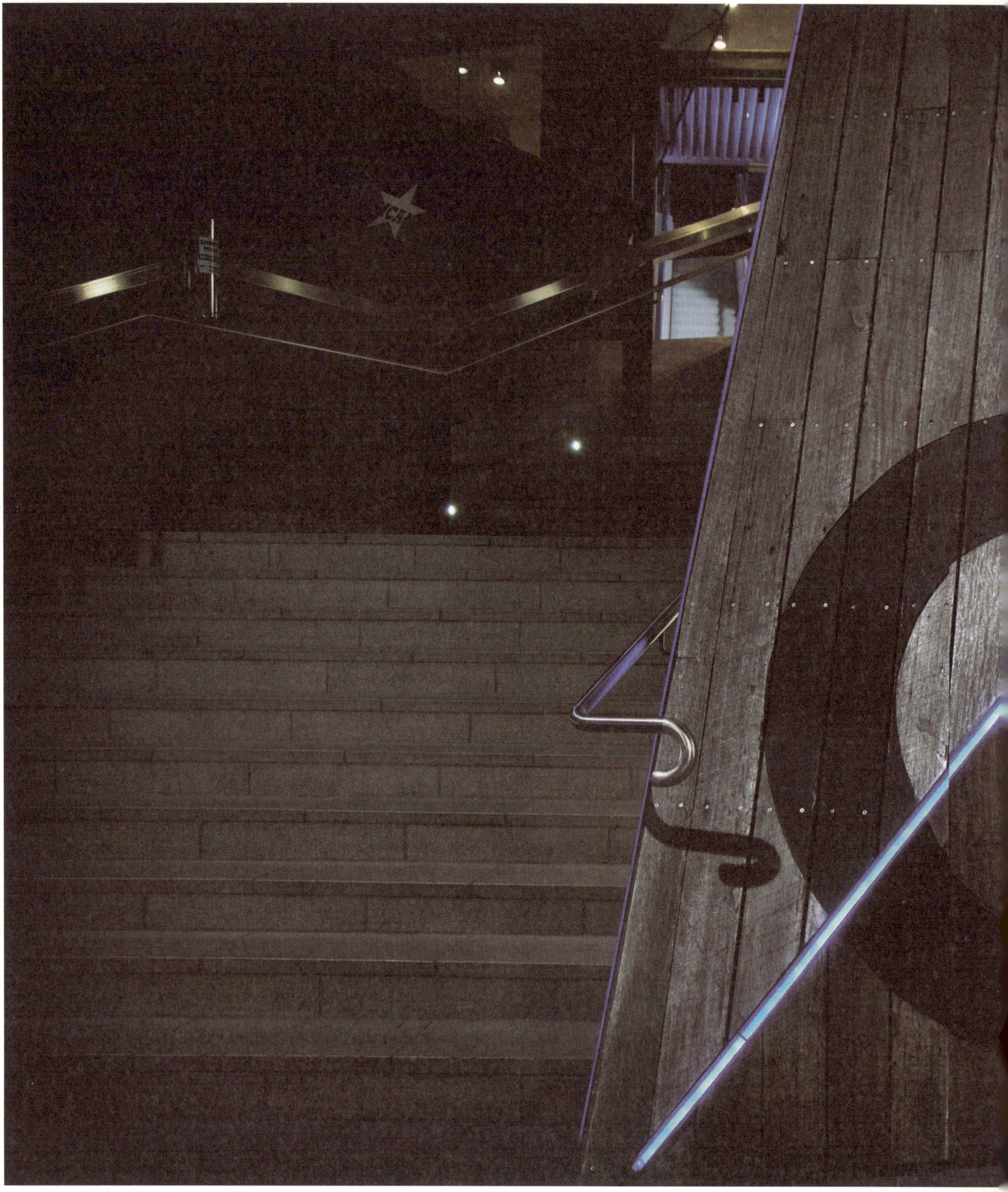

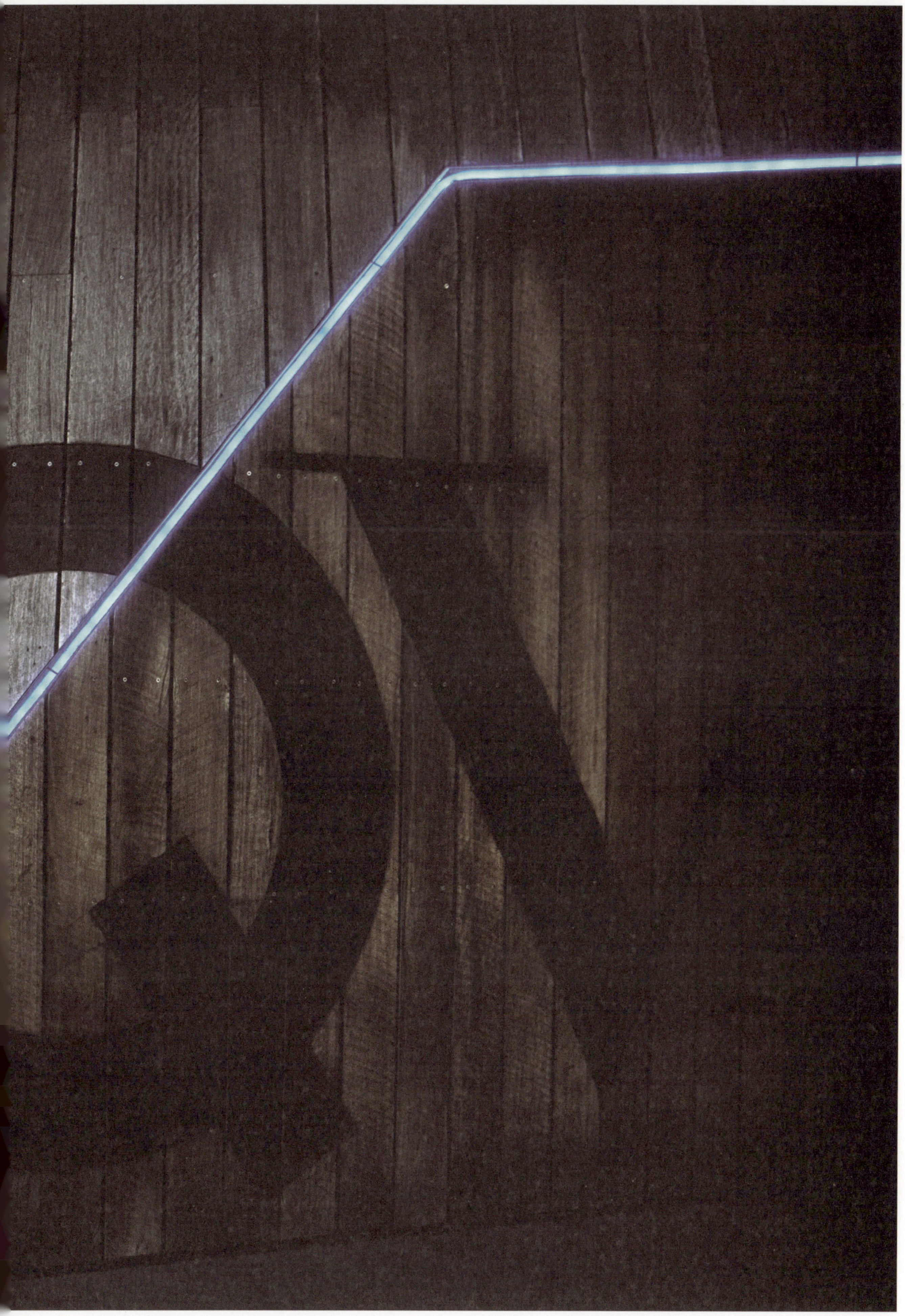

# DUCK DUCK GOOSE BISTRO

31 - 37 Artemis Lane
03 9005 0888
www.au-ddg.com

One of the latest additions to Melbourne's restaurant scene is the innovative project of the Duck Duck Goose restaurant, housed in a new laneway, Artemis Lane. Launched as part of QV Melbourne, both laneway and restaurant are an inspiring variation to those traditionally found in Melbourne.

Offering a bistro, restaurant and bar this exciting concept offers diners the Yin and the Yang of dining – in terms of flavours and dining styles. It was introduced to Melbourne in 2010 by one of the highest regarded Cantonese restaurateurs from Sydney, Edward Ng.

Edward says "Duck Duck Goose was set up with everything and every idea I had. It is my salute to the industry and should fill a gap in the Melbourne restaurant scene."

Edward gave well known architects, BURO, the go ahead to make each side of the large space at QV different, yet complementary in their union. The multi-level bistro offers more relaxed dining in a modern-chic, white zone that incorporates a yum cha bar, mezzanine and terrace, combining to make the bistro the ideal location for quick dumplings, family dining or night time revelry over tapas and cocktails.

Familiarise yourself with the bistro menu and you will find the contemporary and relaxed world of Pan-Asian food that spans Asia in its variety and taste, retaining strong Chinese influences with European tweaks. You will experience food from throughout Asia with Mapo Tofu Taiwanese–style, Teriyaki Salmon, Korean Bibimbab and original, dry style Peking duck.

The hand-made dim-sum ranges from all varieties of dumplings, wontons and other popular yum cha items. Dumplings include pork, Thai beef, prawn, shark fin and all kinds of vegetarian mixtures, which can be ordered pan-fried, poached or fried. There is also a choice of noodles, including udon, ramen and laksa.

The lavish number of tea options will keep lovers of tea in raptures, with teas such as elderflower, rice, grapefruit, mandarin and oolong, as well as the stronger, puerh teas.

The fusion of Asian influences at the Duck Duck Goose bistro will awaken your senses. It is a great place to meet friends for lunch, dinner or a slow Sunday brunch. The prices are low, the food is fresh, fast and flavoursome, the atmosphere relaxed and the service textbook.

77

# DUCK DUCK GOOSE RESTAURANT

31 - 37 Artemis Lane
03 9005 0888
www.au-ddg.com

The Duck Duck Goose restaurant is an exciting night-time venture into the yang of traditional cuisine. From Paris via Hong Kong to Melbourne, Duck Duck Goose's dark side is a testament to owner, Edward Ng's passion and vision.

He is already one of Sydney's most highly-regarded Chinese restaurateurs, and now he combines this honour with his successful entry into French-fusion cuisine. Whether its a selection from the à la carte menu or a full degustation meal, you will experience the pinnacle of fusion food being created in Australia today.

Move through the Champagne Bar to the exquisitely decorated dining room, and you will discover Edward's passion. Nothing has been spared in this captivating room, complete with a water feature large enough to swim in. Black marble table-tops are beautifully set, ready and beckoning you to enjoy a very special evening or to make an ordinary evening special.

Head Chef, Ryo Kitahara, was trained by Iron Chef, Sakai Protégé, in Japan. He now combines ingredients such as quail, beef, duck and dhufish to bring spine-tingling meals to the table.

Ryo says, "The menu is based on strong classic French traditions and techniques, but the food is uniquely Duck Duck Goose. We believe we are pioneering a new wave of inspired French food here in Melbourne and it's really exciting".

Your first foray into the restaurant's French gastronomic menu, which is laced with Eastern highlights, will leave you in full agreement with Ryo and craving for more.

Firm favourites from the dinner menu are the Slowly Cooked Duck Breast and Crisp Ravioli, served with spicy sesame sauce. However with alternatives like the Braised Ox-tail and Foie Gras Mille-Feuille, confit potato, yuzu porto sauce - return visits are a foregone conclusion.

**EDWARD NG'S PRIDE SHINES THROUGH WHEN HE SAYS, "THE RESTAURANT IS A TRUE REFLECTION OF A JOURNEY TO FRANCE THROUGH THE EYES OF AN ASIAN RESTAURATEUR".**

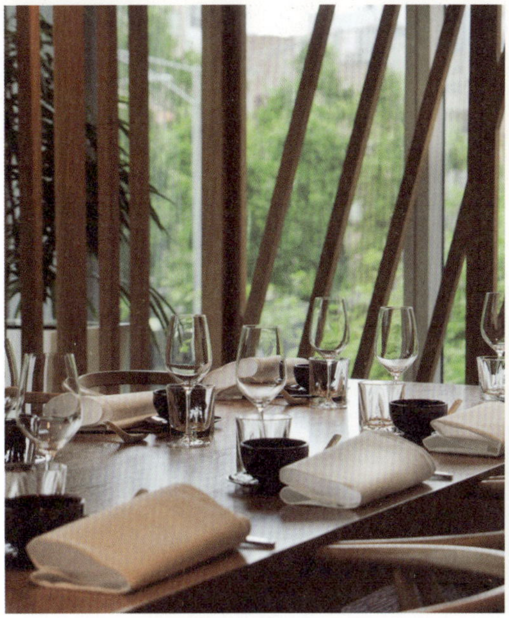

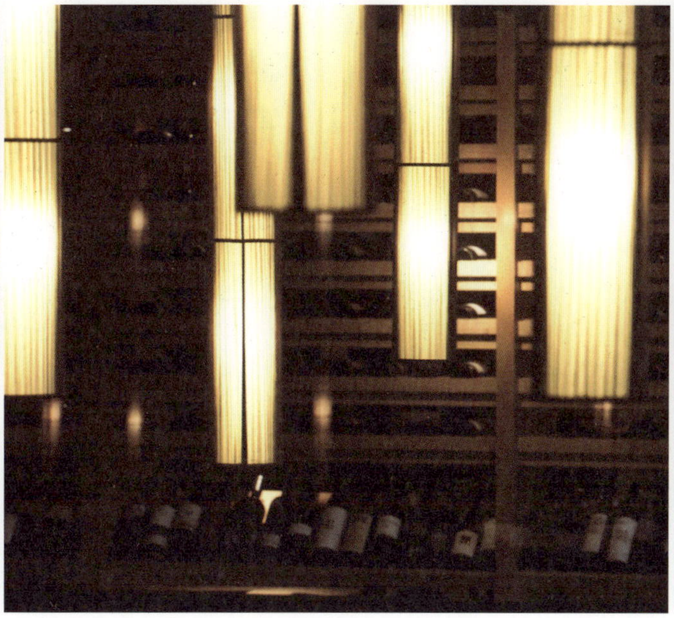

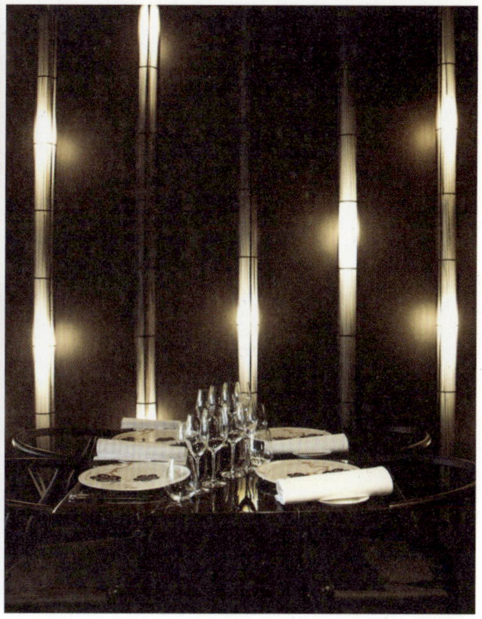

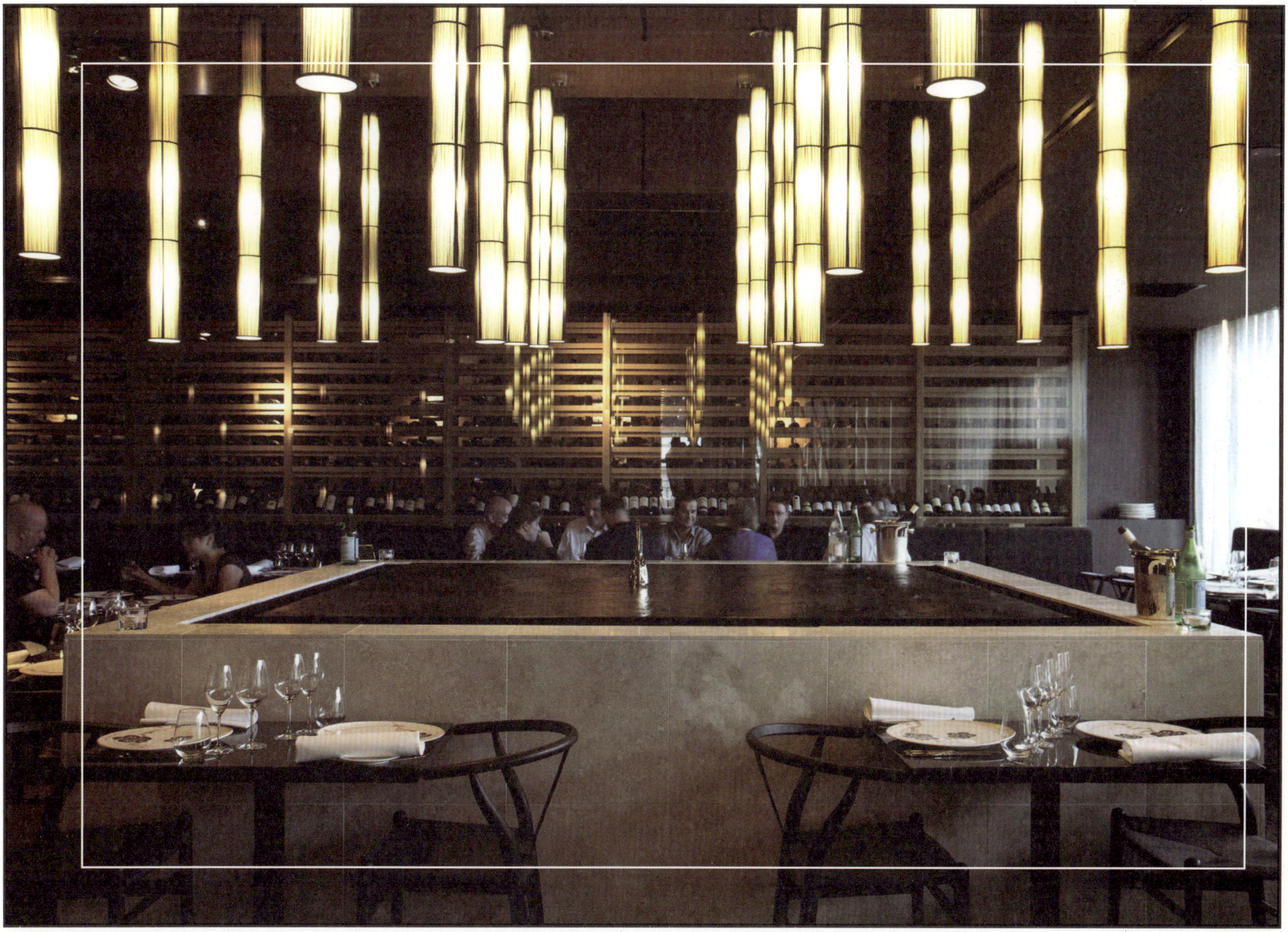

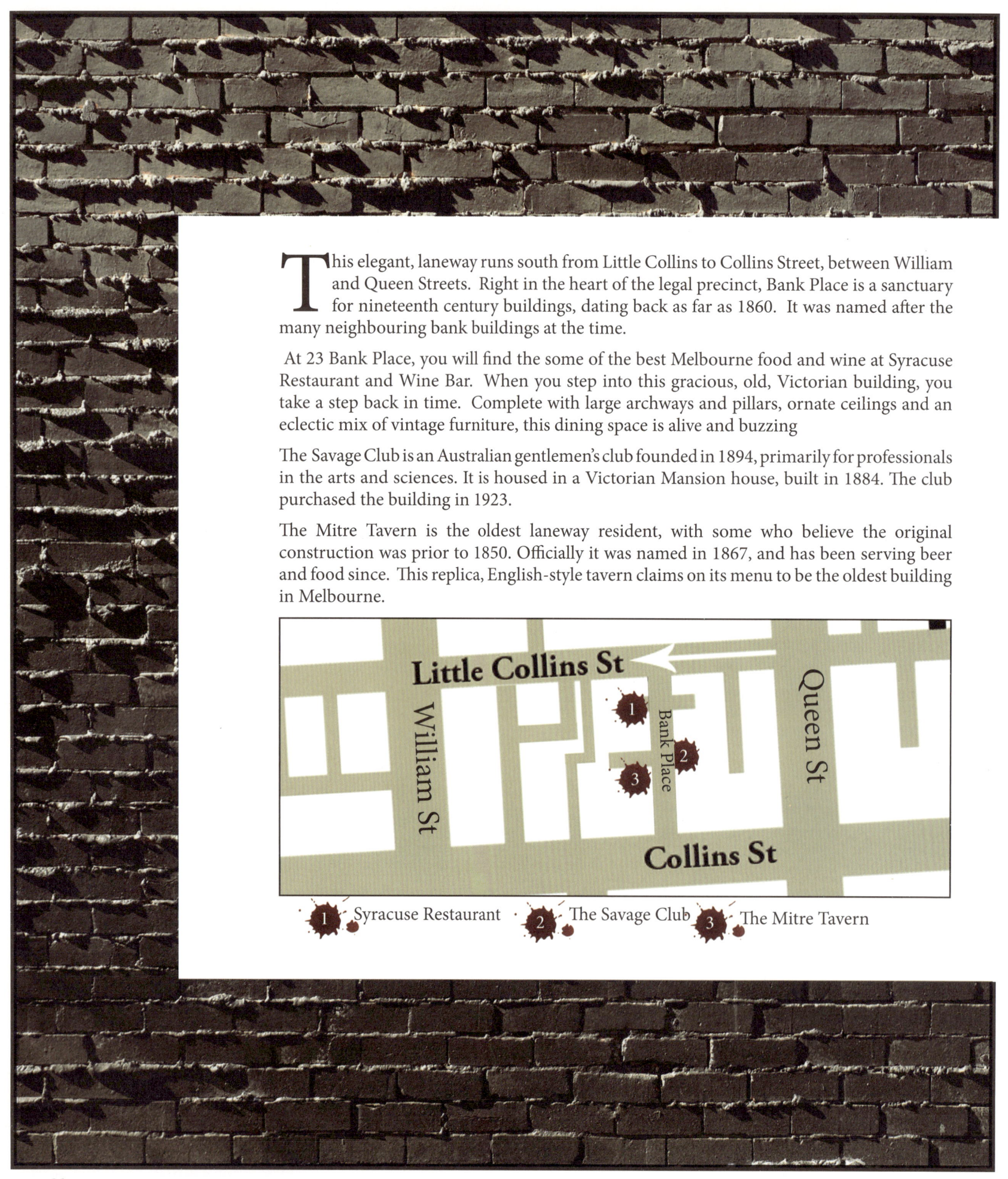

This elegant, laneway runs south from Little Collins to Collins Street, between William and Queen Streets. Right in the heart of the legal precinct, Bank Place is a sanctuary for nineteenth century buildings, dating back as far as 1860. It was named after the many neighbouring bank buildings at the time.

At 23 Bank Place, you will find the some of the best Melbourne food and wine at Syracuse Restaurant and Wine Bar. When you step into this gracious, old, Victorian building, you take a step back in time. Complete with large archways and pillars, ornate ceilings and an eclectic mix of vintage furniture, this dining space is alive and buzzing

The Savage Club is an Australian gentlemen's club founded in 1894, primarily for professionals in the arts and sciences. It is housed in a Victorian Mansion house, built in 1884. The club purchased the building in 1923.

The Mitre Tavern is the oldest laneway resident, with some who believe the original construction was prior to 1850. Officially it was named in 1867, and has been serving beer and food since. This replica, English-style tavern claims on its menu to be the oldest building in Melbourne.

1. Syracuse Restaurant    2. The Savage Club    3. The Mitre Tavern

# BANK PLACE

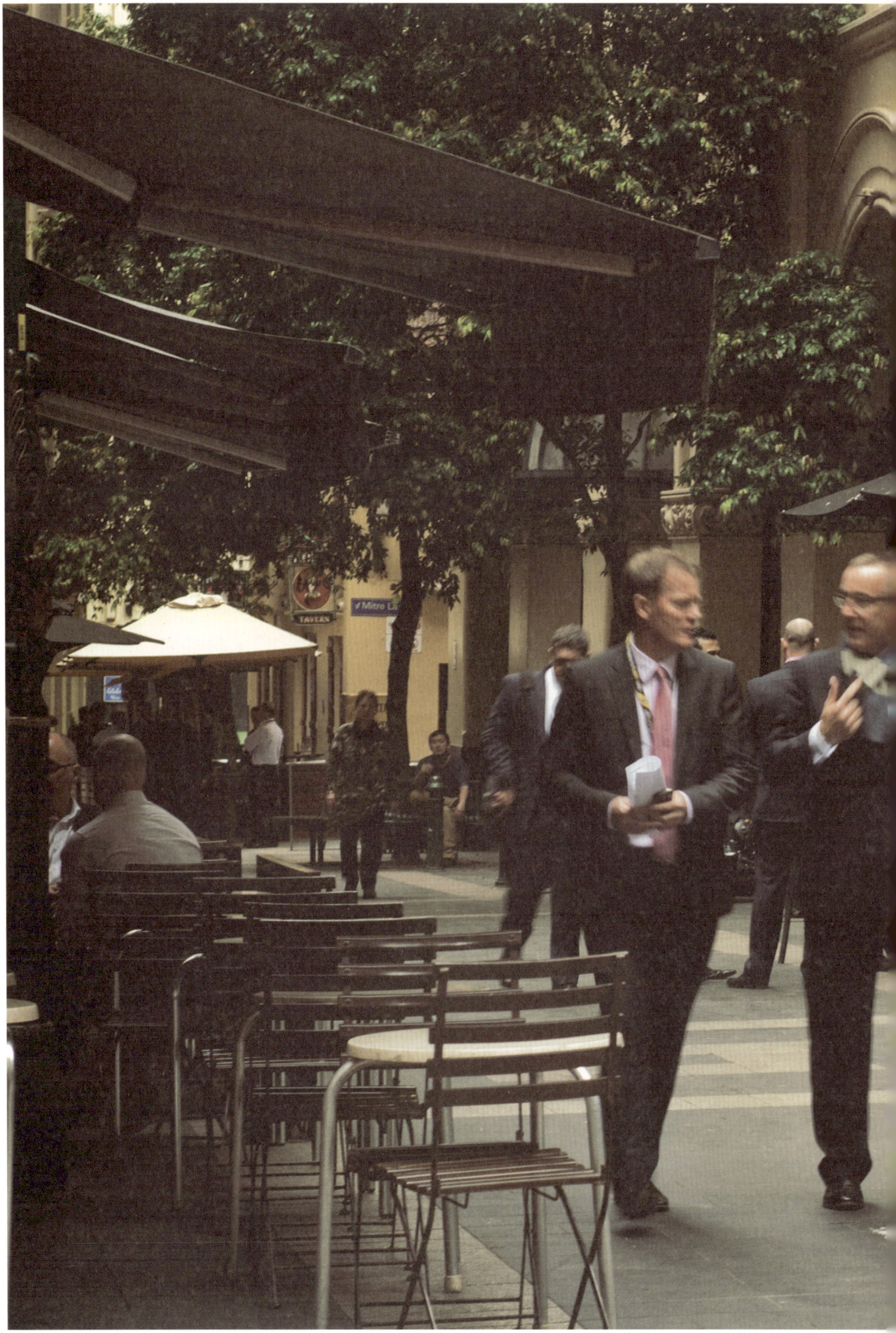

ORTIGIA

# SYRACUSE RESTAURANT & WINE BAR

23 Bank Place
03 9670 1777
www.syracuserestaurant.com.au

When you step into this gracious, old, Victorian building, you take a step back in time. Complete with large archways and pillars, ornate ceilings and an eclectic mix of vintage furniture and ornaments, this dining space is alive and buzzing.

Taking its place amongst Melbourne's finest dining establishments, Syracuse takes its food and wine seriously. The all-day restaurant starts its day with clientele from the local legal precinct, and flows on through lunch and dinner with a fusion of tourists and Melbourne city diners.

Local clientele commence their working day with a fine selection of breakfast treats like *Red Hill Muesli with yoghurt and fruit* or something more substantial like *Eggs on Concotte, with confit lamb, tomato jam and pecorino*.

Rolling on from here, guests can treat the room as a wine lounge or step it up a notch and stay for a business lunch or celebratory dinner. Lunch in this warm and inviting restaurant can be simple tapas plates to share, or chosen from a more generous selection like *Scotch fillet with oxtail ragout, buttered potato and grapefruit marmalade*.

Wine buffs will ogle at the racks and racks of wine bottles, become bemused with the old and rare wine bottles sitting on the window sills and become engrossed in the extensive wine list. However, the winning participants in this scenario are the foodies who expect excellence in their dining experience.

Chef, Michael Harrison, brings his experience from Attica in Ripponlea and, more recently, Ice in Prahran, where he learnt inspired techniques that make the most of unique ingredients from foraged to high end.

Syracuse's dinner menu includes shared plates as well as outstanding dishes like *"Ko" shaved foie gras, peach, pistachio, praline and sauternes granita* or *Suckling pig, young vegetables, morcilla, apple and pork jus*.

The restaurant was established in September 1996, and according to the owners, "Syracuse's longevity and loyal customer base is a testament to our emphasis on good food, wine and service".

---

FROM A '66 CHATEAU PETRUS POMEROL (BORDEAUX), A '71 PENFOLDS GRANGE (BAROSSA VALLEY), AN '88 SANTA SOFIA AMARONE (VENICE) TO A '98 BINDI 'BLOCK 5' PINOT NOIR (MACEDON).... YOU WILL FIND THE WINE LIST AT SYRACUSE RESTAURANT A VERITABLE "WHO'S WHO" OF GENERATIONS OF EMINENT WINEMAKERS.

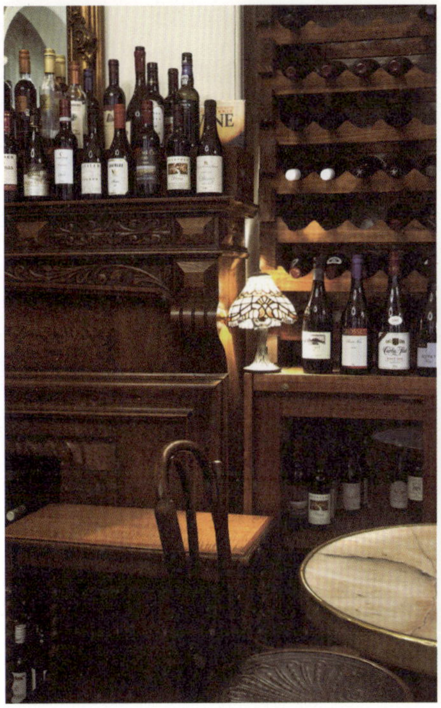

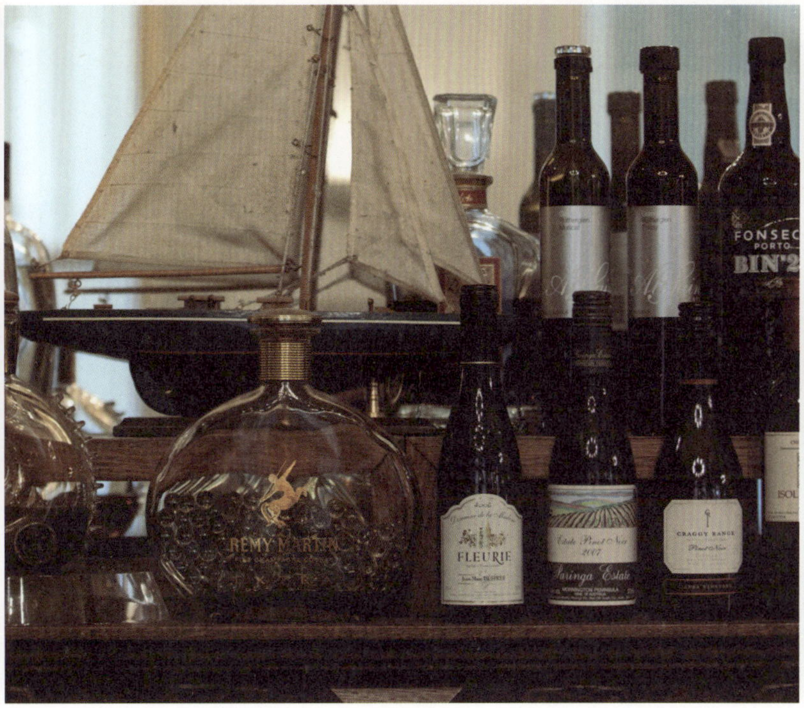
FLEURIE

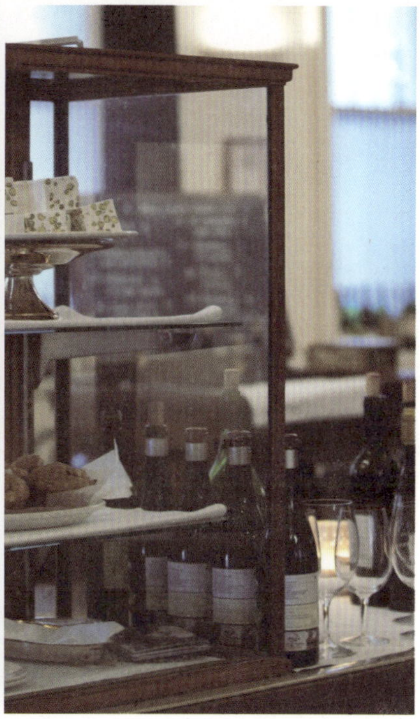

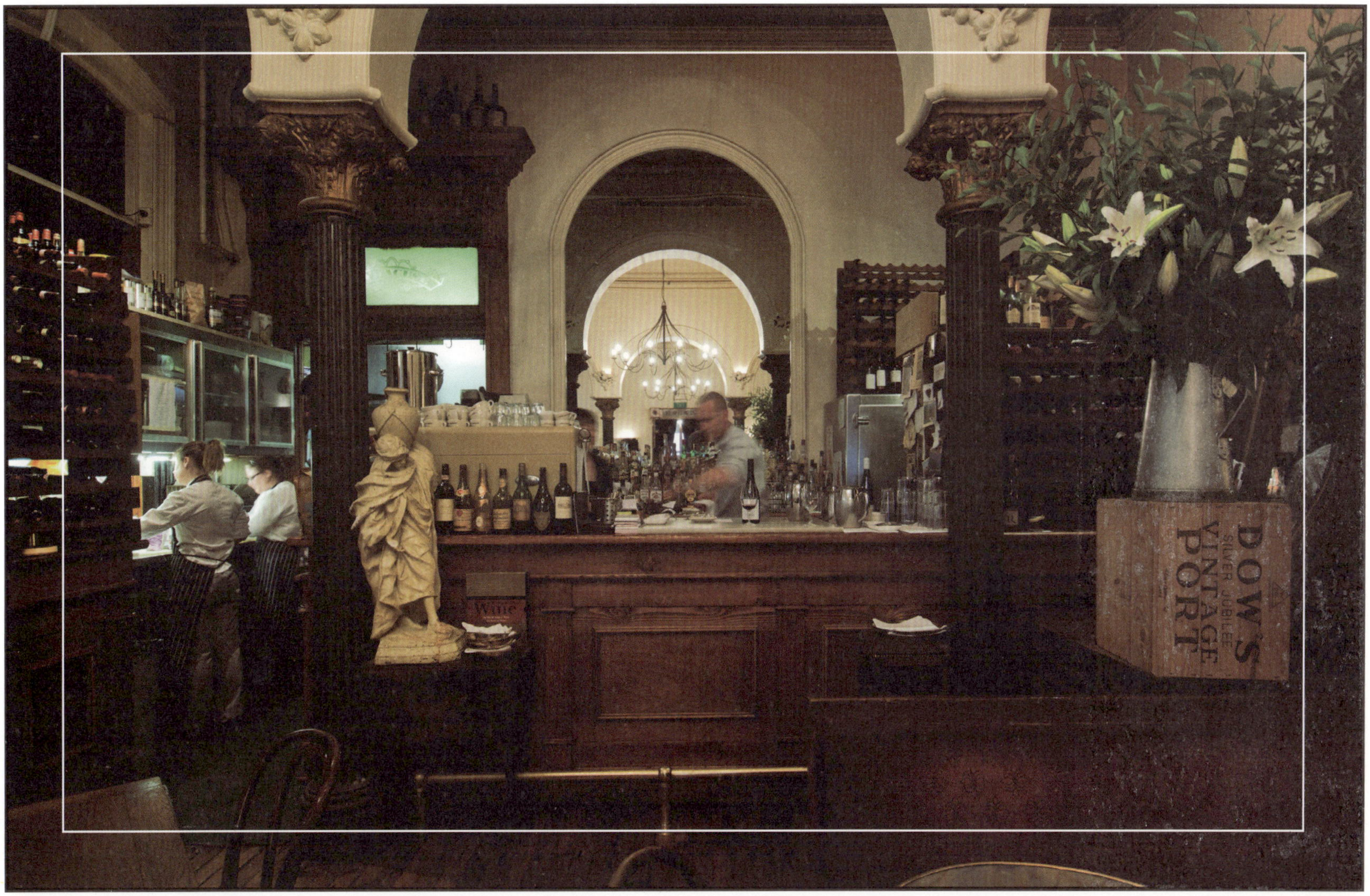
DOW'S
SILVER JUBILEE
VINTAGE
PORT

BANK PLACE BANK PLACE BANK PLACE BANK PLACE BANK PLACE BANK PLACE BANK PL

# THE MITRE TAVERN

5 Bank Place
03 9670 5644
www.mitretavern.com.au

Take a little detour off the downtown end of Collins Street to discover the oldest building in Melbourne, according to Melbourne City Council records. In 1868, Mr. Henry Thompson became the first of many publicans at the Mitre Tavern where today you can still enjoy a drink in the largest open air drinking space in the CBD. An alternative to the surrounding bars and cocktail lounges, the Mitre Tavern draws the crowds looking for an English-style "pub". Savour you beer, wine or cocktail in the laneway beer garden or sit in a rustic chair downstairs. Upstairs you will find a delicious steakhouse and grill meal in the leather-seated restaurant. The Mitre Tavern's kitchen offers succulent Australian-only meats and an assurance that any special dietary needs can be accommodated.

# THE SAVAGE CLUB

12-16 Bank Place
03 9670 0644
www.melbournesavageclub.com

This heritage listed club is a functioning piece of Melbourne's history. Occupied since 1923, this regency style house is one of the few remaining mansion houses in this part of the city. Unfortunately members and guests-only are welcome to enter, but it is worth a look from the outside. The club is named after the minor eighteenth century poet, Richard Savage and its early members who, with a Bohemian spirit, agreed to demonstrate an appreciation for music, art, drama, science and literature. Both my daughters had their Christening parties in the massive downstairs drawing room, complete with two massive fireplaces and beautiful antique furniture. In hindsight, it was an appropriate place to Christen girls in this creative yet "savage" ambience, to pass on the gift of a love for science and the arts. I have fond memories of sitting in the dining room under the punkahs (a type of fan), which ventilate the dining room, prior to an evening with David Williamson, the great Australian playwright.

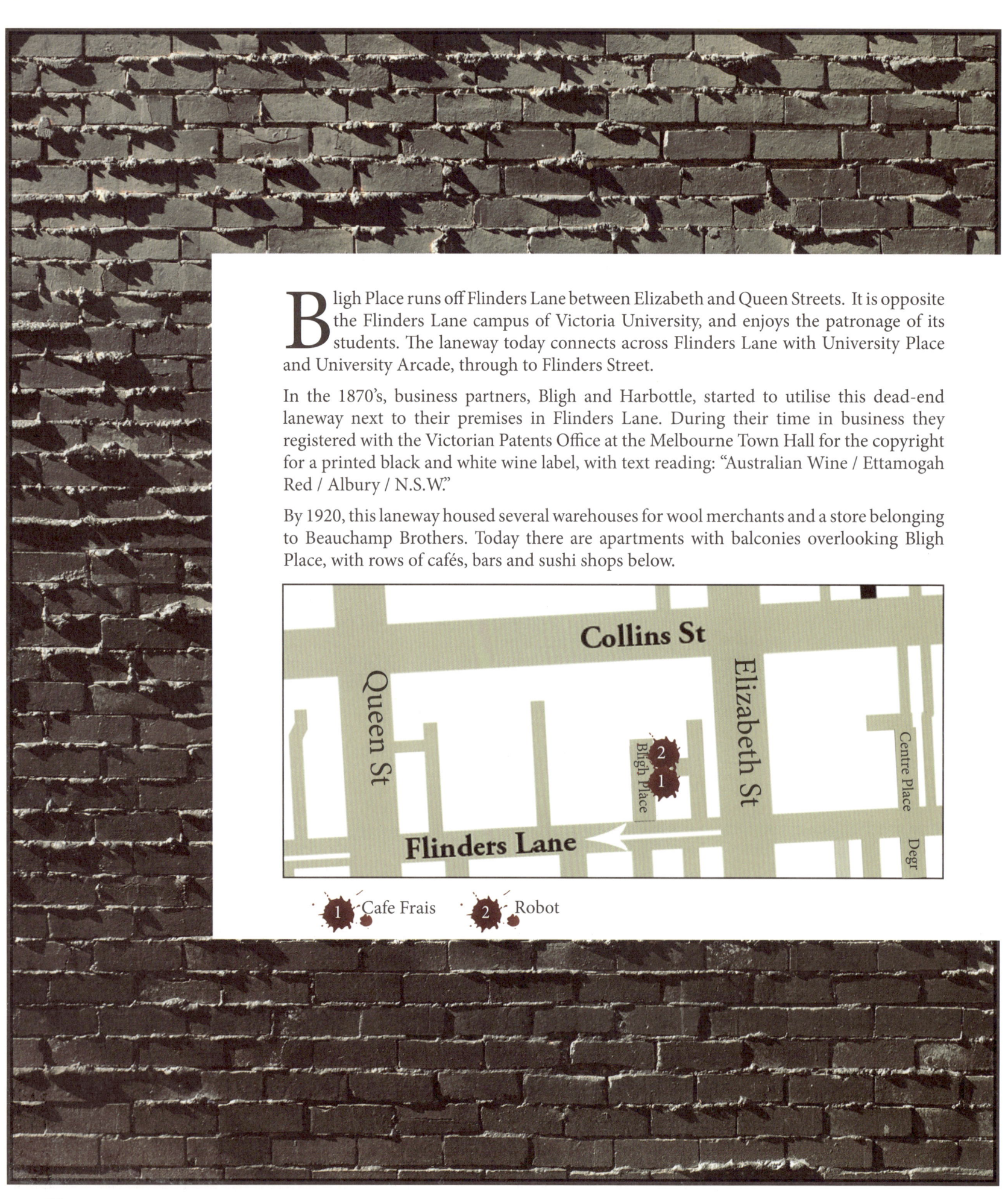

Bligh Place runs off Flinders Lane between Elizabeth and Queen Streets. It is opposite the Flinders Lane campus of Victoria University, and enjoys the patronage of its students. The laneway today connects across Flinders Lane with University Place and University Arcade, through to Flinders Street.

In the 1870's, business partners, Bligh and Harbottle, started to utilise this dead-end laneway next to their premises in Flinders Lane. During their time in business they registered with the Victorian Patents Office at the Melbourne Town Hall for the copyright for a printed black and white wine label, with text reading: "Australian Wine / Ettamogah Red / Albury / N.S.W."

By 1920, this laneway housed several warehouses for wool merchants and a store belonging to Beauchamp Brothers. Today there are apartments with balconies overlooking Bligh Place, with rows of cafés, bars and sushi shops below.

1. Cafe Frais    2. Robot

# BLIGH PLACE

BLIGH PL.
CLOSED TO
VEHICULAR
TRAFFIC
12 MID NIGHT

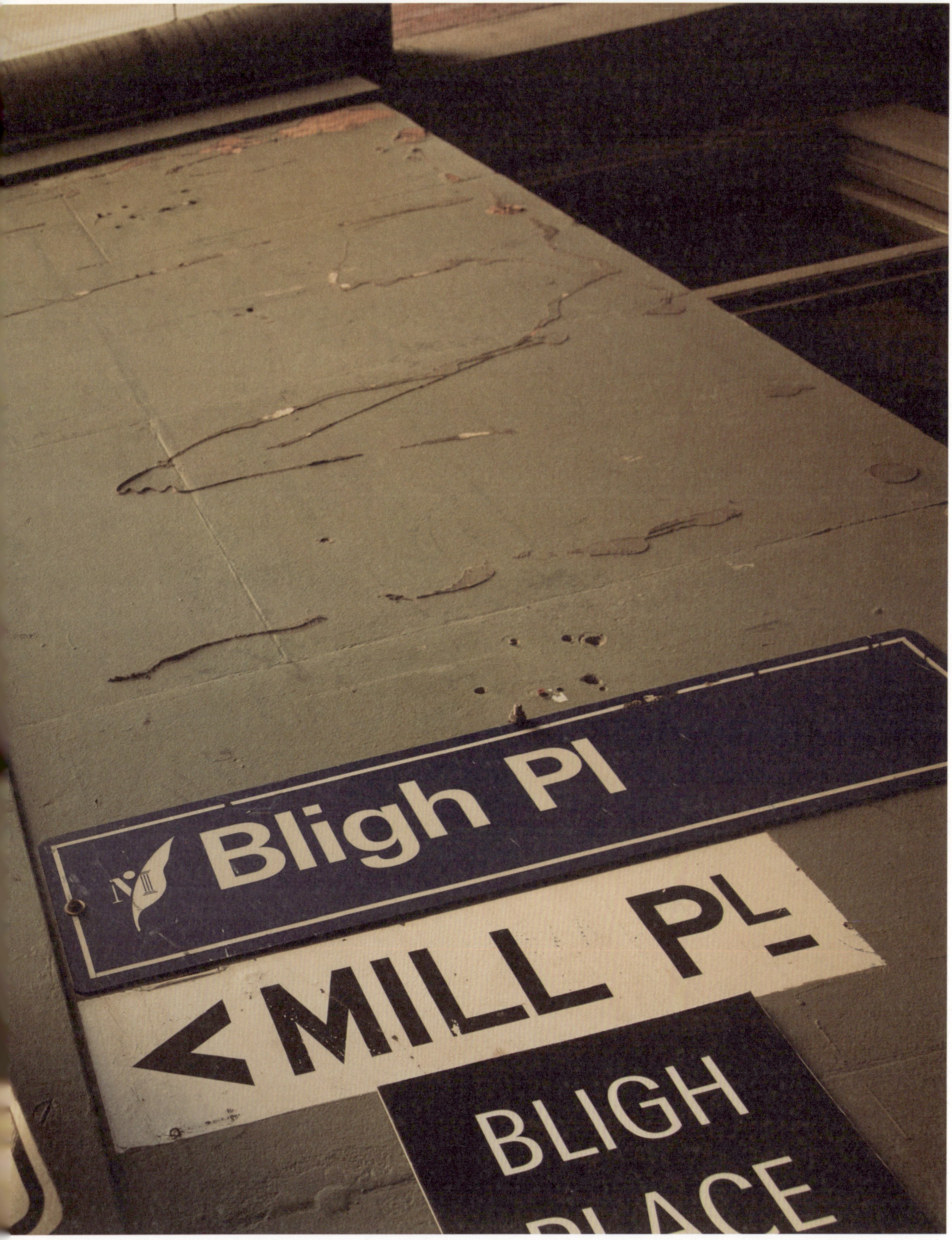
Bligh Pl
MILL PL
BLIGH

# ROBOT BAR

12 Bligh Place
03 9620 3646
www.robotsushi.com

Robot is somewhat different, even for Melbourne - a piece of Neo-Tokyo merged into Melbourne's laneway scene. As you walk into this Japanese pop culture bar, you will be put at ease by what feels like a hip yet minimalist, split-level Japanese apartment. Robot excels in sake and Asian beers, although the odd Australian brew is thrown in for those with tastes closer to home. All the favourite Japanese ales are on the list. You will also see representatives from Indonesia, Thailand, Vietnam, Singapore and Hong Kong. There is a good range of coffee, tea and Japanese style snacks on offer and on some nights you might even be in for a little manga. In the warmer months, chairs and tables are provided outside for people to spill over into the laneway and enjoy a beer garden vibe.

# CAFÉ FRAIS

10 Bligh Place
03 9620 7177

Tucked away off Flinders Lane near Elizabeth Street, Café Frais offers both daytime and night time delights. If you are thinking fresh and mouth watering, as you walk in past the stylish gallery work, you are heading in the right direction. The French inspired café tantalises with quiches, puff pastries, delicious tarts, summer salads, gourmet baguettes and treats for the sweet tooth. Even those in search of a gluten-free option will not be disappointed. At night time, from Wednesday to Friday, take the opportunity to enjoy a wind-down drink with tasty tapas in the beautiful outdoor area.

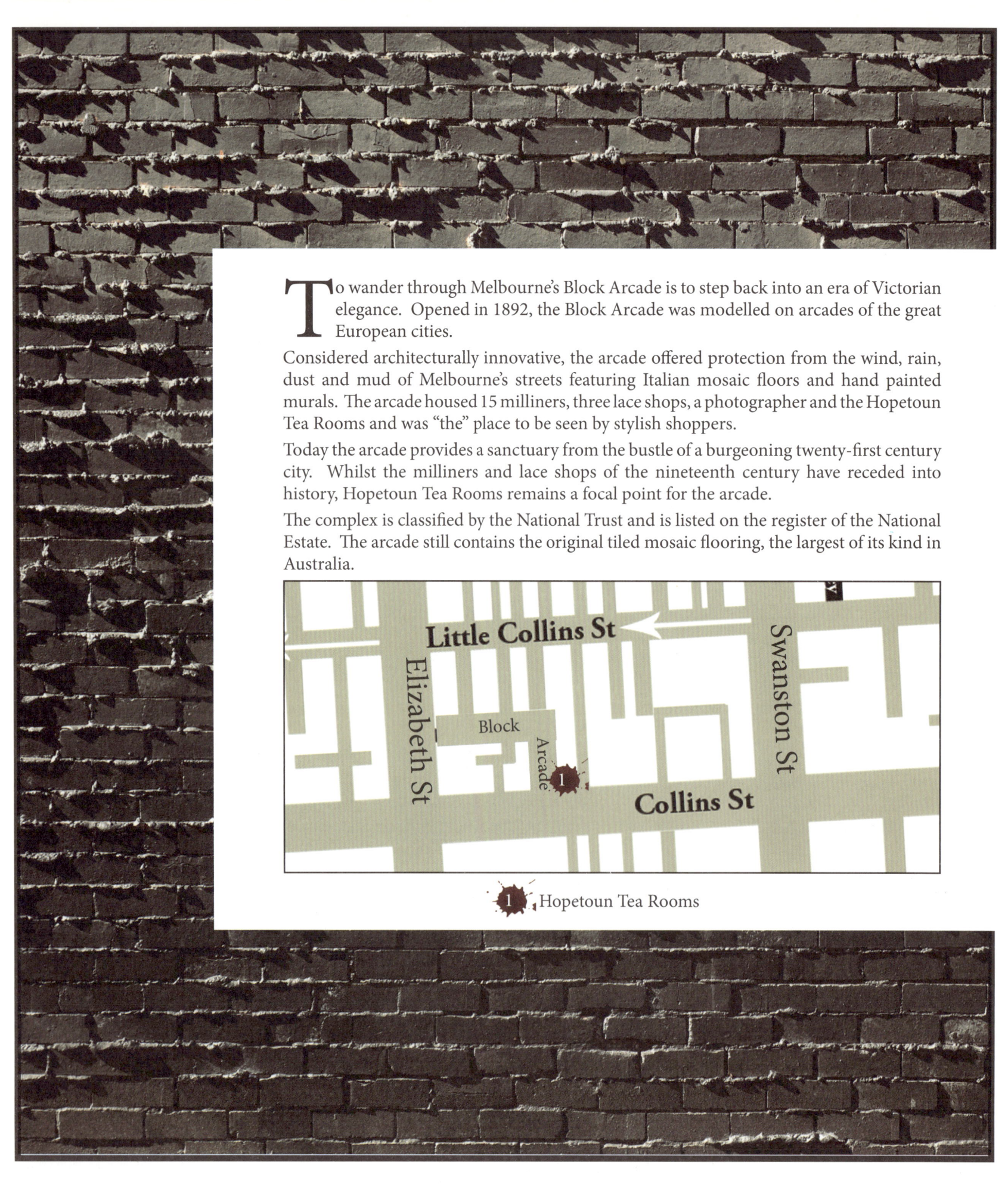

To wander through Melbourne's Block Arcade is to step back into an era of Victorian elegance. Opened in 1892, the Block Arcade was modelled on arcades of the great European cities.

Considered architecturally innovative, the arcade offered protection from the wind, rain, dust and mud of Melbourne's streets featuring Italian mosaic floors and hand painted murals. The arcade housed 15 milliners, three lace shops, a photographer and the Hopetoun Tea Rooms and was "the" place to be seen by stylish shoppers.

Today the arcade provides a sanctuary from the bustle of a burgeoning twenty-first century city. Whilst the milliners and lace shops of the nineteenth century have receded into history, Hopetoun Tea Rooms remains a focal point for the arcade.

The complex is classified by the National Trust and is listed on the register of the National Estate. The arcade still contains the original tiled mosaic flooring, the largest of its kind in Australia.

1. Hopetoun Tea Rooms

# BLOCK ARCADE

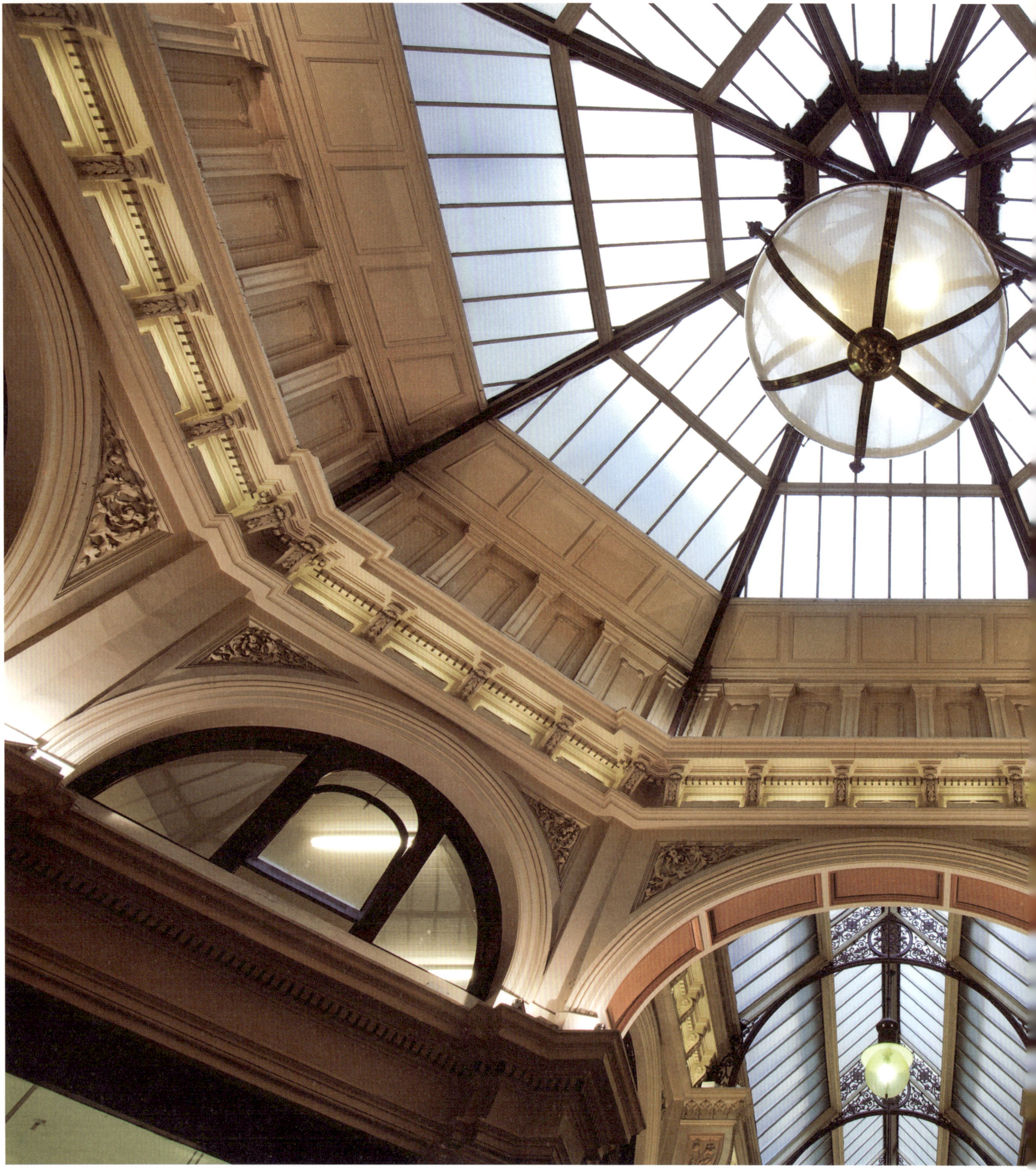

97

# HOPETOUN TEA ROOMS

Shop 1, The Block Arcade
03 9650 2777
www.hopetountearooms.com.au

Step back in time and discover the delights of a bygone era when entering the Hopetoun Tea Rooms in the Block Arcade. Gone are the milliners, lace shops and ladies of the nineteenth century. What remains is the dining room which has been serving generations of Melbournians since the late 1800's.

In the early days, the Hopetoun Tea Rooms was the meeting point for the Victorian Ladies Work Association (VLWA). Many a cup of tea was served to Melbourne's gentry while they discussed ways of helping the poor and destitute women of the country. An initiative of the Victorian Governor of the time's wife, Lady Hopetoun, the VLWA had rooms set-up as a place where women were taught and provided work in embroidery and needlework for nearby tailors. At the time, some of the finest workmanship available anywhere in the world was coming from this precinct. When the VLWA was abandoned in 1907, the Tea Rooms were named after its benefactor, Lady Hopetoun. Then, a stroll around the block of Collins Street, from Swanston to Elizabeth and back along Collins Street to Swanston, was called "doing the block".

After the Block Arcade was opened in 1892, the route changed to include the Arcade and Elizabeth Street. Locals would dress up in their finest clothes and hats and parade around "The Block" before being seated at one of the restaurants and tea places, the Hopetoun Tea Rooms being one of them.

Today you will find the ambience has not changed much since the early days. The Hopetoun Tea Rooms' delightful front window display-case highlights the eclectic assortment of classical, French, English and European cakes which accompany the breakfast and lunch menus.

Once seated, you will marvel at the old world look and feel of how it may have been so many years ago. Heritage listed artefacts including regency wallpaper; designed by Florence Broadhurst, and a vast etched mirror, ensure the historic beauty of the Tea Rooms will be preserved for future generations.

Traditional favourites such as asparagus roll, pinwheels, ribbon sandwiches, hot scones and pikelets still feature on the menu alongside a number of fresh luncheon additions including smoked salmon fritters, shepherd's pie and spinach & ricotta filled zucchini flowers.

Head chef, Harry Hajisava, works well and truly behind the scenes in his basement commercial kitchen. Harry served his apprenticeship under the Roux brothers at the famous Waterside Inn at Bray - UK, and has also worked at Fanny's, Glo Glo's, O'Connells, Momo's and at the Rose & Crown.

The Hopetoun Tea Rooms is open for breakfast, lunch and afternoon tea and offer a mouth watering menu, all served with either a great selection of organic teas or impeccably prepared coffee that should please even the most discerning of Melbourne's coffee drinkers. Dining at the Hopetoun Tea Rooms is a little like returning to an old friend's home. Staff are friendly and inviting, service is efficient yet unobtrusive and the company is grand.

High Tea is enjoyed by people reminiscing about days of old, shoppers taking a well earned rest from the sales and professionals sneaking a break from the demands of corporate life. And amongst the buzz of the conversation, you can hear silver-haired grandmothers joyfully recalling childhood visits to the Tea Rooms. Some things never change.

HOPETOUN TEA ROOMS

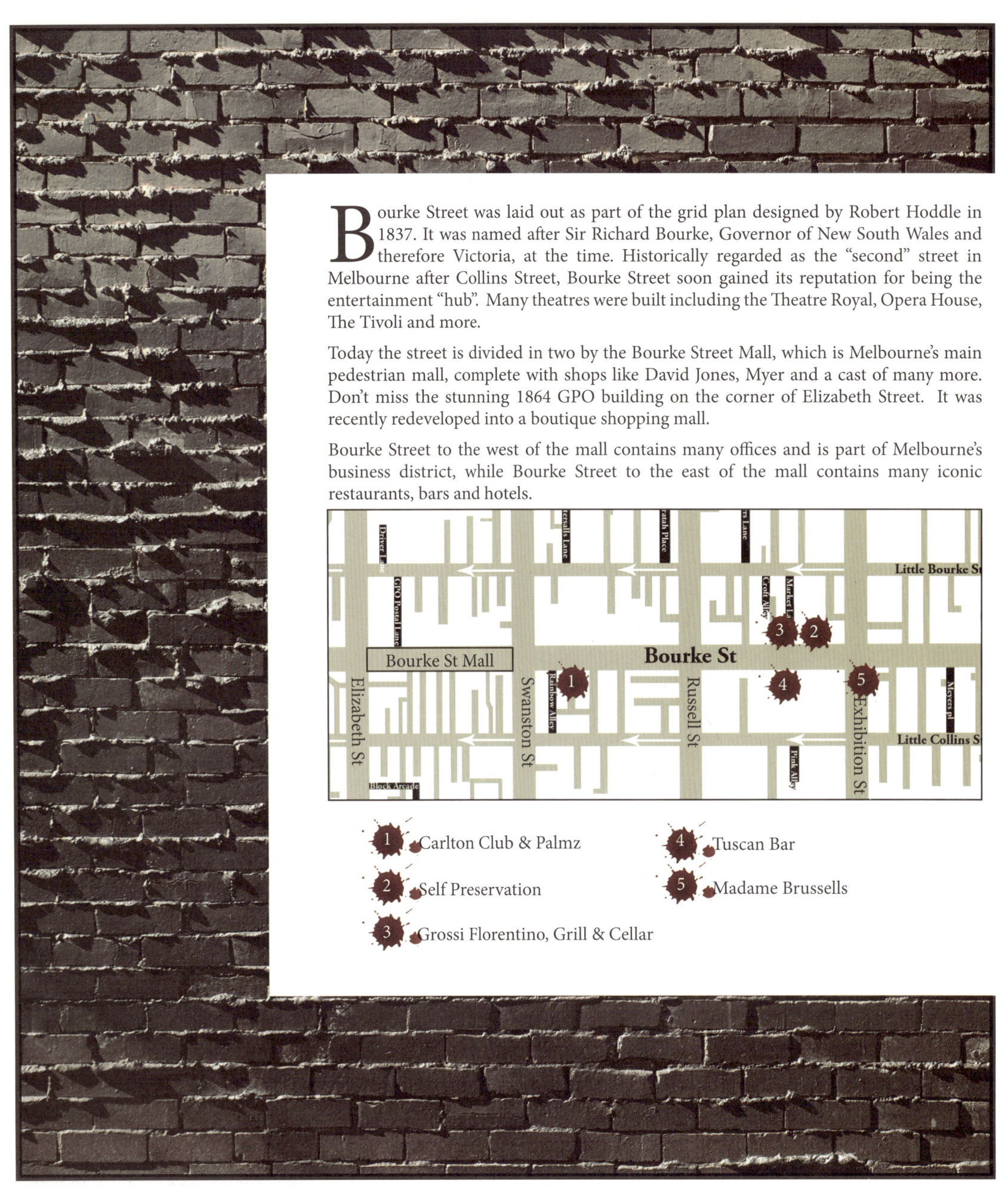

Bourke Street was laid out as part of the grid plan designed by Robert Hoddle in 1837. It was named after Sir Richard Bourke, Governor of New South Wales and therefore Victoria, at the time. Historically regarded as the "second" street in Melbourne after Collins Street, Bourke Street soon gained its reputation for being the entertainment "hub". Many theatres were built including the Theatre Royal, Opera House, The Tivoli and more.

Today the street is divided in two by the Bourke Street Mall, which is Melbourne's main pedestrian mall, complete with shops like David Jones, Myer and a cast of many more. Don't miss the stunning 1864 GPO building on the corner of Elizabeth Street. It was recently redeveloped into a boutique shopping mall.

Bourke Street to the west of the mall contains many offices and is part of Melbourne's business district, while Bourke Street to the east of the mall contains many iconic restaurants, bars and hotels.

1. Carlton Club & Palmz
2. Self Preservation
3. Grossi Florentino, Grill & Cellar
4. Tuscan Bar
5. Madame Brussells

# BOURKE ST.

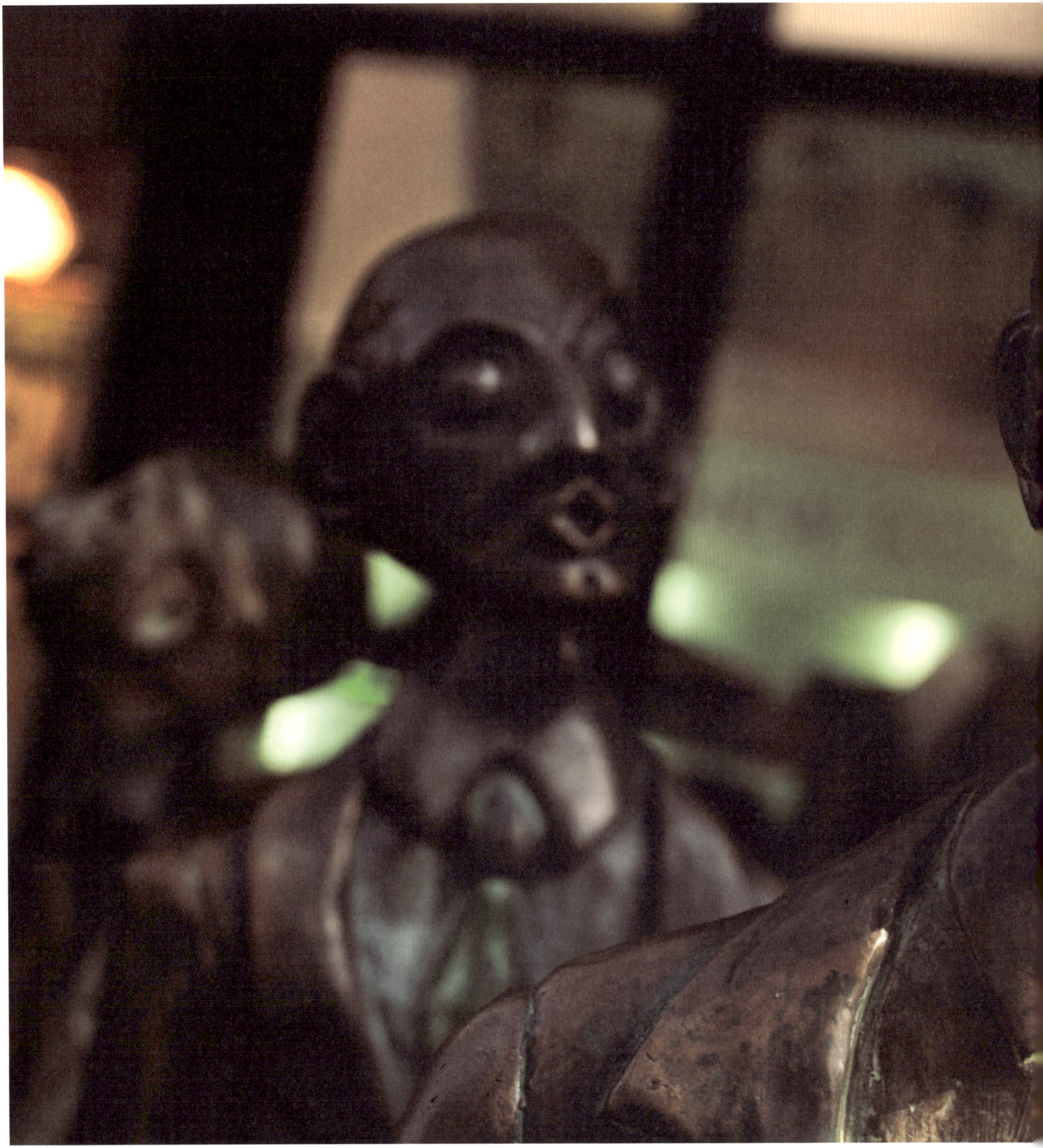

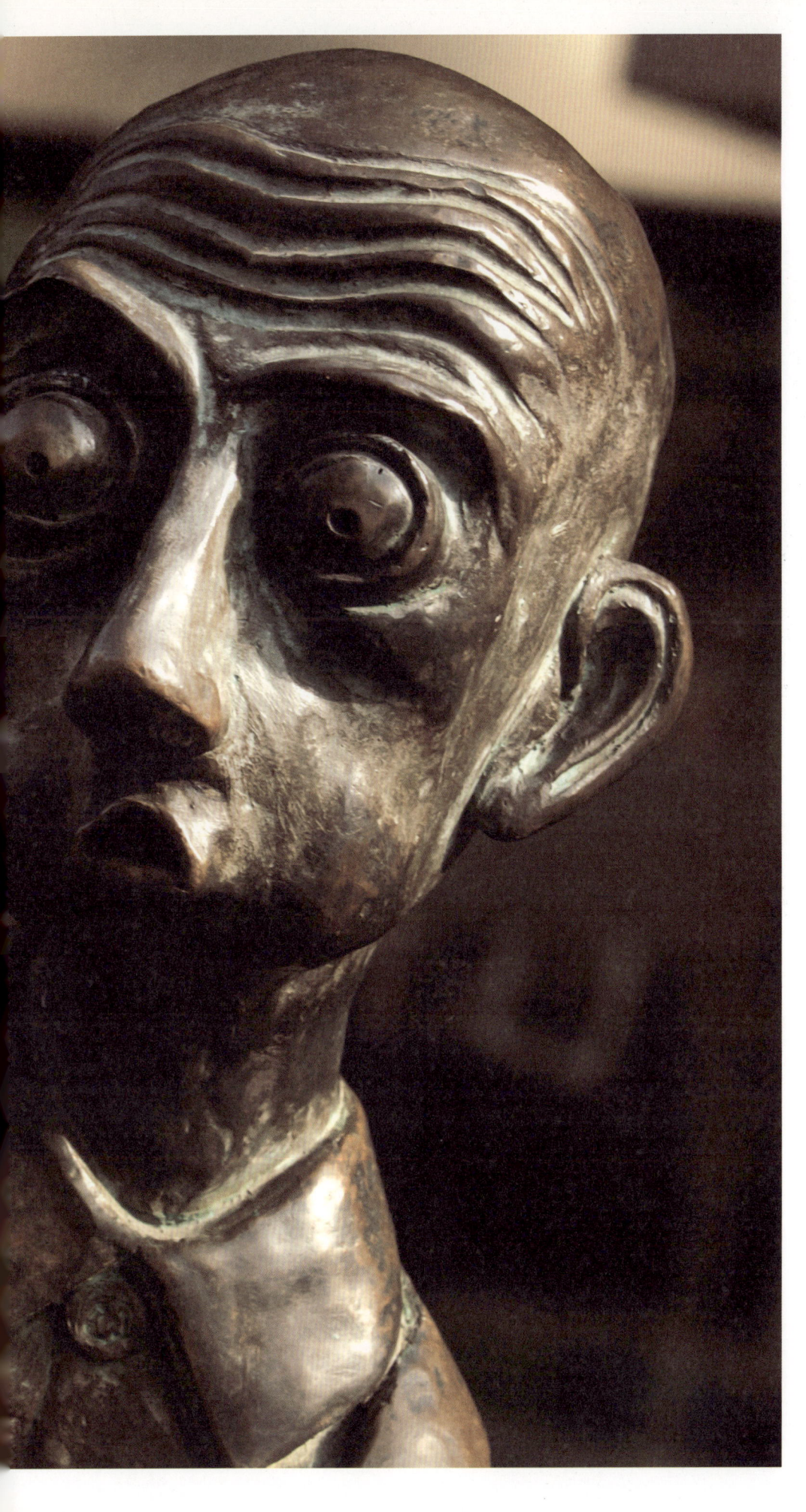

# THREE BUSINESSMEN WHO BROUGHT THEIR OWN LUNCH: BATMAN, SWANSTON AND HODDLE

Alison Weaver and Paul Quinn
Bronze sculpture, 1993
Corner of Swanston and Bourke Streets

# THE CARLTON HOTEL

193-197 Bourke St
03 9663 3246
www.thecarlton.com.au

Appearances can be deceiving, and it has never been truer than in the case of the Carlton Hotel. A nondescript wooden door at street level opens to a staircase that leads to a far-from-typical mid-city bar. Flock wallpaper, sprouting greenery and a zoo of taxidermy creatures – an ostrich, giraffe and peacocks among them – have transformed the bar from down at heel to over the top since owner, Tracey Lester, took over the establishment in 2005.

Once a gathering place for some of Melbourne's less salubrious characters, the Carlton now plays host to a wide variety of punters, from city types looking for post-work refreshment to creative's, musicians and hipsters, who revel in the unusual surroundings. As well as the eclectic interior, there's also a large deck (a retractable awning protects those who prefer the outdoors even when the weather is inclement) that overlooks the Bourke Street bustle.

From the huge wooden bar, choose from the eight beers on tap, an extensive wine list (there are 20 available by the glass) or a range of cocktails that traverses the traditional – Cosmopolitans, martinis and the like – and branches out to include Stuart Woods' creative creations. Particularly popular are the cocktail jugs; My Mother's Ruin is a twist on the gin and tonic, with elderberry liqueur added, that's designed to share with friends.

Offering innovative cuisine is chef Tristan Newman, who trained at Tetsuya's and more recently worked with Andrew McConnell at Cutler & Co and Cumulus Inc. His seasonal menu takes pub classics and gives them a new spin. Choose from a light bite of local wild mushrooms, white asparagus, polenta, rocket and Pecorino cheese or free-range chicken parma to have in the tucked-away dining room with its candlelight and cabinet of curiosities. While the music is always a feature, DJs take over later in the evening playing everything from indie rock to happy house (and plenty of styles in between). Also keep an eye on the website and Facebook page for upcoming special events, such as the regular Danger Record Fair.

"BE AWARE OF WONDER. LIVE A BALANCED LIFE. LEARN SOME AND THINK SOME AND DRAW AND PAINT AND SING AND DANCE AND PLAY AND WORK EVERY DAY SOME!" ROBERT FULHUM

105

106

# PALMZ AT THE CARLTON

193-197 Bourke St
03 9663 3246
www.thecarlton.com.au

High above the city's stores and footpaths is a tropical world that belies its Melbourne locale. The five storeys of stairs leading to the first of two Palmz rooftop bars (the name does give the vibe away somewhat) do tend to scare a few punters away, but the effort is well worth it and only makes the drinks at the destination even more appreciated. Just ask one of the many regulars.

Despite its outdoors location, this is no average beer garden. The setting is a totally tropical bar – wooden decking, bamboo and thatching, full-sized palm trees, bougainvillea climbing the walls and flocks of flamingos set the mood – with a Gotham City backdrop of lit skyscrapers. Nowhere else in the city will you find anything like it. Climb the final set of steps to reach the second Palmz bar and you're right on top of the building, enjoying the breeze and staring out over the urban skyline. Even when the weather is far from perfect, gas heaters help the temperature remain at a sultry level.

The fully stocked bar, housed in a hut not unlike something you might have seen on Gilligan's Island, offers a selection of tap and bottled beers, wines, spirits and cocktails. Match the ambiance with a retro offering; piña coladas or daiquiris, perhaps – or try one of the latest creations. The Amy Winehouse Experience is a blend of Belvedere Black Raspberry vodka, Hennessy VSOP cognac and Chambord, shaken with blueberries, lemon juice and a touch of absinthe. Like its namesake, it has addictive qualities.

This is a glorious spot to catch up with friends as the sun falls over the city and night sets in. The vibe is relaxed and the music is never too loud, allowing for in-depth conversation. As the night wears on, you could also head downstairs to the Carlton for dinner and, even later, some dancing and people-watching. The Palmz rooftop areas, holding up to 300 people in total, can be booked for private parties during the day or evening.

# GROSSI FLORENTINO

80 Bourke St
03 9662 1811
www.grossiflorentino.com

There are not many in Melbourne who don't know the "Guy". In his restaurants, on television, in newspapers, live at shows.... we just can't get enough of him, or his illustrious food.

Guy Grossi – the well-known and leading Australian chef, food and media personality - is the owner and head chef of the Grossi Group of Restaurants, including the esteemed, international and Australian restaurants Grossi Florentino, Mirka at the Tolarno Hotel in St Kilda, Grossi Trattoria in Bangkok and Merchant Osteria Veneta at Rialto in Collins Street.

Grossi Florentino Restaurant is Guy's gastronomical and architectural heart. Stepping up the curved stair case to the two opulent rooms on the first floor, is to be embraced by Italian hospitality as it has been practiced six days a week for over seventy-five years.

You could say the history of Grossi Florentino really began in 1871 when Samual Wynn took over the building and ran the business as a wine shop. His family lived upstairs in a room that is now named after him – the Wynn room. Samuel prospered, and expanded the shop with a café called Café Denat.

Rinaldo Massoni purchased the cafe in 1928 and changed the name to Café Florentino, and the style of food to Italian. The restaurant was hugely successful and by the end of the 1930's was enjoying an international reputation.

In 1935 the property adjoining Florentino was purchased and the upstairs dining room was extended and reopened in time for Australia's 150th birthday celebration. Today, this is the home of Grossi Florentino, with Guy adding his family trademark name on the original.

Grossi Florentino is a place where tradition and progress intertwine, to create a sanctuary for food, art and wine. Inspired by years of the Renaissance, Grossi Florentino lives on in that tradition, bringing to you, with passion and Italian flair, the best in food and wine.

Always changing but forever constant, Grossi Florentino is a Melbourne icon that inspires, exhilarates and seduces. The Grossi Florentino Restaurant menu is a celebration of seasonal produce that brings to the diner a memorable experience.

Using Italian culture, and the fundamental simplicity of "la cucina Italiana" as the corner stone on which to build, Guy uses the best local and imported products to design a wonderful, fresh and innovative cuisine that is distinctly Italian.

Tradition guides, yet does not shackle, the well trained brigade which is directly managed by Guy and brother in law Chris Rodriguez. Depth of knowledge and a passion for ingredients provide an ever changing list of daily dishes.

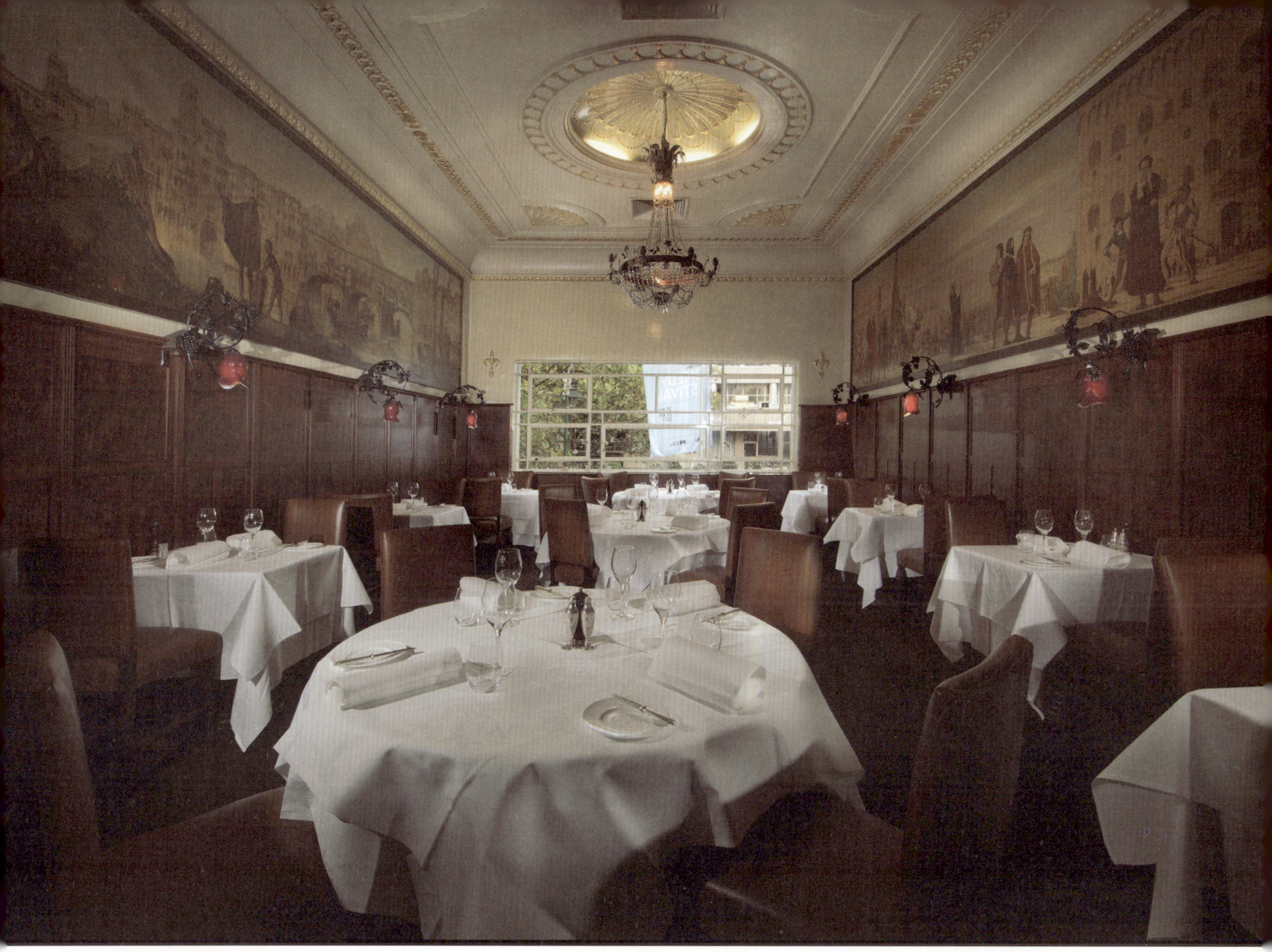

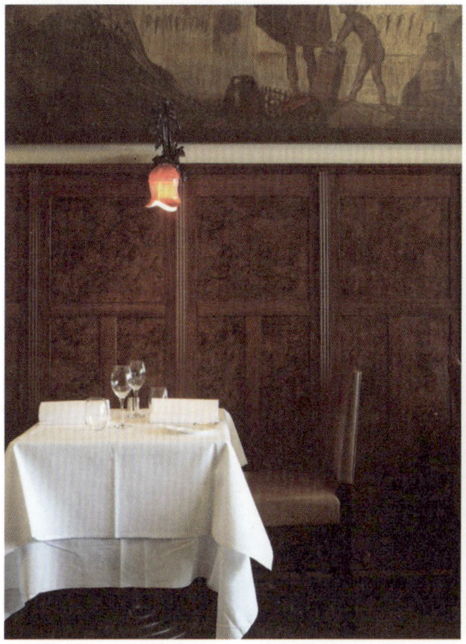

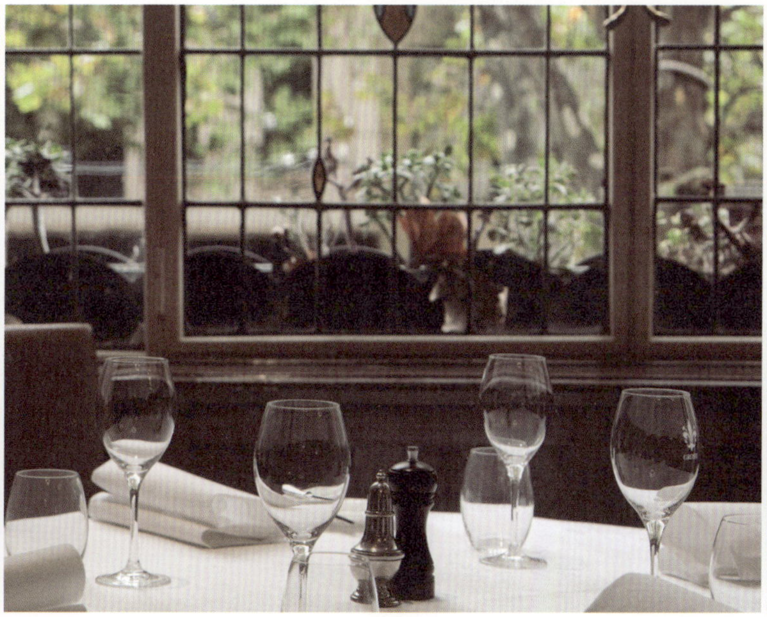

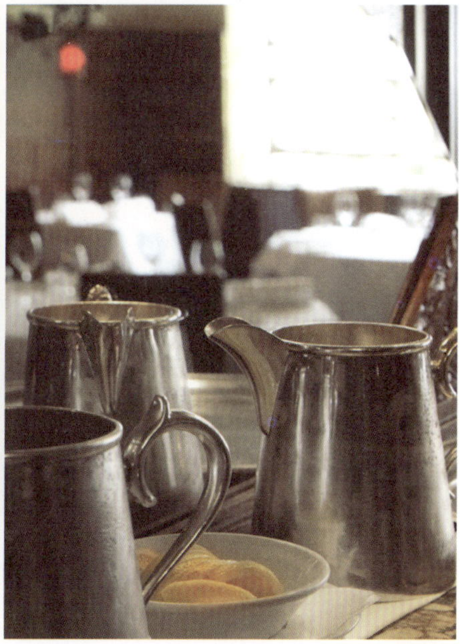

# GROSSI GRILL & CELLAR

80 Bourke St
03 9662 1811
www.grossiflorentino.com

The Grossi Florentino Cellar Bar is the shopfront to the Grossi establishment. A high traffic area where the mood is always changing - bustling and business like in the morning, assertive and noisy at lunchtime and sexy and romantic in the evening. It is the stage upon which Melbourne's café society struts its stuff.

From the day it re-opened in the mid 1950s, it has been a magnate for the habituates of high and low bohemia, politicians, artists, taxi drivers and actors. The menu is proudly Italian, bound by a tradition that transports you to a bar somewhere in Milan or perhaps Fiorenza. Guy's approach here is quality and simplicity.

A typical enoteca, the Cellar Bar menu has a list of food to go with your wine, rather than the other way round. An excellent glass of wine first, then match it with a plate of pasta or some small dishes that can be turned into a lavish dinner.

Or perhaps you will move on to Grossi Florentino Grill – the modern face of the organisation. The epitome of sophisticated, contemporary dining, Italian-style, its aim is to serve simple food based on fresh, local ingredients with sleek, quick service. Using the finest produce, Guy and Chef de Cuisine, Matteo Tine, bring to life the rustic Italian bistro that has won Melbournians hearts with its traditional cuisine and hospitality. Its 'pure' Italian food is an extension of Guy's own childhood experience.

"In my earliest memories of childhood, I can see the kitchen, a place where all would come, filled with these familiar smells, and the laughter of people that love each other and with the anticipation of flavours to come".

The buzz of the open kitchen in the Grossi Grill creates a magnificent atmosphere, one that is centred around 'La Griglia', where the Grill derives its name, always full of the finest aged meats. The constant quest here is for the best quality ingredients which is a fundamental to the Grossi philosophy.

111

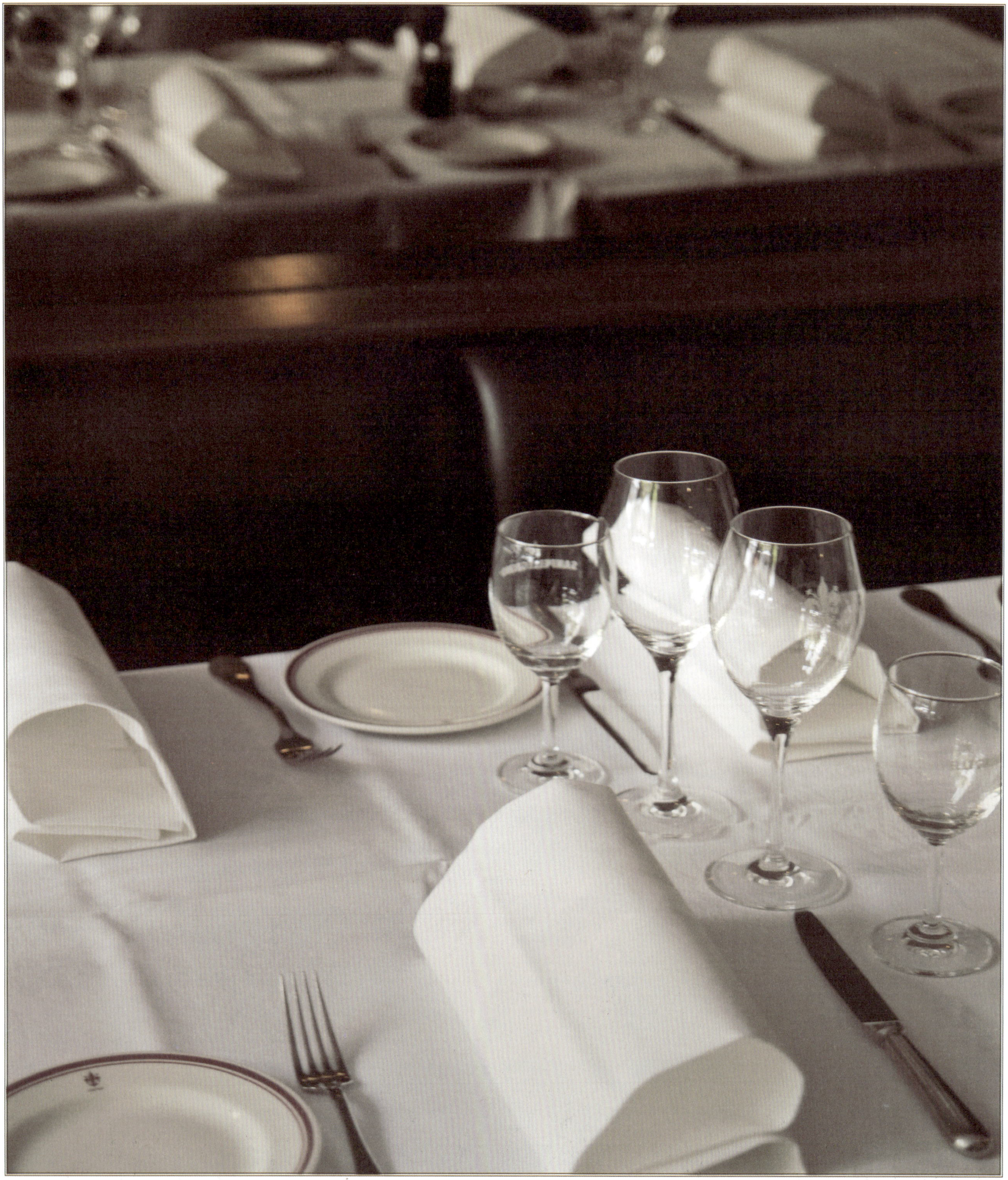

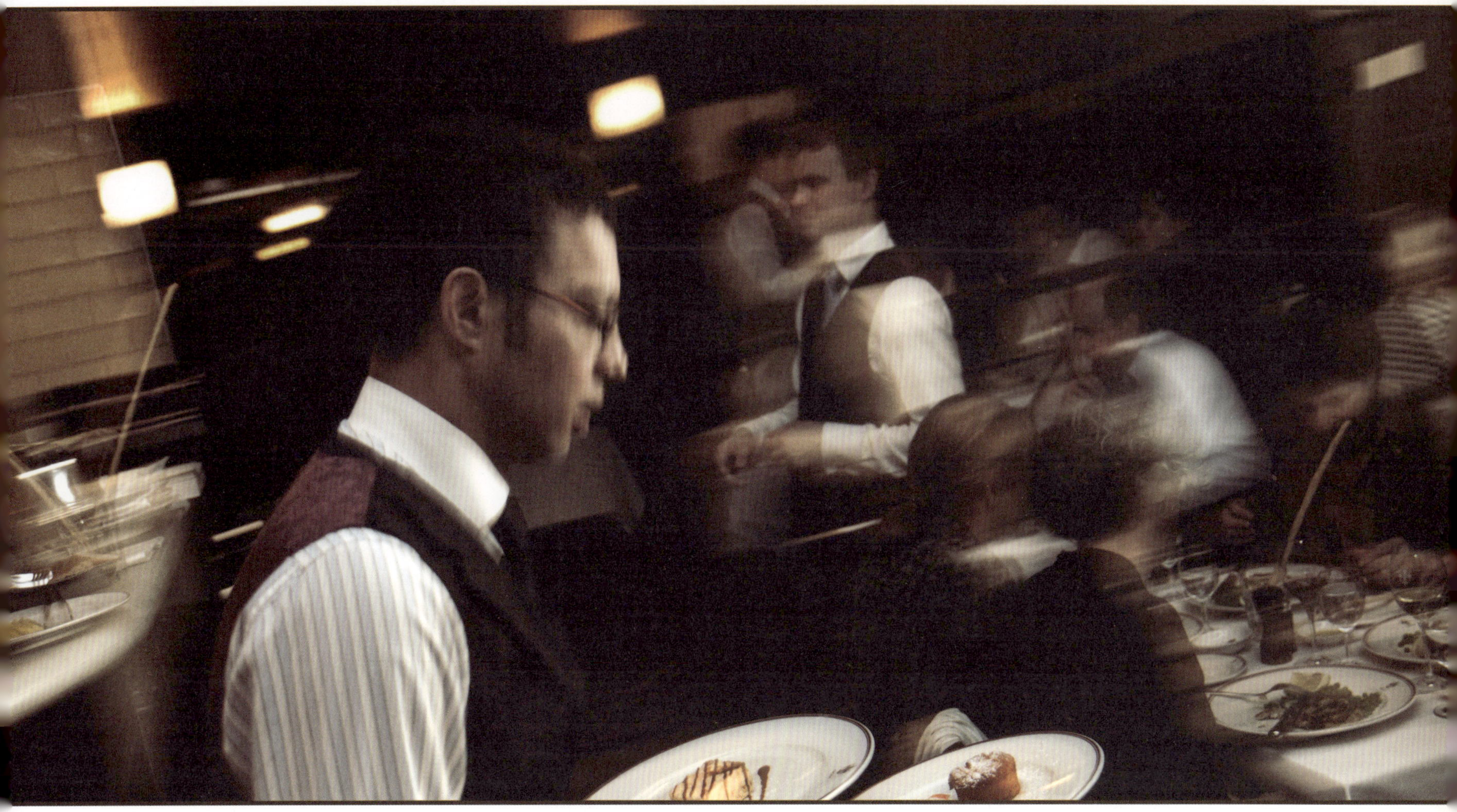

# MADAME BRUSSELS

Level 3, 59 Bourke St
03 9662 2775
www.madamebrussels.com

Who and what is Madame Brussels? You may well ask! With only discrete signage at the street, and a journey upwards via one of the world's ugliest lifts, it's a fantastically trippy relief to land amid this rooftop version of one of Alice's strange adventures. Even for those in the know, Madame Brussels is one of Melbourne's more obscure elevated bars: difficult to find again, because you're brim-full of her famously eccentric hospitality when you leave, and never quite sure whether the last few hours could really have been so ridiculous.

The original Madame Brussels was a notable 19th Century character, famous for laying on hospitality of an altogether more intimate variety. Having been left a widow and mother when only 28, she applied her charms and business acumen to fill an aching void in the marketplace. Such was the demand for her special brand of hospitality, she developed a chain of successful brothels around the eastern fringes of Melbourne city, maintaining decades of busy employment for the ladies in her charge.

The good Madame's reputation is honoured by the more recent institution which bears her name. Still providing individual attention to the needs and special requests of customers, and striving to bring joy and delight to their experiences, Madame Brussels now specialises in serving fabulous cocktails, jugs of punches and Pimms, in surroundings that blend the salubrious with the surreal.

There's an indoor hedged bar wreathed with trelliswork, where nearby garden chairs beckon with their promise of a garden party complete with pink beverages and frosted cupcakes! Handsomely attired staff - seemingly on their way to a social hit of tennis - sparkle and flirt, leaving a gladdened trail of smiles in their wake.

Hidden beyond the garden gates is a room of mystery and intrigue, called The Parlour "up the rear of Madame Brussels". Warmly panelled, plush and indulgently Bavarian, this den of iniquity is home to a head-spinning collection of rare dark spirits and cabinets bristling with crystal decanters, where dedicated clients store their favoured tipple. Whilst often reserved for private functions, The Parlour plays host to a winter season of bizarre special events, when you can join in a crochet-circle, learn the art of fondue fabrication, or dabble in the mysteries of strip-tease!

Best of all, though, is the Madame's ample unclothed frontage, thrusting its doubly splendid balcony over the top end of Bourke Street. No matter how unseemly the weather, there are warm and sheltered corners of the outdoor terrace, with additional fluffy pink blankets and hot-water bottles on request. And where else would you want to be on any warm Summers' evening, other than catching a zephyr curling through the latticework of the uppermost balcony, your frosty libation in hand? What more could you possibly desire? So, what are you waiting for? In time-honoured fashion, Madame Brussels beckons…

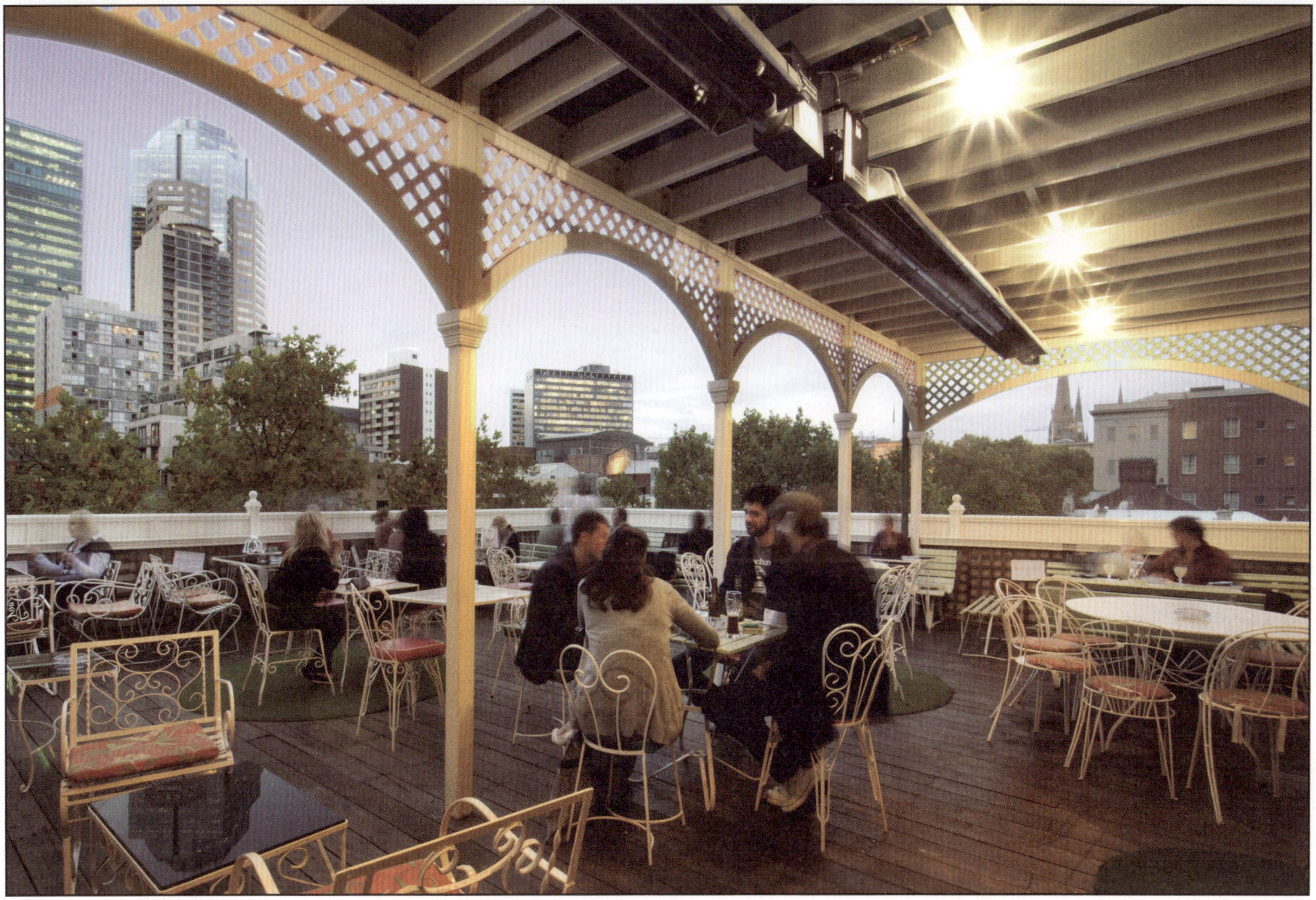

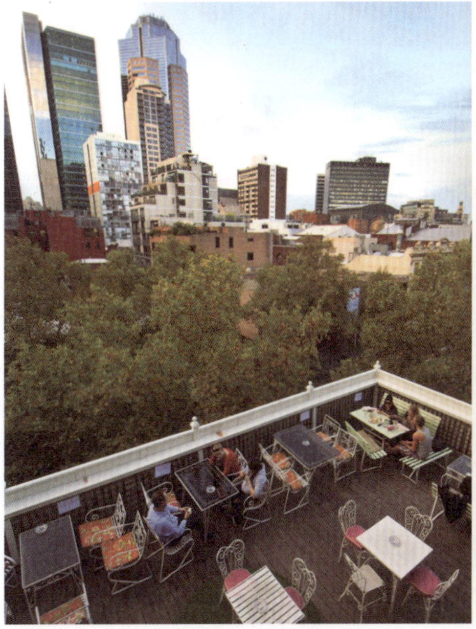

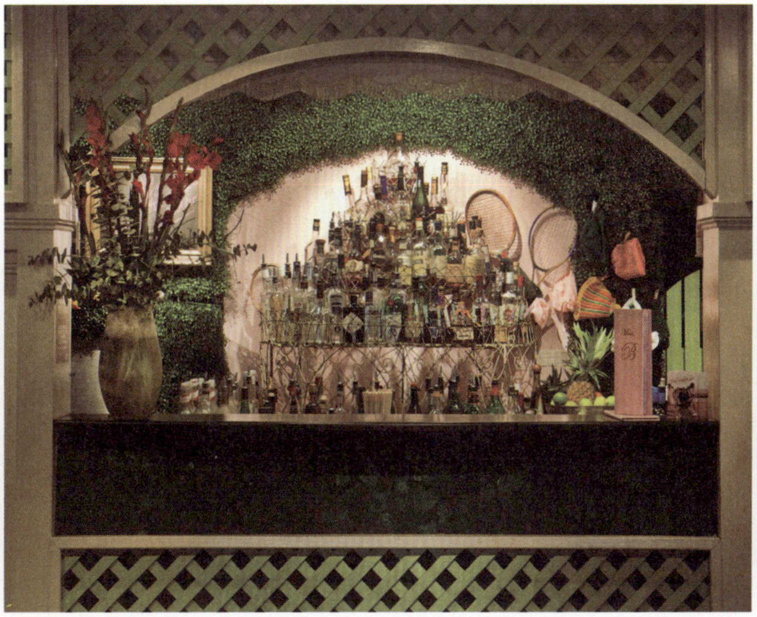

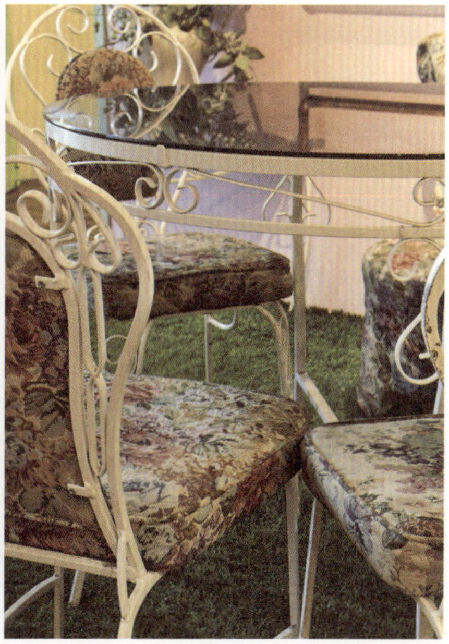

# SELF PRESERVATION

70 Bourke St
03 9650 0523
www.selfpreservation.com.au

Co-owners Anitsa Connor and Con Christopoulos opened Self Preservation in June 2007. This unique space combines the most important facets of Melbourne's CBD: great food, dining, art and shopping. Derived from the ancient idea of jewellery having protective powers, the name Self Preservation is now embodied by a contemporary space with a timeless feel, where exceptional coffee, dining, jewellery and art can be equally enjoyed in a friendly, creative atmosphere.

The high-ceilinged, concrete-floored space is elegantly appointed. Beautiful old tiles decorate the entrance and a neat little marble bar dominated by a coffee machine takes precedence as you step inside. The café flirts with European style using folding wood and metal French café chairs both on the street and in the gallery.

Self Preservation offers a compact but dynamic menu, specialising in turning the best seasonal ingredients into exciting yet simple dishes. The menu, the brainchild of Sam Kenway, reflects the changeable nature of Melbourne's weather and is designed to suit the freshest available produce.

Sam is a familiar and well-respected face on the Melbourne restaurant scene, having cooked for 14 years in a number of well-known Melbourne establishments.

A favourite dish which always brings the customers back for more is the organic minute steak with celeriac remoulade and roasted mushrooms. Thoughtful breakfast options and delicate pastries are also on offer and these make a delicious accompaniment for the well-made coffee and potted tea. There is also an intriguing selection of wine and beer to keep things interesting.

Self Preservation showcases independent, designer and vintage pieces of jewellery. The gold and silver masterpieces range from the purely aesthetic to the downright clever. One range of rings featured the chemical formula for caffeine. The showcases are not purely reserved for jewellery and boast a range of ready-to-hang and affordable artworks.

As a hybrid establishment, Self Preservation attracts a diverse clientele including the lunchtime business crowd, inquisitive tourists and those 'in the know'. Owner Anitsa Connor says, "…what we love about being here is the combination of intimacy and European sophistication, which is all thrown in with a stylish yet down-to-earth sensibility that is unique to Melbourne." That is exactly why you will love being here too.

Crumbed Sea
grilled
orange
Organic
celeriac
& roasted
mushrooms

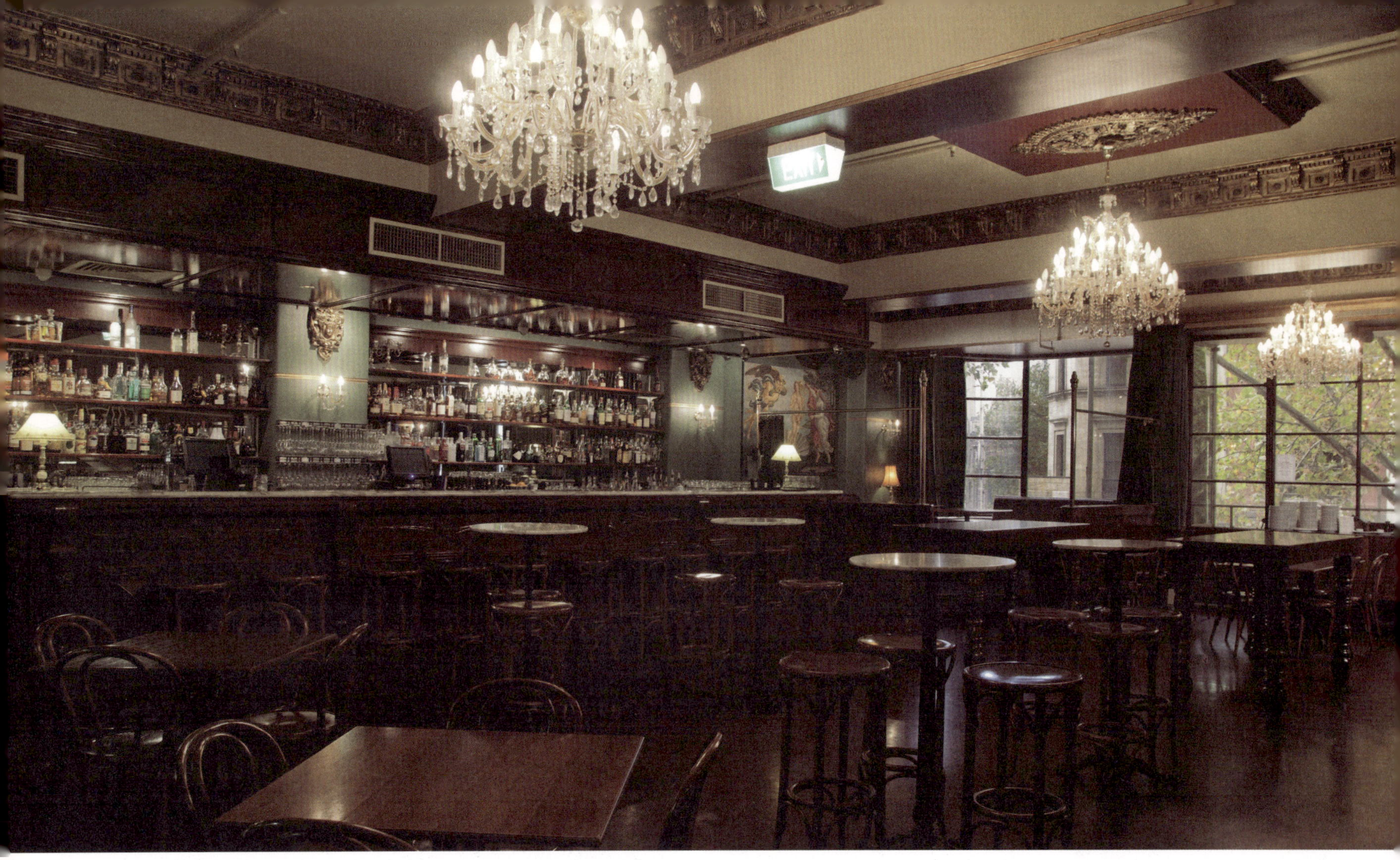

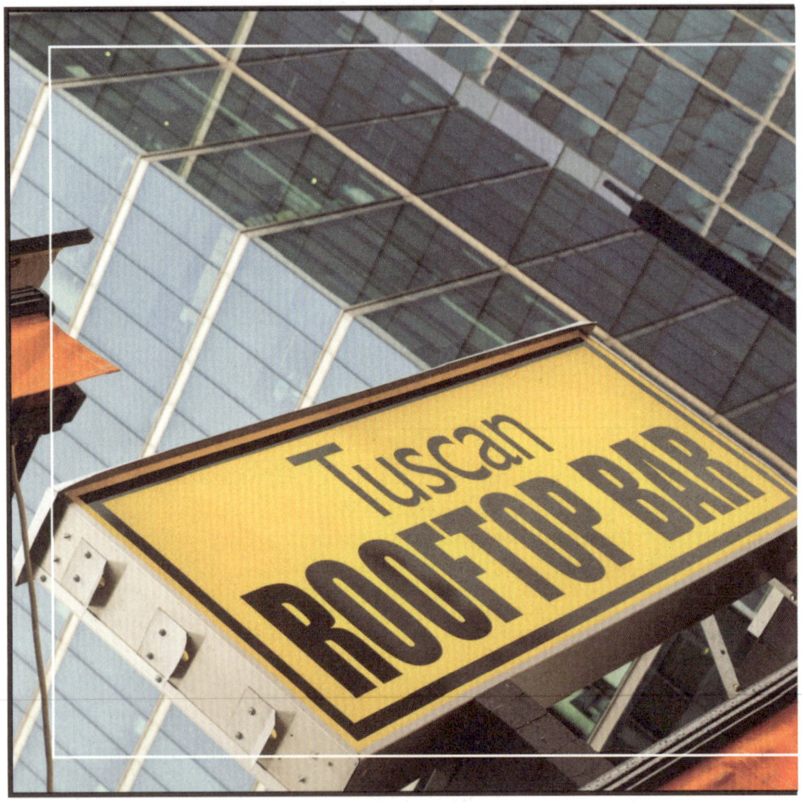
Tuscan
ROOFTOP BAR

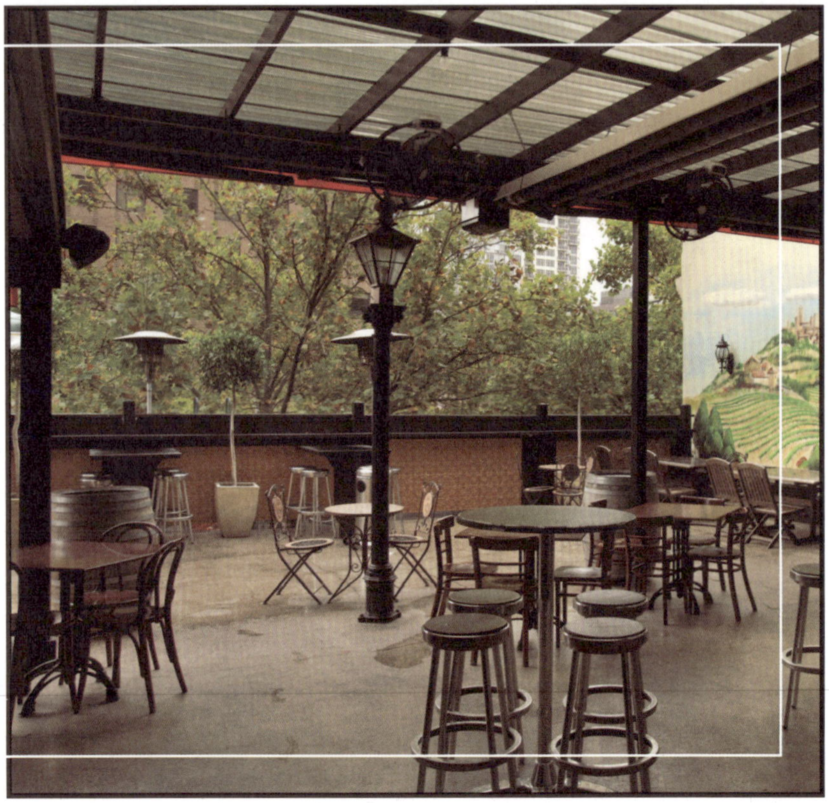

# TUSCAN ROOFTOP BAR

Level 1 & Rooftop
79 Bourke St
03 9671 3322
www.tuscanbar.com.au

"I love being at this end of town where all the established theatres, eateries and bars are," says owner of the Tuscan Bar, Fabbio Navarroli. With the bar and its rooftop setting on Bourke Street, between Exhibition and Spring Streets, Fabio says that this end of town has "a culture and refinement that we try to reflect at Tuscan Bar".

Fabio sees the bar as a place for connecting professionals from a variety of work places. He welcomes Melbourne's professionals and parliamentarians, as well as people from the theatre, including the casts and crews, theatre goers and comedians. They all enjoy the ambience of Tuscan Bar.

And as talk flows, so do the skills of Bartender, Ajay Rose, who amuses clients with his artistic skills. Try out his most noted cocktail, Lemoncello Torta.

Established in 2007, the Tuscan Bar added a Rooftop Garden in 2008. Now you have the choice of the quiet ambience of the first level bar and lounge, or work your way to the top to join in the revelry of a Friday night after work.

You will find creative Italian cooking to share or sit down for a full meal. The atmosphere is relaxed and diners can relish a shared dip, some pasta or a traditional main course. The aroma of Italian cooking greets you on a cold winter's night, and so will the extraordinary cheese selection to enjoy with a good red.

To finish your night, don't miss out on a Tuscan specialty like the housemade vanilla panna cotta, cinnamon and ricotta doughnuts, mixed berry crumble or an affogato shot of sapore espresso coffee.

No wonder, first time visitors find themselves retracing their footsteps through the same door. Indeed, taste buds remember road maps and a foodie mind has its wish granted.

BOURKE ST BOURKE ST BOURKE ST BOURKE ST BOURKE ST BOURKE ST BOURKE ST BOUR

# PELLEGRINI'S

66 Bourke St
03 9662 1885

Step away from the modern, carefully-styled restaurant and back to a time where wholesome flavoursome food was valued over pizzazz. In a one word description that few will dispute, Pellegrini's is an "institution". Pellegrini's has been serving Melburnians for over fifty years and still serves great coffee, great home-made Italian food and provides consistent service. You will find a range of customers from city professionals and theatre goers to students who have come to rely on the good value, honest Italian food. Especially if it is your first visit, keep an eye on passing meals to preview many items that are not listed on the menu, such as the traditional Friday gnocchi or the watermelon granita that appears in the Summer. Dig into an enormous bowl of spaghetti or melting lasagne or alternatively drink your coffee Italian style, on a stool at the bar.

BOURKE ST BOURKE ST BOURKE ST BOURKE ST BOURKE ST BOURKE ST BOURKE ST BOUR

# SOCIETY RESTAURANT

23 Bourke St
03 9639 2544
www.societyrestaurant.com

Established by Guiseppe Codognotto, the restaurant which moved to 23 Bourke Street in 1932 is one of Melbourne's oldest Italian dining institutions. Guiseppe's son, Rino, steered Society through its glory days from 1940 to the 1980's, becoming one of Melbourne's original "Spaghetti Mafia" for providing the city with the finest Italian food and service. After Rino's retirement in 1984, Society saw various changes to name and form until it was brought back to its roots by the DiMattina Group in 2007. Today you will find a lovingly restored restaurant filled with classic charm and luxurious style. The cuisine, while holding true to rustic and flavoursome creations, follows a modern tailored menu that avoids being unnecessarily grandiose. The wine list incorporates a satisfying fusion of Australian and Italian wines, with a large enough variety to please those with a taste for good wine.

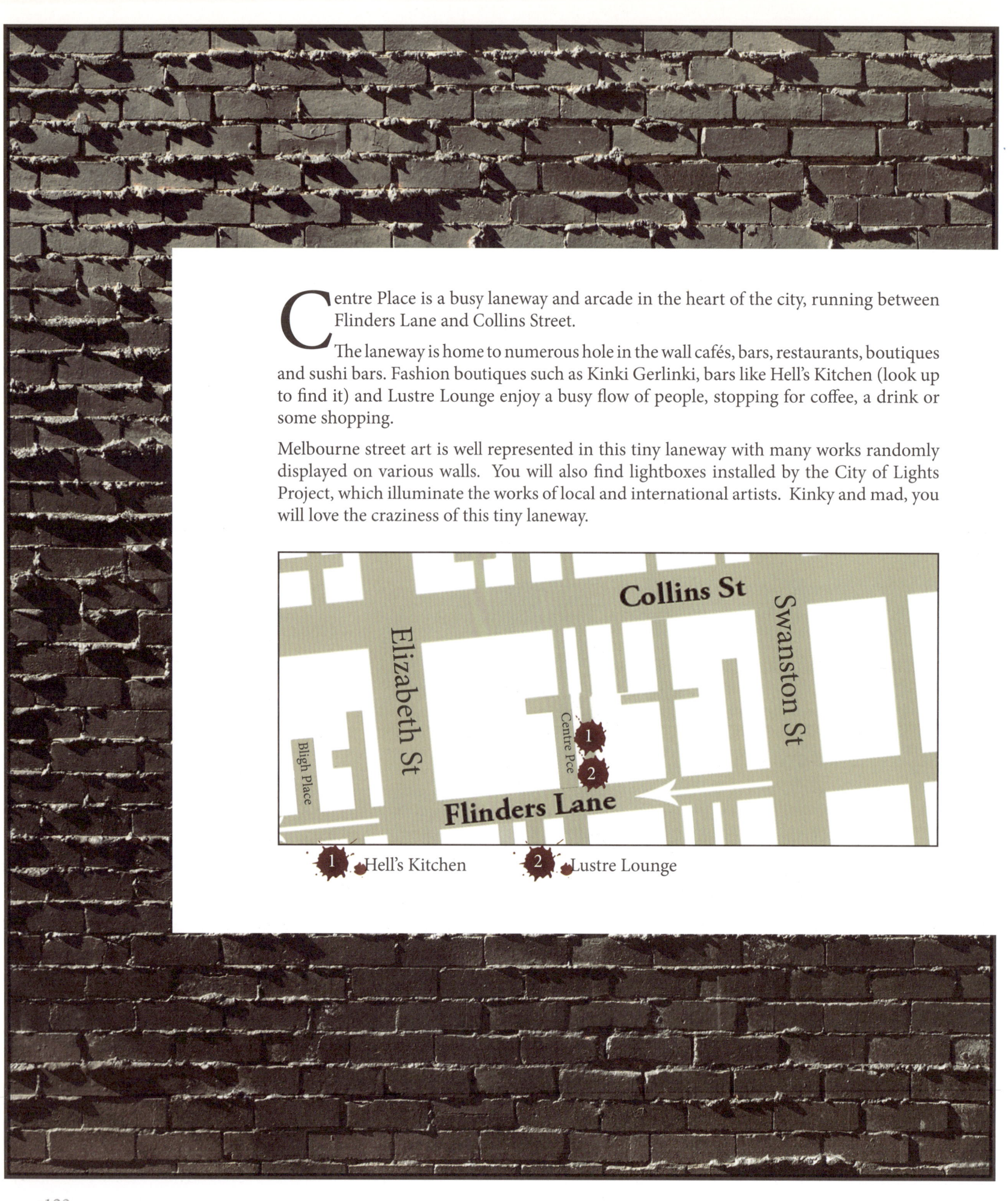

Centre Place is a busy laneway and arcade in the heart of the city, running between Flinders Lane and Collins Street.

The laneway is home to numerous hole in the wall cafés, bars, restaurants, boutiques and sushi bars. Fashion boutiques such as Kinki Gerlinki, bars like Hell's Kitchen (look up to find it) and Lustre Lounge enjoy a busy flow of people, stopping for coffee, a drink or some shopping.

Melbourne street art is well represented in this tiny laneway with many works randomly displayed on various walls. You will also find lightboxes installed by the City of Lights Project, which illuminate the works of local and international artists. Kinky and mad, you will love the craziness of this tiny laneway.

1. Hell's Kitchen
2. Lustre Lounge

# CENTRE PLACE

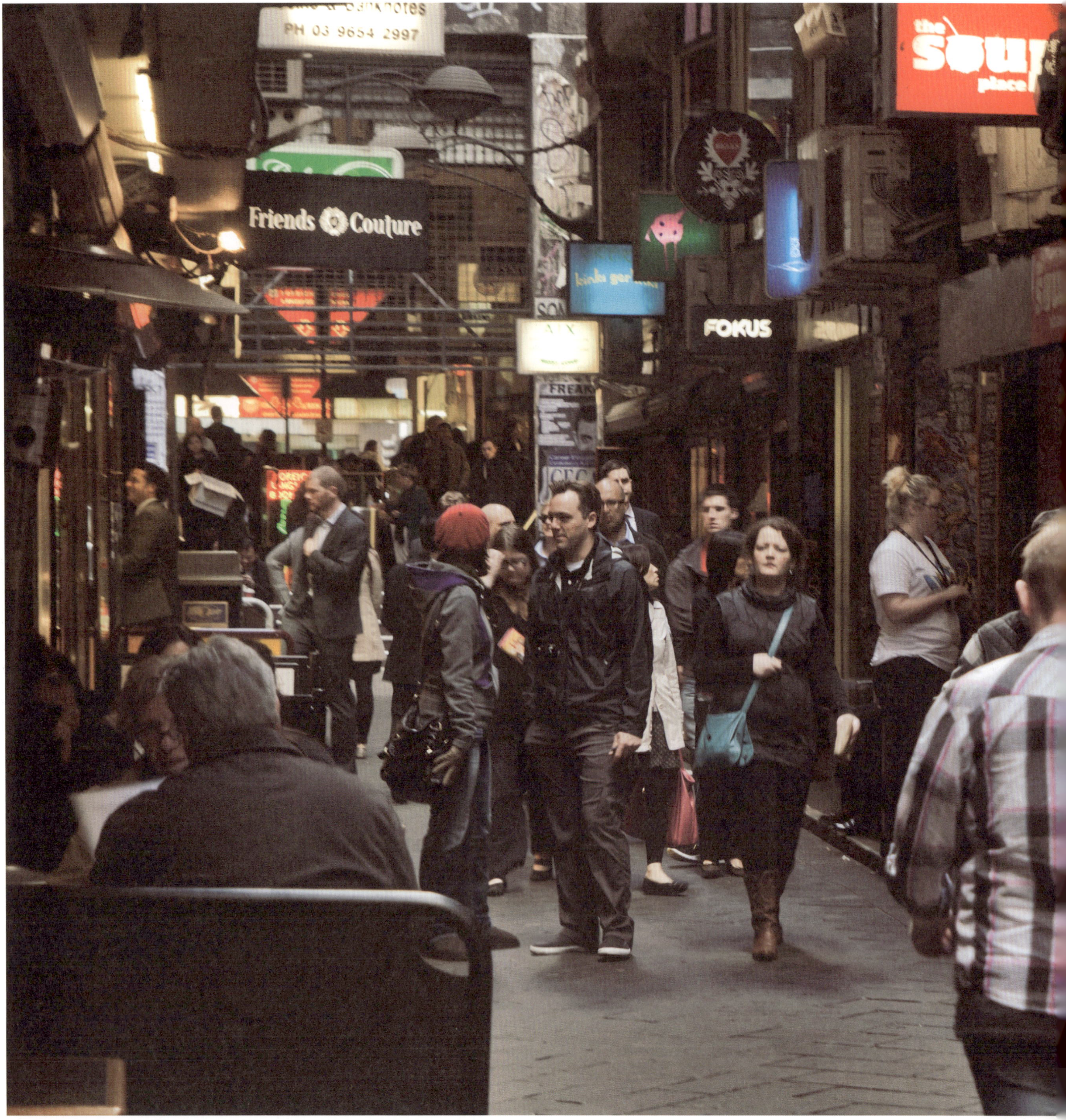
PH 03 9654 2997
Friends Couture
FOKUS

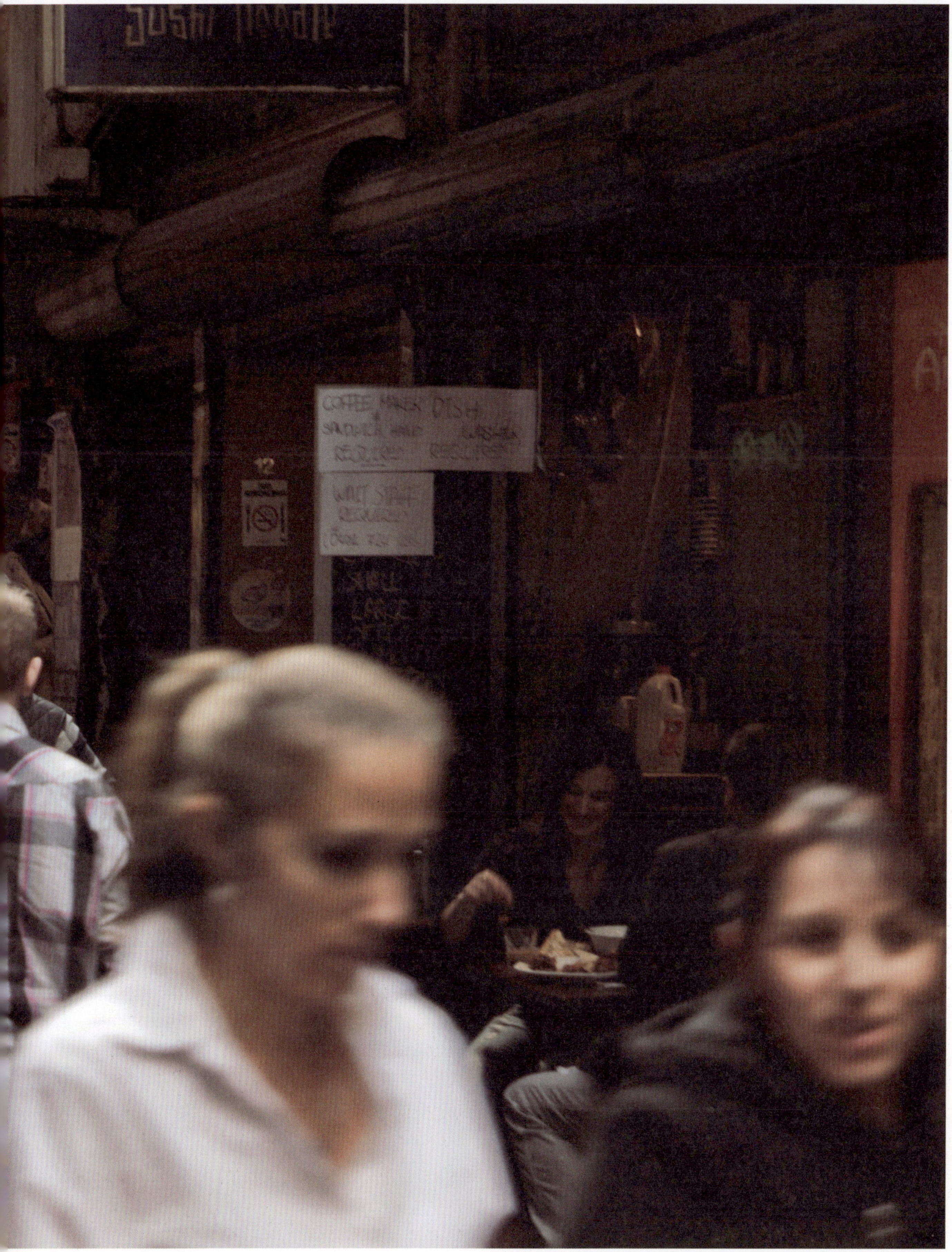

# HELLS KITCHEN

20 Centre Place
03 9654 5755
www.hellskitchenmelbourne.com

Hidden between Elizabeth and Swanston Streets and tucked off Flinders Lane is a one of Melbourne's secret cocktail/wine bars. "Look up!" is all I can say, while you ramble down this tiny laneway with pop-up cafés and tiny shops dotted along its side walls. Follow the sign and up the narrow staircase and you will escape to Hells Kitchen.  Claim your place at the window overlooking Centre place and you will find yourself amongst a mix of post-work and arty types. The bar is a cosy place to enjoy not only the Carlton Draught and Cooper's Pale on tap, but the vodkas that are infused in-house with delicious flavours including chilli, lime, honey and ginger, lemon and coffee. If you are feeling peckish you should be able to find something to satisfy yourself.  The menu is simple but still manages to provide a number tasty vegetarian dishes. Hell's Kitchen is a great no-fuss retreat above the work bustle.

CENTRE PLACE CENTRE PLACE CENTRE PLACE CENTRE PLACE CENTRE PLACE CENTRE

Level 1, 252 Flinders Lane
03 9671 3371
www.lustrelounge.com.au

# LUSTRE LOUNGE

Lustre Lounge is another of Melbourne's hidden secrets. At the entry of Centre Place, keep an eye out for the silver balcony overlooking the corner of Flinders Lane and Degraves Street. Of course, the white, round light hanging above the entrance that says "Lustre Lounge" is a dead give-away, once you know where you are going.

Polished wooden floors, peach walls and oversized couches produce a glowing, psychedelic, 70's feel. The range on the drinks menu should cater to most palates, in particular premium spirits and good champagne, yet encouraging the cocktail bias. The feel of the bar, like its location is a step away from the grungy laneway below, making this an unpretentious night time spot for professionals, locals and all who appreciate a drink with a view.

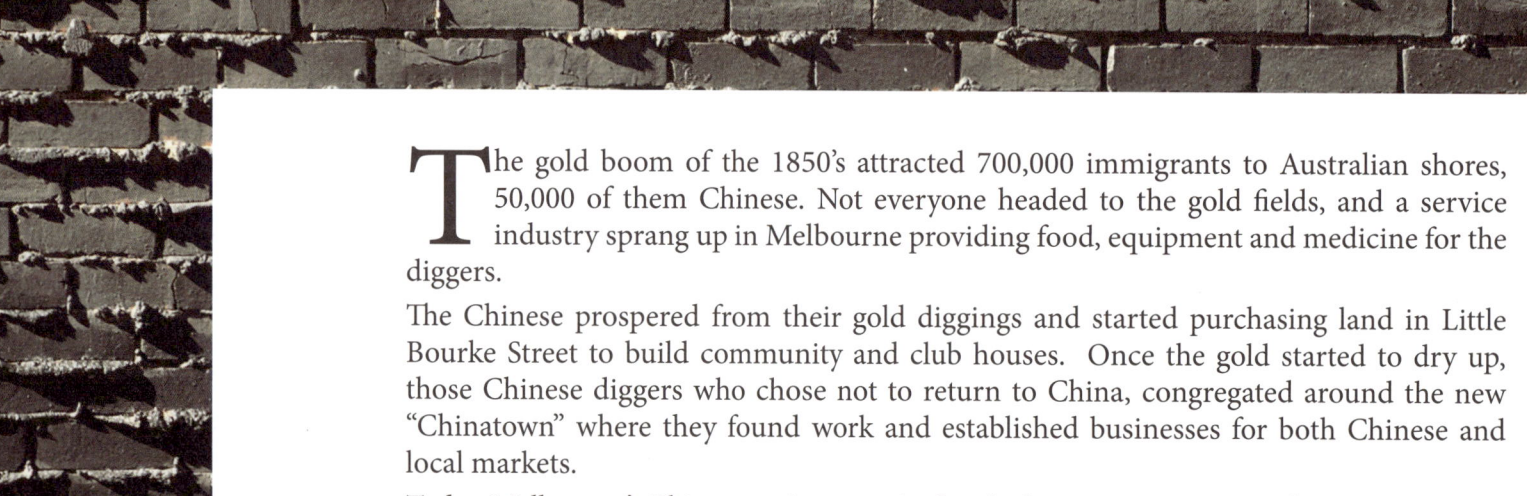

The gold boom of the 1850's attracted 700,000 immigrants to Australian shores, 50,000 of them Chinese. Not everyone headed to the gold fields, and a service industry sprang up in Melbourne providing food, equipment and medicine for the diggers.

The Chinese prospered from their gold diggings and started purchasing land in Little Bourke Street to build community and club houses. Once the gold started to dry up, those Chinese diggers who chose not to return to China, congregated around the new "Chinatown" where they found work and established businesses for both Chinese and local markets.

Today, Melbourne's Chinatown is recognised as the longest, continuous Chinese settlement in the western world. It is a busy hub for the Chinese community, and one of the most endeared strips of restaurants, noodle houses, Asian grocery stores, Chinese medicine and herbalist centres, bookstores and fashion boutiques in the city today.

Greeted by five key arches, clearly announcing the entrance to Chinatown, the precinct extends along Little Bourke Street, from Swanston Street to Spring Street. Not purely Chinese, you will also find cuisines from other cultures including Thai, Japanese, Malaysian, Vietnamese, Contemporary European and Australian to tempt your taste buds.

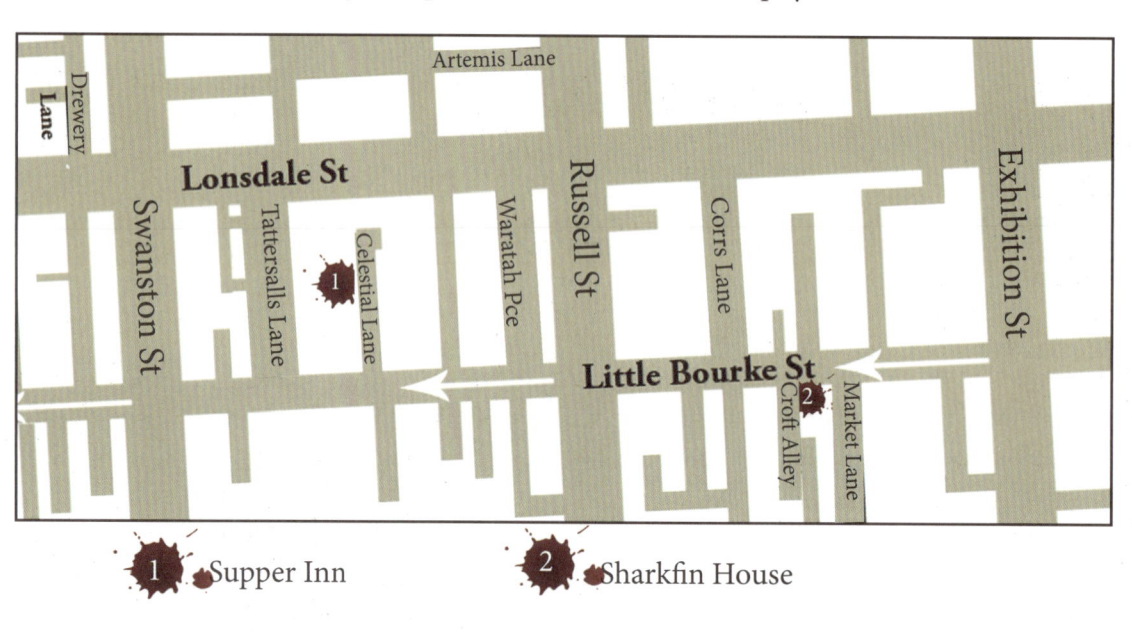

1. Supper Inn
2. Sharkfin House

# CHINATOWN

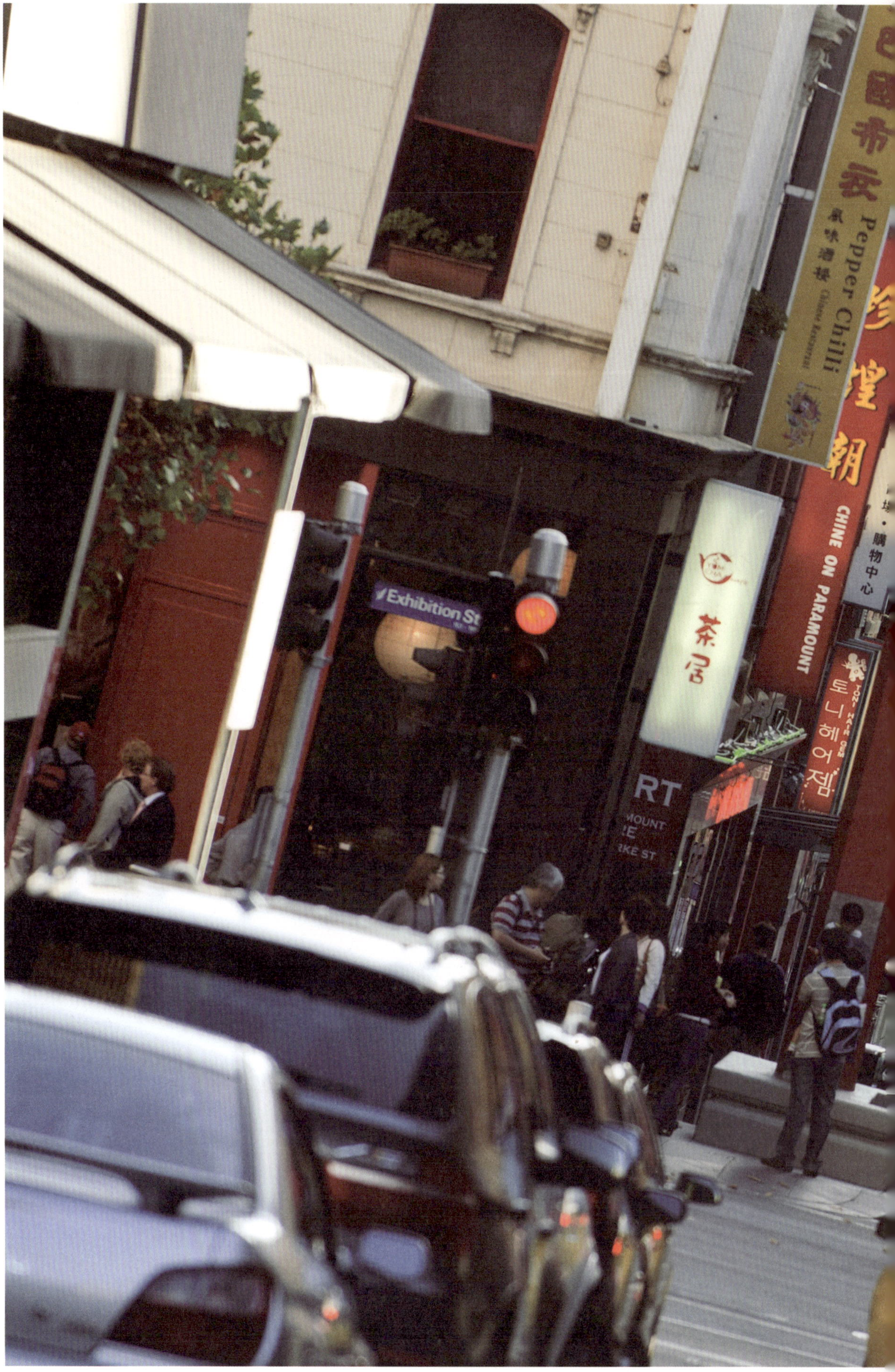
Exhibition St
Pepper Chilli
CHINE ON PARAMOUNT

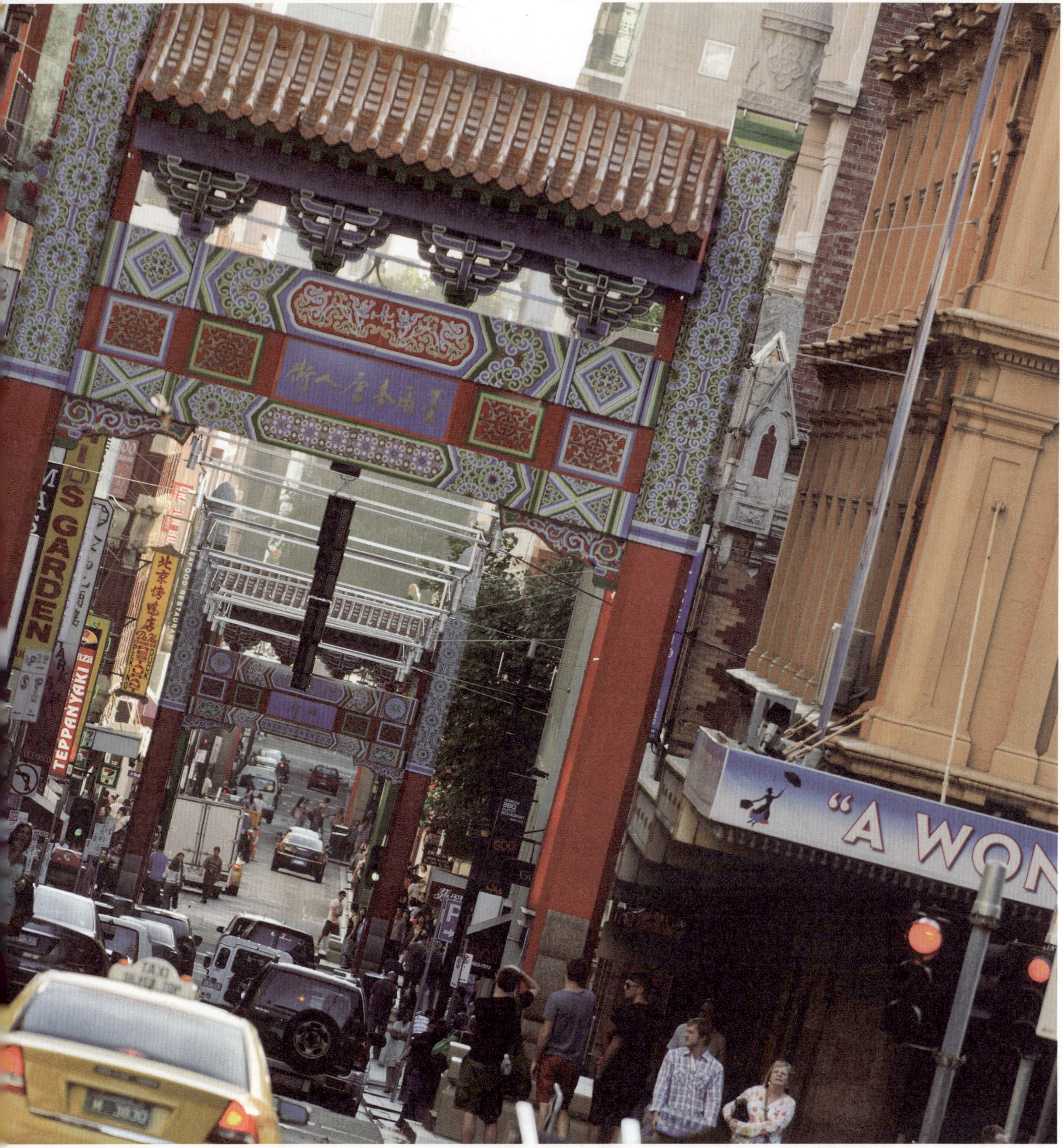
GARDEN
TEPPANYAKI
TAXI
“A WON

# SHARKFIN HOUSE

131 Little Bourke St
03 9663 1555
www.sharkfin.com.au

Shark Fin House has earned a glowing reputation for its authentic and delicious Chinese dishes. So popular, in fact, it opened a second restaurant in the city, one at either end of China town. As soon as you walk through the doors you will become immersed in the Mandarin background chatter. Many local Chinese eat here to find traditional Chinese meat, noodle or rice dishes including shark fin meals on the extensive menu. Open until the early hours of the morning, there is no excuse for missing the delicious yum cha or the dumplings, which are a specialty. This is one of those much-loved places that you will need to book in advance, but the first bite of the fresh seafood makes securing a table well worth the effort.

CHINATOWN CHINATOWN CHINATOWN CHINATOWN CHINATOWN CHINATOWN CHINATOWN

15 Celestial Ave
03 9663 4759

# SUPPER INN

Almost hidden from China Town's sight is this infamous local restaurant, Supper Inn. Half-way between Russell and Swanston Street you will turn off Little Bourke Street and into Celestial Avenue. Look up, and you will see the long-standing sign of a Melbourne favourite - one of the gems of Chinatown. Open until 2.30am everyday, you will find genuine Cantonese cuisine at very affordable prices. As you walk up the wood panelled stair case, you will find a typical looking Chinese restaurant, but don't let that mask your view of the place. Celebrate with specialties like pickled and roasted Suckling Pig, Combination Seafood in a clay pot or Stuffed Scallops with minced Calamari and Prawns. If you are a drinks connoisseur and worried about the wine list, don't be. Another perk of Supper Inn is that you can bring your own.

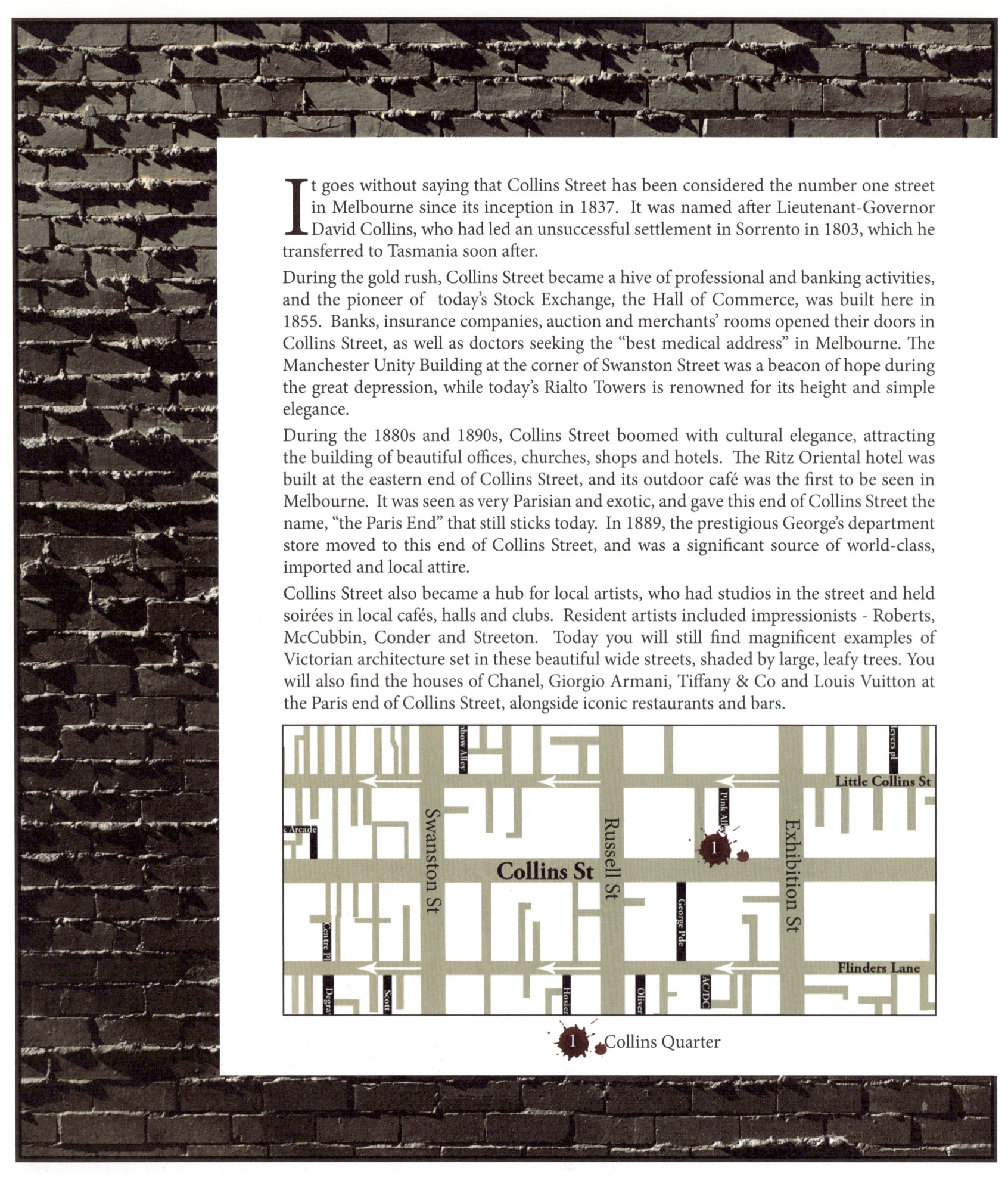

It goes without saying that Collins Street has been considered the number one street in Melbourne since its inception in 1837. It was named after Lieutenant-Governor David Collins, who had led an unsuccessful settlement in Sorrento in 1803, which he transferred to Tasmania soon after.

During the gold rush, Collins Street became a hive of professional and banking activities, and the pioneer of today's Stock Exchange, the Hall of Commerce, was built here in 1855. Banks, insurance companies, auction and merchants' rooms opened their doors in Collins Street, as well as doctors seeking the "best medical address" in Melbourne. The Manchester Unity Building at the corner of Swanston Street was a beacon of hope during the great depression, while today's Rialto Towers is renowned for its height and simple elegance.

During the 1880s and 1890s, Collins Street boomed with cultural elegance, attracting the building of beautiful offices, churches, shops and hotels. The Ritz Oriental hotel was built at the eastern end of Collins Street, and its outdoor café was the first to be seen in Melbourne. It was seen as very Parisian and exotic, and gave this end of Collins Street the name, "the Paris End" that still sticks today. In 1889, the prestigious George's department store moved to this end of Collins Street, and was a significant source of world-class, imported and local attire.

Collins Street also became a hub for local artists, who had studios in the street and held soirées in local cafés, halls and clubs. Resident artists included impressionists - Roberts, McCubbin, Conder and Streeton. Today you will still find magnificent examples of Victorian architecture set in these beautiful wide streets, shaded by large, leafy trees. You will also find the houses of Chanel, Giorgio Armani, Tiffany & Co and Louis Vuitton at the Paris end of Collins Street, alongside iconic restaurants and bars.

1. Collins Quarter

# COLLINS ST.

30%
SCOTCH&SODA
AMSTERDAM COUTURE
LAST ITEMS
30%
70%
SALE
50%
40%
30%
30%

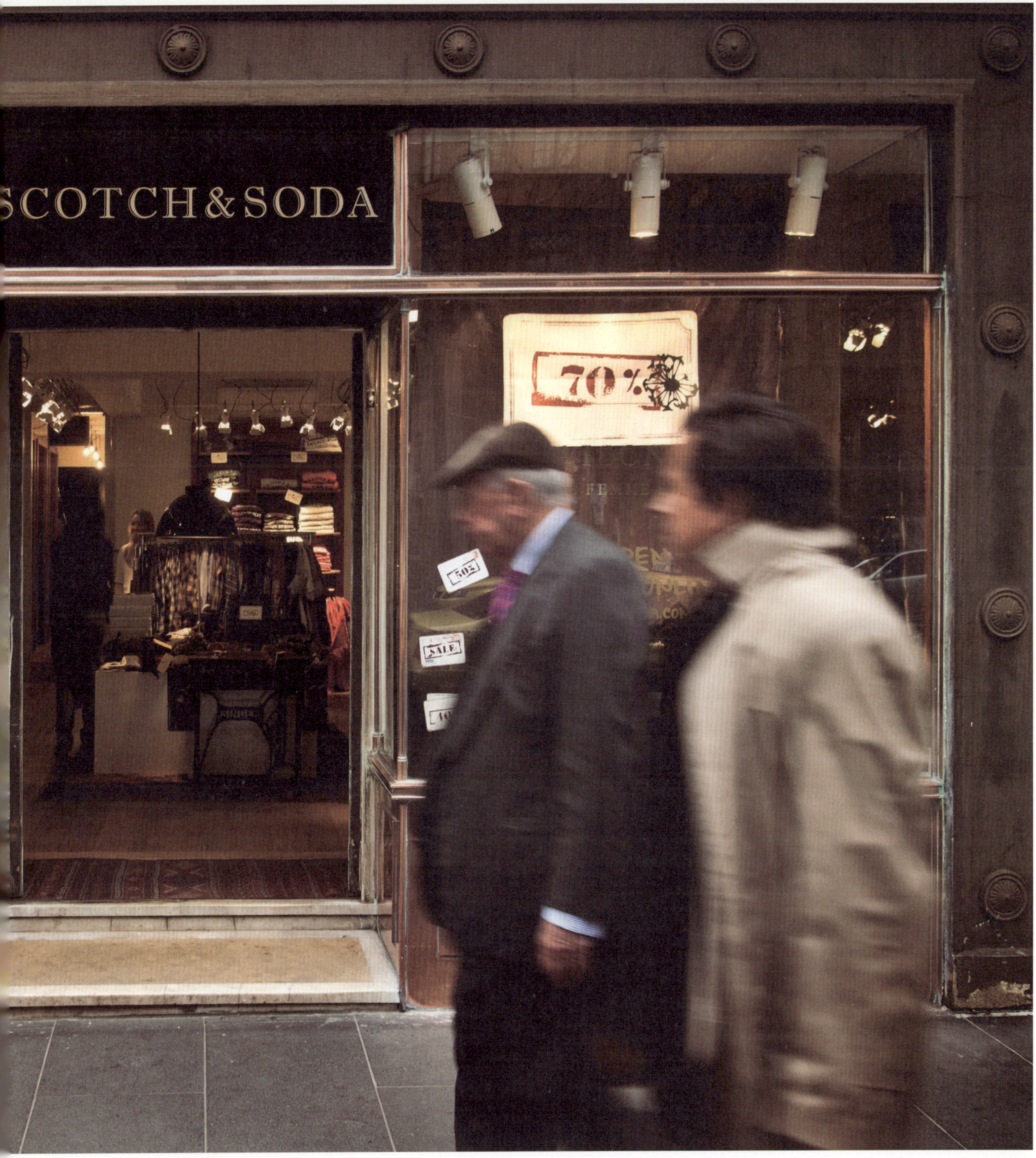
SCOTCH&SODA
70%
SALE

# COLLINS QUARTER

86 Collins St
03 9650 8500
www.collinsquarter.com

Transforming one of Melbourne's old pubs into an inspired blend of 19th and 21st century space, has given the top end of Collins Street a modern destination, with a variety of settings for almost every occasion.

Collins Quarter occupies a space that was originally two Victorian terrace houses, 86 and 88 Collins Street, built in 1872. Today, Collins Quarter has four defined 'quarters' which consist of Colin's Pub, The Magnolia Courtyard, Blind Alley Bar and Ra.

The Collins Street entrance takes you into a newly renovated pub area known as Colin's Pub. Here you will find a mixture of lounge, dining and standing areas and a long list of tap and bottled beers. The pub opens onto the Magnolia Courtyard with its distinct, retractable glass roof - a handy addition to protect from the unpredictable Melbourne weather. The courtyard shares its name with the venue's centerpiece, a large Magnolia Tree which is encased by its very own planter box made from solid slate flagstones used originally to pave Collins Street.

Food is taken quite seriously at Collins Quarter with head chef, Michael Nunn, toiling day and night to put together seasonally inspired creations including delights such as their Mountain Goat Steam Ale braised beef cheek and mushroom pie, the pine mushroom and baby onion ragu with marinated Yarra Valley goats cheese tart or their crispy confit duck leg with drunken quince and grilled piadina flat bread.

With the sharing concept kept as a constant reminder here, try dividing the suckling pig spit roast, the grilled local squid and the spiced Berkshire pork belly between some friends.

Head bartender, Scott Reed, has had 15 years experience in the industry and has worked in some of the top bars in Melbourne including Black Pearl, Ginger and Lotus, to name a few. He is backed by the extensive experience and enthusiasm of Johnny Sit (also having 15 years experience) and Storme Wilde.

One of Scott's favourite cocktails on the constantly changing list is Berry Delish, a classic daiquiri with raspberry, a hint of basil and touch of balsamic. Whatever your reason for visiting Collins Quarter, your wishes can be realised at one or the other of its fabulous quarters.

**NEW MIXES WITH OLD AS THE MAGNOLIA COURTYARD CREATES A SPECTACULAR CENTREPIECE, MARRYING THE 19TH CENTURY GRANDIOSITY OF COLIN'S PUB WITH THE 21ST CENTURY RAZZLE-DAZZLE OF BLIND ALLEY BAR.**

139

# MERCHANT

The Rialto, 495 Collins St
03 9614 7688
www.merchantov.com

The inspiration for the Merchant evolved from the rich, Venetian culture of Guy Grossi's family ancestry plus those of his partner, the Grollo family.

"I found myself engrossed on a recent trip back to Veneto, the region where both Grossi and Grollo families come from," said Guy Grossi. "The gothic buildings, an abundance of water and boats, food and wine being consumed with gusto - to me it seemed this was the glue that held this happy and social lot together. I was filled with a desire for a piece of this spectacular place to be brought back to Melbourne".

In the heart of the financial district, there is no better place for this concept than within the Rialto Towers forecourt. The building's name is the perfect reference to Venice's first harbour and the set of Shakespeare's story by the same name. Merchant is aptly named, occupying the red brick building in Collins Street with its gothic architecture of Venetian origin, first built as a trading house. Its cobblestone laneway runs around the perimeter of the building allowing for horse and carts to bring produce to its trading floors.

In Italy an Osteria is a place for food, wine and the company of others. It is not a restaurant of rigid style, but a relaxed informal environment to drink or eat. Merchant is a place that is exciting and authentic from the minute you walk through its doors. With great emphasis placed on the Venetian tradition, Merchant represents a casual space that allows for all types of dining experiences.

Design has been a 2-year project with Mills and Gorman employing the use of rich materials to provide bold warmth and manifest Guy's vision. Inspiration was drawn from many seductive eating spaces in the northeast of Italy. There is also a hint of 1950s style American cocktail bars in spaces, which are sexy, relaxed and moody.

The colors are water, mist, moody, mystical and chic. See them come to life on the west wall mural that lures you into the select few hidden booths. There is a chair for everyone. Some may be seated in view of white-jacketed barmen and others may be seated in front of the open kitchen as plates of food are served and taken to tables to be shared.

The menu is, of course, strictly Italian, filled with authentic, northern recipes. Try starting with some small bite size snacks called 'cichetti'. These are designed as antipasto to share, or perhaps a nubble at the bar with a cocktail before your meal. You will find a delightful selection such as Aranzini de zafferan (Saffron Arancini), Patède figà de anara (Duck Liver Pate) or you can share a platter of Cioco conservà (Preserved Artichokes). And don't worry if your Italian is not up to scratch, there are translations on the menu and your waiter can help you with your choices.

Of course, the mains are a joy just to read. Imagine authentic Figà a la Venezian (Calves liver, onions and sage), Luganeghe in graela (Char-grilled Pork sausages) or the Conejo a la vecia (Braised Rabbit, pine nuts and sultanas). Of course there are some local favourites, like the Scamone de buò Wagyu (Char-grilled Ranger's Valley Wagyu rump) and the Scota deo (Char-grilled lamb cutlets.

The wine culture at Merchant is strong with a list that pays homage to the great wine regions of North Eastern Italy. Merchant has much to offer in its dimly lit chamber. An exciting and energetic place to have a pound of fun.

141

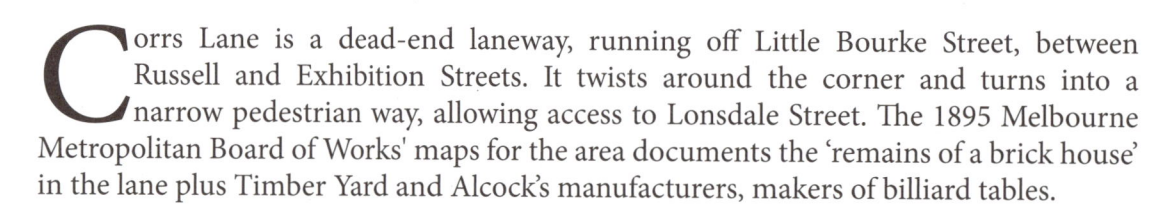

Corrs Lane is a dead-end laneway, running off Little Bourke Street, between Russell and Exhibition Streets. It twists around the corner and turns into a narrow pedestrian way, allowing access to Lonsdale Street. The 1895 Melbourne Metropolitan Board of Works' maps for the area documents the 'remains of a brick house' in the lane plus Timber Yard and Alcock's manufacturers, makers of billiard tables.

Today, Corrs Lane contains a quirky mix of restaurants and bars. Chinese, Japanese, German and contemporary art – all packaged in one neat, little laneway. At the southern end you will find traditional Chinese under the curious name, Ant's Bistro. To the north of the lane, is Yamato Japanese Restaurant, an intimate space with authentic Japanese food.

In between north and south, you will find the new German-inspired, Berlin Bar, which is divided into east and west. This quirky venue brings together today's united Germany with its list of German, Austrian and Belgian beer – and you can chose to drink on the east or west themed sides.

For lover's of art is the local artists' hangout – FAD Gallery – an art gallery in a bar, or is it the other way around? Wine, beer or champagne while you enjoy an eclectic mix of ever-changing paintings, photographs and other artistic works.

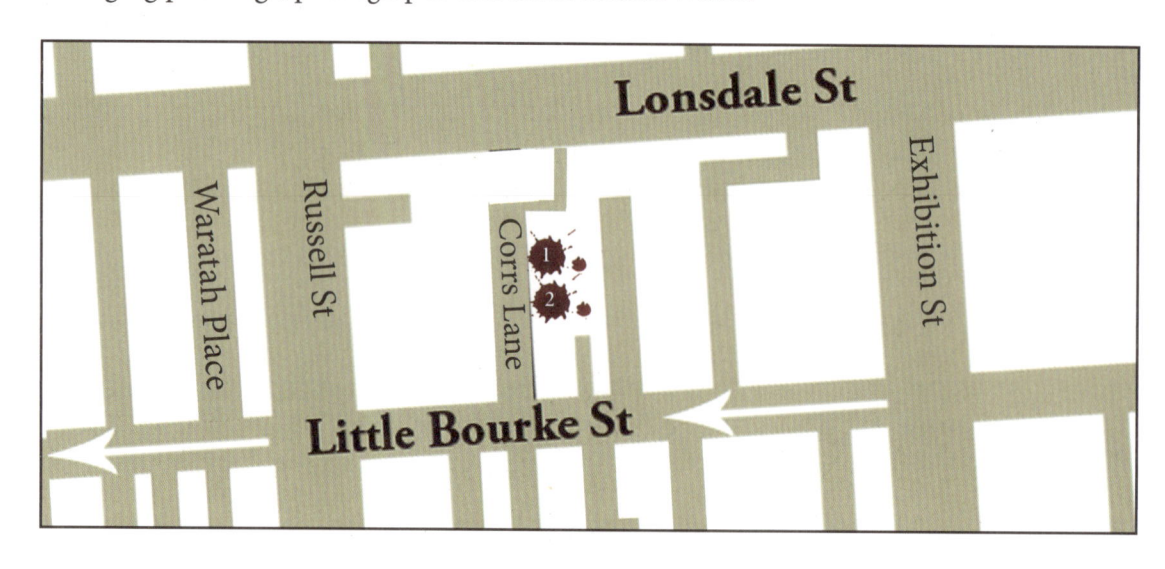

1. Berlin Bar   2. Fad Lounge & Bar

# CORRS LANE

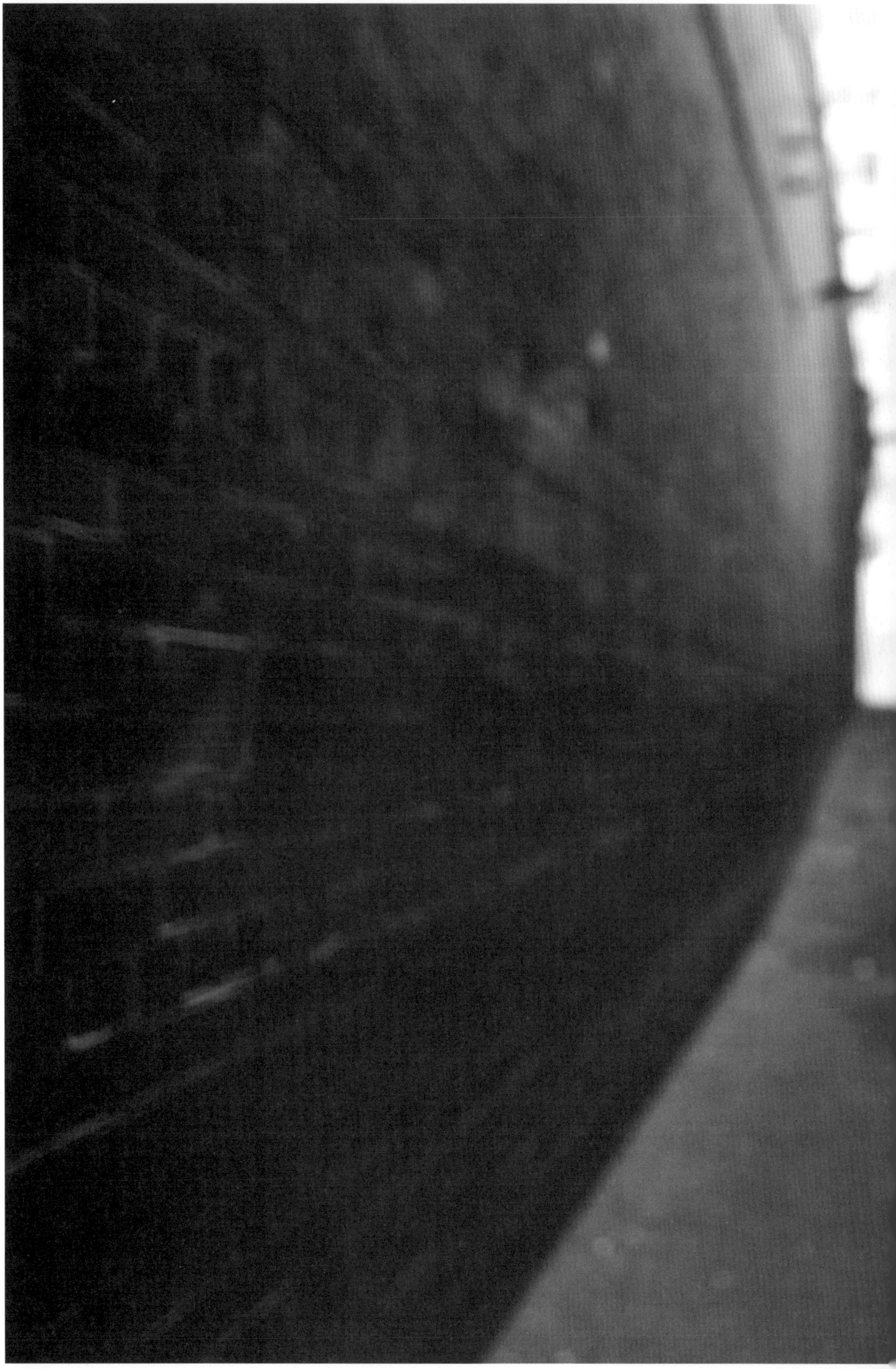

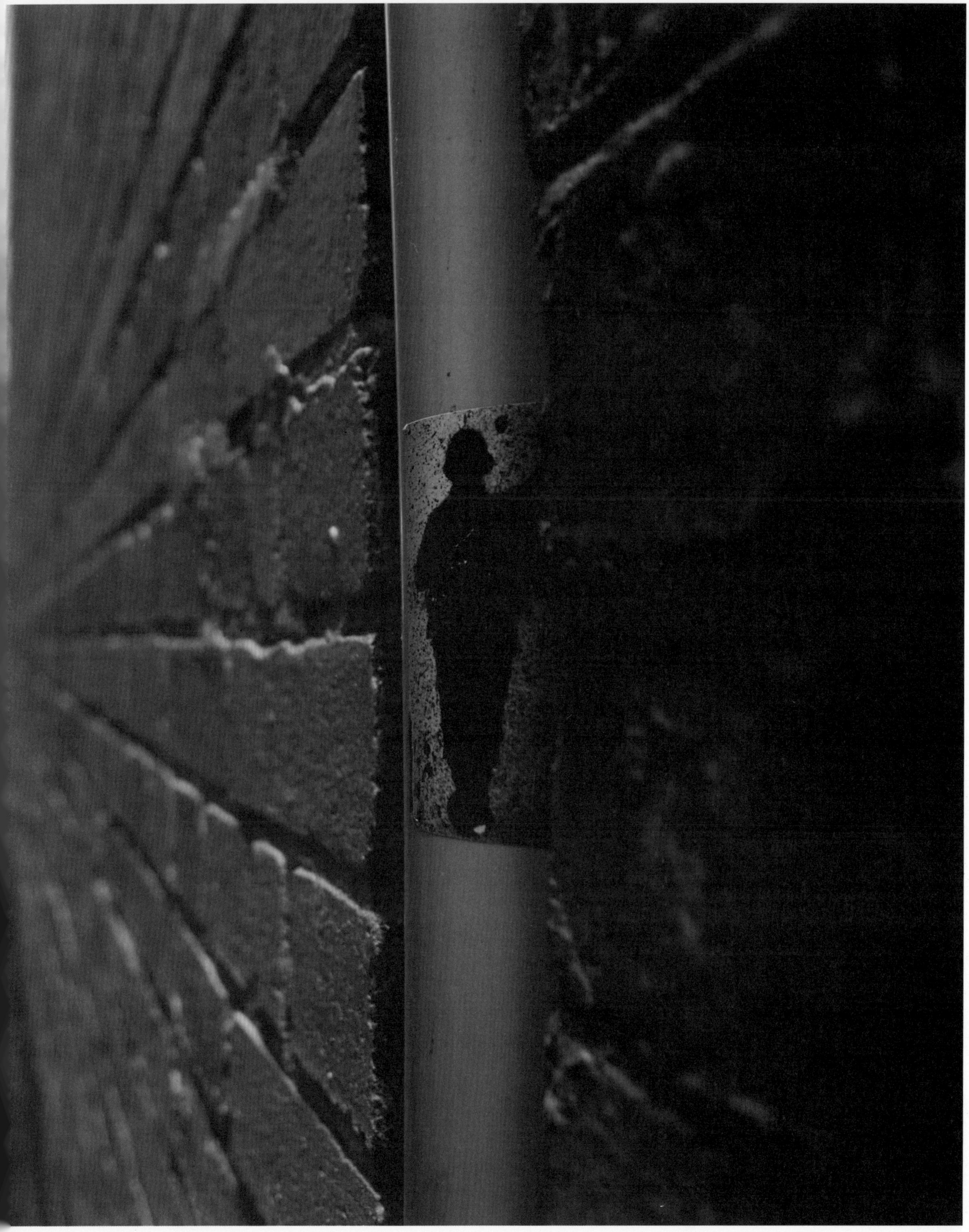

# BERLIN BAR

16 Corrs Lane
03 9639 3396
www.berlinbar.com.au

Neatly hidden above the laneways off Little Bourke Street, the unique nature of Berlin Bar makes it well worth the hunt. Don't be put off by the closed door and the German-speaking doorman peeking through the slit in the door. If you walk on through you will be in for an interesting night. Divided into two halves where east meets west, Berlin Bar captures both the opulence and ostentatious nature of a West German Parlour and the contrasting austerity of an East German bunker. However the Berlin bar is not all about its looks. The extensive drinks menu ensures that all visitors will find something to take their fancy, from the theme inspired cocktails to fine spirits, respected wines and champagne. Clever décor includes a table made from a bathtub and a replica of the Berlin wall.

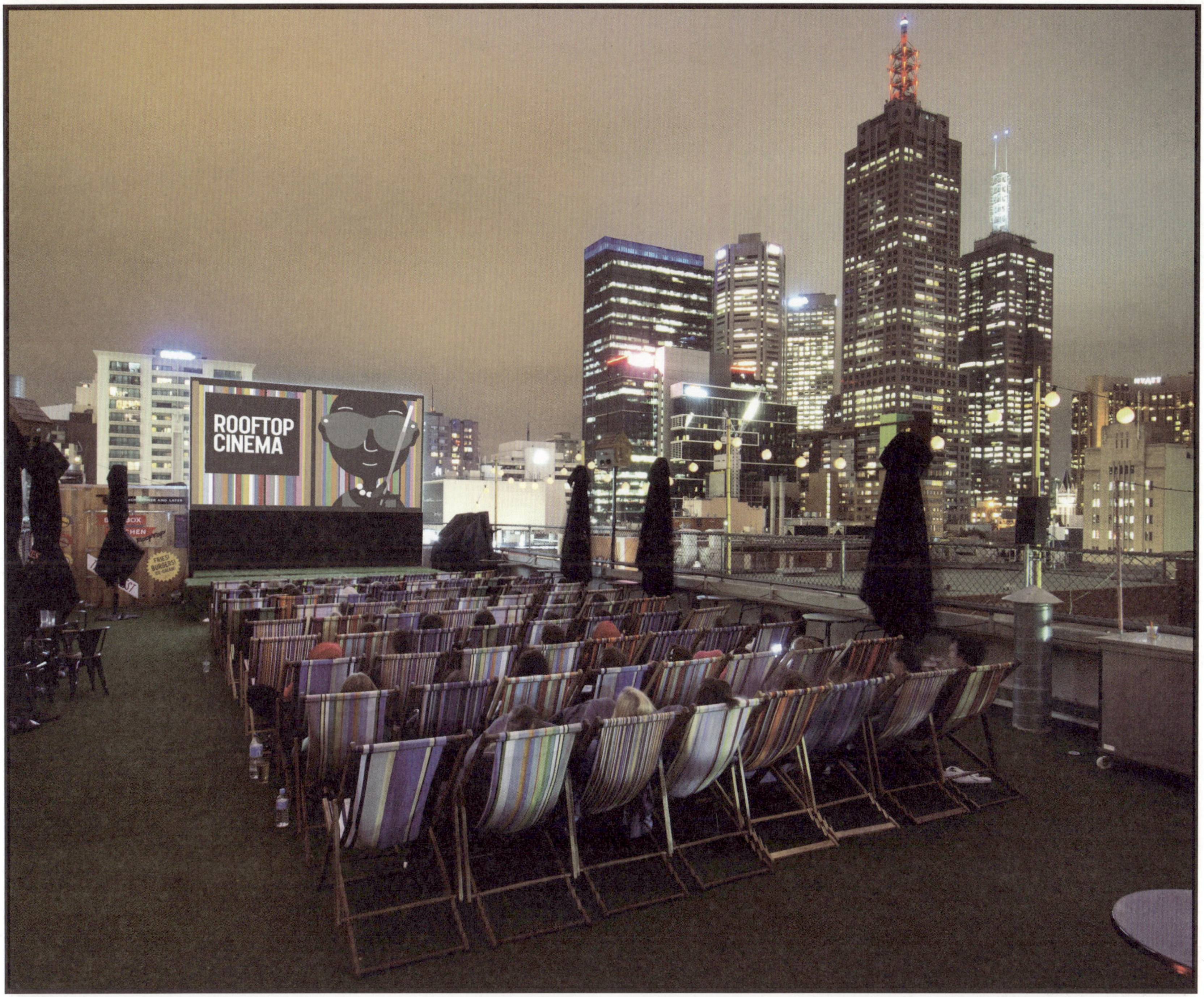
ROOFTOP
CINEMA

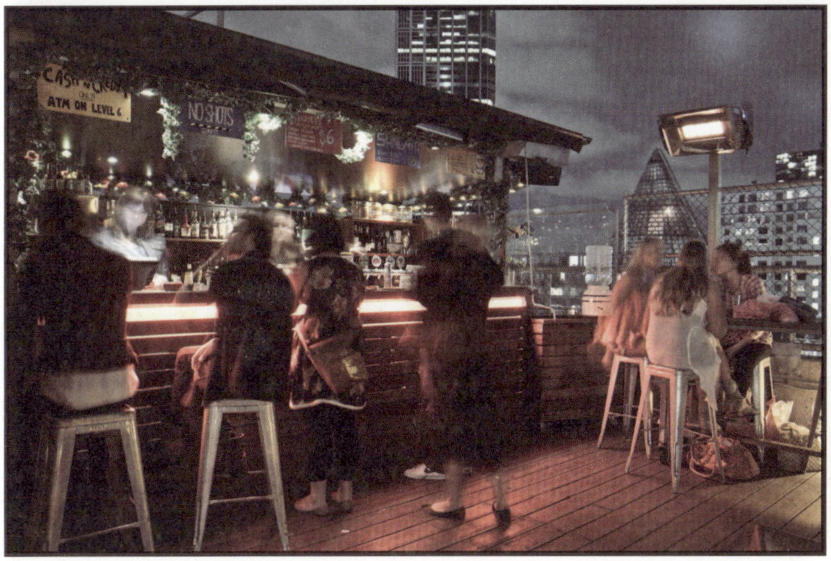

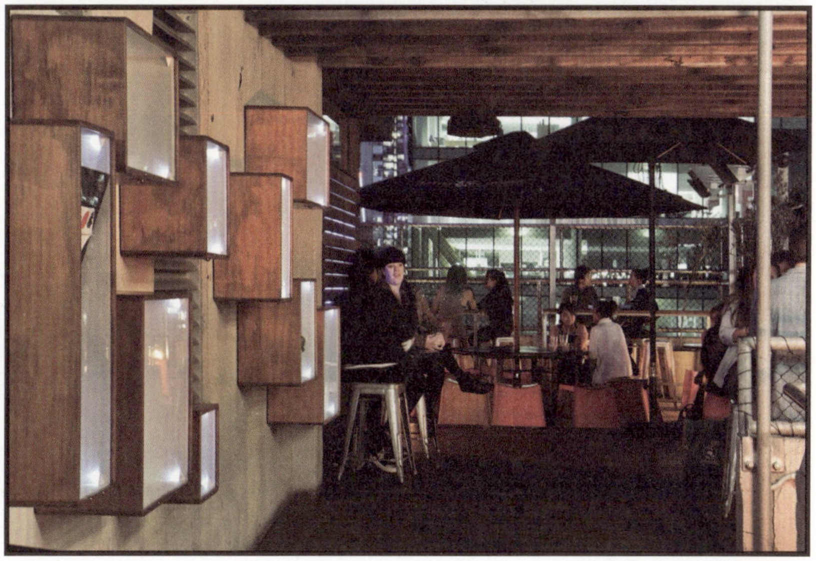

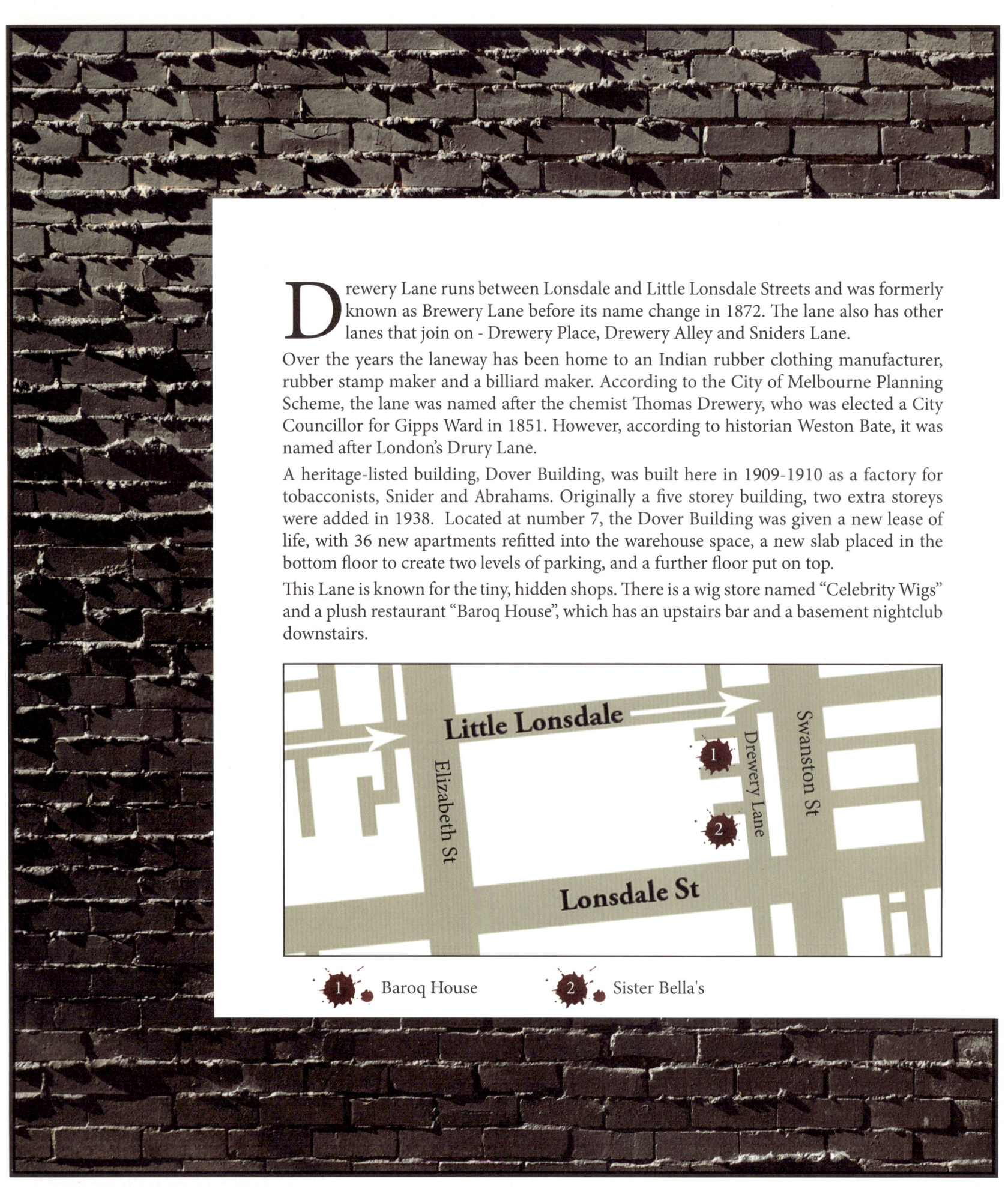

Drewery Lane runs between Lonsdale and Little Lonsdale Streets and was formerly known as Brewery Lane before its name change in 1872. The lane also has other lanes that join on - Drewery Place, Drewery Alley and Sniders Lane.

Over the years the laneway has been home to an Indian rubber clothing manufacturer, rubber stamp maker and a billiard maker. According to the City of Melbourne Planning Scheme, the lane was named after the chemist Thomas Drewery, who was elected a City Councillor for Gipps Ward in 1851. However, according to historian Weston Bate, it was named after London's Drury Lane.

A heritage-listed building, Dover Building, was built here in 1909-1910 as a factory for tobacconists, Snider and Abrahams. Originally a five storey building, two extra storeys were added in 1938. Located at number 7, the Dover Building was given a new lease of life, with 36 new apartments refitted into the warehouse space, a new slab placed in the bottom floor to create two levels of parking, and a further floor put on top.

This Lane is known for the tiny, hidden shops. There is a wig store named "Celebrity Wigs" and a plush restaurant "Baroq House", which has an upstairs bar and a basement nightclub downstairs.

1. Baroq House
2. Sister Bella's

# DREWERY LANE

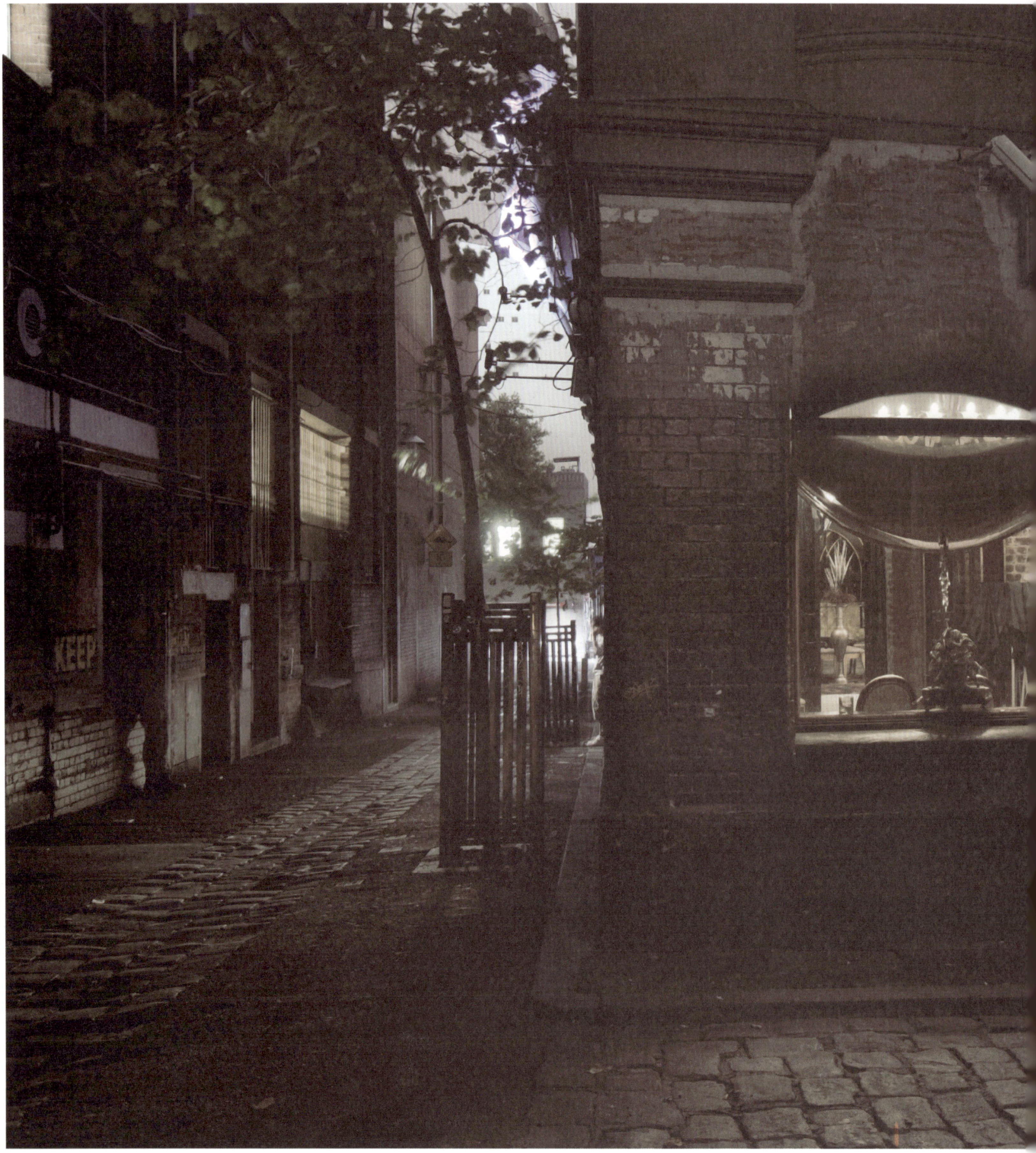
KEEP

LOADING ZONE
15 MINUTE
ALL OTHER TIMES
HARSTEL HOUSE
LEVEL THREE
Celebrity Wigs
Glamour Wigs
HACHEM

# SISTER BELLA

22 Drewery Place
No phone number

Sister Bella is a lost "secret" that we are glad to have found, making it a honey jar for Melbourne's different scenesters. It is a good thing this split level bar is quite hard to find, hidden at the end of two unassuming alleys, because Sister Bella's is becoming the place to be. From the same owners as St Jeromes, Sister Bella's has taken on an op-shop chic style of its own. During the day you can settle into a booth couch and soak up the atmosphere over a coffee, drink or a cheap bite. Bring your laptop and take advantage of the free wireless in the ultimate hideout. At night, under lantern light, chill out in the bohemian atmosphere, sharing spirits, beers and snacks with friends.

DREWERY LANE DREWERY LANE DREWERY LANE DREWERY LANE DREWERY LANE DREWERY

# BAROQ HOUSE

9-13 Drewery Lane
03 8080 5680
www.baroqhouse.com.au

Think "dress to dazzle", A-lister, party style and from the moment you walk in you can't help but be impressed as you are transported back to the lavish 16th and 17th Centuries. Baroq house prides itself on being "inspired by a classic period of extravagance", its "opulent décor and furniture" and its "celebration of the arts". The two level baroque mansion-style bar and lounge provides a high-end nightlife experience. The basement is divided between a beautifully styled bar area and a dance floor that is cleverly sidelined by a daybed area where you can lounge as you summon reserves for the next round of dancing. The ground floor is larger with a lounge room and another bar where you can indulge in the signature cocktails. Treat yourself to a Baroq Deluxe such as the Dom Perignon Classic Champagne cocktail for the luxurious price of $150.

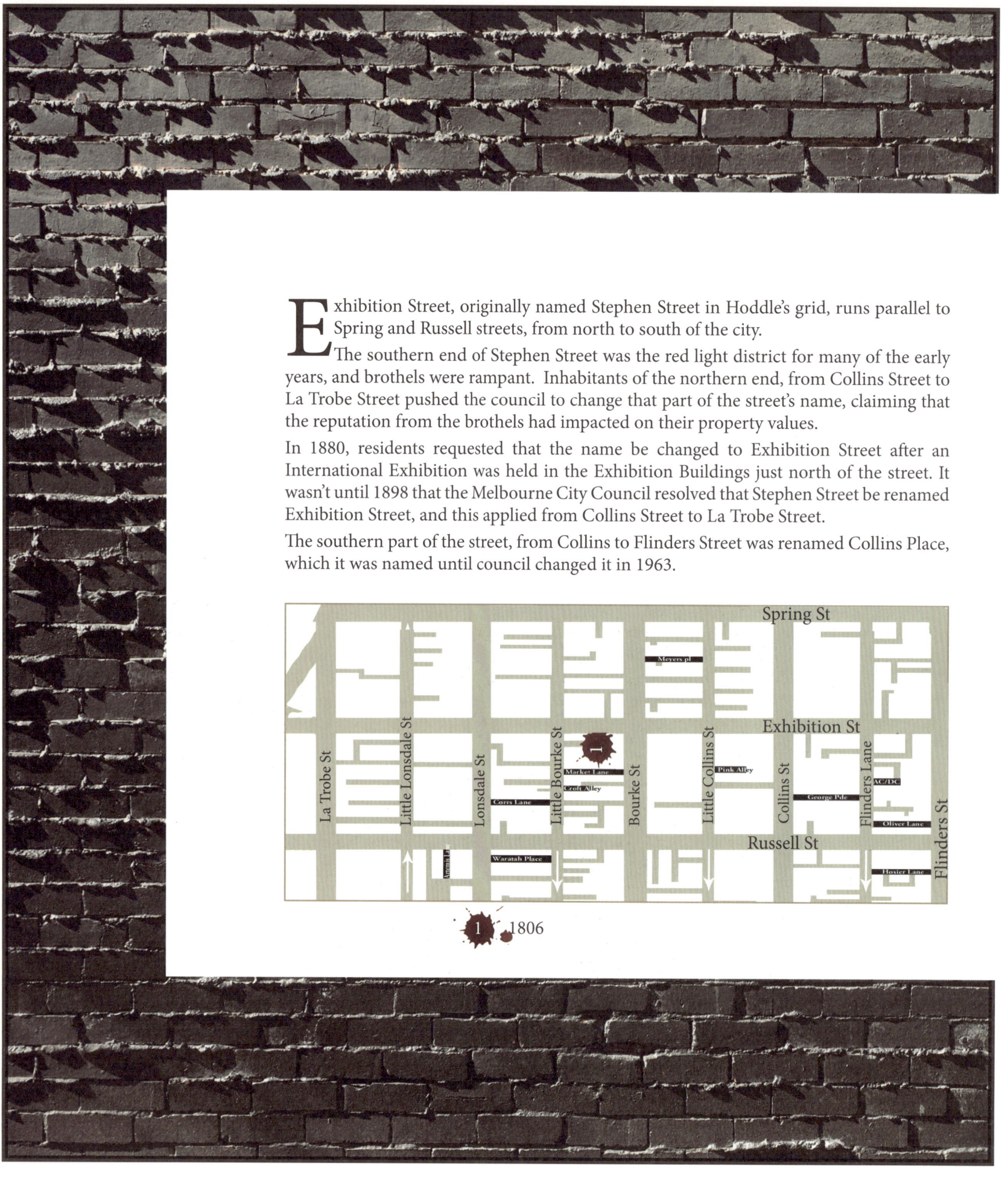

Exhibition Street, originally named Stephen Street in Hoddle's grid, runs parallel to Spring and Russell streets, from north to south of the city.

The southern end of Stephen Street was the red light district for many of the early years, and brothels were rampant. Inhabitants of the northern end, from Collins Street to La Trobe Street pushed the council to change that part of the street's name, claiming that the reputation from the brothels had impacted on their property values.

In 1880, residents requested that the name be changed to Exhibition Street after an International Exhibition was held in the Exhibition Buildings just north of the street. It wasn't until 1898 that the Melbourne City Council resolved that Stephen Street be renamed Exhibition Street, and this applied from Collins Street to La Trobe Street.

The southern part of the street, from Collins to Flinders Street was renamed Collins Place, which it was named until council changed it in 1963.

1. 1806

# EXHIBITION ST.

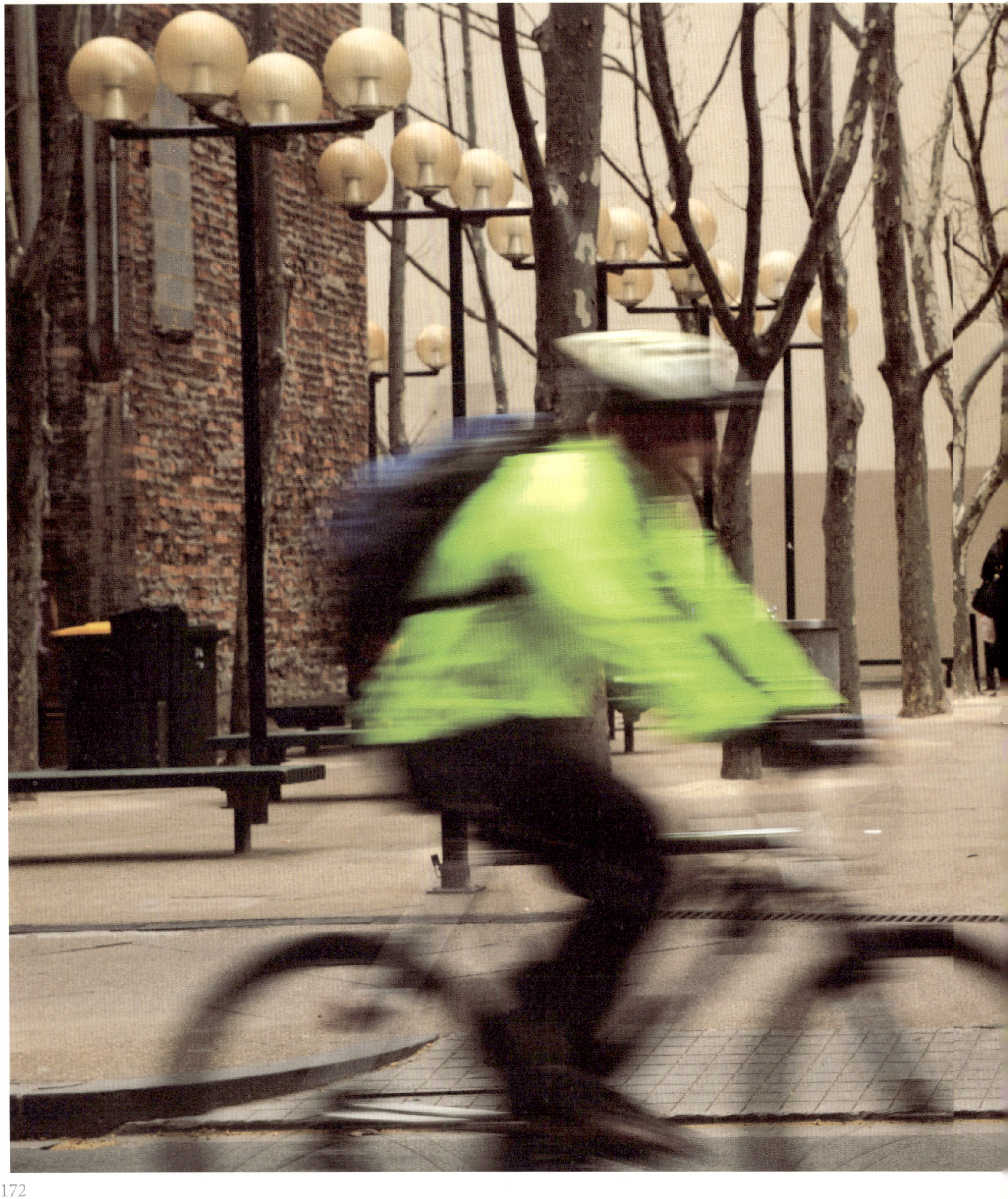

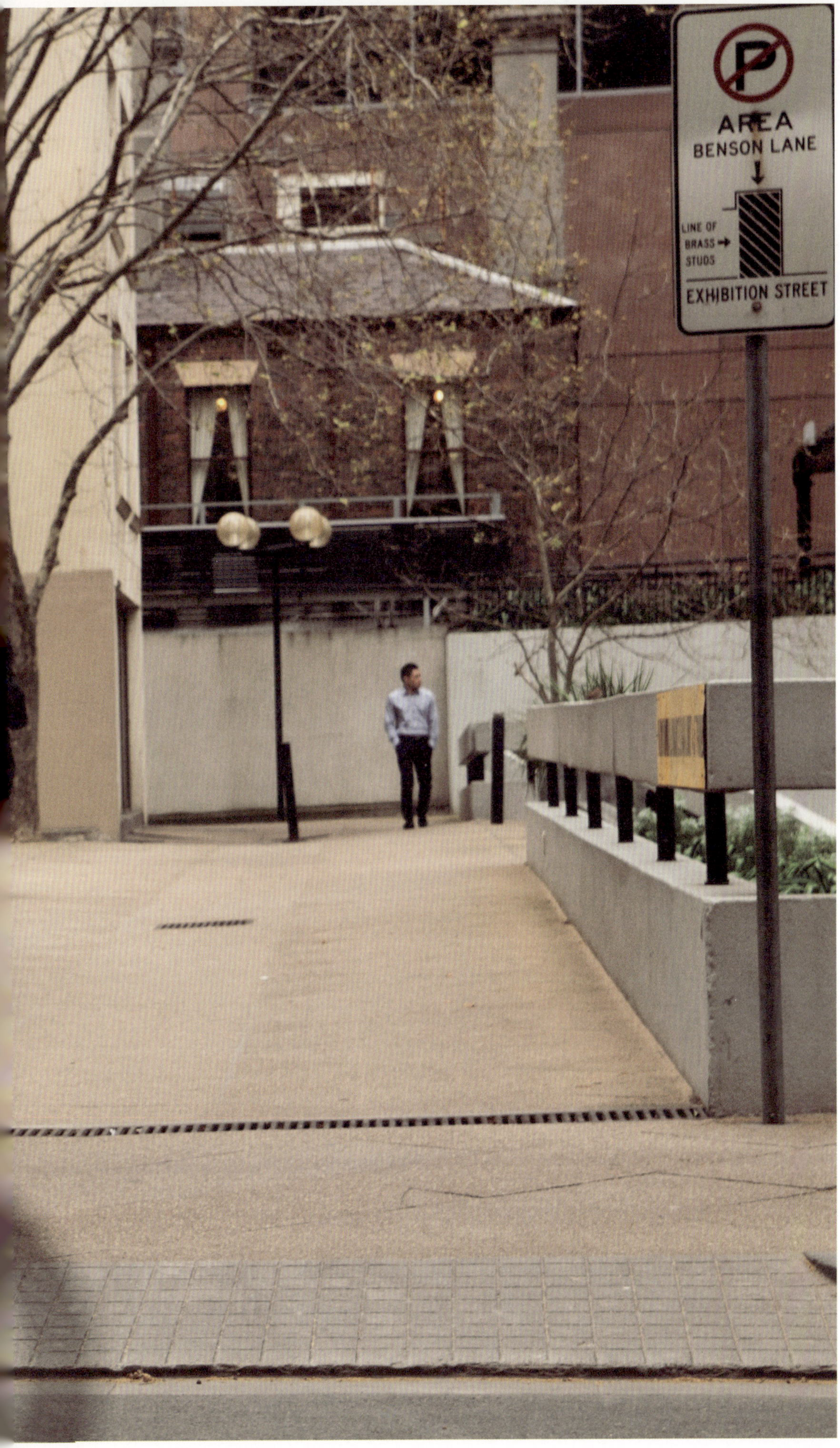
P
AREA
BENSON LANE
LINE OF
BRASS
STUDS
EXHIBITION STREET

# BAR 1806

169-171 Exhibition St
03 9663 7722
www.1806.com.au

It has been near on four years now since 1806 opened its doors, albeit in a very clandestine manner, and the bar has gone from strength to strength ever since. The interesting name is derived from the year in which the word "cock-tail" was defined in print, way back in the year 1806.

This appreciation of history is a theme that carries throughout the venue making every experience one for the books. The award winning menu itself is an impressive compilation of the best and most popular drinks from every decade since the 18th century, complete with interesting anecdotes about each entry.

This virtually allows you to take a delicious journey through time, though it might take you a few sittings. The one drawback of such an extensive selection can be that it is too intimidating for the everyday consumer to even know where to start, however the team at 1806 have made this a non sequitur.

1806 is a table service venue where, like a restaurant, you must be able to be comfortably seated in order to gain entry. One is then waited on hand and foot by the energetic and extremely knowledgeable floor staff who make the aforementioned journey through time as simple as a walk in the park, with an emphasis on good old fashion customer service and the right drink for the right customer every time.

Owner Lisa Kelly is supported by two of Melbourne's most talented bartenders who manage the venue and keep it at the forefront of the Australian bar scene. Andy Wren and Nick Reed have both spent a number of years honing their skills in the U.K. Andy is a native Scotsman and Nick was lured to Edinburgh 4 years ago and recently returned.

Nick was a finalist at this years 42bELOW cocktail World Cup and his winning drink the "Lets get Fizzical" is the newest addition to the hallowed pages of the 1806 menu. A twist on the Ramos Gin Fizz, it combines Passionfruit vodka, citrus, vanilla, homemade raspberry syrup and cream, and is shaken for 5 straight minutes before being served in an old baked bean tin.

You can join on of the Cocktail Classes held once a month at 1806 or one of the group /team building packages, such as the 1920's themed Murder Mystery night complete with gangsters, guys and dolls.

Hot off the press – 1806 is pleased to announce their newest bar addition, "The Understudy", an underground experience that lives up to the unique vibe of this Melbournian institution.

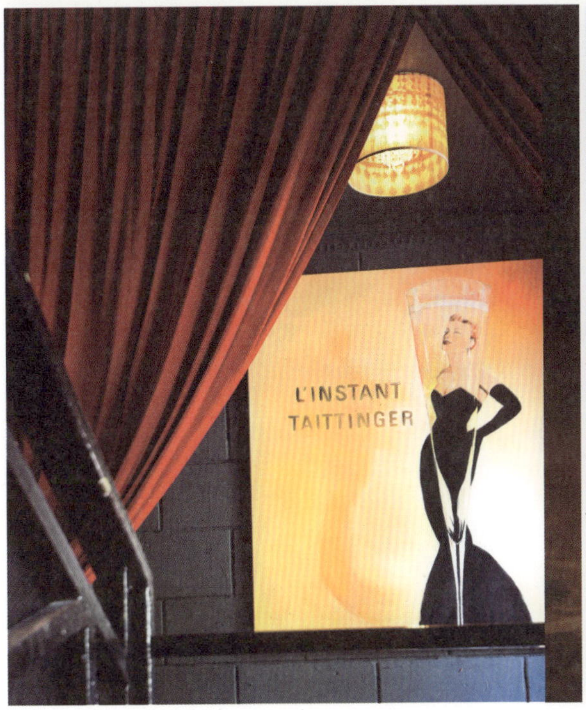
L'INSTANT
TAITTINGER

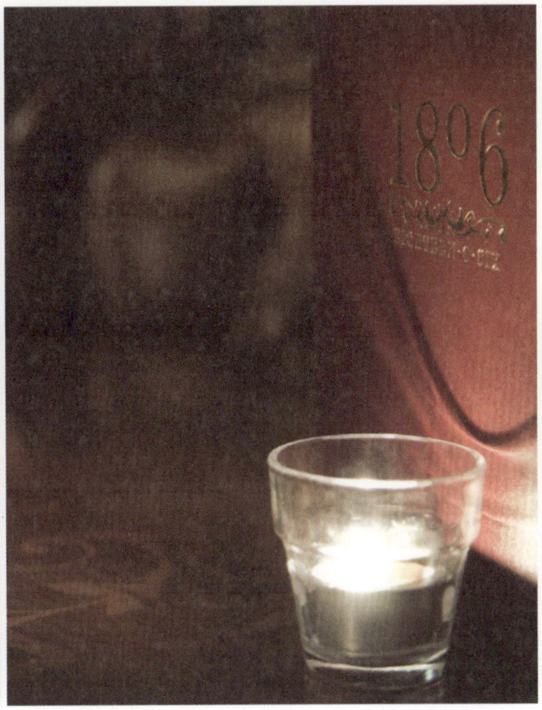
1806

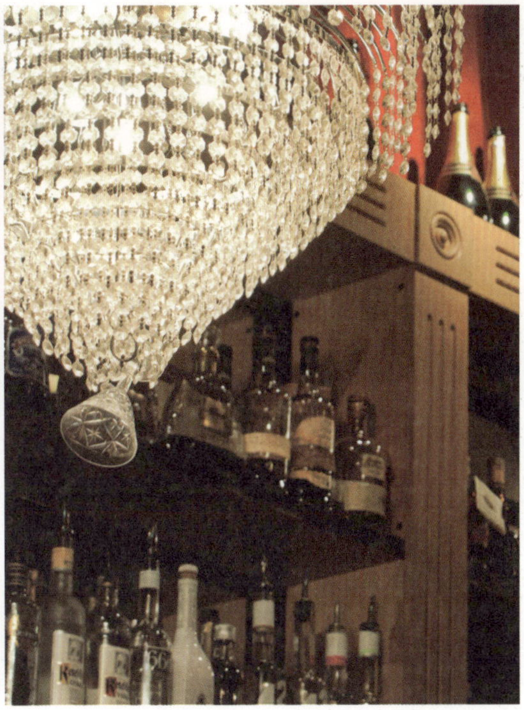

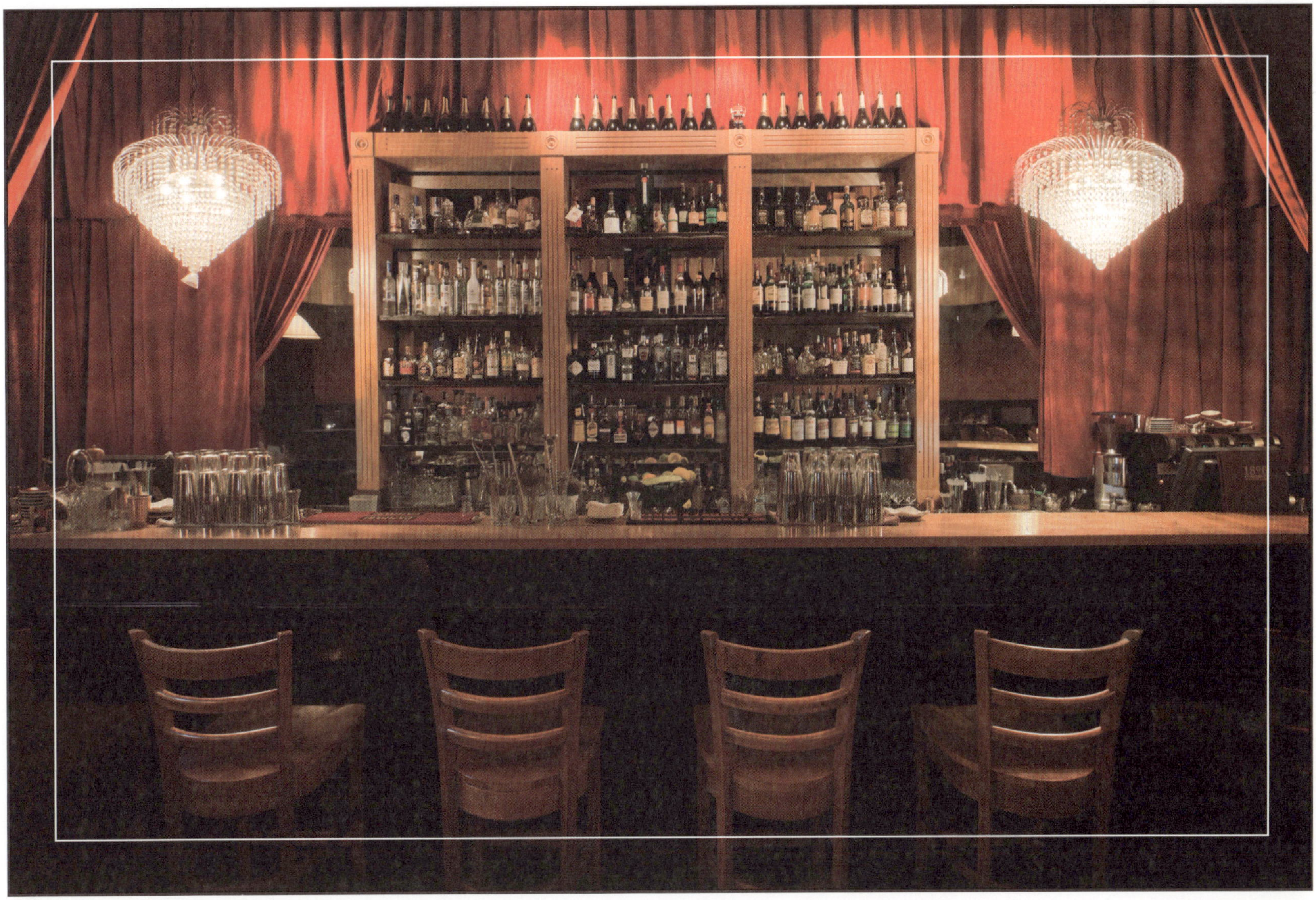

Love it or hate, the design of Melbourne's public space, Federation Square, has created enormous debate from its very conception. One thing is for sure, the concept, the design, the construction and eventual result are "outside the square" in more ways than one.

Firstly, the location is outside the original CBD grid that Hoddle planned in 1836. Argument for the building of a public place for many years, was that the central business district lacked "soul". It needed a place for its inhabitants to relax, enjoy some greenery and hold public gatherings. After much discussion, City Square was built between Swanston Street, Collins Street, Flinders Lane and the Westin Hotel. To accommodate the new space, council purchased and demolished a number of buildings, most notably the Queen Victoria Buildings (1888), to make way for the new square. However, the plan was dogged with controversy and deemed by many as a failure.

Despite attempts to revive the square in the 1900's, Jeff Kennett demanded a solution when he stepped into government in the mid-1900's. Thinking outside the square, it was decided that the ugly twin towers of the former Gas and Fuel Corporation and the old Princes Street railway station could be demolished and a new "square" built over the Jolimont Yard railway lines.

A competition was held to design the new square, and the funny part is – there was nothing square about the result. The design included several five-storey "shards", intertwined with open spaces with laneways and stairs leading to the river and to Flinders Street Station across the road. Today, Federation Square is home to a wide range of restaurants, cafés, bars, visitor services and shops.

1. Chocolate Buddha  2. Riverland Bar  3. Transit

# FEDERATION SQUARE

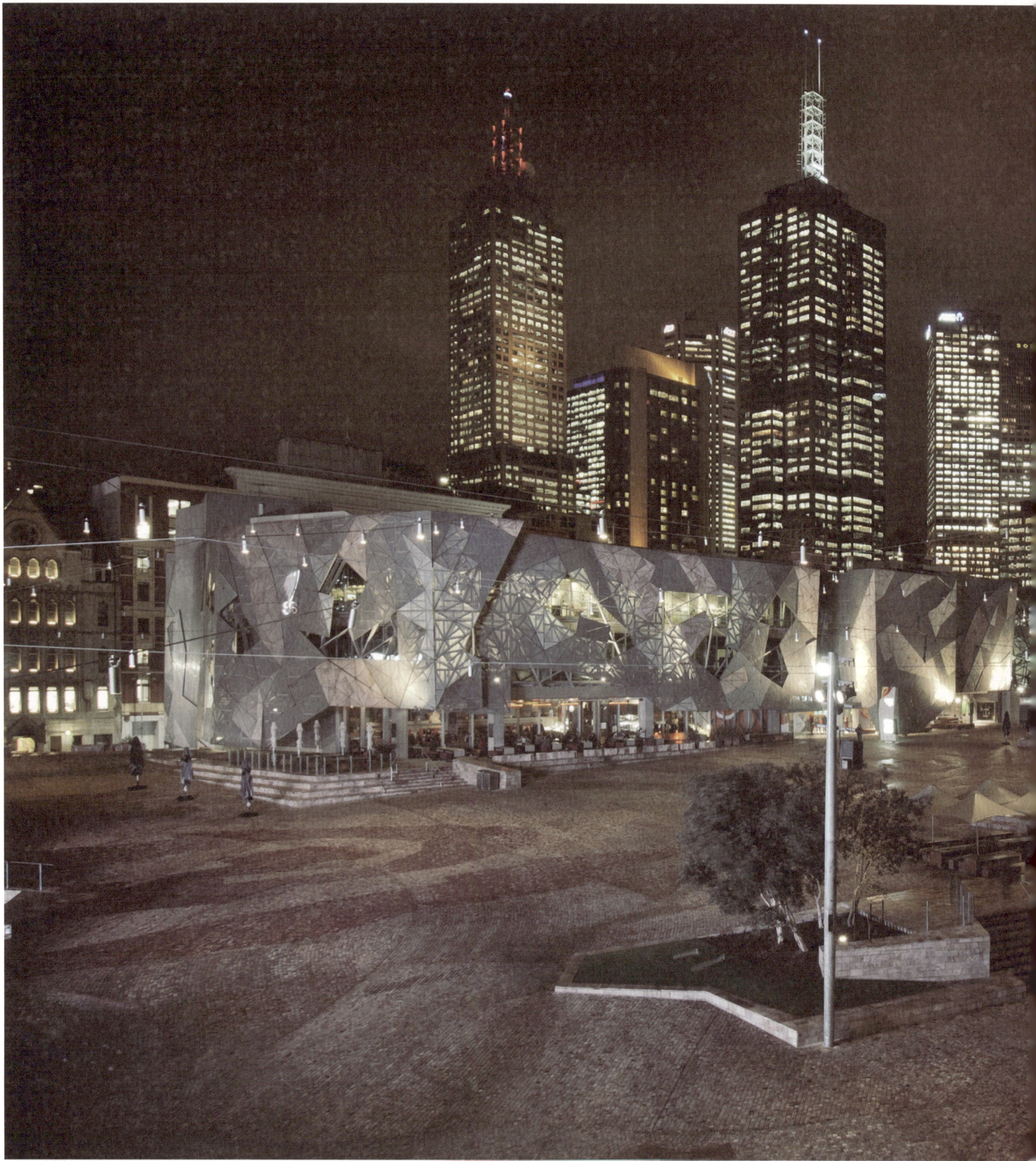

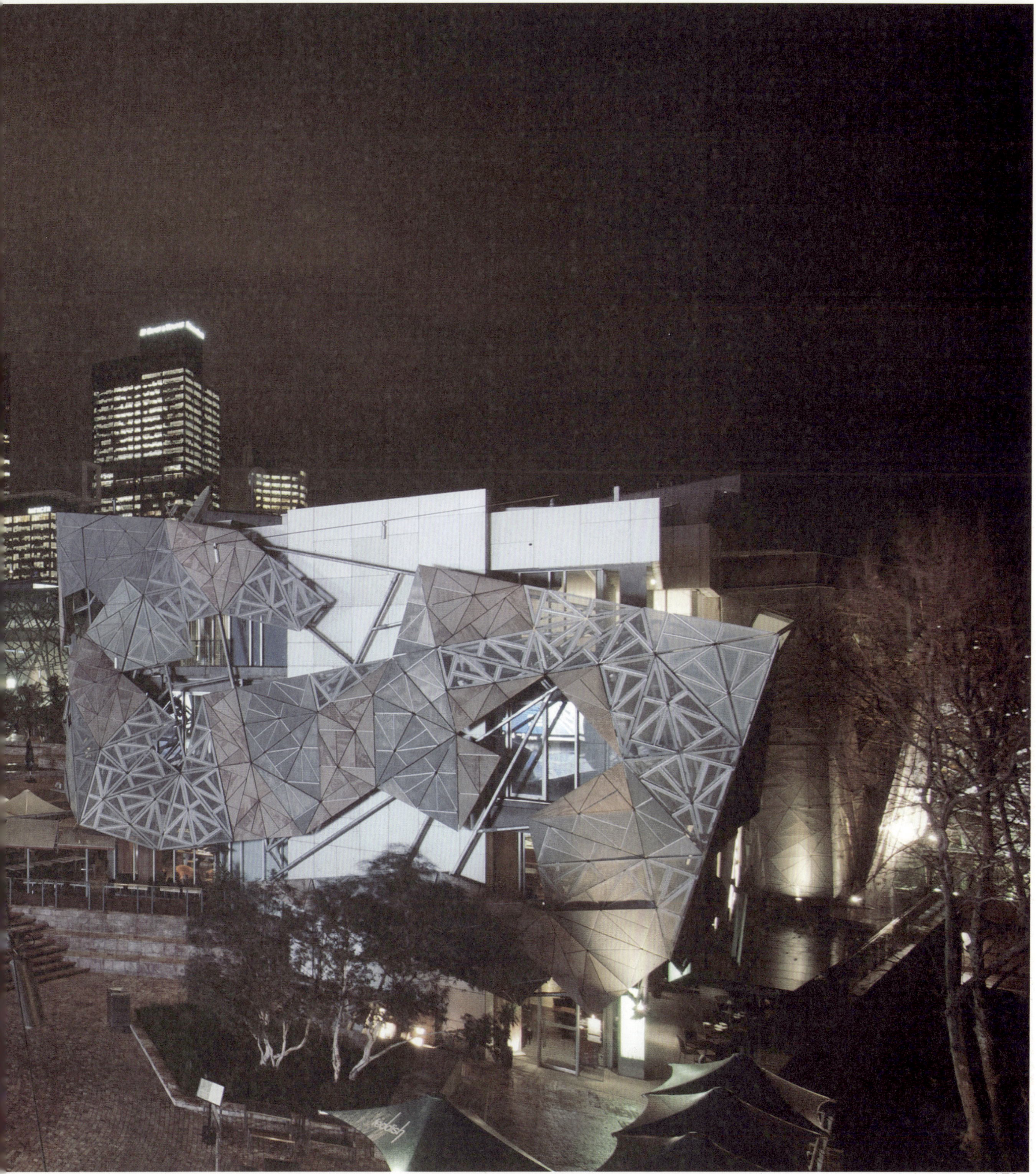

# CHOCOLATE BUDDHA

Federation Square
03 9654 5688
www.chocolatebuddha.com.au

Leader in communal dining since 2002, Chocolate Buddha opened its doors to an adoring clientele of Melbournians and visitors, looking for a unique Japanese experience. The clean, sharp lines of the dining room are minimalist, typical of the discreet style which permeates the Japanese culture. No flashy gimmicks here, just long, lean tables, neatly set, with accompanying multi-coloured, cushion-top stools.

People come here for the food and the head chef makes sure they get what they expect. The kitchen produces most of the staple foods eaten in Japan, including Ramen, noodles in soup stock with a variety of ingredients, Donburi, rice in a bowl with toppings, as well as traditional sushi and sashimi. The menu also includes some local and international food to make the most of the freshest, seasonal ingredients available locally.

Try starting with a lemon iced tea, which is crisp and refreshing and not overtly sweet. If you enjoy a Japanese classic, try the delicious deep-fried silken tofu with fresh snow peas and baby corn, menma, wakame and spring onion in a fresh vegetable soup with ginger, sesame and chilli oil over hand-made soba noodles.

Chocolate Buddha was taken over by Angela Mathioudakis and George Incretoli in 2005. Their vision for Chocolate Buddha was heavenly sent. You can't get anything more perfect than a Buddha or chocolate – and the combination of the two is what is represented in the restaurant.

The unique experience of sharing their space while dining, creates a friendly, relaxed atmosphere where everyone chats with each other. Plates are shared amongst friends, and the great selection of wines, sake, beer and spirits combine perfectly with the Japanese food.

Open until 11pm, this funky Japanese canteen is set in the heart of Federation Square.

chocolate buddha

# RIVERLAND BAR

Vaults 1-9 Federation Wharf
03 9662 1771
www.riverlandbar.com

This bar is one of Melbourne's hidden jewels. As you cross the Swanston Street Bridge, keep your eyes pealed for the beautiful old brick arches surrounding large, warmly-lit windows. In 2006, Riverland bar was lucky enough to snap up the location of the historic Federation Wharf vaults which were built in 1889 on the banks of the Yarra River. Find a seat outside by the grill and try the trademark organic sausages with onions and sauerkraut as you get lost in thought, gazing across the river. Alternatively investigate further into the stunning old-world stone vaults and get caught with the problem presented by all good menus, choosing only one meal. Have one of the tap beers or take your pick from the more extensive range of red, white and sparkling wines and enjoy one of the most picturesque restaurant/bars in Melbourne.

FEDERATION SQUARE FEDERATION SQUARE FEDERATION SQUARE FEDERATION SQUARE FED

Level 2, Transport Hotel
03 9654 8808
www.transporthotel.com.au

# TRANSIT

Transit cocktail lounge is the perfect central hub for any good night out. With its convenient location in Federation Square above Transport Hotel, Transit really takes full advantage of its blessings, combining live music and great cocktails with stunning views. Find yourself a place on one of the comfortable black leather couches, silently cheering the table service that lets you spend more time with your friends rather than lined up at a bar. Alternatively peruse the endless wine list and order some comfort food before strolling onto the terrace to see what else Transit has to offer. With sweeping views over the MCG, along the Yarra River and over the Arts Centre spire, those that aren't transfixed will certainly not be at a loss for conversation.

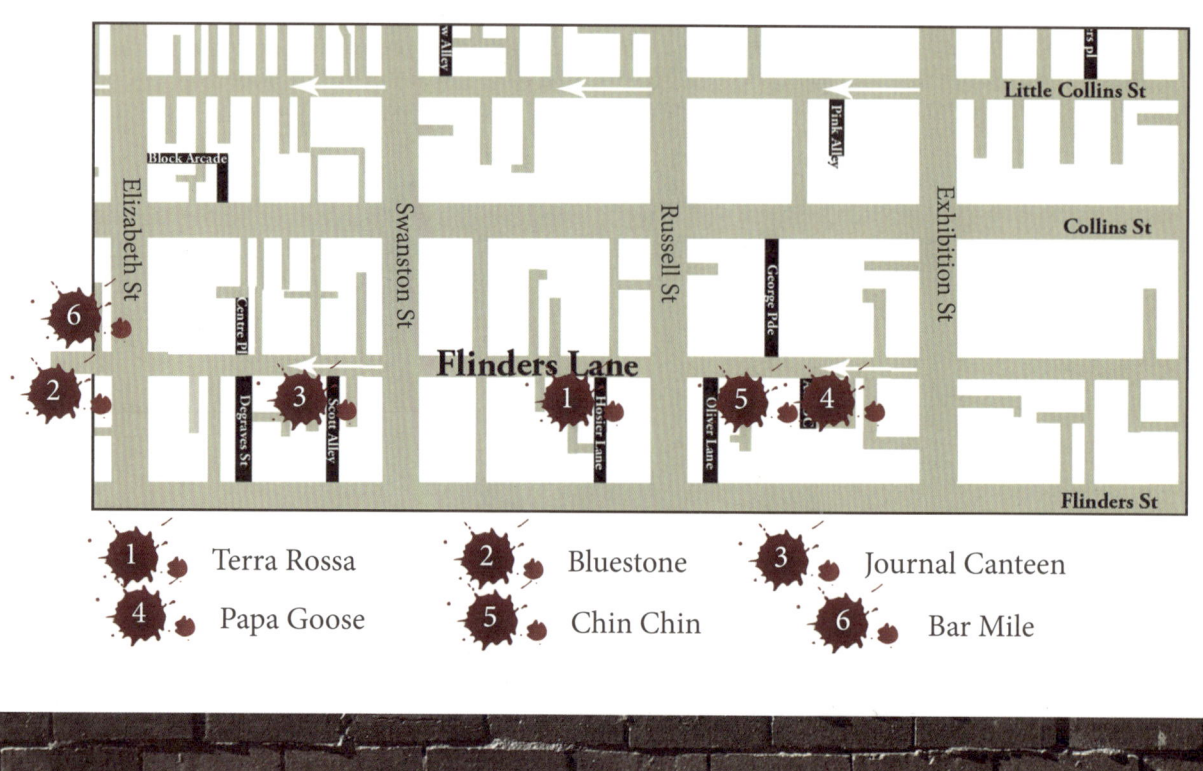

Flinders Lane runs from one side of the city to the other – a one-way bustling strip from Spring to Spencer Streets. As part of the original Hoddle Grid, the lanes and little streets were designed for out of sight duties, including rubbish and night soil collections. However, in the 1860's, Flinders Lane was upgraded and warehouses were built, with the lane gaining the reputation as a wholesale district, mostly trading in imported goods brought in through nearby wharves and railway stations.

For a large part of the 20th century, post WWII, immigrant and refugee Jews set up the highly regarded garment industry along the lane. For over a hundred years, 'The Lane', as it was called, became an Australian icon, becoming the heart of Australian fashion manufacturing.

Its position couldn't have been better - close to shops, department stores, transport terminals and a pool of labour . Buyers could 'do' the Lane in one session. Comparison buying became important as buyers checked the market and then placed orders. There was a real sense of community between rival companies – they all knew each other and their families. Often favours were asked and given, components lent and borrowed. These manufacturers knew their trade, and were very good businessmen.

The number of clothing firms reached 610 in 1939, and this level of activity was maintained until the early 1960s. However, rising rents and traffic congestion saw the industry begin to move to the suburbs. A new breed of entrepreneurs descended on the strip, including designers like Prue Acton, Geoff Bade, Kenneth Pirrie and Thomas Wardle.

Today, the area is home to many boutique hotels, "loft style" apartment conversions, cafés and bars. The lane also connects with a number of smaller lanes, including Degraves Street, ACDC Lane and Manchester Lane which weave their way through the city.

1. Terra Rossa
2. Bluestone
3. Journal Canteen
4. Papa Goose
5. Chin Chin
6. Bar Mile

# FLINDERS LANE

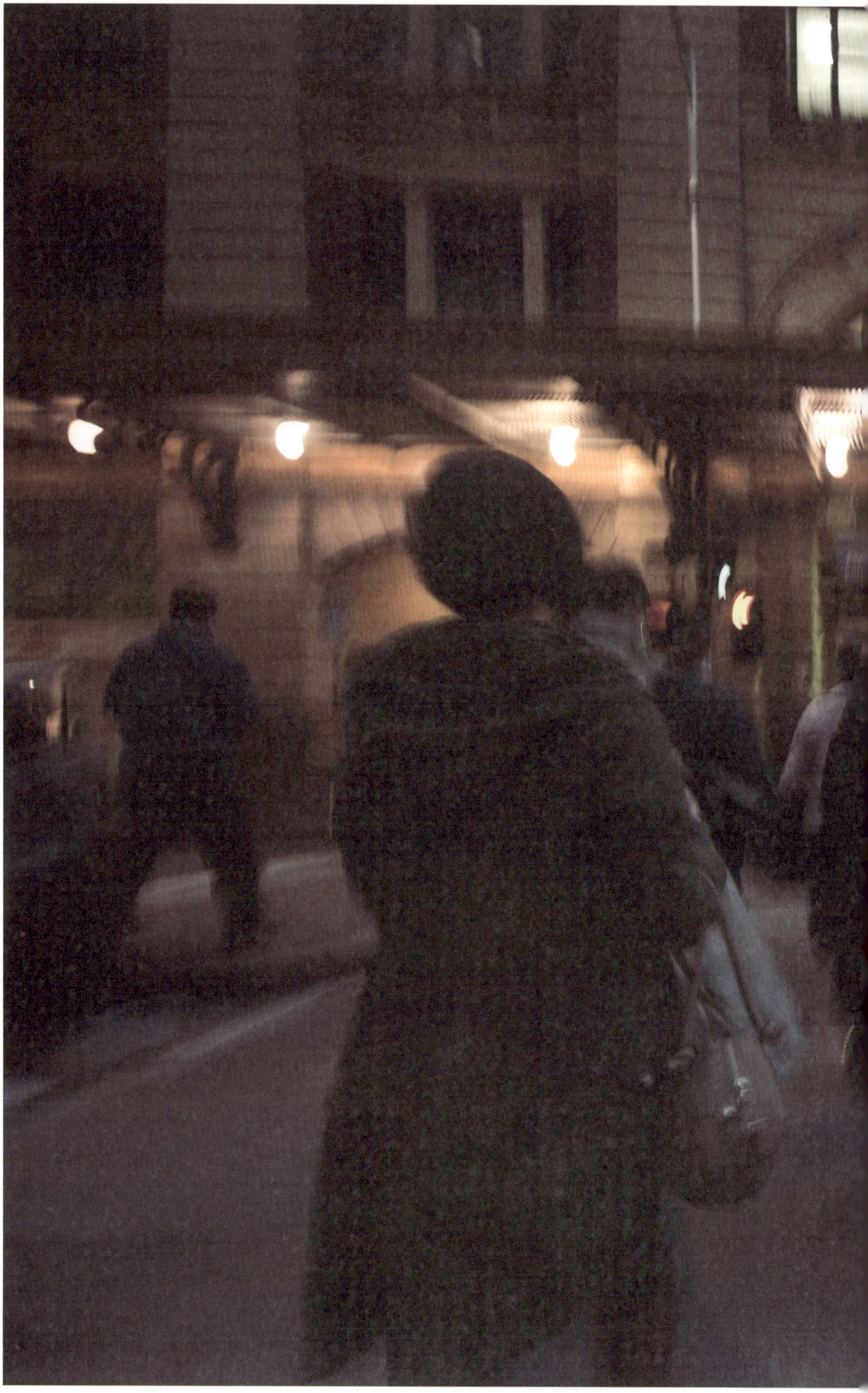

# TERRA ROSSA

87 Flinders Lane
03 9650 0900
www.terrarossarb.com.au

In an area that was originally home to Melbourne's best textile, hosiery and tailor businesses – is the historic building that now houses the Terra Rossa restaurant and bar. After doing time as a Chinese laundry until the 1950's, being destroyed by a fire and rebuilt in the late 1950's as Victoria's Swiss Club, in July 2007 the space was eventually converted into a sleek modern restaurant. This conversion included the restoration of the interior and exterior of the building to its original condition, combined with contemporary interior designing.

The revamp was certainly undertaken with style, as the red walls and dark furniture now set an intimate mood. The venue is made up of a restaurant, a bar, and rather uniquely, a cheese room. Some of the more striking décor includes an open fire with an impressive feature wall of stacked logs surrounded by beautiful Chesterfield sofas and chairs. Exposed brickwork has been used to full effect throughout, as has chandelier lighting that gleams off the wooden furniture.

The novelty of this place is the cheese room with its great variety of cheeses and condiments that can be tasted alongside a carefully selected bottle of wine from the bar. You will regret not reserving for the restaurant if you are staying for dinner. The cuisine is multifarious Mediterranean, with an extensive tapas selection, deliciously complemented by contemporary pasta dishes. The main fares section incorporates delightful incarnations of favourite meat dishes such as tomato and balsamic slow roasted chicken, pimento almond crusted lamb rack and Madeira winter duck Ragu. The vegetarian dishes are so delectable that even the strictest carnivores may start to sway.

The versatility of the menu makes Terra Rossa a convenient and attractive option day or night. The weekday lunch specials which offer great value are a particular bonus. Breakfast is also available with a variety of options that are sure to make your morning seem brighter.

The bar list is extensive with a strong showing of Australian produce interspersed with high-demand international guests. The cocktail list is sufficient to sooth most taste buds, while the wine list includes recommendations to accompany the main courses. A strong list of spirits is included as by-the-fire soothers, the beers cover a wide spectrum and even the ciders have a respectable showing.

The buzz, the excellent wine list and the positive atmosphere are enhanced by great service, combining to draw an eclectic mix of people which keeps them coming back for more.

189

# JOURNAL CANTEEN

Level 1, 253 Flinders Lane
03 9650 4399

Walk up the stairs from Journal Café and you will be rewarded by the enticing aromas from Rosa Mitchell's menu of the day. The authenticity and simplicity of Rosa's Sicilian inspired cooking is evident in her high quality provincial cuisine that has turned the Journal Canteen into an eating hot-spot, even in the restaurant capital of Australia. Rosa's antipasto – a constant on the ever-changing menu – is a form of art, exhibiting excellent flavour and seasonal produce with the Chef's own homely flair and style. There are always a handful of delicious meals available on the chalk board, which are finished off delightfully with a stove-top coffee. Or if you are looking for a little indulgence you could always order the four course "degustation" that will fill you with flavour from tip to toes.

# FLINDERS LANE FLINDERS LANE FLINDERS LANE FLINDERS LANE FLINDERS LANE FLINDERS

# PAPA GOOSE

91-93 Flinders Lane
03 9663 2800
www.papagoose.com.au

Right at the back door of the distinctive 101 Collins Street building, Papa Goose is has a large corporate following as well as visitors to town. This ground floor restaurant offers diners the option of a main floor table or a private dining table. Chef and owner Neal White, offers a wide range of meals, designed around local produce whose true flavours are preserved as the central focus of each dish. The cocktail bar, Loose Goose, is on the first floor and provides a well-represented Australian wine list, while still giving international options including a selection of French champagne. Unwind after work over delicious classic or contemporary cocktail while grazing from the small plates menu. If cocktails are not your style there is Peroni on tap as well as a wide range of beers and spirits.

# BLUESTONE

349 Flinders Lane
03 9620 4060
www.bluestonerestaurantbar.com.au

This Melbourne icon is situated in the downtown end of Flinders lane between Queen Street and Elizabeth Street. Heritage listed for its elegant bluestone walls and expansive ceilings, reminiscent of its earlier woodshed days, its old-world features include grand gilt mirrors, plush fabrics and ambient colours. Combined with renowned chef, Jason Smythehas' innovative and contemporary menu is the owner, Jason McLean's lovingly selected wine list of Australian and International premier wines. Dine upstairs or chill out at Bluestone Downstairs in the New York style bar/lounge where you can enjoy sumptuous tapas or an award winning wood-fired pizza with your designer cocktail or wine. There is also the more exclusive option of private dining in the plush surrounds of the private dining area or in the more casual red section of the lounge.

# BAR MILE

308 Flinders Lane
03 9620 7122

Gracing the corner of Flinders Lane and Bligh Place is Bar Mile. Few people have broken the cone of silence on this great find, but those that have are unanimous with profuse praise. When walking down Flinders Lane you are unlikely to miss the big, arched windows in the Edwardian influenced façade. Inside Bar Mile is a beautiful large open space, decorated with interesting light fixtures, inspired by a farm theme and wrapped with square fencing material. Taking full advantage of the location, the café/bar also provides an outdoor seating area in Bligh Place. The cuisine is modern Australian cuisine and it is complemented by an excellent list of well priced wines.

# CHIN CHIN

125 Flinders Lane
03 8663 2000
www.chinchinrestaurant.com.au

Chin Chin is casual yet stylish dining to a tee, taking on an Asian street-style food approach. With its opening in early 2011, it has made its name on Flinders Lane as an eating hall not to be missed. Chris Lucas's new Thai eatery is making waves in Melbourne with ex-Botanical chef, Chris who has navigated away from all formalities you find in a fine dining restaurant. Sharing is his main emphasis with items like crunchy school prawns, suckling pig pancake rolls and an array of assorted dumplings. Chris has stuck to an all-Australian wine list – supporting local producers by using their names on the menu.

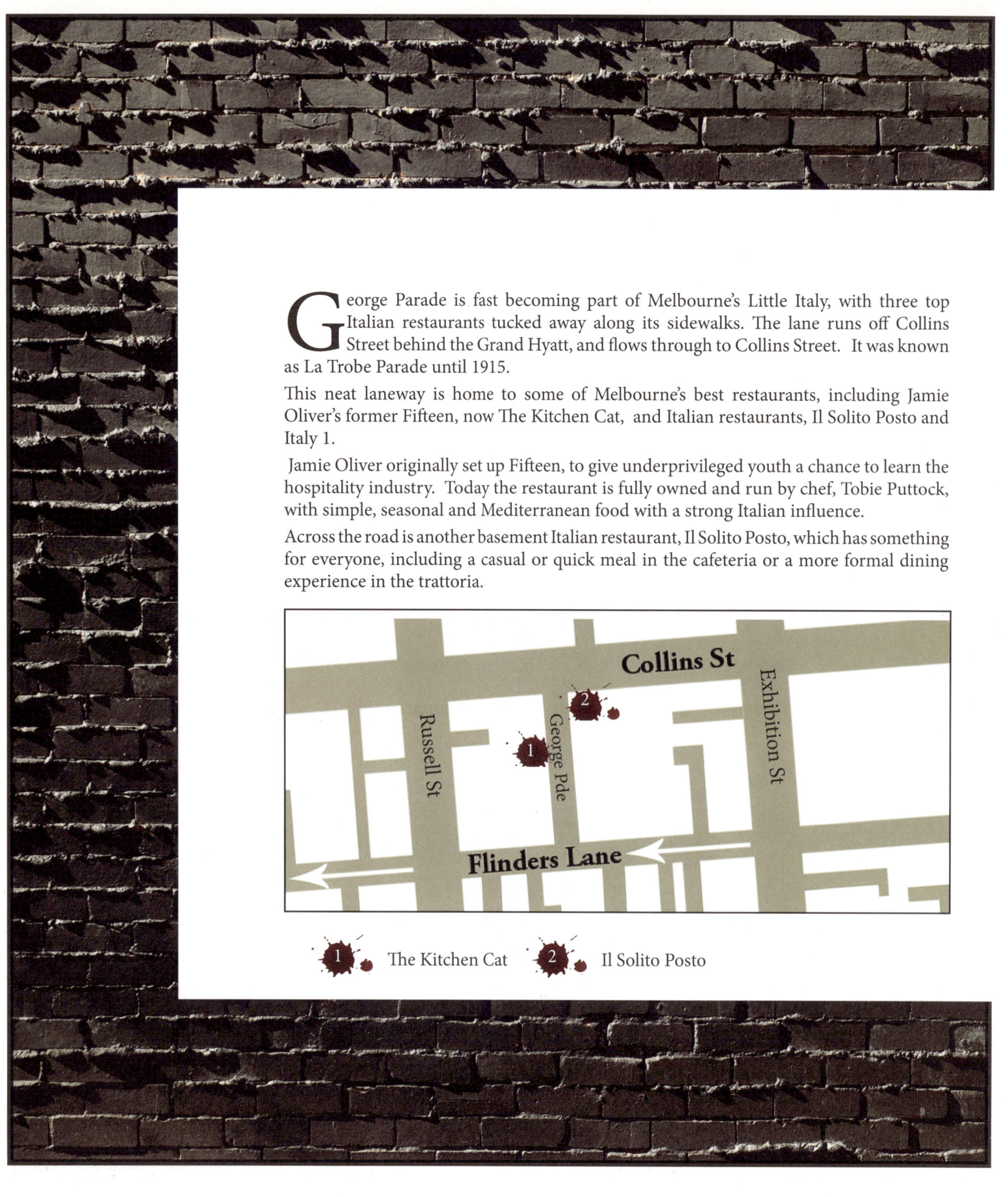

George Parade is fast becoming part of Melbourne's Little Italy, with three top Italian restaurants tucked away along its sidewalks. The lane runs off Collins Street behind the Grand Hyatt, and flows through to Collins Street. It was known as La Trobe Parade until 1915.

This neat laneway is home to some of Melbourne's best restaurants, including Jamie Oliver's former Fifteen, now The Kitchen Cat, and Italian restaurants, Il Solito Posto and Italy 1.

Jamie Oliver originally set up Fifteen, to give underprivileged youth a chance to learn the hospitality industry. Today the restaurant is fully owned and run by chef, Tobie Puttock, with simple, seasonal and Mediterranean food with a strong Italian influence.

Across the road is another basement Italian restaurant, Il Solito Posto, which has something for everyone, including a casual or quick meal in the cafeteria or a more formal dining experience in the trattoria.

1. The Kitchen Cat    2. Il Solito Posto

# GEORGE PDE

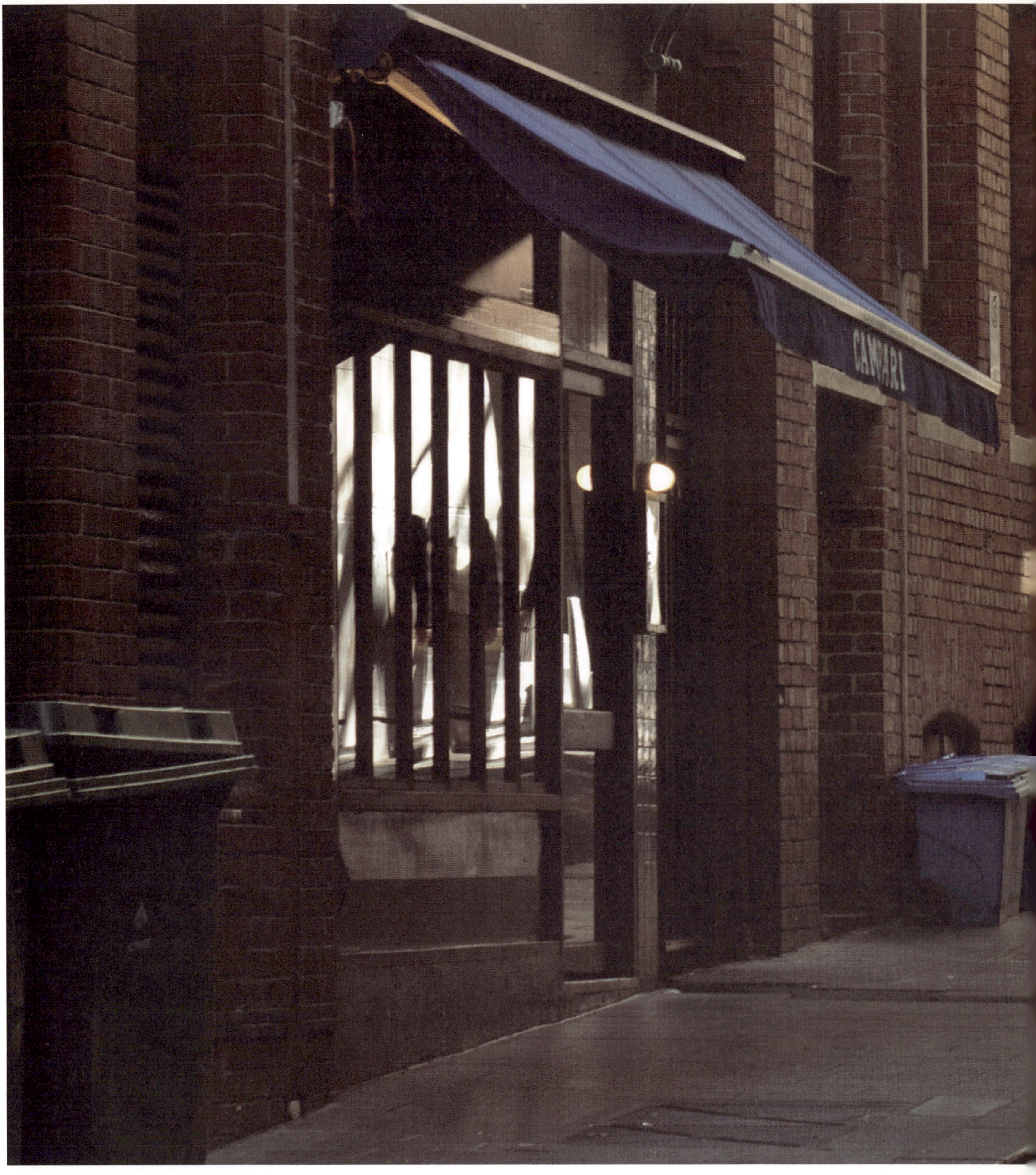
CAMPARI

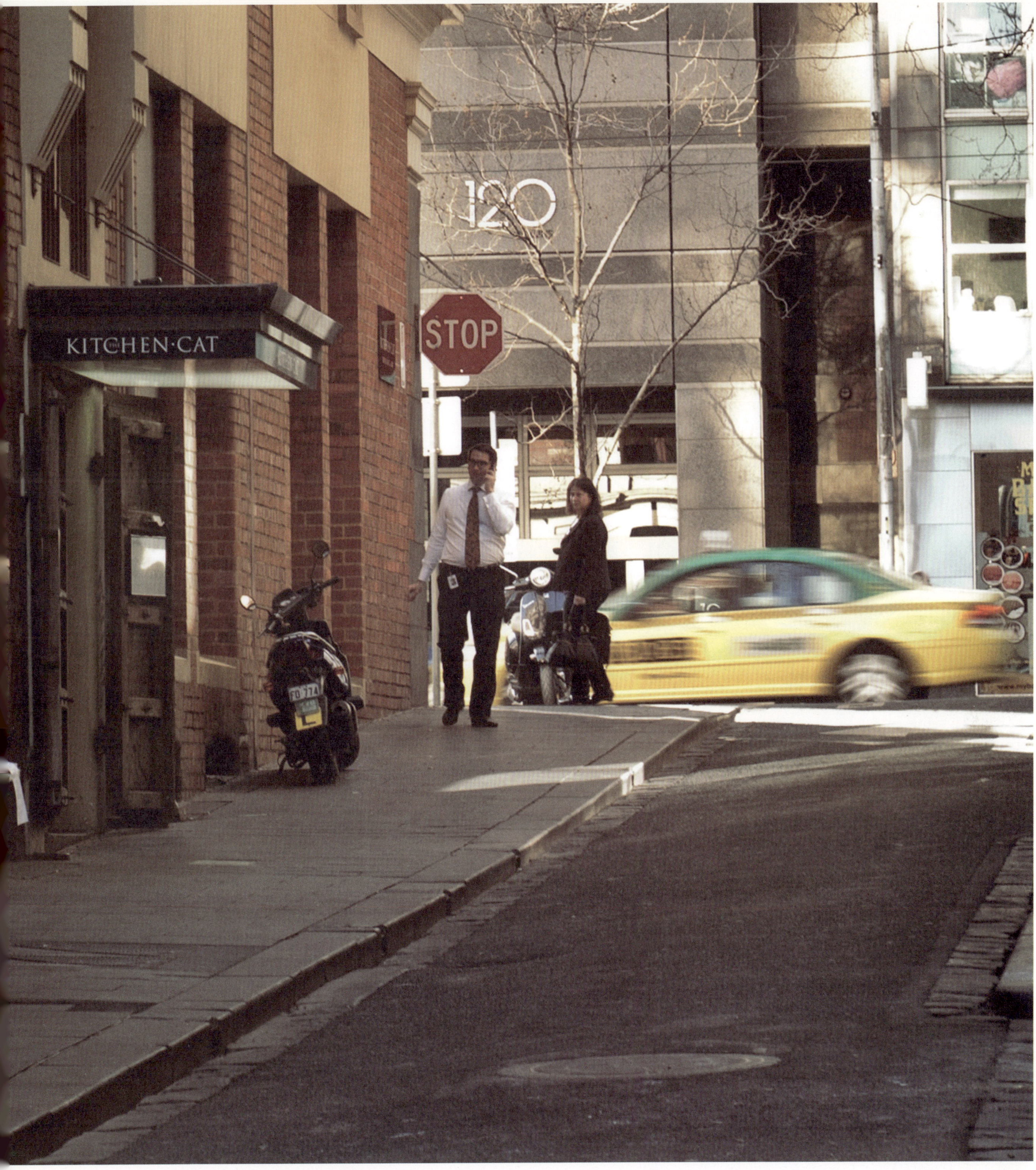
KITCHEN·CAT
STOP
120

# IL SOLITO POSTO

Basement, George Parade
03 9654 4466
www.ilsolitoposto.com.au

Looking through the glowing windows into the sub-basement off George Parade, you will discover Il Solito Posto. An aptly named establishment offering both a cafeteria and a trattoria has become "home" for those in the area seeking a great Italian meal. If you are in search of an Italian fine dining experience, Il Solito Posto is not one to miss. It combines great service with fresh and delicious traditional food that can certainly be deemed value for money. An important feature is the owner's passion for wine. Lose yourself in the extensive wine list which incorporates top quality, local Australian and imported Italian and French wines, while specialising in older iconic Australian wines and a wide selection of champagne and sparkling whites.

# THE KITCHEN CAT

Basement, George Parade
03 1300 799 415
www.thekitchencat.com.au

The Kitchen Cat is the fruition of Jamie Oliver's Fifteen restaurant. Taken over by Fifteen's head chef, Tobie Puttock, the Kitchen Cat serves simple and elegant Italian, European and Mediterranean dishes. The restaurant is in a basement area with an open kitchen and has been refurbished in a bright and modern European style. Diners can take full advantage of the open kitchen by booking to sit at the chef's table where you will certainly be in for an entertaining evening. The crowning glory of the Kitchen Cat is Tobie Puttock's amazing meat cuts and cured meats and sausages, some of which are proudly on show as you walk down the entrance staircase. The extensive wine list provides the perfect balance of Australian and European vintages.

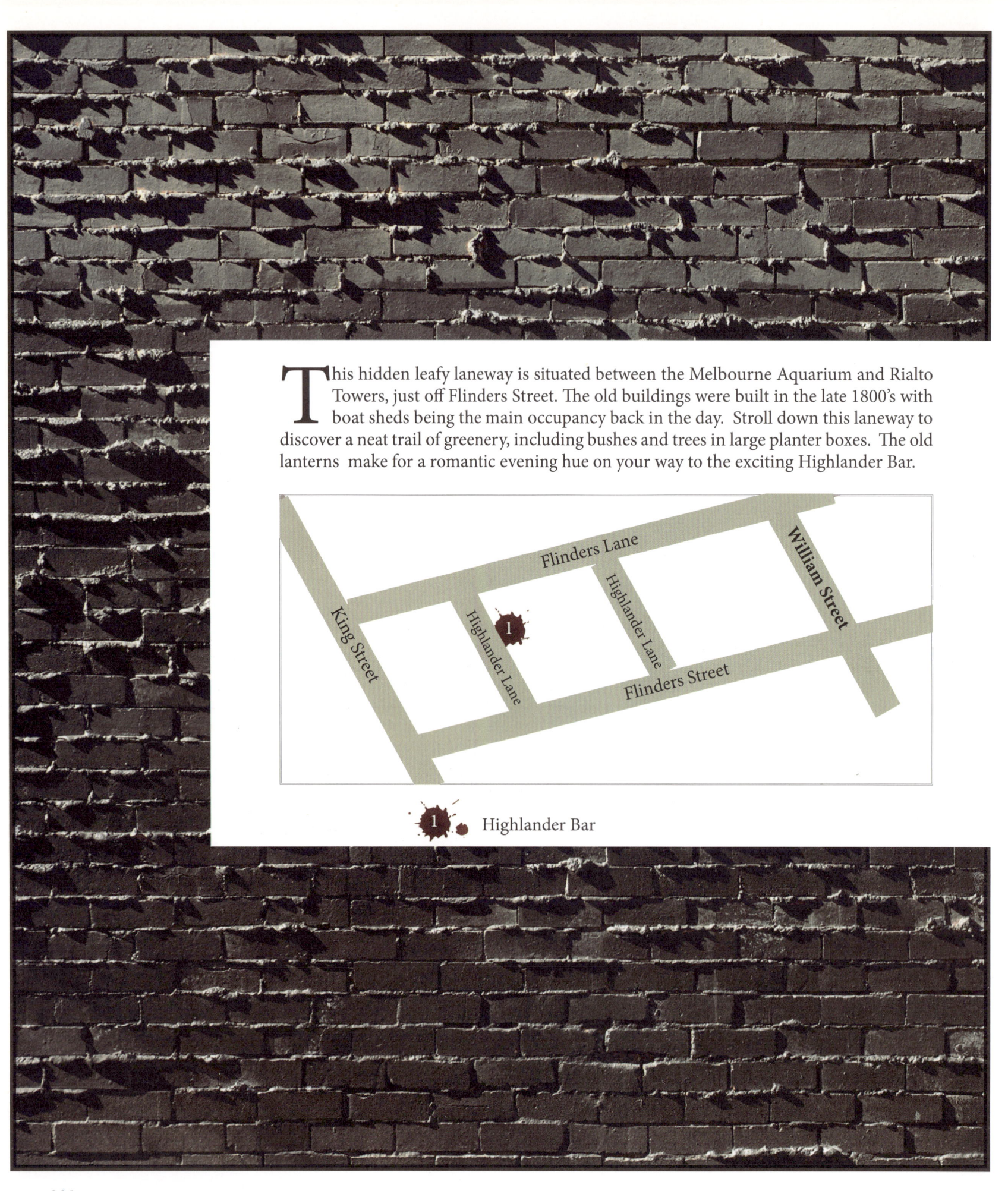

This hidden leafy laneway is situated between the Melbourne Aquarium and Rialto Towers, just off Flinders Street. The old buildings were built in the late 1800's with boat sheds being the main occupancy back in the day. Stroll down this laneway to discover a neat trail of greenery, including bushes and trees in large planter boxes. The old lanterns make for a romantic evening hue on your way to the exciting Highlander Bar.

1. Highlander Bar

# HIGHLANDER LANE

204

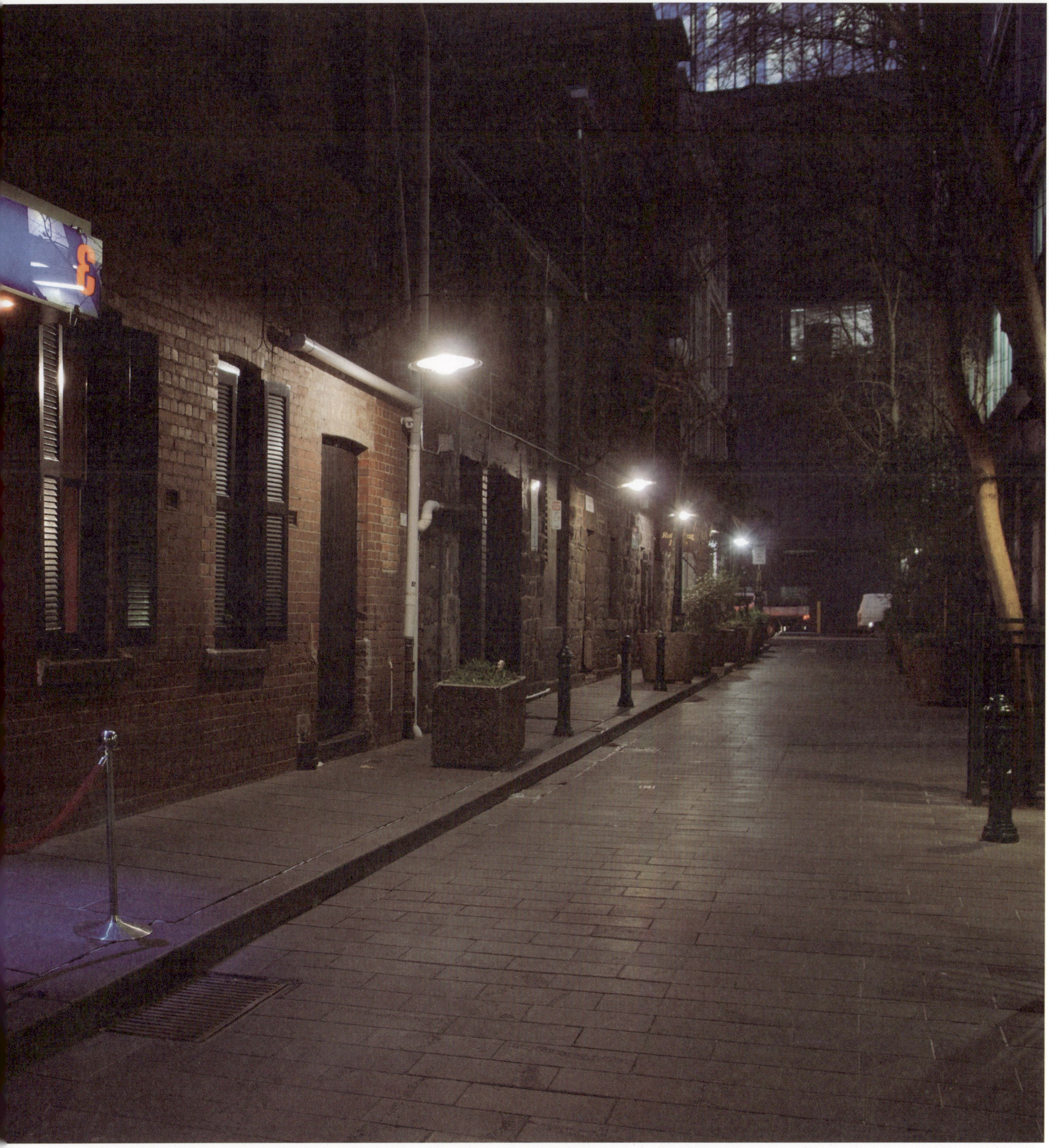

# HIGHLANDER BAR

11 Highlander Lane
03 9620 2228
www.highlanderbar.com.au

From the outset, Highlander bar is something different - hidden in a leafy laneway between the Melbourne Aquarium and Rialto Towers, just off Flinders Street. The old building dates back to the late 1800's and was once used as a boat storage shed. Since becoming a licensed venue in the 1980's, 11a Highlander lane has worn a myriad of names and guises, before finally becoming the Highlander Bar in 2009. Owner Kate Whillas has turned this space into a hot boutique bar and nightclub.

Highlander is all about the good times. It is spread over two levels with a nice long bar and big spacious dance floor. The lounge area offers ample seating with intimate, velvety couch booths and stools where you can relax and chat in the muted candle and lantern light. Dancing is however a big part of the fun here with great music, a warm vibe and relaxed dress code allowing you to be comfortable being yourself.

The drinks menu covers the spectrum with enough scope to thrill beer lovers and cocktail seekers alike, and with prices to keep your wallet happy. Ask the friendly bar staff for the signature cocktail - a white chocolate and passionfruit martini - and it may even be made for you by Kate herself. If you like to plan in advance check out the website and discover the drink specials and food offers that are often available.

The slightly secluded location means that new customers are usually referred by existing clients, giving this bar a natural advantage of a crowd that is a harmonious mix of like-minded individuals. The Highlander ticks all the boxes in its own relaxed way, satisfying the needs of the local after-work, corporate clientele, as well as providing the perfect haunt for a younger, fun-loving and friendly night crowd, who will always come back for more.

The Highlander's attractive layout and ambience, combined with its convenient walking distance from both Flinders Street and Southern Cross stations, also makes it a very popular venue for private hire, including birthday parties, product launches, dance parties and even art exhibitions.

This is the perfect place to spend the night, with plenty of places to sit and chat earlier on and the promise of a full dance floor and party atmosphere later.

207

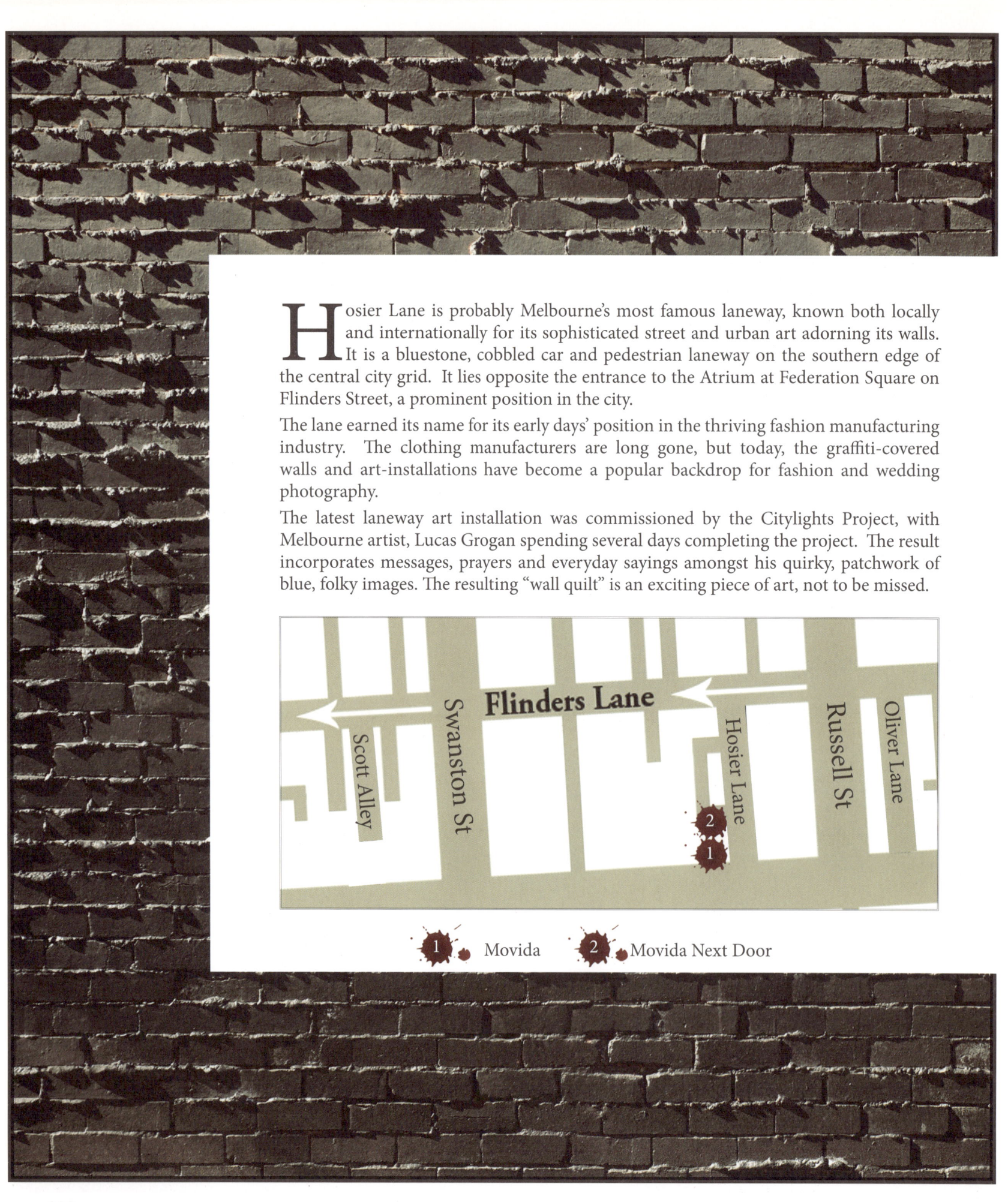

Hosier Lane is probably Melbourne's most famous laneway, known both locally and internationally for its sophisticated street and urban art adorning its walls. It is a bluestone, cobbled car and pedestrian laneway on the southern edge of the central city grid. It lies opposite the entrance to the Atrium at Federation Square on Flinders Street, a prominent position in the city.

The lane earned its name for its early days' position in the thriving fashion manufacturing industry. The clothing manufacturers are long gone, but today, the graffiti-covered walls and art-installations have become a popular backdrop for fashion and wedding photography.

The latest laneway art installation was commissioned by the Citylights Project, with Melbourne artist, Lucas Grogan spending several days completing the project. The result incorporates messages, prayers and everyday sayings amongst his quirky, patchwork of blue, folky images. The resulting "wall quilt" is an exciting piece of art, not to be missed.

1. Movida
2. Movida Next Door

# HOSIER LANE

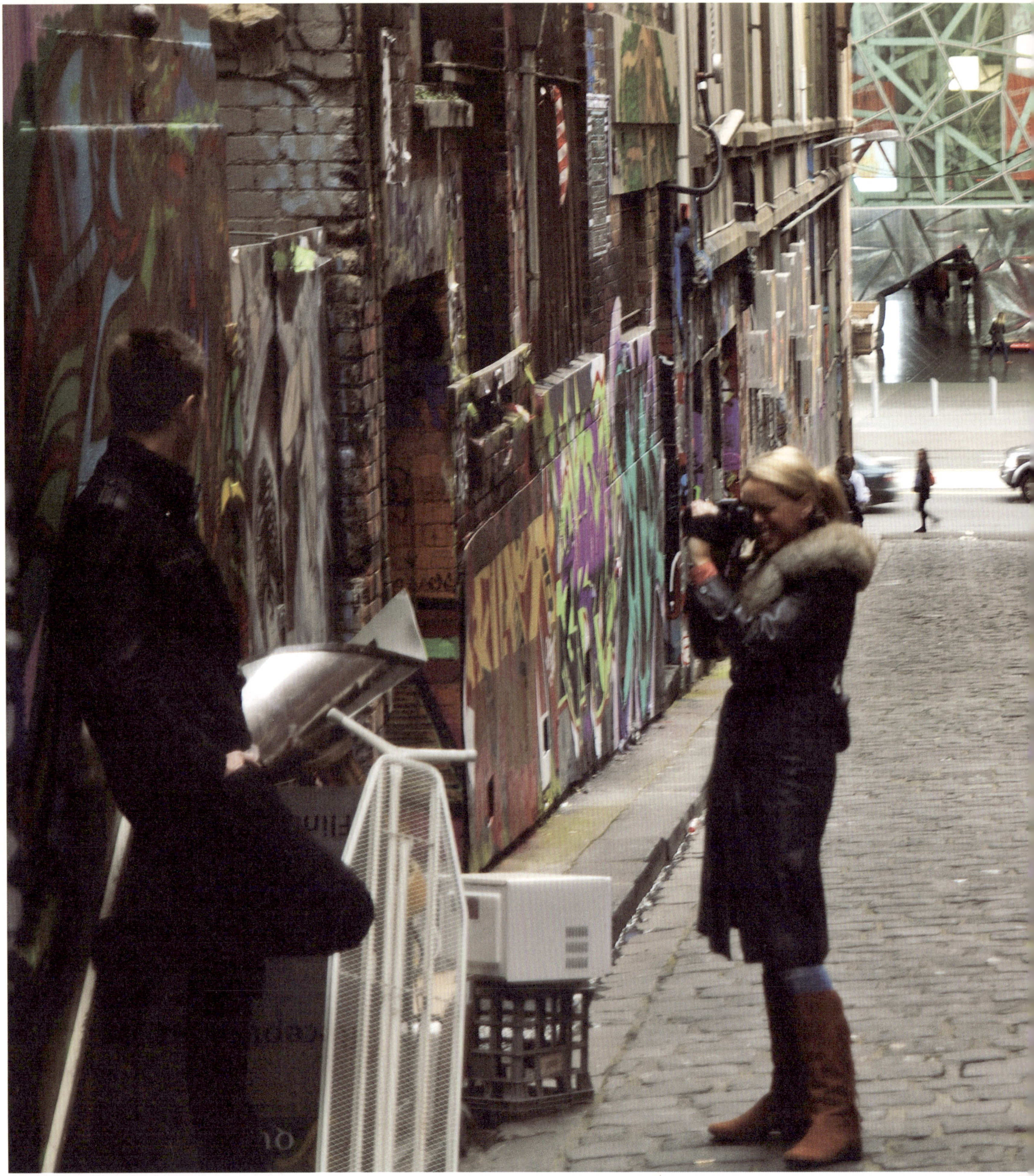

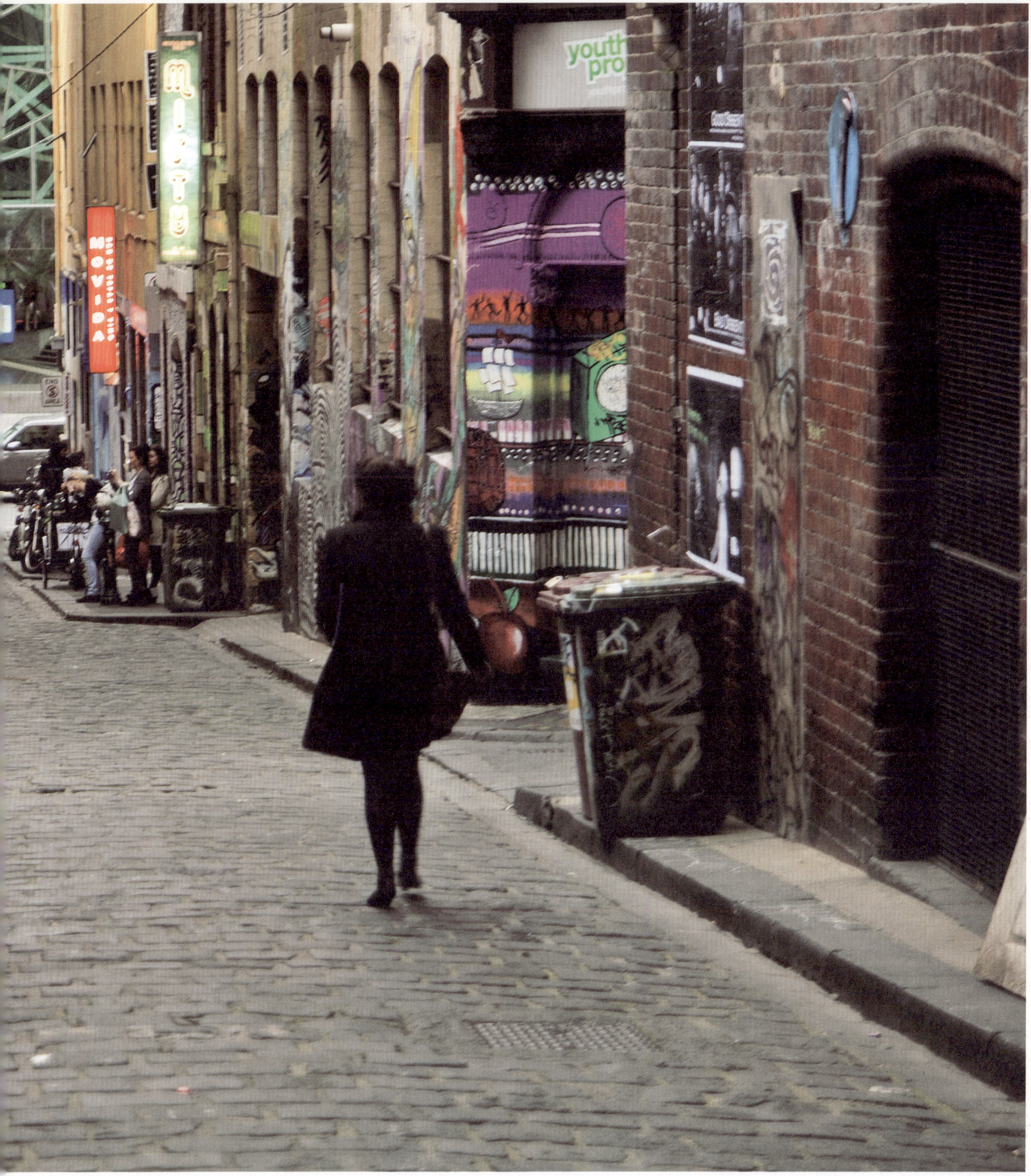
MOVIDA
youth

# MOVIDA

1 Hosier Lane
03 9663 3038
www.movida.com.au

Just a short stroll from Federation Square, Movida is a fantastic Spanish experience in the heart of Melbourne. The wooden furniture, earthy tones and funky tunes give this restaurant/bar a vibrancy and warmth. In true Spanish tradition, Movida offers great beer and top-notch Spanish red wines that can be enjoyed around the bar and complemented with tapas. Slide across to the tables for some shared dishes – like the sumptuous slow braised lamb or the house-made morcilla (blood sausage). If there are more than four of you, trust the kitchen and take advantage of the banquet. Vegetarians are not left out with a variety of options, and everyone with a sweet tooth will smile at the delicious hot chocolate with churros. Movida will take reservations if you don't want to miss out on a table.

HOSIER LANE HOSIER LANE HOSIER LANE HOSIER LANE HOSIER LANE HOSIER LANE HOSIER

# MOVIDA NEXT DOOR

Corner Flinders St & Hosier Lane
03 9663 3038
www.movida.com.au/next_door

Right next door to Movida at the entrance to Hosier Lane, is Frank Camorra's Movida Next Door. It is a more casual, sherry and tapas style bar, designed to complement the traditional focus of Movida. Here you can expect authentic and delicately flavoured food, presented in a simple, rustic fashion. Round off your Spanish beer or favourite sherry with the must-try, stumpy chorizo sausages, which are made to the specifications of Frank's Dad, Juan.

Little Bourke Street runs through the whole city, from Spring Street to Spencer Street. Two grand, red arches claim Swanston to Spring Streets as Melbourne's Chinatown. Home to literally hundreds of restaurants and bars, Little Bourke Street is not just home to Chinese or other Asian inspired food. (see Chinatown pages for more info).

The Spring Street end is close to the theatre district, and it has numerous restaurants catering for pre-dinner drinks or after-theatre tapas. Fine wine and excellent dining can be found at Melbourne's iconic, Punch Lane Wine Bar and Restaurant. And further down towards Elizabeth Street, you will find some of the best coffee in Melbourne in a little café called Brother Baba Budan. Major department stores such as Myer and David Jones have entrances on Little Bourke Street. The back entrance of GPO Melbourne is also on this street.

1. Punch Lane   2. Longrain   3. Brother Baba Budan

# LITTLE BOURKE ST.

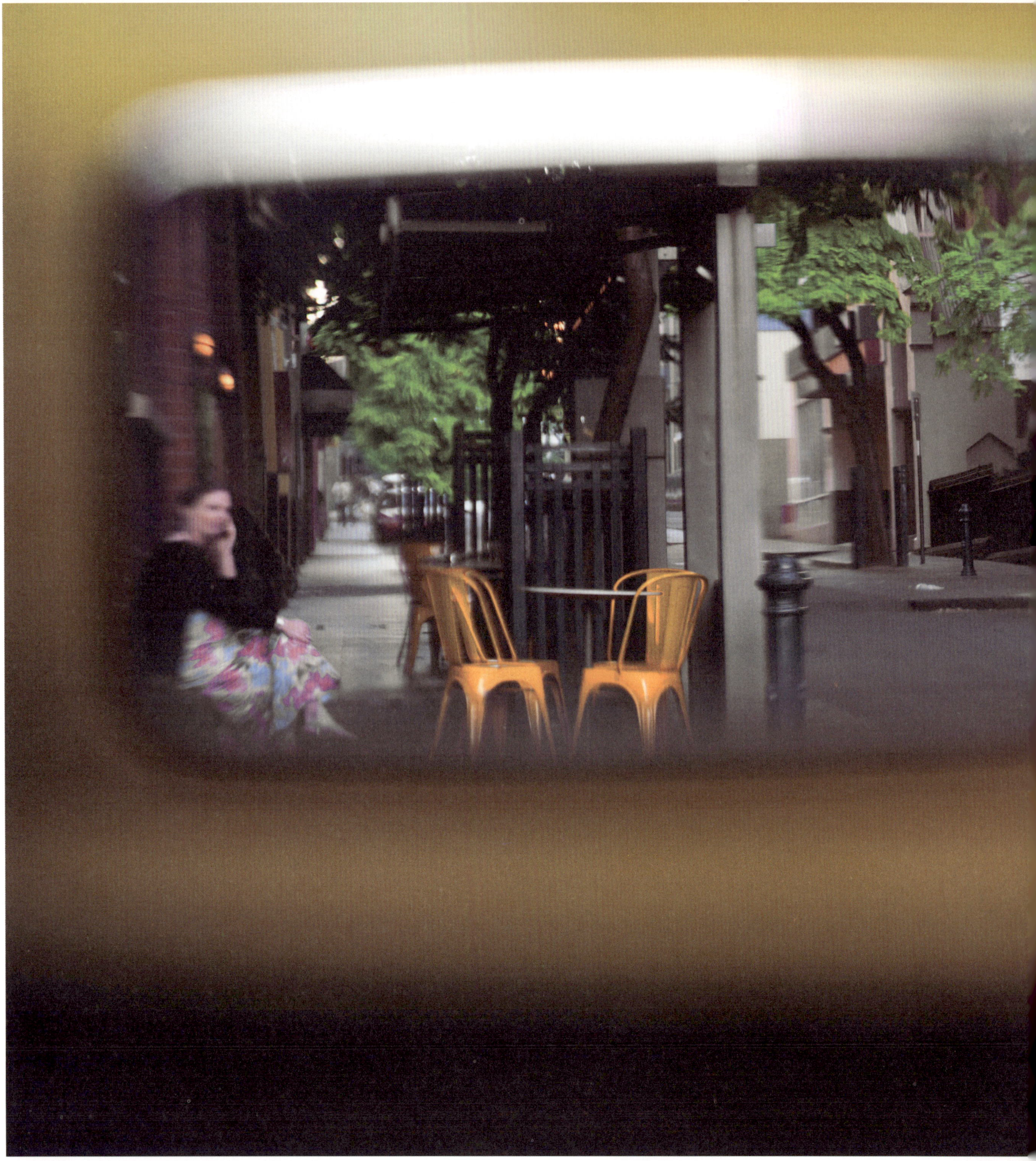

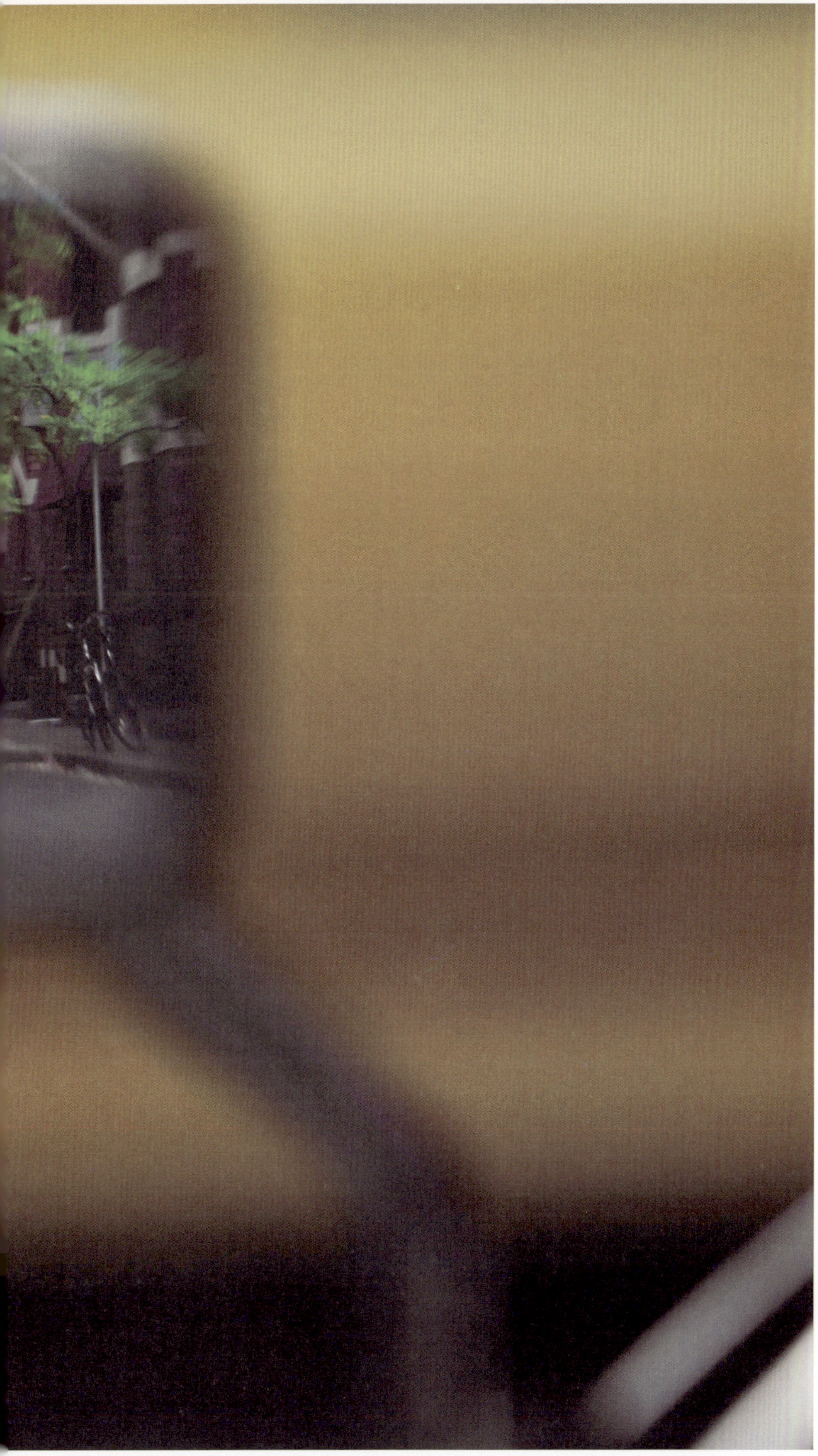

# PUNCH LANE

43 Little Bourke St
03 9639 4944
www.punchlane.com.au

After sixteen years as a Melbourne institution, Punch Lane Wine Bar Restaurant is still "packing a punch." Named after the adjacent laneway, Punch Lane's success is based on good old, fashioned food, wine and service.

Dating back to the days when liquor licenses were limited, owner, Martin Pirc, invited patrons to enjoy a more European, flexible restaurant attitude and dining style. Punch Lane became Melbourne's first boutique wine bar, and a favourite amongst Melbourne's theatre-goers and wine-lovers, who relished the opportunity to eat and drink at a venue which adapted to their moods and catered for either a formal or informal experience; whether it be a business lunch meeting, a quick, pre-theatre dinner, after-work drinks and tapas, or just sit with a book and a glass of wine.

Today, Punch Lane's reputation is based on its seasonal menu, extensive wine list, ambience and service. The calibre of the wine cellar requires no introduction, and consists of a superb collection of Australian classics, including many small boutique producers, as well as many fine wines from New Zealand, France, Italy and Spain.

The menu reflects a modern Australian cuisine, fused with European influences. The menu encourages clientele to "choose their own adventure," offering options such as a cheese platter to share over a bottle of wine, pre-theatre tapas, or a full menu of elegant, tempting dishes. An enormous blackboard showcases a diverse range of cheeses and wines on offer, and wine racks covering the back wall provide a tempting backdrop. For parties of up to 24 guests, a semi-private room is available, featuring a wrought-iron centrepiece, a large handmade mirror, a wall of wine and views of the passers-by on Little Bourke Street.

Begin by sharing the chef's tasting plate, complete with beetroot-cured salmon with dill creme fraiche, house-made labne, Spanish tortilla, marinated mushrooms, sardine escabeche, scotch quail egg, and Sicilian and Ligurian olives. Move on to market fish with confit capsicum, sauteed chats, scampi and chive creme fraiche sauce, or a Black Angus rib eye (350g) steak with red wine shallots and tarragon butter. The desserts are to die for, and feature such beauties as a chocolate sponge, layered with chocolate ganache, served with cherries poached in kirsch and clotted cream, and a rhubarb and vanilla custard tart, served with house-made ginger ice cream. (See chef's recipe next page.)

Punch Lane houses an eclectic collection of furnishings and curios, amongst them a timber bar made from 100-year-old jarrah, floorboards salvaged from an old basketball court in Healesville, a mirror constructed from those same boards, hand-crafted, wrought-iron fixtures and red leather chairs that the Beatles sat on when they visited Australia in 1964. This attention to detail sets the tone for a unique and enjoyable lunch, dinner or drink. Designed by acclaimed Melbourne architects, Jackson, Clements, Burrows, the alfresco dining area on Little Bourke Street provides the perfect aspect to sit and watch the world go by, and its clever design won the 2005 Urban Architecture Award.

With so much to offer, Punch Lane Wine Bar Restaurant is set to impress anyone who is looking for a true Melbourne laneway gem…

Cropwell Bishop Stilton
Soft, sweet and savoury w/ distinct, mild blue mould - England
Garrotxa
Semi-hard goat's milk cheese. Sweet, slightly tart flavour, covered with natural moulds. - Spain
Fleur du Marquis
Classic ewe's milk cheese rich & creamy, savoury
Chardonnay - Vic
2009 Yarra Warra
Pinot Noir Rosé - Vic
2009 Grove Mill
Sauvignon Blanc - N.Z.
2010 Forest Hill
Riesling - W.A.
2009 Sartarelli
Verdicchio Classico
- Italy

Shiraz
Pike & Joyce
Pinot Noir

Tapas to enjoy with a glass of wine
Seared scallop w/ chorizo oil, tomato, capers and mixed herbs.
Olives
Grilled turkish bread w/ dips

# BROTHER BABA BUDAN

359 Little Bourke St
03 9606 0449
www.brotherbababudan.com.au

Melbournians display their loyalty for this little gem with many return visits. At first glance through the window, this espresso bar, Brother Baba Budan piques your curiosity with the school chairs on the ceiling, but as you draw closer to the door you are entranced by the enticing coffee aromas. Sister to the popular Seven Grains espresso bar in Fitzroy, Brother Baba Budan is dedicated to the 17th Century surfer Baba Budan. Revered by Muslims, Hindus and now all coffee drinkers in Melbourne, Baba Budan was said to have introduced the coffee plant to India in the form of seven beans transported from the port of Mocha in Yemen. Baba Budan is a true shrine to coffee, from the coffee bean door handle to the beans from St Ali where several origins and blends are roasted.

# LONGRAIN

44 Little Bourke St
03 9671 3151
www.longrain.com.au

Partners Martin Boetz and Sam Christie have outdone themselves with this superb, Thai/Asian influenced restaurant and bar. Utilising the heritage look of the old stable building and combining it with classy wooden features including rows of long tables and simple chandeliers. The restaurant seating is designed for Longrain's distinctive banquet style eating, and the generous main dishes should be combined and shared. Longrain's bar, a centre piece dividing the restaurant from the cocktail lounge, speaks for itself being voted one of Australia's best bars in the "Best of The Best" edition of the Australian Gourmet Traveller magazine. The mainly Victorian wine list was selected to complement the hot, salty, sour and sweet flavours of the food.

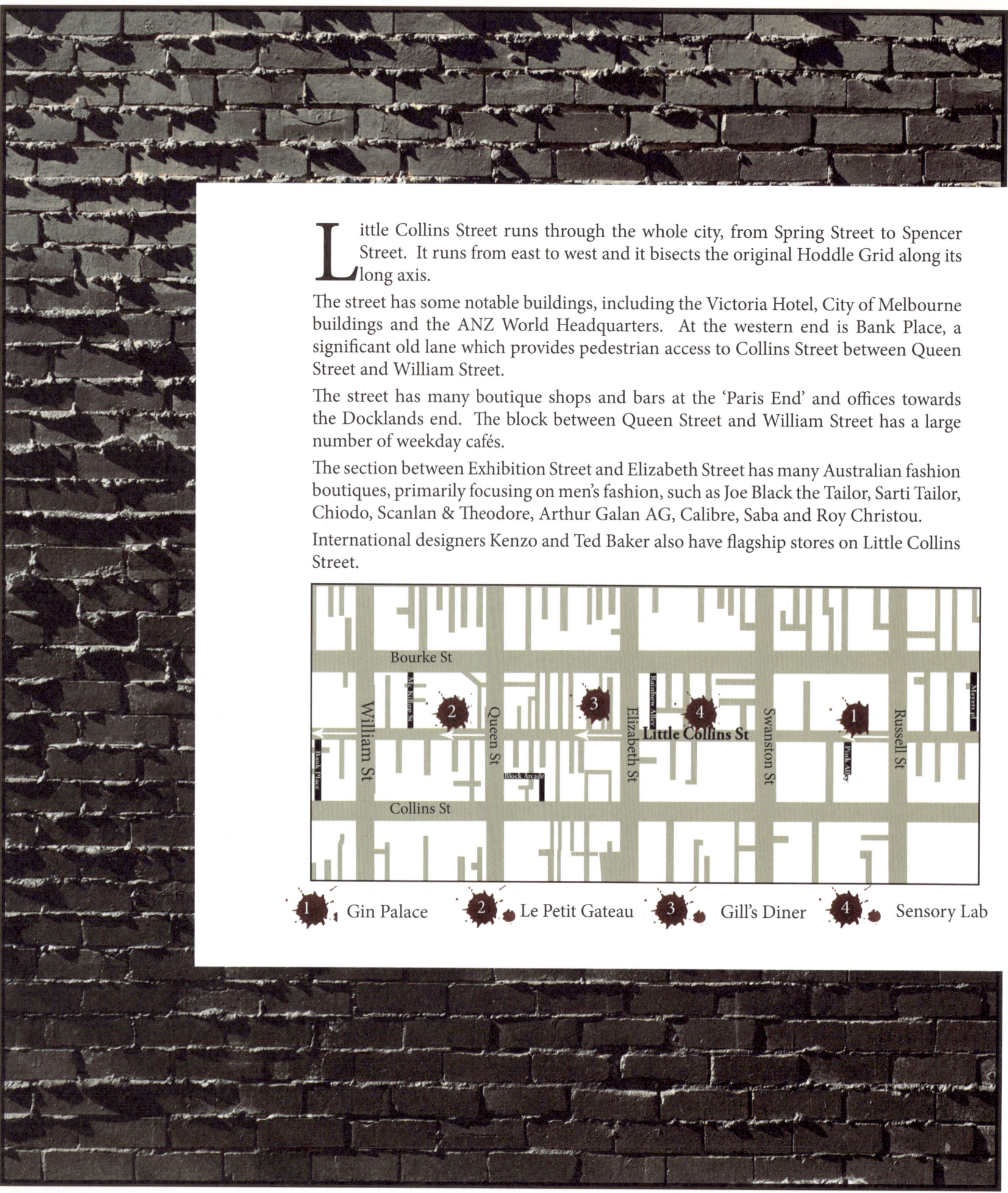

Little Collins Street runs through the whole city, from Spring Street to Spencer Street. It runs from east to west and it bisects the original Hoddle Grid along its long axis.

The street has some notable buildings, including the Victoria Hotel, City of Melbourne buildings and the ANZ World Headquarters. At the western end is Bank Place, a significant old lane which provides pedestrian access to Collins Street between Queen Street and William Street.

The street has many boutique shops and bars at the 'Paris End' and offices towards the Docklands end. The block between Queen Street and William Street has a large number of weekday cafés.

The section between Exhibition Street and Elizabeth Street has many Australian fashion boutiques, primarily focusing on men's fashion, such as Joe Black the Tailor, Sarti Tailor, Chiodo, Scanlan & Theodore, Arthur Galan AG, Calibre, Saba and Roy Christou.

International designers Kenzo and Ted Baker also have flagship stores on Little Collins Street.

1. Gin Palace    2. Le Petit Gateau    3. Gill's Diner    4. Sensory Lab

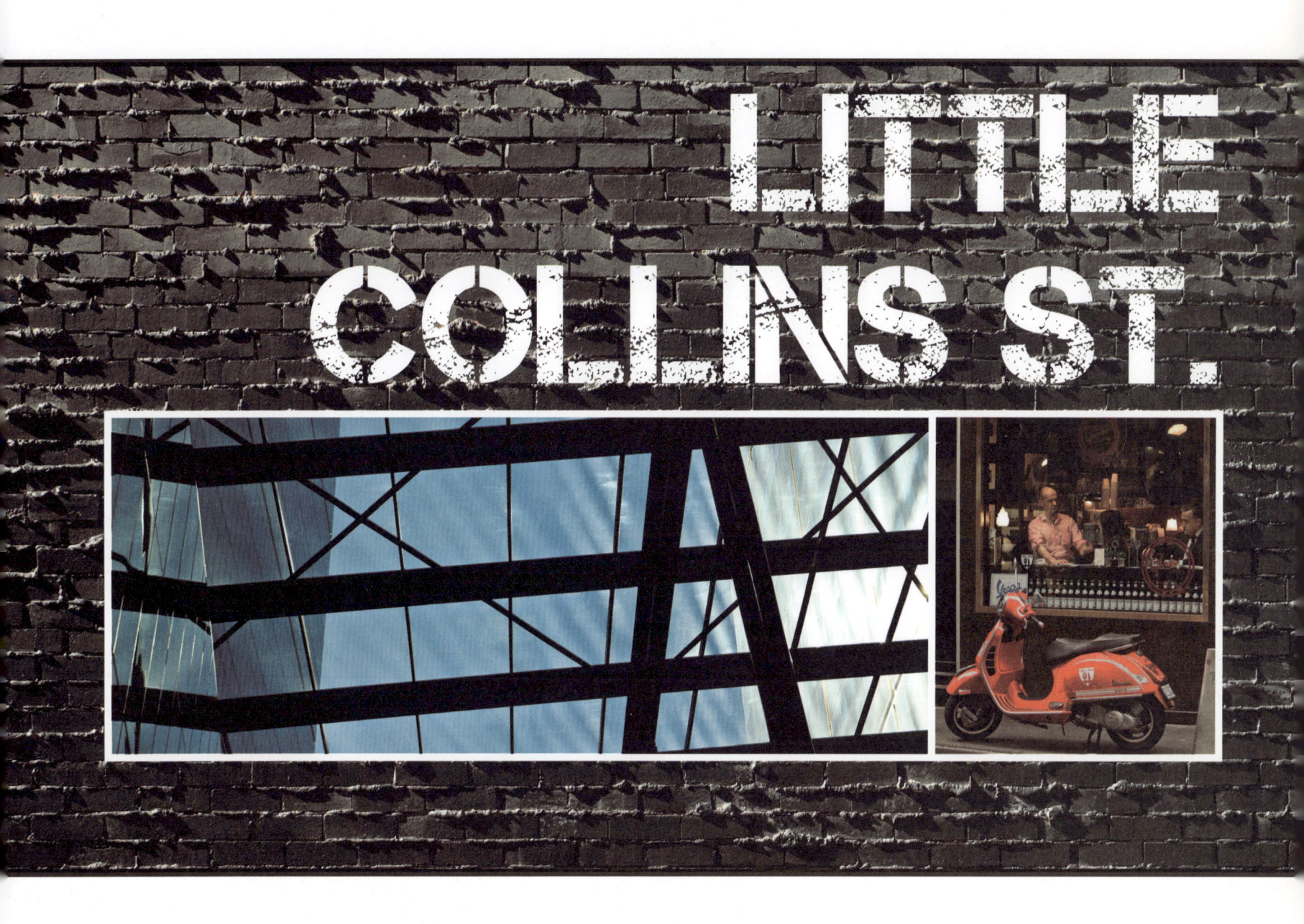

# LITTLE COLLINS ST.

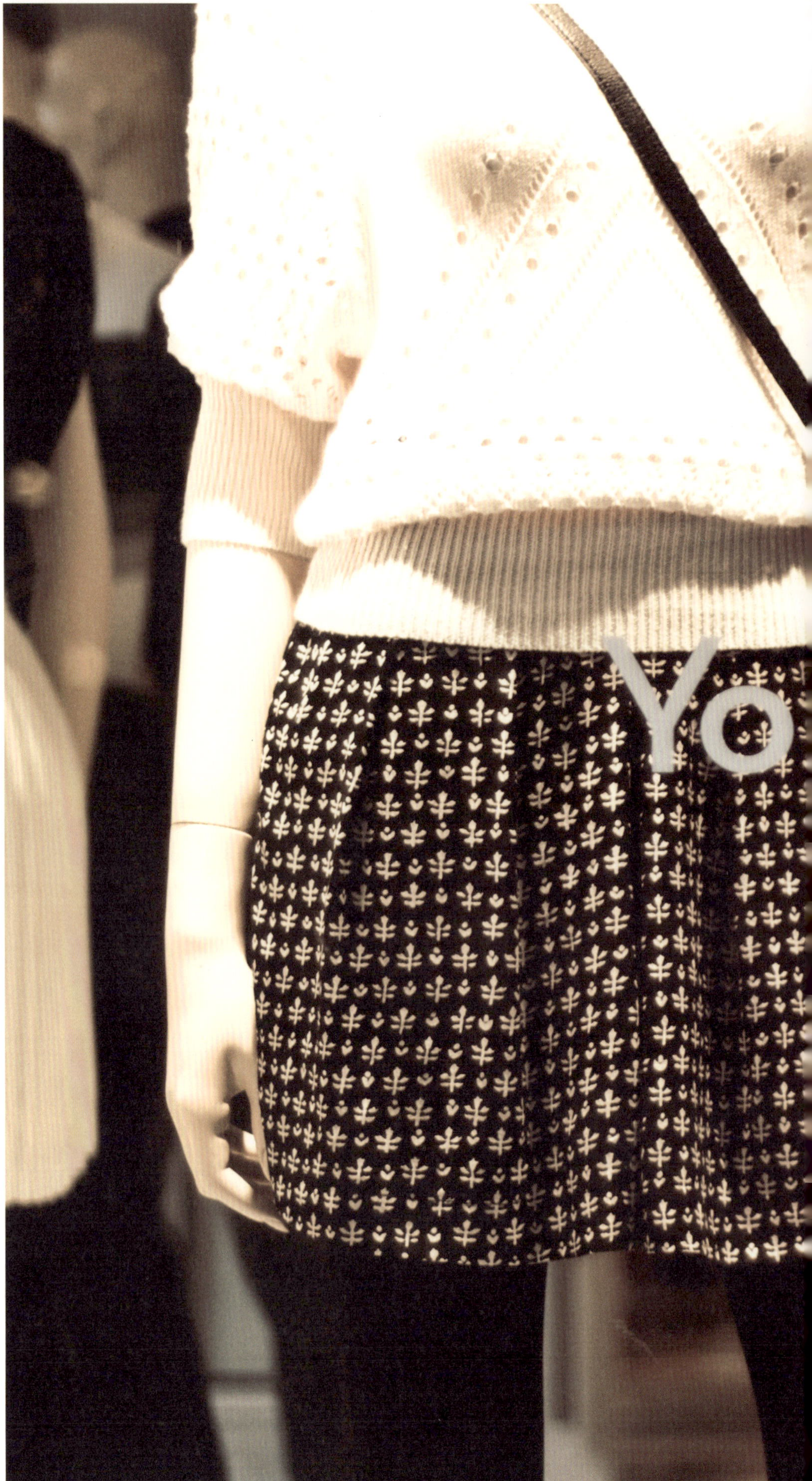
Yo

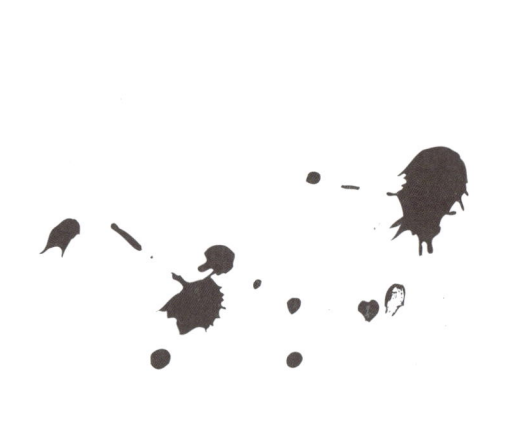

u are woman?

# LE PETIT GATEAU

458 Little Collins St
03 9944 8893
www.lepetitgateau.com.au

With so many irresistible pastries, tarts, cakes and desserts on show, you simply must have a coffee and a look at Le Petit Gateau in Little Collins Street. A well known part of the RACV City Club, the pastry shop makes everything in-store and you can watch the team preparing and cooking through a large glass window.

The award-winning French pastry chef, Pierrick Boyer, has worked alongside some of the most internationally renowned chefs including Alain Ducasse, Christophe Michalak, Pierre Marcolini and Stephane Leroux. He brings a wealth of experience to Melbourne's pastry and cake scene and he is making a name for himself throughout Australia with his novel cuisine.

You can order a special cake, something for the next office party or simply drop in to discuss any special order you may have. While you are there try one of his sweet collections in the showcase. You will become addicted and have to come back for more!

Pierrick says his creations are all from original recipes and are purposefully minimalist and contemporary. Each exquisite item features fresh, distinctive flavours that have been chosen specifically to satisfy all tastes and suit every occasion.

Try taking home a Brownie and Passionfruit Chocolate Gâteau – with a brownie base, crunchy praline passionfruit custard and chocolate mousse - offering a delicate balance of rich and refreshing flavours. Or impress everyone at your next dinner party with the tempting layers of the Cosmopolitan – a carrot cake base topped with white chocolate cheesecake and raspberry jam.

Tantalise your chocolate-loving friends with the pure indulgence of a Praline Mud Cake, with its smooth hazelnut chocolate icing to melt the strongest resistance.

What brings Melbourne's "sweet-tooths" clammering back to Le Petit Gateau is the cutting edge ingredients, preparation and design of Pierrick's cakes. At Easter, you have to admire his shop full of house-made, chocolate Easter eggs and other shapes.

Being a part of the RACV, Le Petit Gateau is also a cozy place to meet for business, morning coffee, or a late afternoon catch up with friends. Whatever the occasion, there is always a reason to drop by Le Petit Gateau. But let me warn you, you will come away saying, "I have never tasted anything like that before!"

Make sure you follow Pierrick Boyer's creations on Twitter and Facebook - he will keep you updated with his latest adventures and creations!

Cake photos by Brent Parker Jones

# GILLS DINER

360 Little Collins St
03 9670 7214

See the white neon "Italian Espresso" sign with "AND BAKERY" written below in red capitals? You are almost there. Although officially off Little Collins, you will have to wander down dead-end Gills Alley and past the window bar's outdoor stools to find the entrance to Gills Diner as it is tucked behind its counterpart, the Commercial Bakery. The restaurant oozes old-school charm serving a rustic and satisfying Italian and French style cuisine created by Chris Kerr and Head Chef Kyle Doody. Enjoy the warehouse/schoolroom/candlelit grotto style décor while scanning the back wall blackboard for the menu. Take the opportunity to try a beverage from one of the smaller producers, who Gills Diner is helping to break into the general market with a wine list that avoids any of the larger commercial brands.

# SENSORY LAB

297 Little Collins St
03 9645 0065
www.sensorylab.com.au

Welcome to the freshest ground coffee you have tasted! Owned and roasted by St Ali, Sensory Lab's beans are only roasted to first crack, which gives the coffee a much smoother texture and uncovers the true flavour of the bean. Located at the Little Collins Street entrance to David Jones, the coffee wonderland is a true laboratory of tastes. Upon arrival into this retro minimalist café, you will have the opportunity for a lab assistant to take you through the single-origin tasting notes and the reserve selection to uncover your palate preferences. Four types of brewing methods are used and a chart is available to help you identify which method enhances the flavour of which beans. This is a first stop for home and office baristas, coffee connoisseurs and all those who like a good brew.

It was Hoddle's idea in the 1837 grid plan that the 'little' streets in Melbourne would all run parallel to each other, including Little Collins, Little Bourke and Little Lonsdale Streets. They all run from Spring to Spencer Streets. Many laneways in Melbourne run off these little streets. In the late nineteenth century Little Lonsdale Street was considered the heart of 'slumdom' – housing only what was considered 'low-life' working class communities.

1. Thousand Pound Bend  2. Horse Bazaar

# LITTLE LONSDALE ST.

WHAT HAPPENS IN THE GUTTER, STAYS IN THE GUTTER.

232

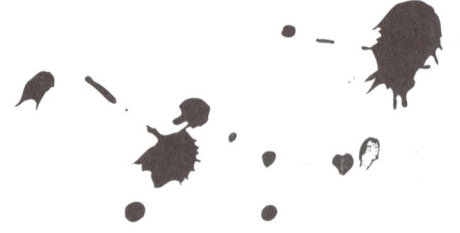

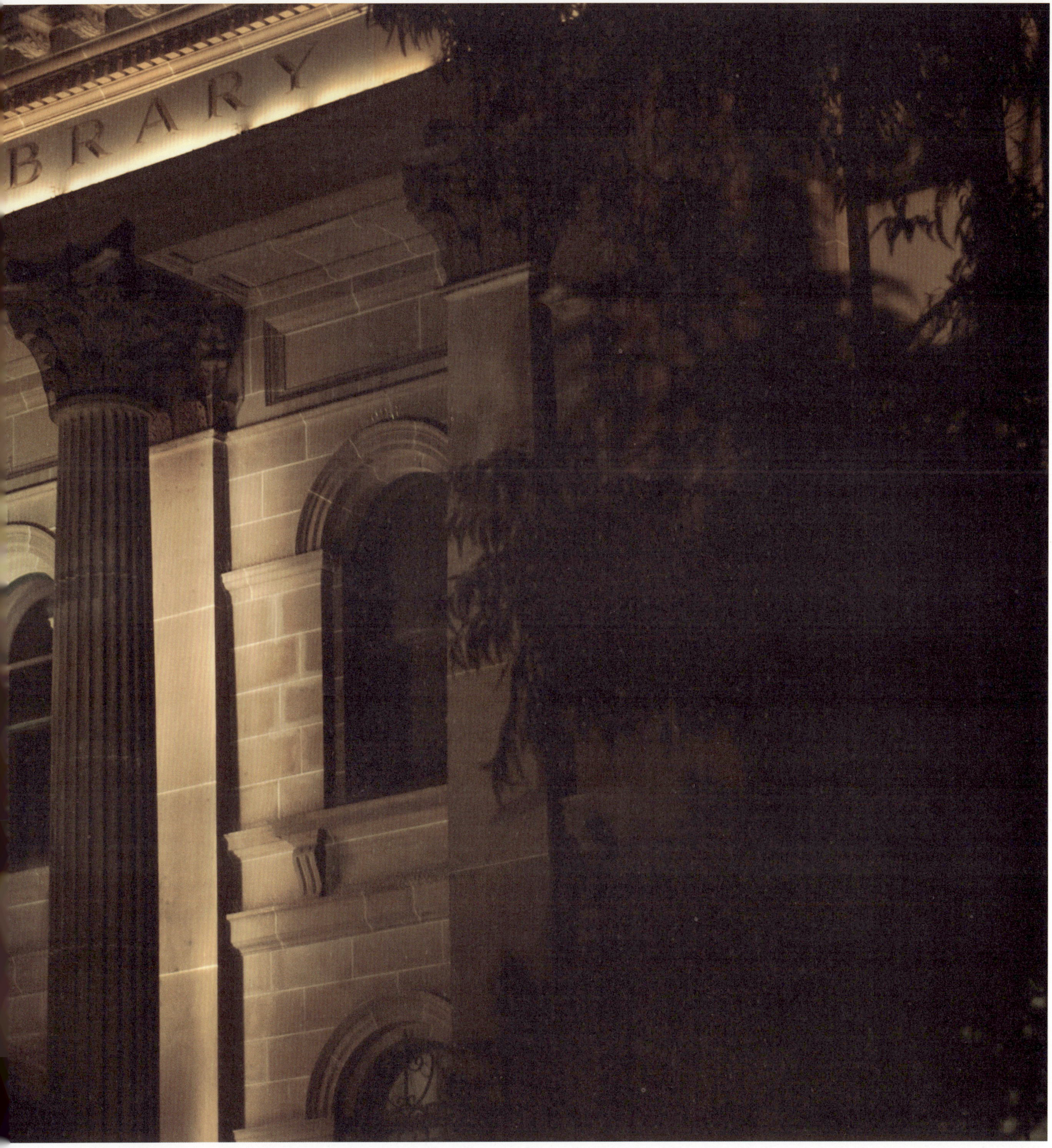
BRARY

# HORSE BAZAAR

397 Little Lonsdale St
03 9670 2329
www.horsebazaar.com.au

From its origins as a saddlery shop in Kirk Lane, Horse Bazaar has evolved into a bar that fuses music, art, technology and alcohol into the perfect cocktail. Escape to this exciting venue with its eclectic music and quality drinks, including classic cocktails and a selection of Australian focused wine. During the day you may prefer the home-spun, kitchen treats and free wireless internet to work or linger in the relaxed atmosphere. You will surprised by the 20 metre digital canvas that continually projects new media and digital artworks. Investigate the toilets and you will see just how far this theme has been take,n with a world first rear projection urinal.

# LITTLE LONSDALE ST LITTLE LONSDALE ST LITTLE LONSDALE ST LITTLE LONSDALE ST

361 Little Lonsdale St
0450 258 730
www.thousandpoundbend.com.au

# 1000 £ BEND

This re-incarnation of St Jeromes is a spacious, revamped warehouse. Its hip, understated style is typical of Jerome Borazio's talent in creating refreshing and contemporary venues in out of the way places. Thousand Pound Bend validates the use of an eclectic mix of retro furniture and artifacts carefully selected from a number of Melbourne antique and op-shops. The overall effect is welcoming and you will share space with a diverse range of Melbournians from hippies to suits. Here, hipsters are served a dose of culture with their lattes, and whether you are grungy, arty or something else entirely you will find this café/gallery/cinema worth a visit. Try the comfortable couches and the free-wireless that you can enjoy with a low-cost coffee. Upstairs the cinema room is furnished with mismatched chairs and comfortable bean bags. The gallery, beyond the café, is home to rotating exhibitions, installations, fashion parades, projections and whatever else comes along.

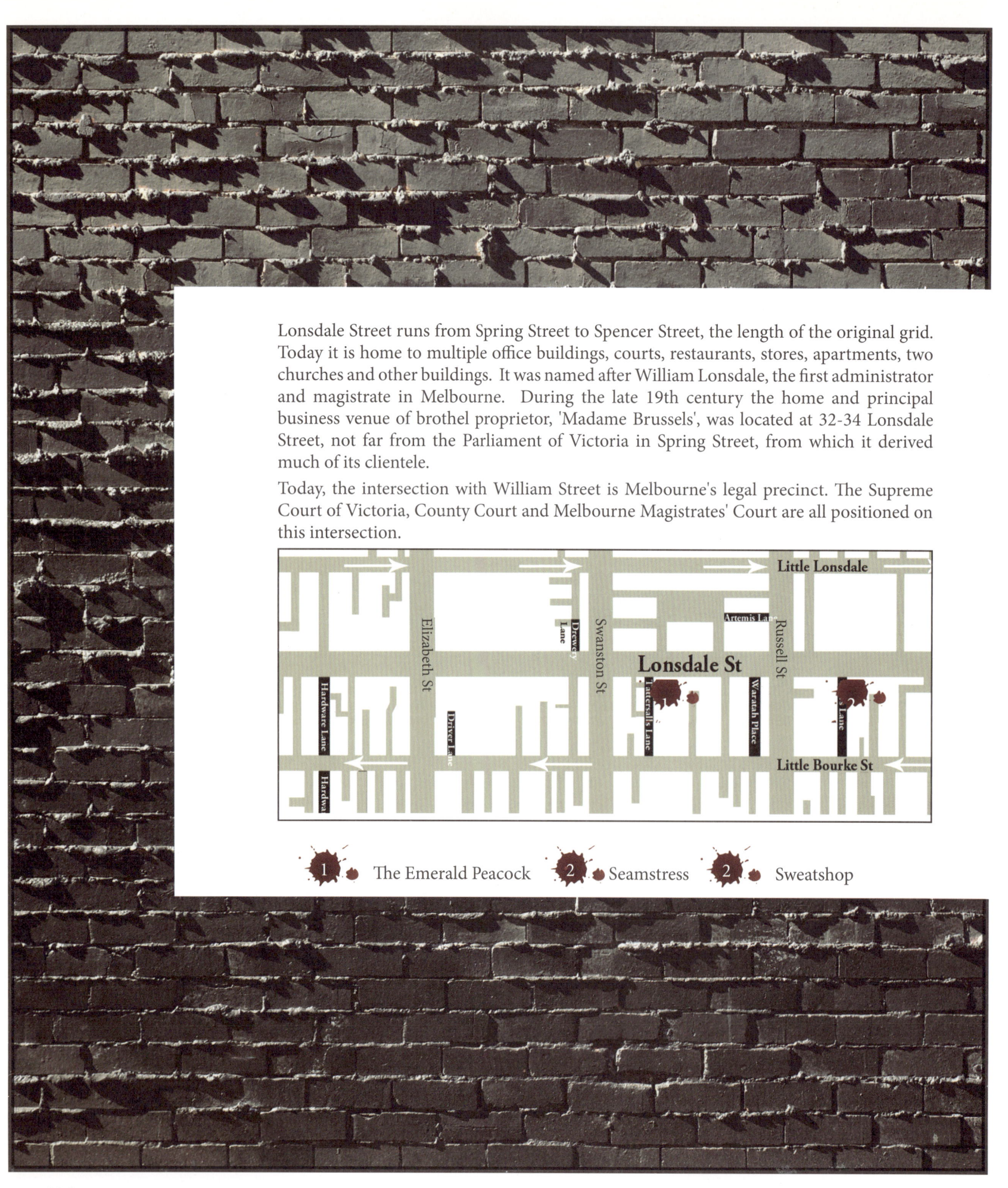

Lonsdale Street runs from Spring Street to Spencer Street, the length of the original grid. Today it is home to multiple office buildings, courts, restaurants, stores, apartments, two churches and other buildings. It was named after William Lonsdale, the first administrator and magistrate in Melbourne. During the late 19th century the home and principal business venue of brothel proprietor, 'Madame Brussels', was located at 32-34 Lonsdale Street, not far from the Parliament of Victoria in Spring Street, from which it derived much of its clientele.

Today, the intersection with William Street is Melbourne's legal precinct. The Supreme Court of Victoria, County Court and Melbourne Magistrates' Court are all positioned on this intersection.

1. The Emerald Peacock   2. Seamstress   2. Sweatshop

# LONSDALE ST.

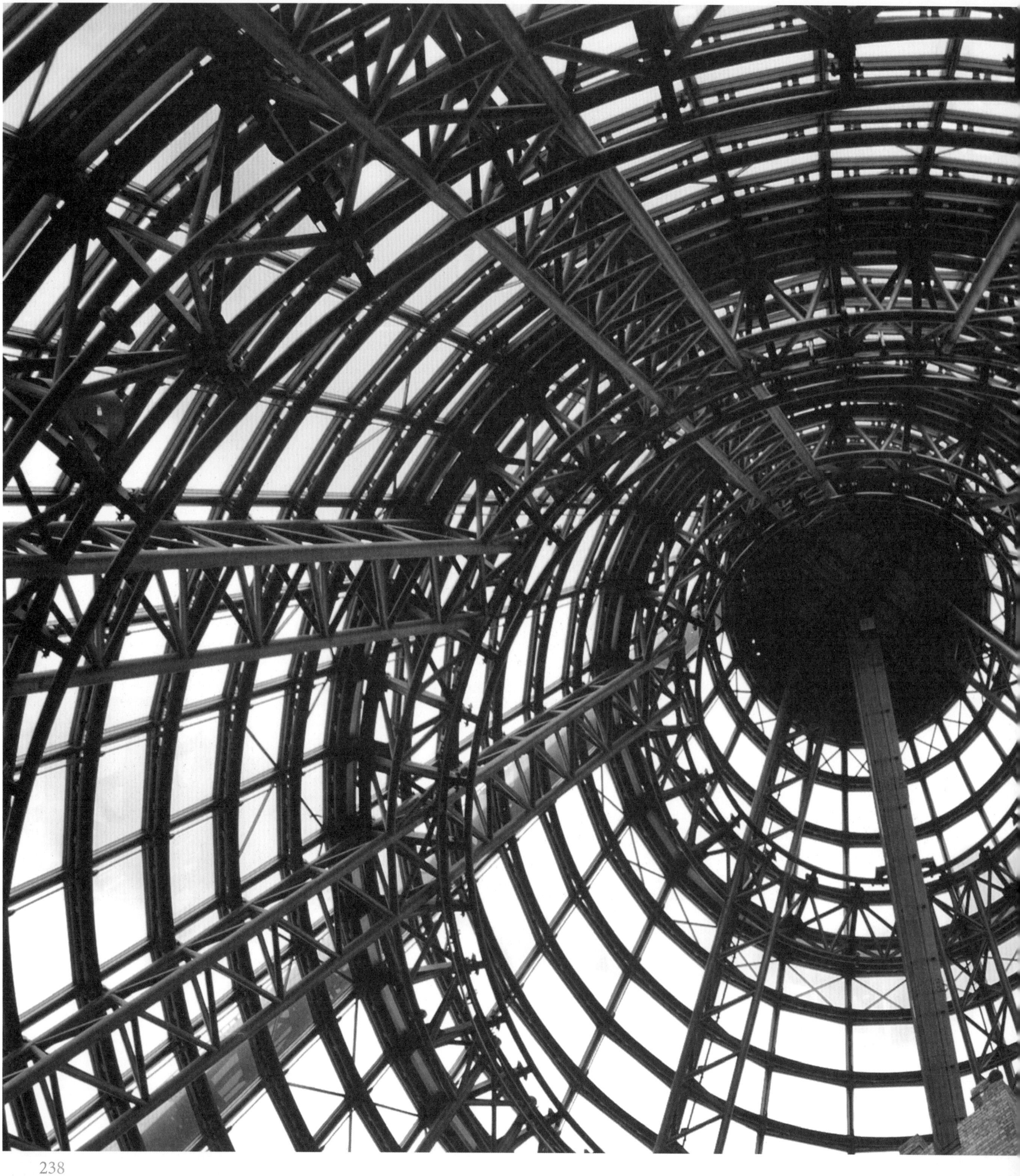

239

# SEAMSTRESS

Level 1
113 Lonsdale St
03 9663 6363
www.seamstress.com.au

Enter this historic, former garment factory in Lonsdale Street, and you will be taken back to the 1800's when this area was renowned for its fine tailoring, equal to the best in the world. Complete with antique sewing machines, heritage yarns and multi-coloured draped fabrics, the décor in this building almost deserves a visit on its own.

The Seamstress dining room plays host to inspired pan-Asian cuisine from a talented kitchen brigade with broad living, working and travelling experiences of the exciting and varied cooking styles of the continent.

The dichotomy of old and new brings this old sewing factory back to life and into the 21st century. It provides a Manhattan-style décor, blending the backdrop of the old factory with a mix of vintage and new furnishings. But best of all, it fuses the ancient arts of Asian cooking with today's ultra-modern kitchen techniques and locally sourced, seasonal ingredients.

The signature recipe on the next page is one of the most popular dishes as the pre "plat principal", part of the restaurant's philosophy of staggering dinner across more than just two or three courses.

The focal point of his menu follows the basics of Asian dining, banquet style sharing. Sharing plates include dishes like twelve hour braised Berkshire pork belly, drunken potatoes and steamed baby bok choy, Slow cooked pork neck tossed with glass noodles, bitter melon, truffle mushroom and a caramelized chili sauce or Pan seared Market Fish of the Day with a tamarind dressed herb salad, coconut milk & tahini tossed soba noodles in a vegetable broth.

Finish with sweet sensations such as five spice chocolate pudding with mandarin parfait and whisky sabayon or Coconut, lime and pandan leaf tart with mango sorbet.

The creative wine and cocktail lists provide flavours to accompany any dish with aplomb. The carefully selected list focuses on aromatic whites, light, easy drinking reds and affordable sparkling treats from the best producers in Australasia as well as a selection of old-world labels helpfully listed by grape varietal rather than the complex classification systems of Europe.

This intimate restaurant seats only 50, so be warned – make sure you book ahead!

# SEAMSTRESS
## restaurant bar

DINING ROOM

# SEAMSTRESS COCKTAIL BAR

Level 2
113 Lonsdale St
03 9663 6363
www.seamstress.com.au

"LANEWAY RESTAURANTS AND BARS ARE WHAT DISTINGUISH MELBOURNE. SEAMSTRESS IS UNASSUMING AT STREET LEVEL, BUT ONCE YOU ENTER THE FRONT DOOR YOU ARE TAKEN ON A JOURNEY UP A FLIGHT OF RICKETY TIMBER STAIRS TO A DINING ROOM ON THE FIRST LEVEL AND COCKTAIL BAR ON THE SECOND, IN INTRIGUING AREAS THAT MIX OLD WITH NEW" - TALLY KONSTAS, OWNER.

Up two rickety flights of timber stairs and on top of a hickledy-pickledy, four level warehouse style attic space, finds the perfect space for a pre-dinner drink. This classic cocktail bar is redolent of a 1930's colonial speak-easy, prominent during the years of prohibition when the sale of alcohol was done from secretive, clandestine nooks and crannies.

Complete with a Chinese laundry hanging from the ceiling, with rows of silk cheongsams of every colour of the rainbow, this bar is poles apart from what you might expect.

The open plan layout lets you either perch at the bar or enjoy attentive table service in one of the classic leather armchairs or private booths. The bar is architecturally charming with its wooden fittings and comfortable timber stools. An extensive classic cocktail list which lays claim to Melbourne's best Martini along with impressive line-ups of spirits, local and international wines & beers. The choices will have you stuttering with their assortment and attention to detail.

A reasonably priced menu of bar food can be ordered to turn your after-work drink into a late-night session.

243

# SWEATSHOP

Basement
113 Lonsdale St
03 9663 6363
www.seamstress.com.au

This former textile factory's basement bar is one of Melbourne's laneway secrets. Set in what was originally a Buddhist temple in central Chinatown, the building was converted to a garment warehouse and a café before it's current incarnation.

The sweatshops of the 19th century would have had rows of women fretting away over treadle sewing machines. Today you will stumble down the age-old staircase to find this hip, underground bar where those in the know share drinks, light dinner, gossip and fun. Sweatshop makes use of its raw warehouse surrounds with oriental fabrics suspended from the ceiling, a blend of old records and exposed wiring around the walls with furniture of dismantled shipping pallets to rest your drink.

DJ's come from around Melbourne to entertain the mixed crowd playing anything from hip-hop, classic RnB and rare grooves. You can venture out in to the back of the laneway to find the smokers courtyard. Enjoy mischievously named drinks from a vinyl sleeve, cocktail menu, such as a Honey Smash – polish vodka, berries, honey, lemon and mint, or a Disco Sour – a playful take on the famous Peruvian Pisco Sour served blue.

Other skillfully made cocktails include a Pina Colada of coconut cream, fresh chunks of pineapple and rums or a Paloma – Tequila, pink grapefruit juice and soda.

Sweatshop also hosts brand launches, corporate dinners, fashion parties, product showcases, artistic workshops and more.

> "SWEATSHOP IS THE MISCHIEVOUS LITTLE BROTHER, SEARCHING THROUGH THE UNDIES DRAWERS OF ITS BIG SISTER SEAMSTRESS. SWEATSHOP IS ALL ABOUT ABSOLUTE QUALITY DELIVERED WITH STYLE, A DASH OF FUN AND PLENTY OF JEST".

245

# THE EMERALD PEACOCK

233 Lonsdale St
03 9654 8680
www.theemeraldpeacock.com

Two years after opening the much loved Red Hummingbird, Taj Hospitality found their next rooftop venue, which is on Lonsdale Street just around the corner from the sister site, The Red Hummingbird. They were lucky to obtain the current heritage building which stood vacant for quite a few years after having served previously as a Buddhist training centre. Perhaps the good karma remains because the Emerald Peacock certainly has a good vibe.

The venue is divided into three distinct areas. The cocktail bar with its irregular wood panelling and vintage highlights is charming with sophisticated glamour. The Peacock Lounge returns to the old world luxe style, with a mixture of elongated communal tables or decadent booths where you can enjoy some food with your drinks.

Upstairs is the "piece de resistance" or the rooftop bar. Giving a more relaxed vibe than downstairs, the rooftop is styled around recycled woods and natural tones, taking full advantage of its lantern lit space and beautiful views of the city skyline. The overall effect is a mixture of retro and eclectic decadence that marries style with a fantastic ambience.

The Emerald Peacock can be relied upon for a true cocktail experience, with well loved classics and ingenious twists and creations. The elegant signature cocktail, "The Emerald Peacock", sets the tone for the bar that is upheld well: a blend of Belvedere vodka, lime juice, elderflower, cucumber and fresh mint. The beer and wine lists are good but it is the cocktails people come here for.

The Emerald Peacock also has a good menu on offer with tapas style sharing options and gourmet pizzas that are delicious and a great accompaniment to the drinks. A clear night on the rooftop with an Emerald Peacock cocktail and a Hummingbird pizza is a good night indeed! On a weekend it is even possible to enjoy a unique girls' picnic at the Emerald Peacock – a booking is required but it is worth it to experience the delights of the bubbles, sweets and savouries found in the high tea with a twist.

In keeping with the careful designing and styling of the Emerald Peacock, the demographic is quite specific as the bar seeks to fill the needs of sophisticated, career oriented, well-travelled, socially and politically aware clients – those with a taste for variety and innovation. The crowd is savvy, loyal and friendly, generally having found the Peacock through recommendation rather than walk-ins.

When asked about the bars in Melbourne, Managing Director Sharan Sagoo said, "Melbourne is an exciting city that is full of little nooks and crannies. Melbournians are so spoilt when it comes to hidden finds as there are lots of treasures nestled in the laneways.

Finding a rooftop is an absolute urban treasure".

247

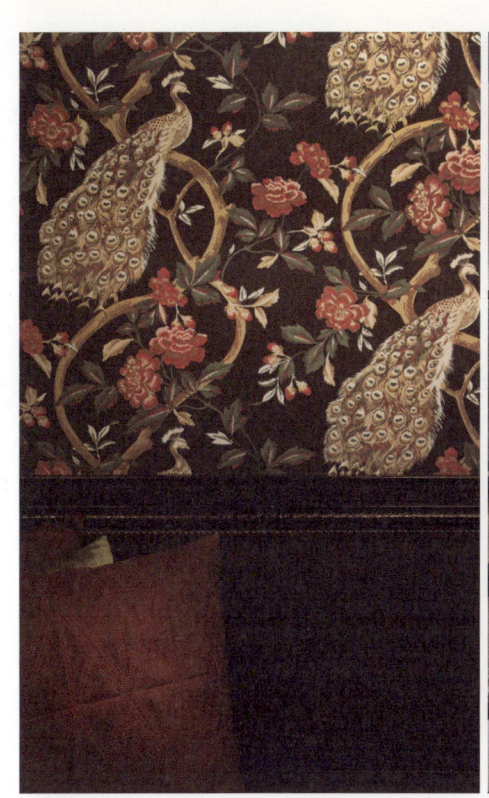

McKillop Street runs off Little Collins and Bourke streets. The first date of it being occupied was 1839 and was named after J.P. McKillop who was an accountant and estate agent in 1865. The street has seen many different eras. In 1910 is was full of manufactures and printers, while today it is occupied by high end restaurants like Red Spice Road and funky bars.

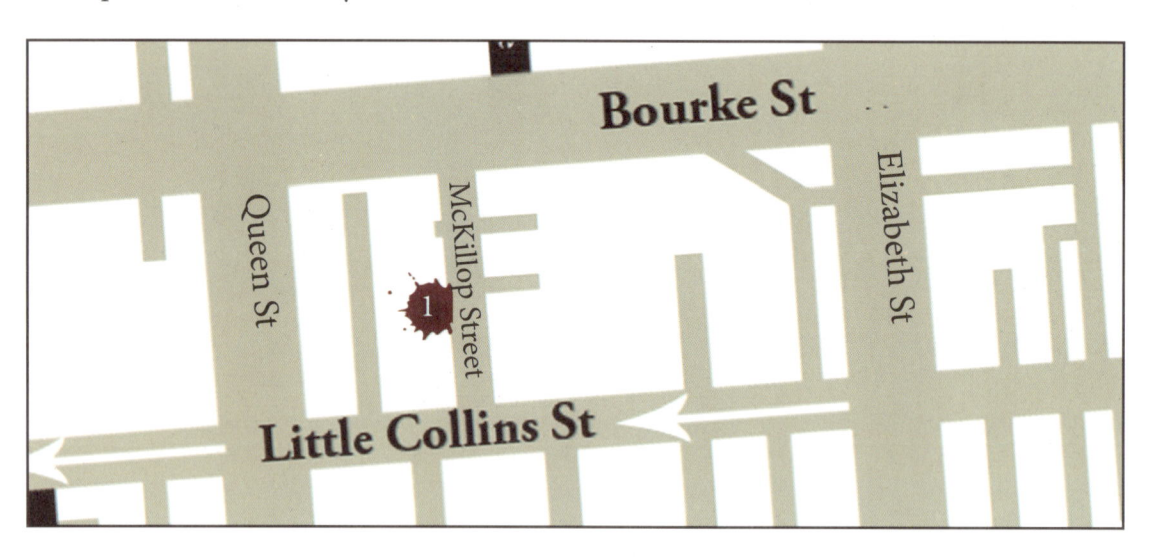

1. Red Spice Road

# MCKILLOP ST.

250

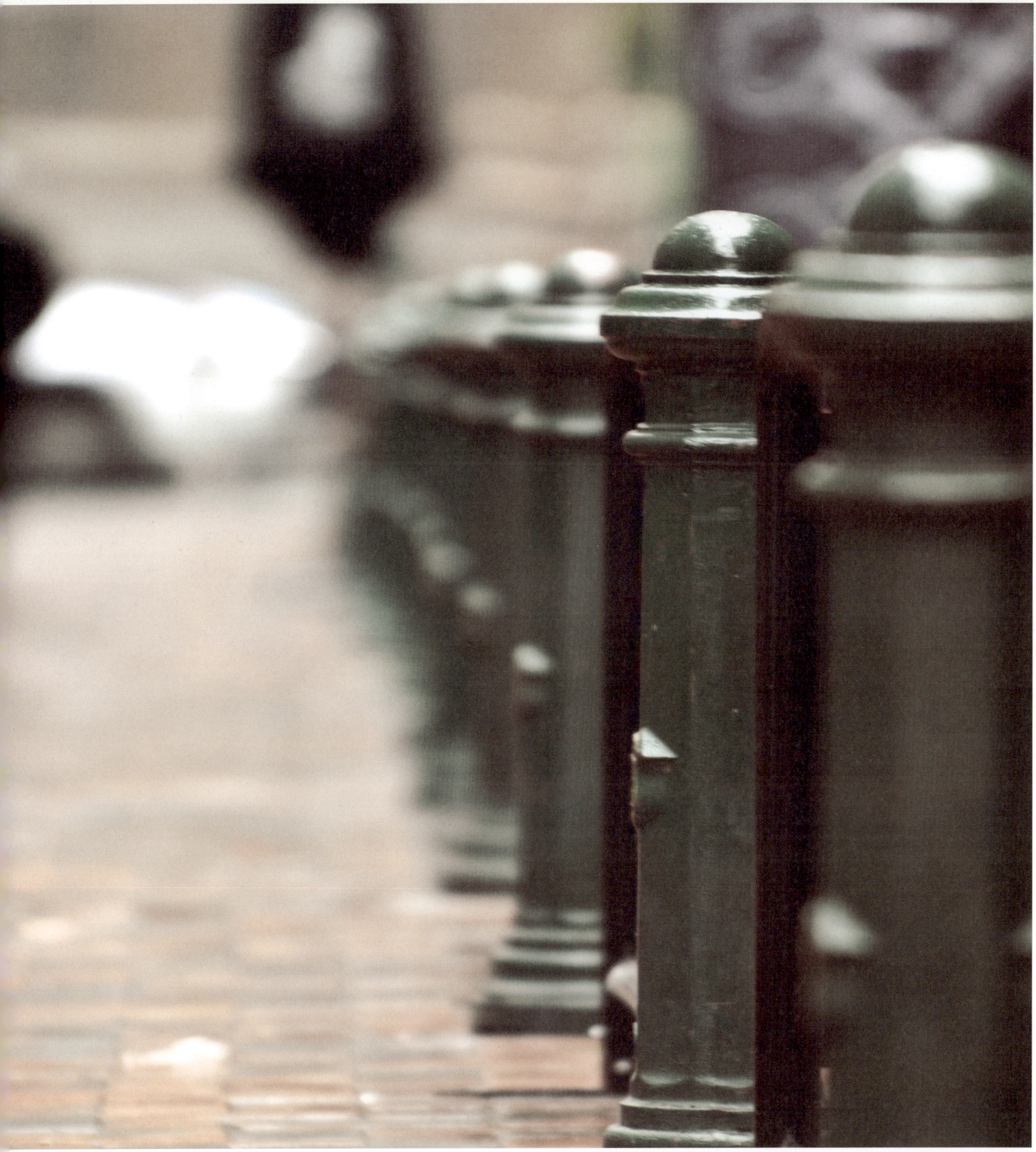

# RED SPICE ROAD

27 McKillop St
03 9603 1601
www.redspiceroad.com

On a small street stretched between Bourke and Little Collins, just down the hill from Queens Street is the highly commended Red Spice Road. McKillop Street is steeped in history with the current restaurant site playing host to a veterinary surgery at the turn of the 20th century. The view from the bar of the beautiful surrounding buildings and the cobbled street below, transports you to another time, an oasis in the middle of the CBD's legal precinct. Red Spice Road has evolved as one of Melbourne's most loved restaurants.

Red Spice Road maintains a high level of quality and style across the board. A sizable establishment that boasts the ability to host large groups, the layout and décor is an inherent part of the charm even before a mouthful passes your lips. The venue is divided into six distinct areas designed around the concept of communal dining and shared dishes.

The Lantern Room, a key defining feature of the restaurant, is one of the largest round tables in Australia seating 60 people and is lit by the largest indoor red lantern. There is a courtyard off the lantern room where you can enjoy al fresco dining in the beautiful South East Asian-inspired surroundings, lit by the glow of warm lanterns.

The Long Room with its polished wood fittings, warm hues and beautiful spider-web orb lighting, features large rectangular tables fitting up to 60 guests. Two private dining rooms are on offer, Lotus 1 and Lotus 2 combined with an opium bed lined Bar Room, decorated with silk cushions and large windows, completes the effect admirably.

The bar is foremost a cocktail bar, with amongst many other beverages including more than 16 Asian themed cocktails and bar snacks. The success of John McLeay's restaurant menu can probably be attributed to his food ideology. When asked what he finds exciting about Asian food he said "I love the balance. Take for example our most popular dish which is pork belly with chilli caramel, black vinegar and cabbage mint salad."

"Now pork belly to me is incredibly rich and so is caramel but you add the black vinegar and the refreshing cabbage salad that has a citrus tang and it becomes balanced. It's pretty much the same for most dishes and there generally is a counter balance in the flavours somewhere."

With tender meats cooked to perfection, refreshing greens and herbs and an ever changing menu led by their signature dishes, John McLeay seems to have his balance spot on.

Although the crowd is predominantly corporate during the day, as can be expected in the CBD, at night the excellent food and buzzing atmosphere draws a wide mix of people.

253

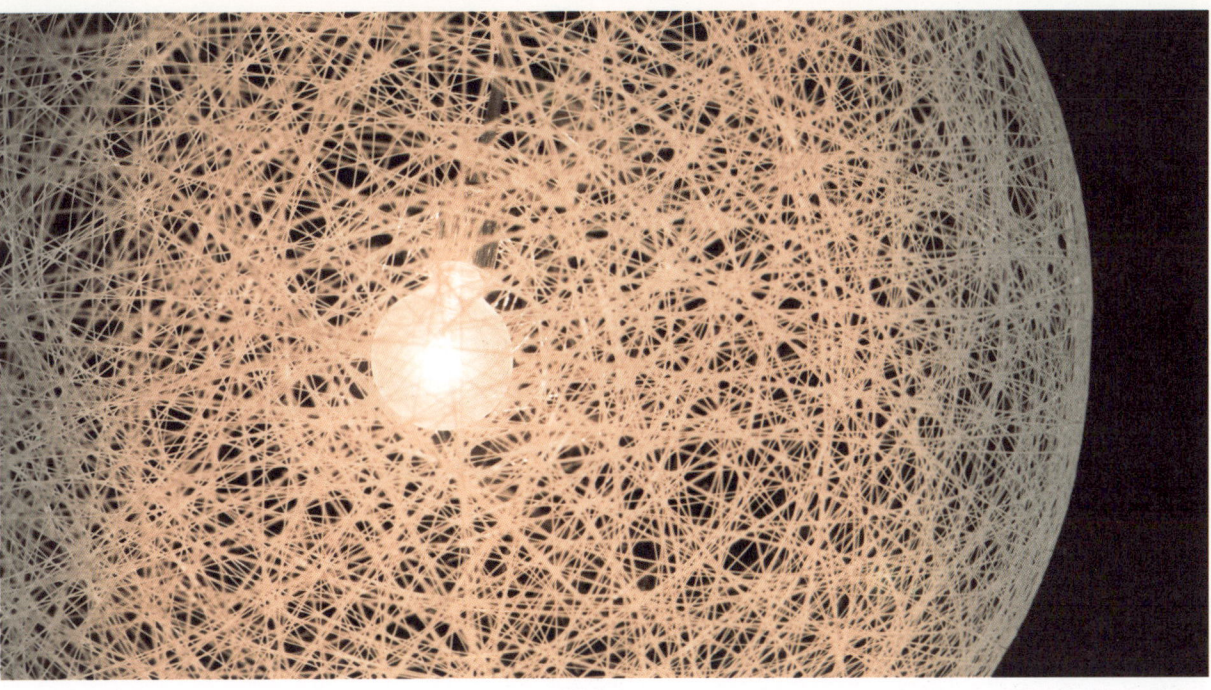

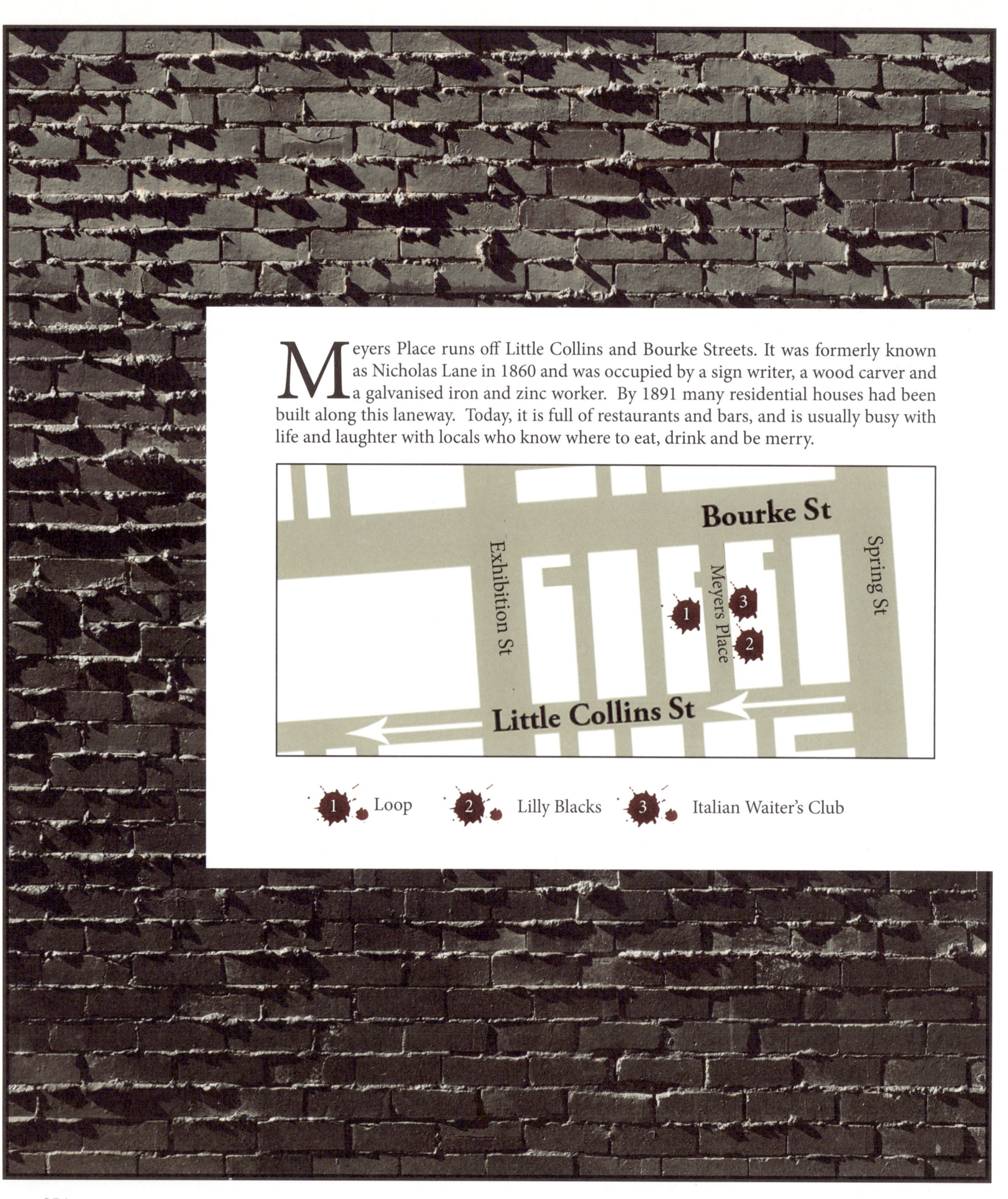

Meyers Place runs off Little Collins and Bourke Streets. It was formerly known as Nicholas Lane in 1860 and was occupied by a sign writer, a wood carver and a galvanised iron and zinc worker. By 1891 many residential houses had been built along this laneway. Today, it is full of restaurants and bars, and is usually busy with life and laughter with locals who know where to eat, drink and be merry.

1. Loop    2. Lilly Blacks    3. Italian Waiter's Club

# MEYERS PLACE

NO DRINKS BEYOND THIS POINT

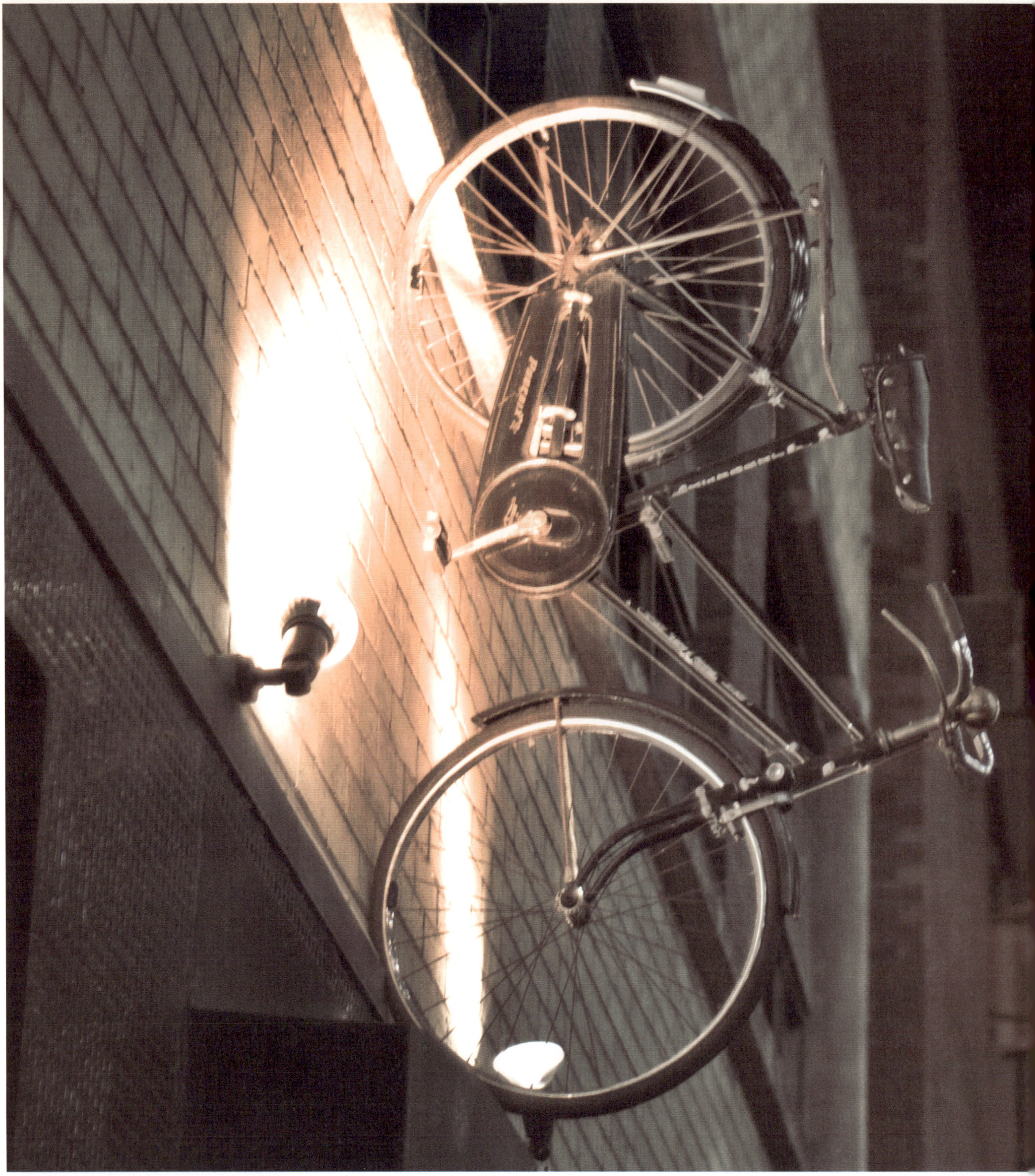

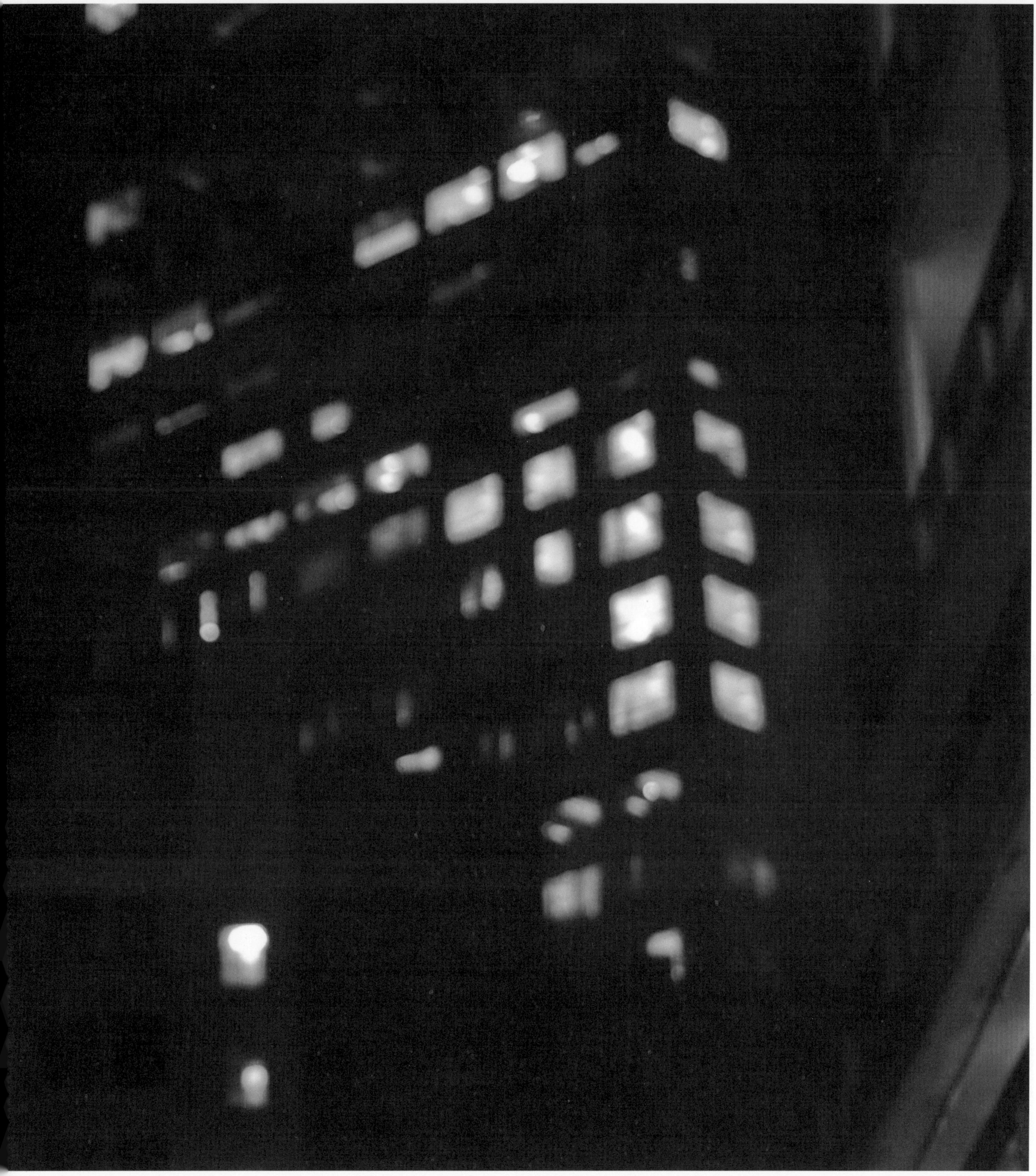

# LOOP

23 Meyers Place
03 9654 0500
www.looponline.com.au

If you want to get into the Melbourne Loop, you can't go past this distinctive bar in Meyers place. Loop is a versatile project space/bar that presents films, audio-visual performances, experimental music and art forums. Their eclectic program ensures the bar reinvents itself nightly, and the venue highlights a diverse range of digital media.

Established in 2003, Loop's owner directors - Adam Bunny, George and Alex Giannopoulos - designed the space wanting to add a unique dimension to the vibrant culture of Melbourne. Two custom-built, large format screens form the backbone of the space, and combined with an expertly engineered sound system and LCD projectors, beam a lush audio-visual experience to diverse audiences.

The bar ambience creates an informal atmosphere where art in a variety of forms can be soaked up in a relaxed, social setting. The monthly 'Process' forum invites young, contemporary Melbourne architects to discuss new buildings and theories, while 'Don't You Have Docs?'- held on the third Monday of every month - supports short documentary film. The recently launched 'LoopdeLoop' hosts an animation challenge on the last Tuesday of every month and on Thursday nights, 'Photography Night Walks' curate spontaneous slide screenings of quirky images, shot that night around Melbourne, in the cozy environs of the cinema space.

If you are not attending an arts event, you can always enjoy the bar, which provides an intimate, sophisticated ambience. Loop offers an extensive drink selection, where guests can enjoy a quiet beer or cocktail with friends on a weeknight, or a more energetic romp soaking up tunes expertly sliced and diced by resident DJs over the weekends. Always accompanied by live visuals on twin massive screens, Loop's weekends provide an exciting club vibe within the confines of a welcoming bar… well into the wee hours of the morning.

Bar Manager Gareth Edser, hailing from the UK, draws on his international experience to create quality cocktails with eye-catching garnishes. Try his latest concoction - the 1801, an agave twist on the classic Old Fashioned.

Project Manager Kristin Bacon, who has been associated with Loop since its inception 8 years ago, draws on her 15 years experience in various Melbourne bars and her performing arts background, to program and oversee all that is Loop.

Loop attracts a broad demographic- film makers, architects, students, academics, local professionals, hospitality staff, bar hoppers and club goers - through its eclectic programming and convivial approach. And the Stop Press! Loop is expanding to the roof top - and taking its philosophy skyward- to combine an outdoor screening venue with a cocktail bar and café- all within the setting of an intimate roof top garden oasis.

Nesting in an environment teeming with creepers, vines and vertical gardens, Loop Roof will offer fabulous city views, guaranteed to delight punters of all feathers.

259

# LILY BLACKS

12 Meyers Place
03 9654 4887
www.lilyblacks.com.au

Exuding a warm ambience with its well balanced 20's décor, Lily Blacks is a cocktail saloon with an eye for quality ingredients and a flair for serving a twist on the classics. Adding to the hum of Meyers place, this bar draws you in with its sizable drinks menu that flirts with a European theme and offers old and new world wines, bottled beer and, of course, cocktails. With the bar open until 3am there is plenty of time to explore the cocktail menu, revisiting classics or testing some of the interesting and unique Lily Blacks creations. The great drinks, modern tunes, well-dressed bar staff and tasty platters can sustain you long into the night.

# THE WAITERS CLUB

20 Meyers Place
03 9650 1508

The Italian Waiters Club is quite simply a Melbourne institution. Possibly the oldest hideaway in Meyers Place, the restaurant was opened in the late 1940's. Originally an exclusive escape for the city's Italian and Spanish hospitality workers, dropping a secret password would gain your admittance upstairs where in the simple surrounds people enjoyed, traditional Italian fare and quality pasta meals at reasonable prices, and could relax into a game of cards over their coffee. Today the club is open to all who can find it but is still run on the same principles of good wine and tasty food in hearty portions and with no need to hide behind embellishments. In keeping with its history the décor is as it would have been back in the 80'w, with the menus written on boards around the restaurant , allowing day-to-day changes.

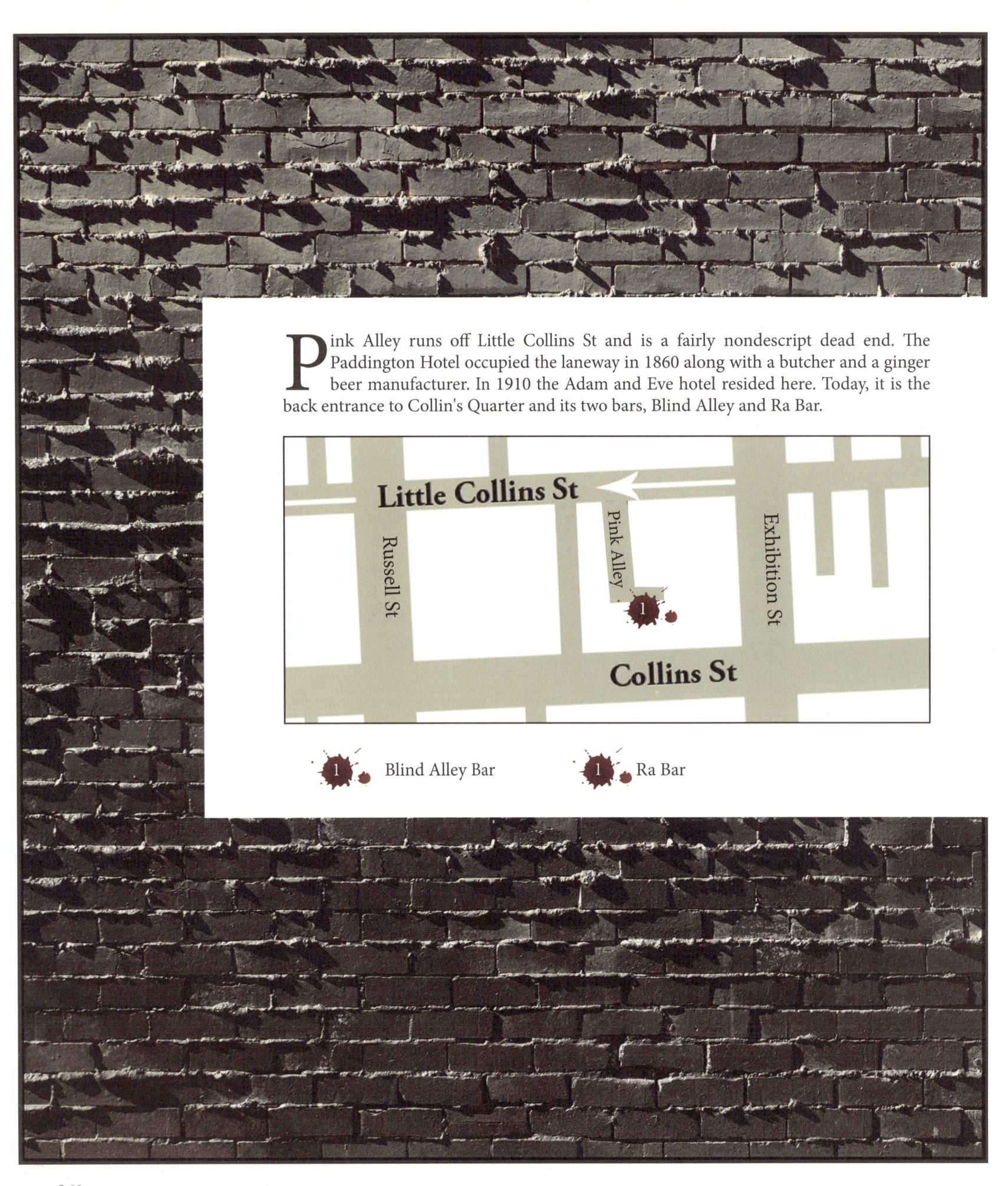

Pink Alley runs off Little Collins St and is a fairly nondescript dead end. The Paddington Hotel occupied the laneway in 1860 along with a butcher and a ginger beer manufacturer. In 1910 the Adam and Eve hotel resided here. Today, it is the back entrance to Collin's Quarter and its two bars, Blind Alley and Ra Bar.

1. Blind Alley Bar
1. Ra Bar

# PINK ALLEY

264

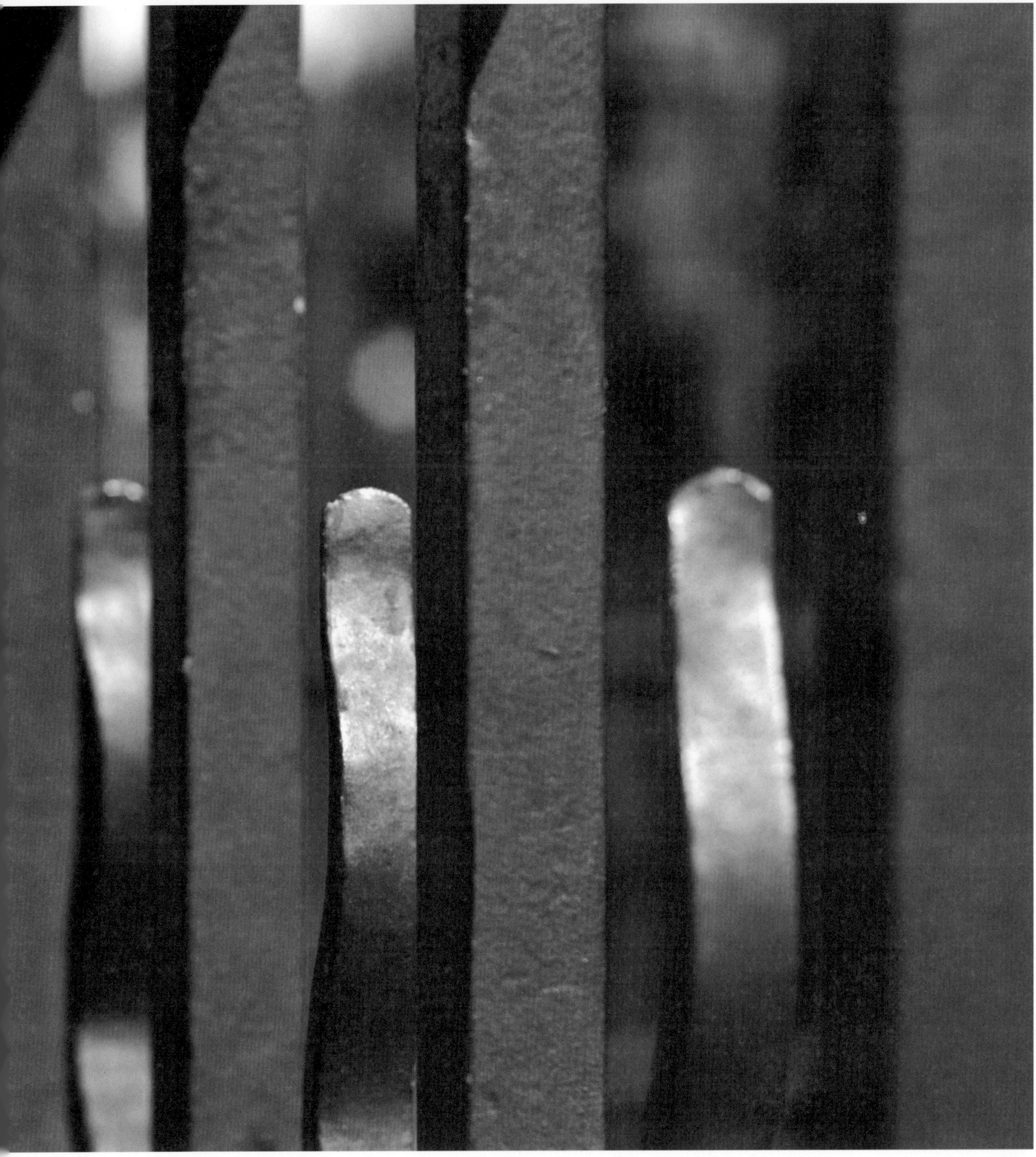

# RA BAR & BLIND ALLEY

1 Pink Alley
03 9650 8500
www.collinsquarter.com

Venture down Pink Alley which runs off Little Collins Street and you will find an exciting architectural masterpiece, designed by the award-winning firm, Jackson Clements Burrows. Look up and you will see a steel marvel which houses the super-exclusive Ra Bar. If you are looking for that hidden treasure you have found it – that unique place where you can sit back and relax knowing you can enjoy some of the most distinctive alcohol products available in Australia today.

Ra Bar isn't cheap, but if you fancy the red carpet treatment, padded couches, fluffy blankets, a cigarette or two with the wafting smell of cigars – here is the spot to enjoy it. Only top shelf beers and spirits are served in this chic bar to give your soul a lift and your mind something totally different to dwell on.

Boasting one of Australia's finest champagne lists, you will also find a range of cocktails and an impressive selection of Australian and European wines.

Travel downstairs and you will find the intimate Blind Alley Bar, adjoining the more casual Magnolia Courtyard named after the huge magnolia tree centerpiece. This is a great place to stop for a drink after work and have a quick drink before entering the 1872 building which now houses, Colin's Pub, for a bite to eat.

CIGARS
CHAMPAGNE
FOIE GRAS
COCKTAILS
CAVIAR

RA

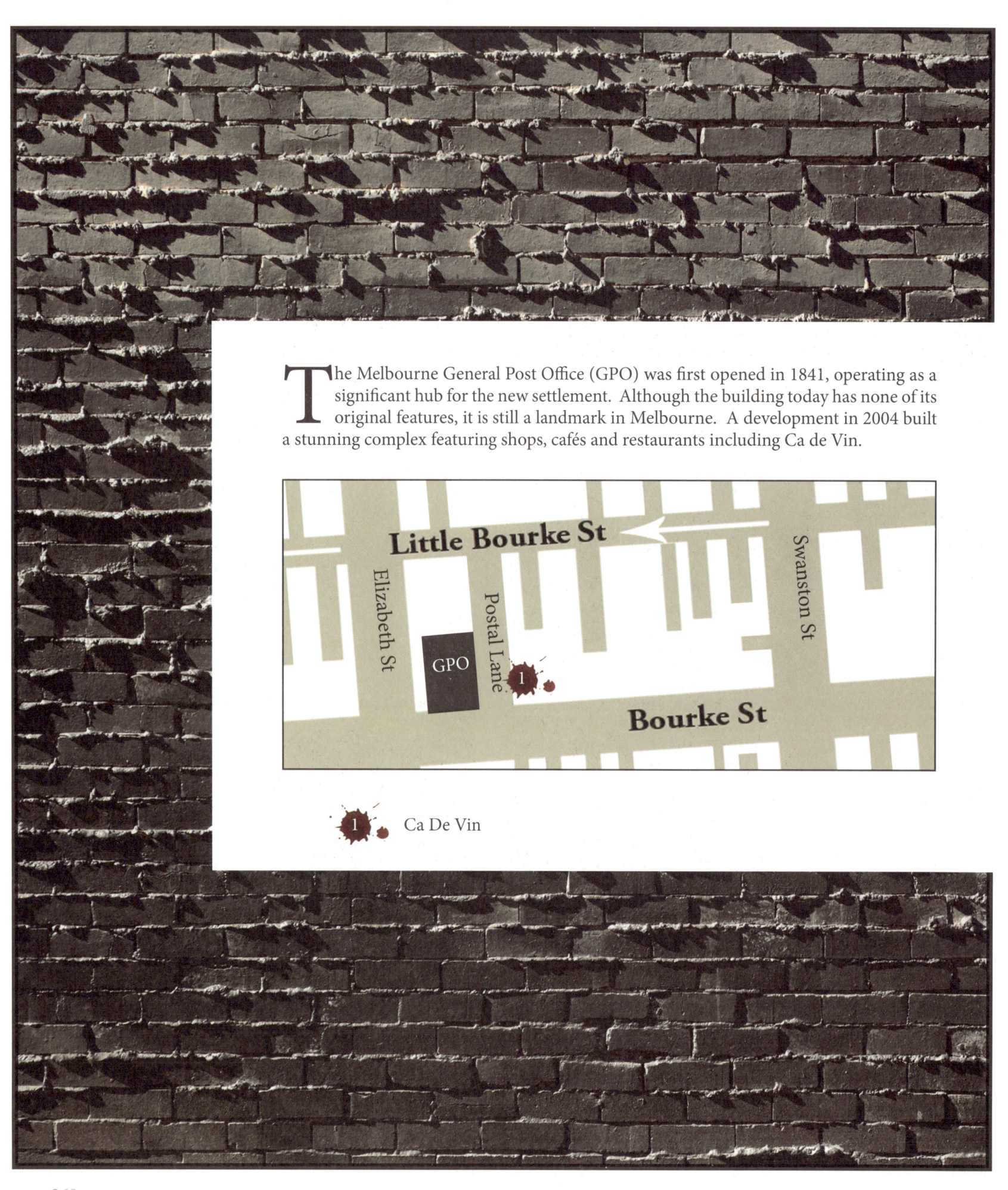

The Melbourne General Post Office (GPO) was first opened in 1841, operating as a significant hub for the new settlement. Although the building today has none of its original features, it is still a landmark in Melbourne. A development in 2004 built a stunning complex featuring shops, cafés and restaurants including Ca de Vin.

1. Ca De Vin

# POSTAL LANE

## POSTAL LANE
· KENZAN · CA DE VIN · RAMEN YA ·

MELBOURNE'S GPO

THE CITY'S FINEST SHOPPING · MELBOURNESGPO.COM

MFI BOURNES
GPO

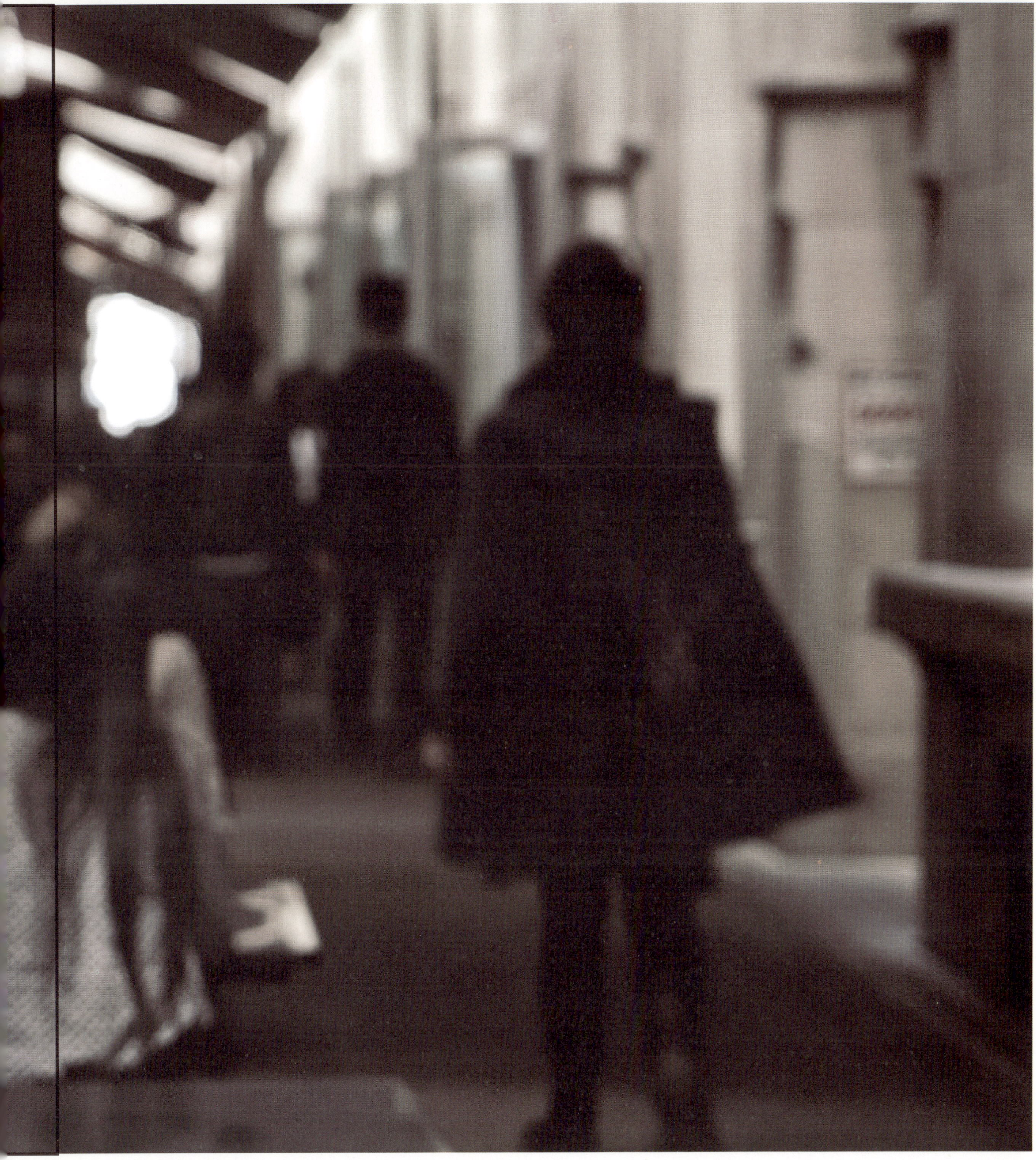

# CA DE VIN

GPO Postal Lane
03 9654 3639
www.cadevin.com.au

Ca de Vin, the house of wine, is strategically placed next to the old Melbourne GPO, in the laneway once used by postal vans. Postal Lane provides a warm and cozy atmosphere with glints of bright sunshine breaking through the high awnings during the day. At night, romance is in the air with tiny candles that glow from every table, through the dark, timber, Austrian bent chairs.

Large, Gothic, wrought-iron gates divide the crazy world of the Bourke Street Mall, welcoming you into a treasured, peaceful space, to sit and have a coffee or enjoy a serious meal. The menu has a solid Mediterranean feel offering Mezze to Pizzas and pastas, and Secondi with Contorni. You have a wide range to choose from.

The specials are listed on a huge blackboard, along with specialty wines by the glass. The place gets fairly busy at lunch and dinner times, and the conversations are usually lively and animated.

Pizzas are the specialty at Ca de Vin as they are the hard-to-find, Italian-style with light, crispy thin crusts. My favourite is the simple Margherita - Napoli, mozzarella and fresh basil. It is what I head straight for on any trip to Italy - I just love the simplicity and blend of fresh authentic flavours. More exotic pizzas include Pepperoncino - Bell peppers, chorizo, bocconcini and parsley on a confit cherry tomato base; or the popular Jamon - Spanish cured ham, fiore di latte, and napoli finished with fresh rocket and parmesan.

If you are not so hungry, try some platters to share like the Eggplant Frites, citrus seasoned and served with a spicy cumin dip. Or share the traditional Greek Saganaki - hot pan-fried kefalohaviera cheese.

Pastas include some traditional favourites plus some exciting novelties like the prawn and caramalised leek ravioli served with a creamy citrus bisque or the Pappardelle with a traditional slow braised veal ragu.

For secondi, you can't go past the veal osso bucco served with risotto Milanese or you could try the Rack of Lamb with beetroot and feta ravioli, sautéed spinach and a red wine reduction.

Thursday is apparently an Italian tradition for gnocchi day, with Ca de Vin serving fresh gnocchi with gorgonzola, sauteed spinach and mushrooms with toasted walnuts.

Contorni consist of dishes to accompany your meal, or try having your salad before your secondi in true Italian style. Sides include rocket, pinenut and parmesan salad with a balsamic dressing and the Insalata mista of radicchio, mixed leaves, fresh basil and Spanish onion topped with grated carrot and red wine vinaigrette.

Away from the bustle of Bourke Street, the crowds and the trams, it is a scene straight out of the Mediterranean – you will think you have travelled to another continent.

273

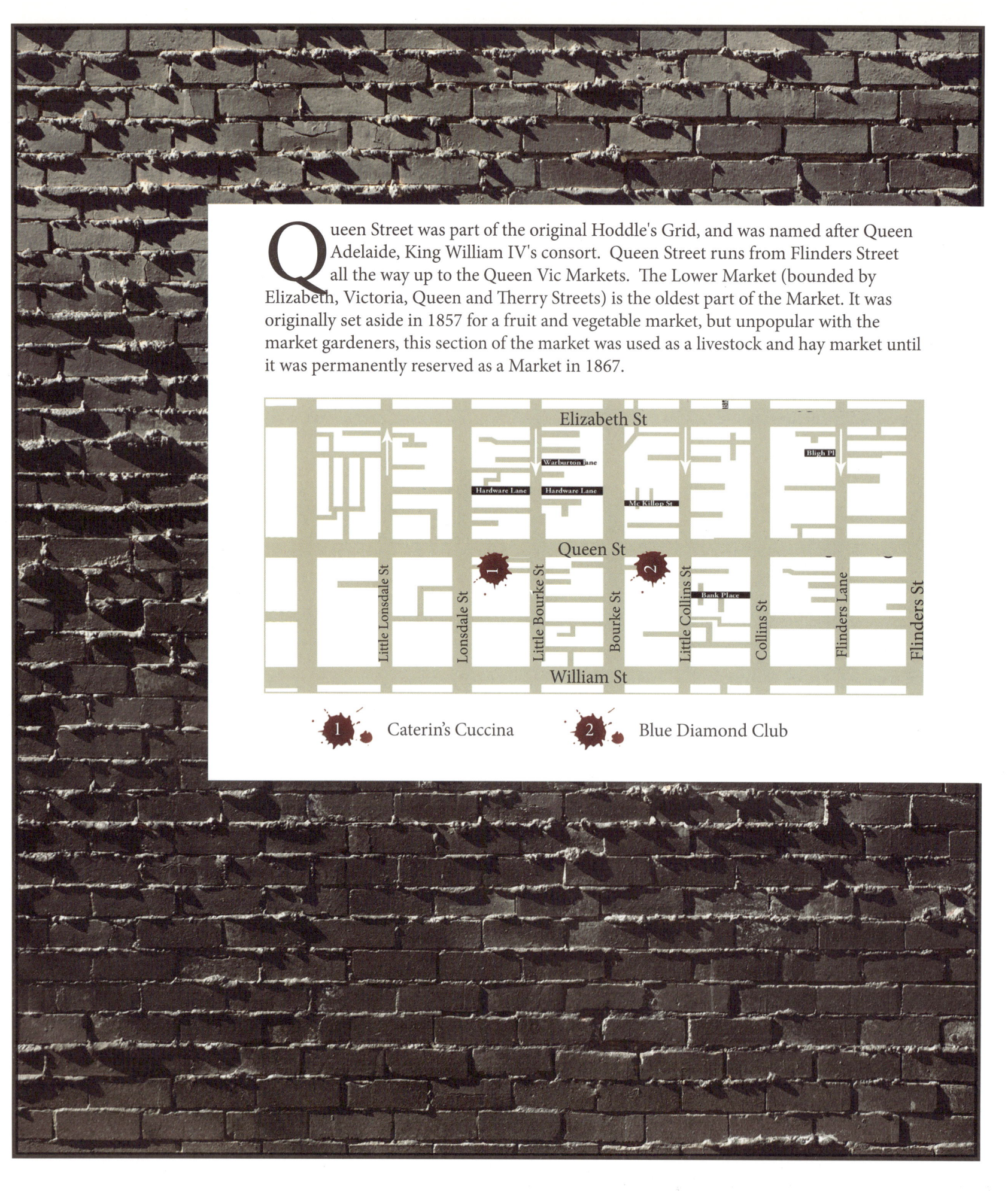

Queen Street was part of the original Hoddle's Grid, and was named after Queen Adelaide, King William IV's consort. Queen Street runs from Flinders Street all the way up to the Queen Vic Markets. The Lower Market (bounded by Elizabeth, Victoria, Queen and Therry Streets) is the oldest part of the Market. It was originally set aside in 1857 for a fruit and vegetable market, but unpopular with the market gardeners, this section of the market was used as a livestock and hay market until it was permanently reserved as a Market in 1867.

1. Caterin's Cuccina
2. Blue Diamond Club

# QUEEN ST.

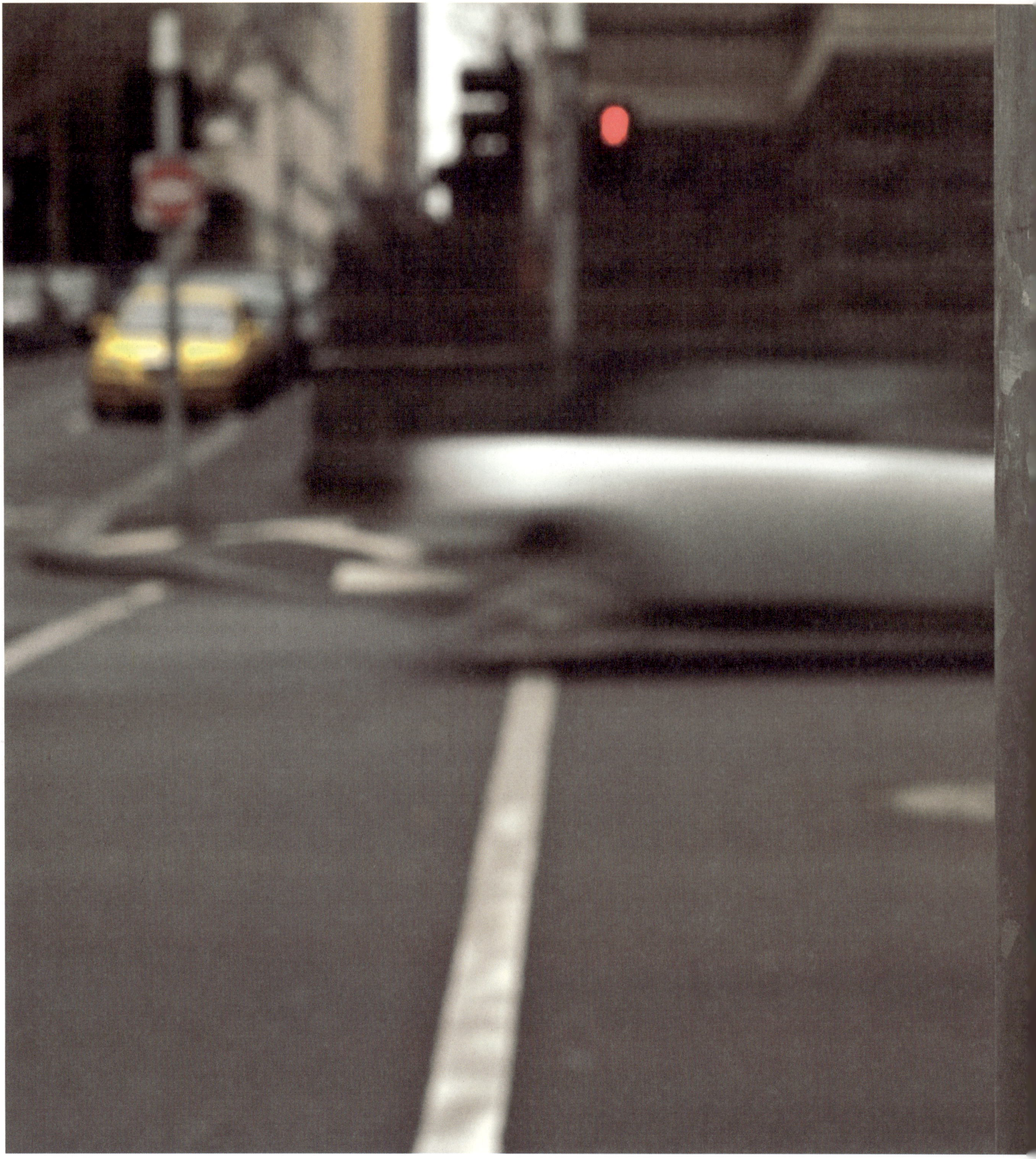

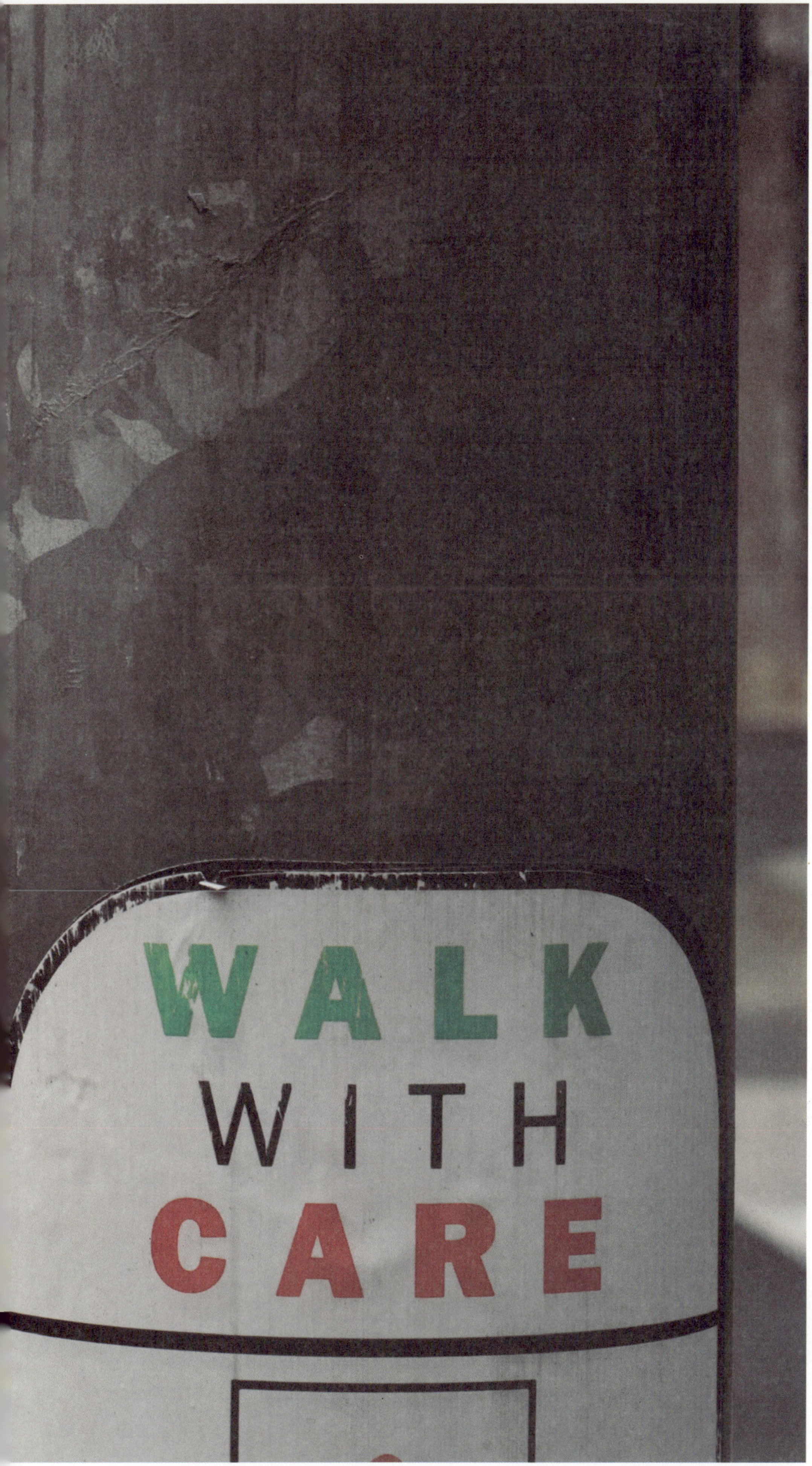
WALK
WITH
CARE

# BLUE DIAMOND CLUB

Level 15, 123 Queen St
03 8601 2720
www.bluediamondclub.com.au

If you haven't heard about one of Melbourne's rooftop secrets, you would need to fly a helicopter to discover it. Hidden on top of an office block, you need to travel level after level to reach the penthouse, before discovering this dynamic rooftop secret, Blue Diamond Bar.

Perched rooftop and sky-high, Blue Diamond takes in breathtaking views of Melbourne's skyline from its lively bar and eagle-view balconies. Leaving the lift on Level 15, you enter a new world of opulence and Manhattan glamour.

The red carpet is already rolled and awaiting your arrival. Sumptuous and large leather lounges beckon for you to tumble into after a long day at the office. Why not try a classic or Blue Diamond signature cocktail from the extensive list. Just order a cocktail from Blue Diamond's "Mauritian Magician", Warrence Moorghen, and his professional team and you will discover a creation to take you to higher places, where only the sky is the limit. And if cocktails aren't your thing then the huge selection of local and international wines, beers and spirits are sure to satisfy.

The balcony and new corner terrace are ideal spaces to enjoy your drink "el fresco" or to savour a fine Cuban cigar in unparalleled style. For the peckish, a tasty bar menu of hot and cold, small and large dishes through to party platters is always available and sure to please all tastes.

Live music and top D.J's gets this bar shaking even further, with very funky and very danceable tunes. Other live events include comedy nights, burlesque and degustation dinners.

Blue Diamond is also available for a range of private functions and corporate events.

"SURE, MELBOURNE IS FAMOUS FOR SMALL UNDERGROUND BARS, BUT I THOUGHT IT DESERVED A LARGE PENTHOUSE-STYLE BAR WITH AMAZING VIEWS," SAYS ANDREW LEONEDAS, OWNER OF BLUE DIAMOND BAR.

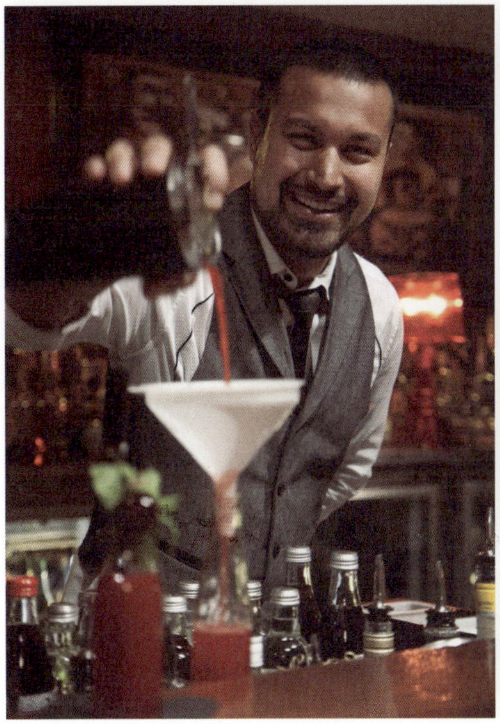
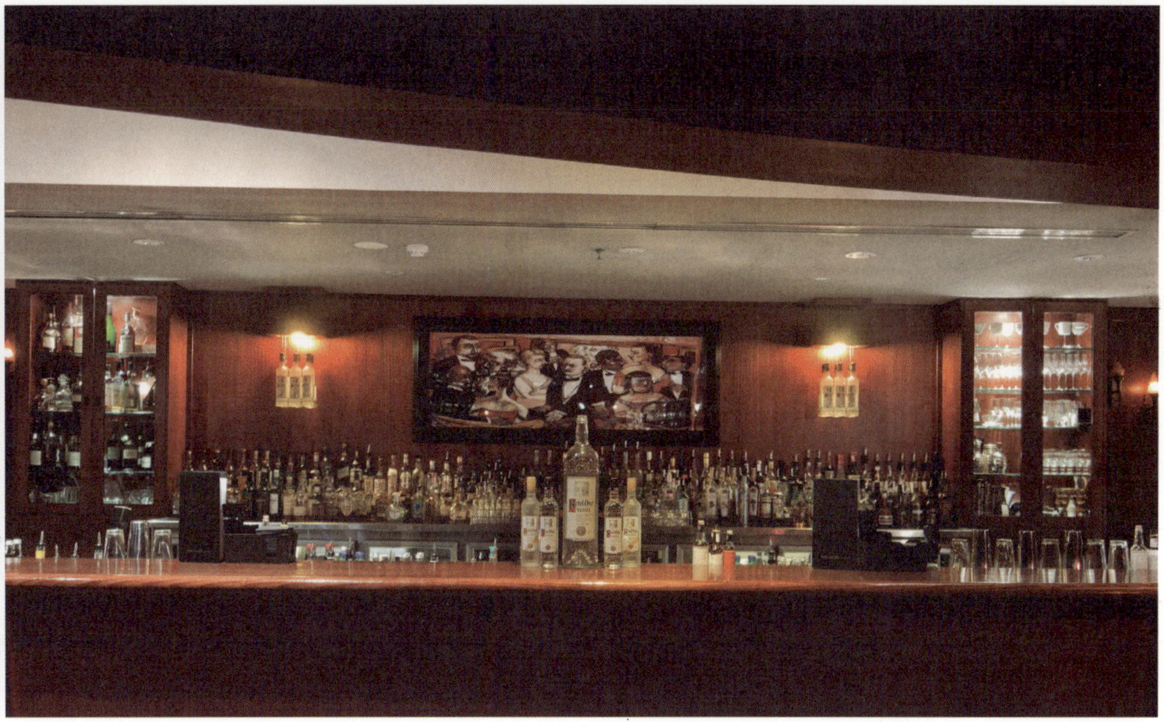
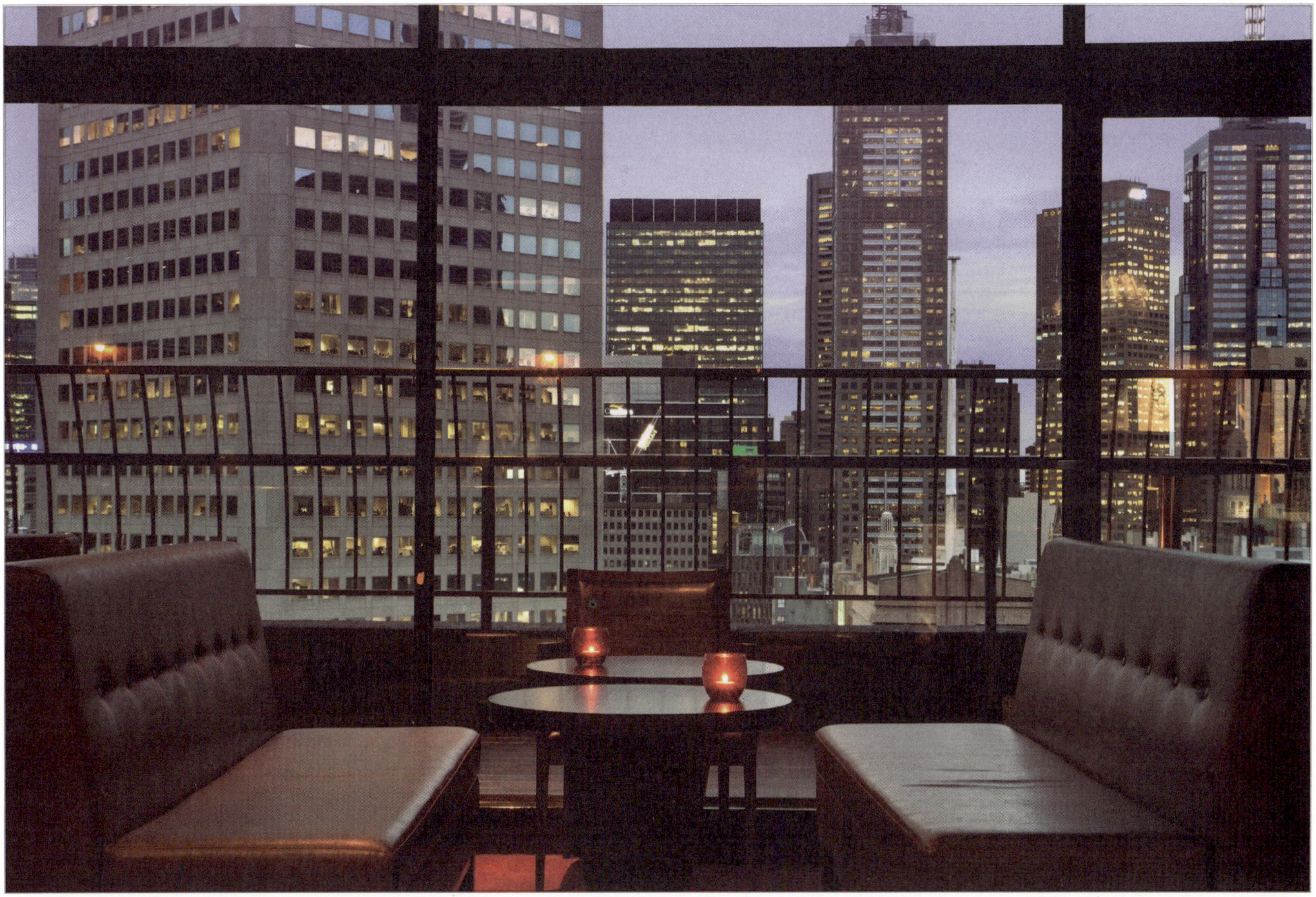

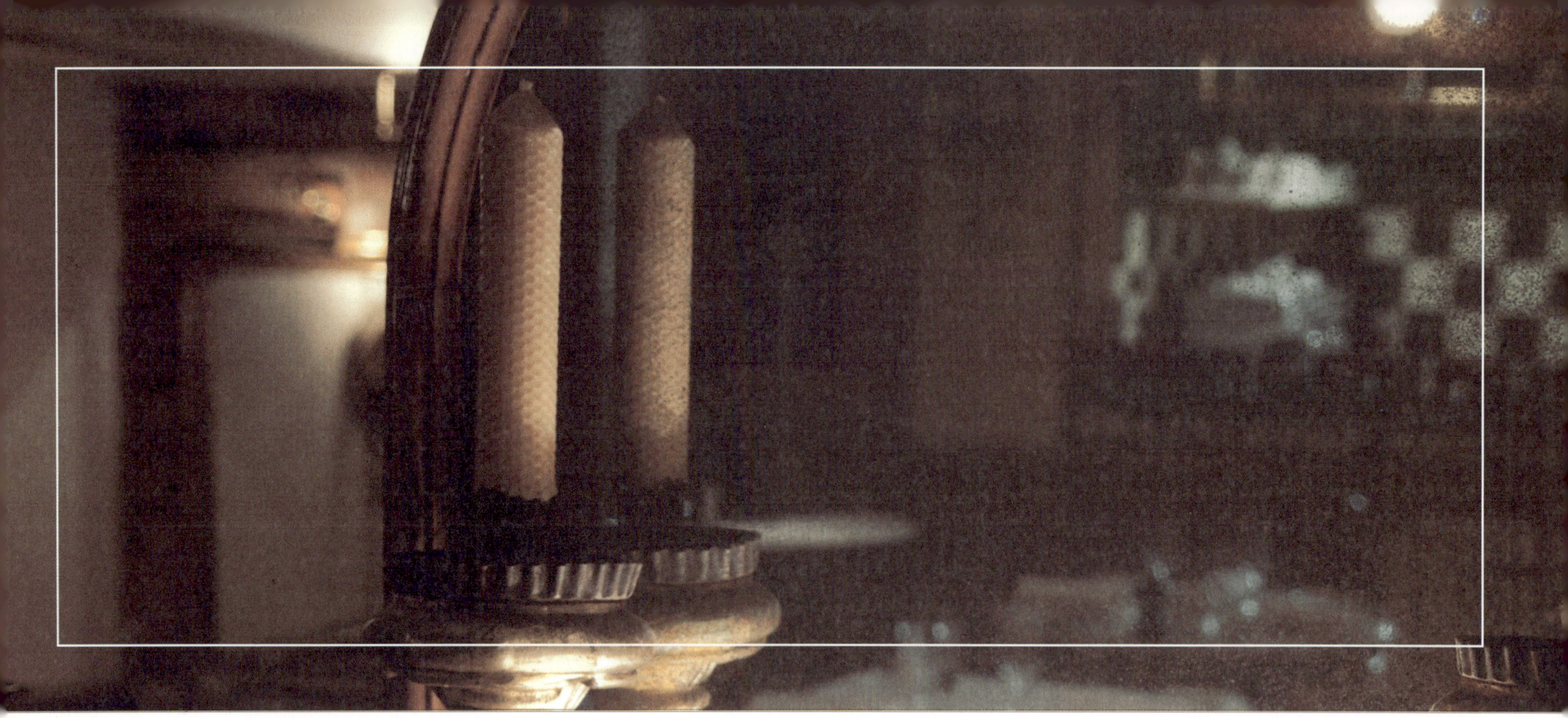

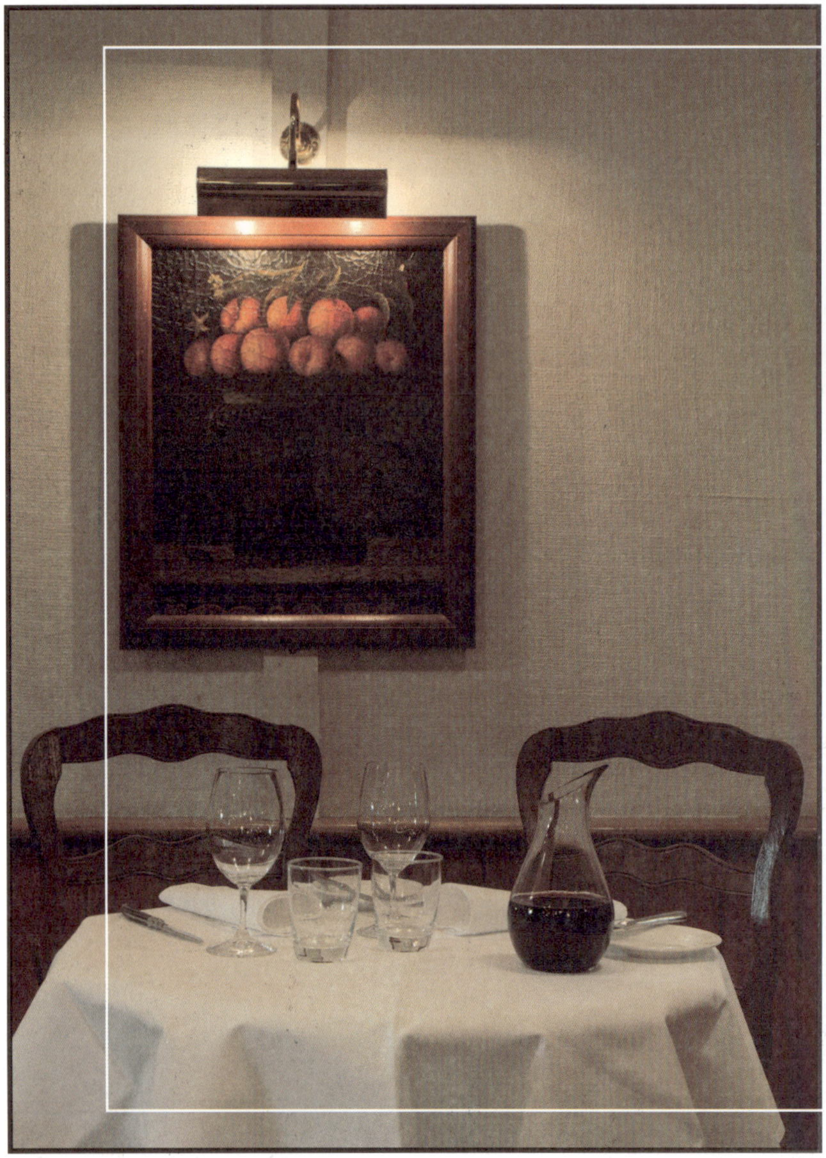

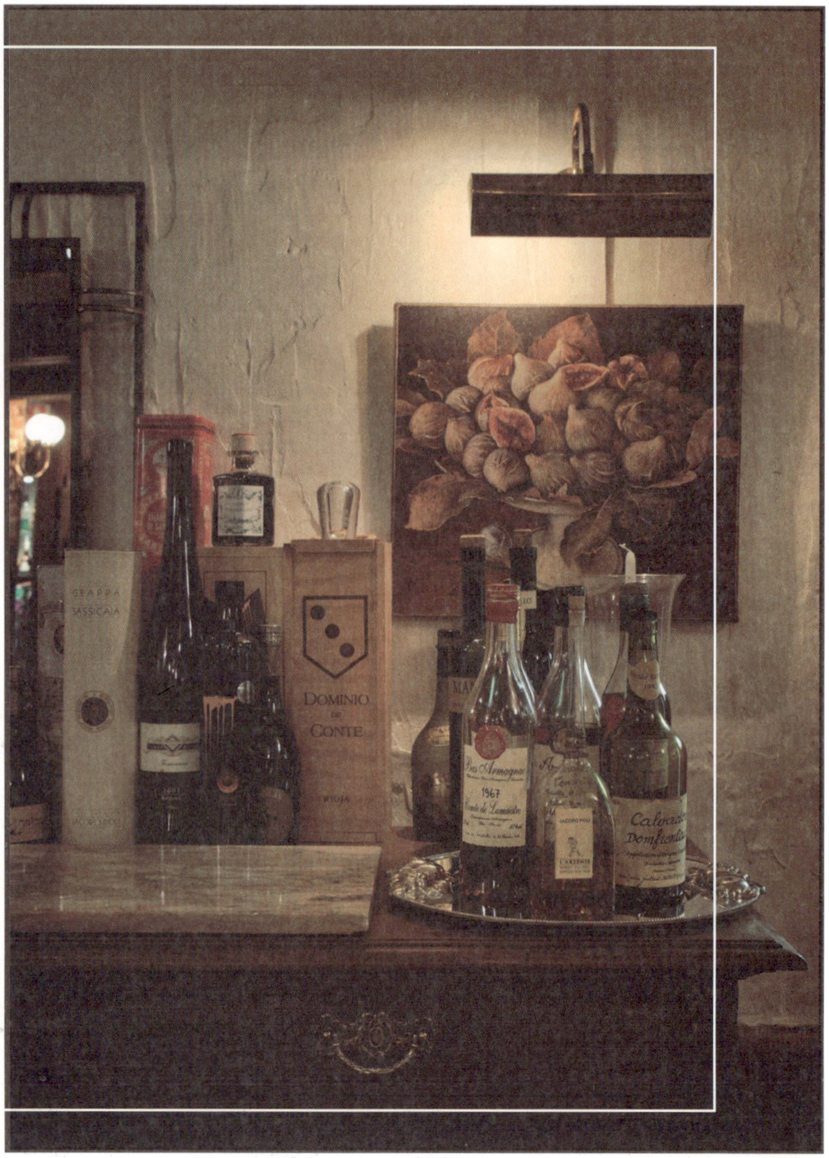
GRAPPA
SASSICAIA
DOMINIO
CONTE
1967

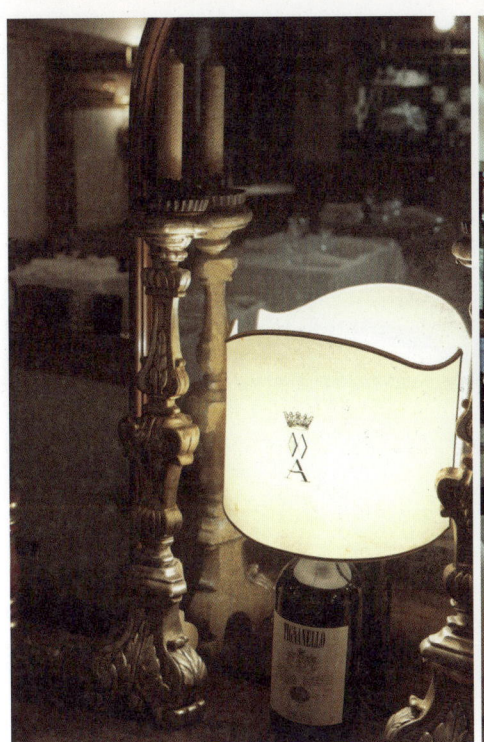

# CATERINA'S CUCINA E BAR

Basement Level, 221 Queen St
03 9670 8488
www.caterinas.com.au

Underground and private, Caterina's Cucina e Bar, is an exciting lunch-only restaurant, frequented by business high-flyers, and others looking for that unique Italian experience. It does a roaring lunch trade invigorated by the chef's expertise in regional Italian food. He is also assisted by a variety of fresh Italian talent, harnessed straight off the boat. That ensures authenticity and up-to-date ideas from the mother country.

The marble and formally clothed tables, antique mirrors and Venetian masks combine to create an ambience of an Italian opera, with scene changes from buzzing and romantic to the outlandish Italian, depending on the occasion. Specials are recited by professional and informed staff and a local and international wine list complements the menu. With 400 wines on the main list and a dozen or so by the glass, Caterinas is certainly serious about their wine. It is also dedicated to serving Northern Italian food reflecting the restaurant's heritage as well as spanning the length of the boot.

You may find an authentic vialone nano risotto, traditional braises using a variety of game such as hare in salmi with cacao, rabbit on soft polenta bramata and slow roasted venison in nebbiolo wine, or simply a cured delicacy of local red mullet in the form of a carpaccio. Daily housemade breads, cutting edge pastas utilising squid ink or roasted chestnut flour and the obligatory biscottini complete the story. Fresh, seasonal produce, some straight from the farmer's gate, pays homage to Caterina's Gippsland farming roots, as well as ensuring the ongoing support for small local producers.

A regular stable of permanent staff provides consistently competent and friendly service, and suggestions about the right kind of options to suit the individual needs. The ambience is relaxed, with mellow music and subtle lighting – a welcome break from the corporate world upstairs.

Caterina Borsato, who launched her restaurant back in 1994, is well-known from her weekly cooking show on Channel 31, called 'Regional Italian Cuisine'. True to form the show is about acknowledging the contributions of her migrant heritage. Old recipes that are not found in books, engaging stories that reaffirm culture and traditions, and every now and then, the odd "Saluté"! Caterina's Cucina e Bar is the perfect venue for hosting a corporate event, private dinners and functions or simply, an elegant wedding. These events can be booked outside the normal lunch trading periods. The restaurant can seat 90 people and can cater for parties up to 150.

Rainbow Alley is located off Little Collins Street. It was named after the Rainbow Hotel in 1856 which stood on the corner of Swanston and Little Collins Streets. A cider manufacturer, George Hopkins ran his company from Rainbow Alley in the 1860's. By the nineteenth century the laneway was considered a place of filth and back-street crime. Dumpsters are still dotted through the lane amongst a bunch of hidden bars, cafes and coffee shops. Don't miss the hidden gem, Cabinet Bar!

1. Cabinet Bar

# RAINBOW ALLEY

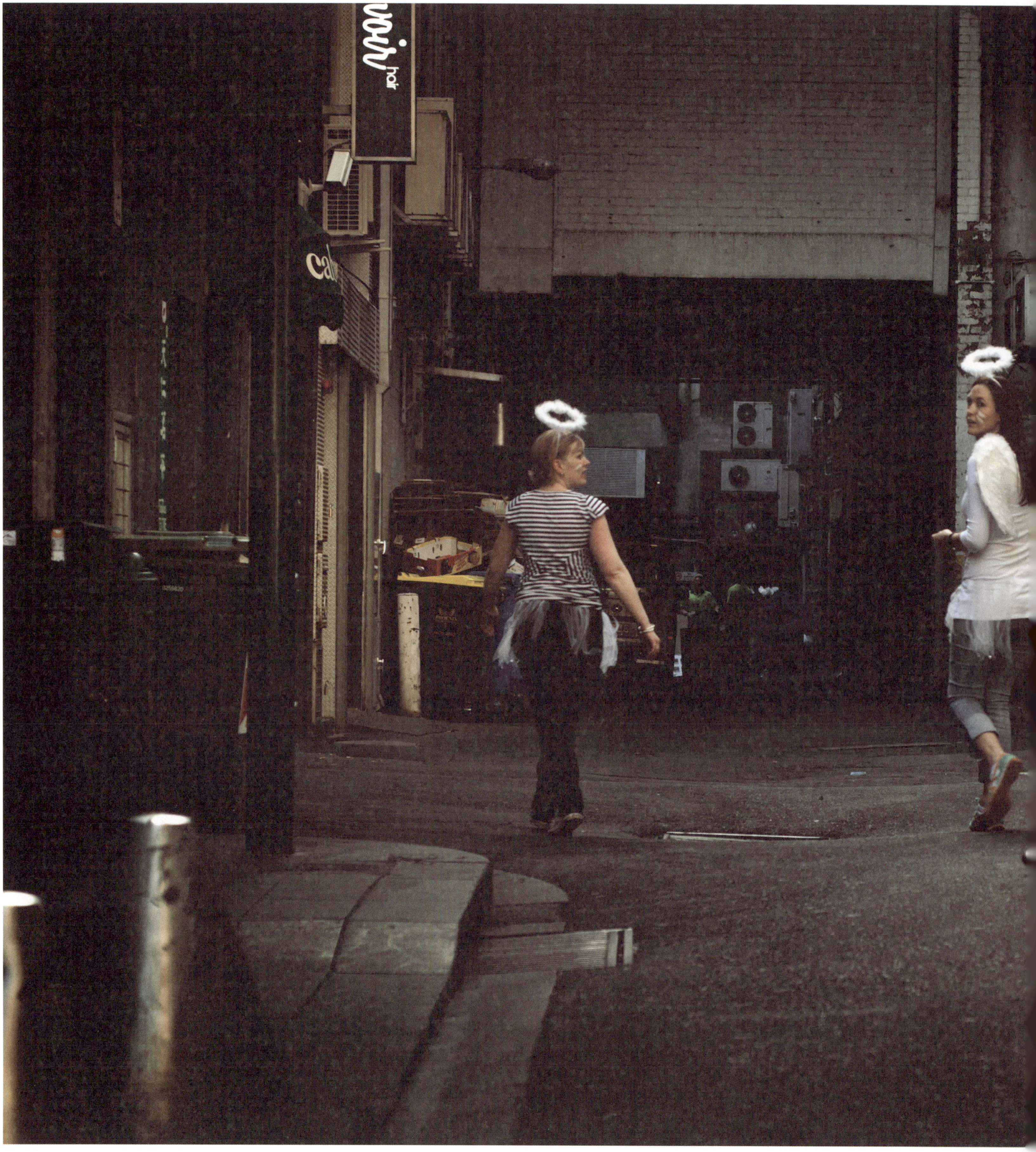
hair

!WARNING!
PRIVATE PROP
UNAUTHORISED VEHIC
WILL BE WHEEL CLAM
AND OR TOWED AWA
NATIONA
GUARDIA
SECURI
(03) 9729 8

# CABINET BAR & BALCONY

11 Rainbow Alley
03 9654 0915
www.cabinetbar.com.au

You will want to lock the door, throw away the key and settle in for the evening in Rainbow Alley's intimate Cabinet Bar. Tucked behind Little Collins Street and next to the Melbourne Town Hall, this welcoming, laneway space is reminiscent of a softly-lit, Parisian night club, decorated with a blend of European furnishings and retro-chic décor.

Kath Lunny and Alan Bell established Cabinet Bar in 2007 to create an exclusive place, cherished by those "in the know". It is nearly hidden down Rainbow Alley, a laneway which was named pre-1856 after the nearby Rainbow Hotel.

You will find tiny tables for two, comfy sofas and a large table to share. It is the perfect venue for a meet, greet, eat and drink. There is also a balcony with wonderful views over Swanston Street, with passers-by oblivious to the revellers above. You can watch the sun go down here while you enjoy a cocktail, wine or a meal.

Head barman, Alan Bell, lights up the night with his creative and ingenious recipes for an assortment of cocktails. These are served well into the night and include Cabinet's signature 'Johan's Java Jive' (photo on the opposite page) which consists of Montenegro, Lemoncello, vanilla and mint.

Blackboards direct you to the seasonal menu which changes often. Cheese, sweets, flatbreads and share-style plates can be ordered to go with your drink, or you will find something more substantial like the seafood salad with chili prawn, tuna and salmon.

Kath said they named the bar after a cabinet which literally means 'small room'. She said, "Unlike other Australian cities, Melbournians loves to hide away in a small bar or restaurant. We are also confident to walk down any dark, seedy laneway, knowing a 'pot of gold' awaits."

Stop by during the day for a selection of lunch-time treats, or after hours for a home-cooked meal like Mum used to make.

> UNLIKE IN OTHER CITIES, MELBOURNIANS LOVE TO HIDE AWAY IN A SMALL BAR OR RESTAURANT. WE ARE CONFIDENT TO WALK DOWN ANY DARK, SEEDY LANEWAY, KNOWING A 'POT OF GOLD' AWAITS.

287

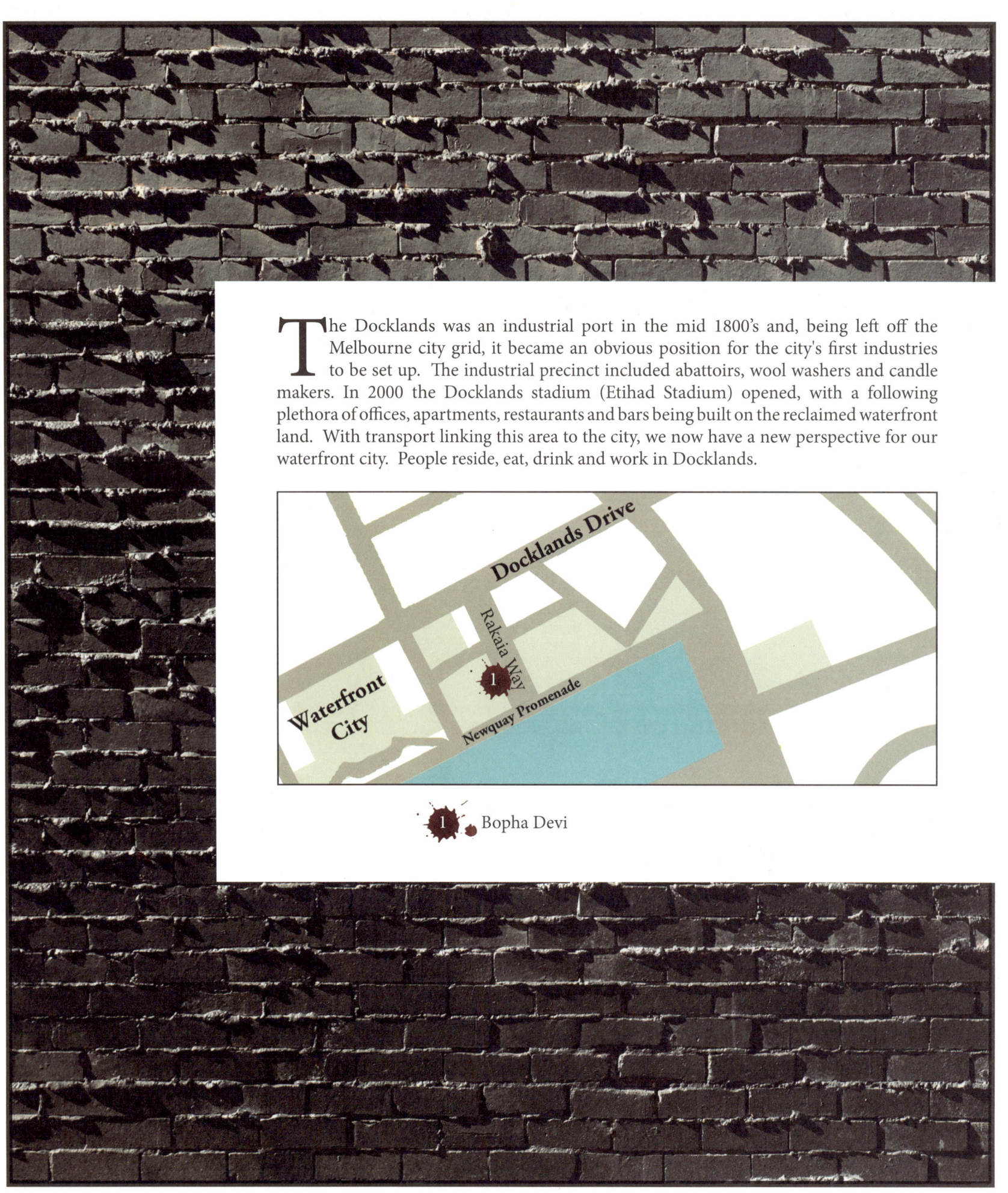

The Docklands was an industrial port in the mid 1800's and, being left off the Melbourne city grid, it became an obvious position for the city's first industries to be set up. The industrial precinct included abattoirs, wool washers and candle makers. In 2000 the Docklands stadium (Etihad Stadium) opened, with a following plethora of offices, apartments, restaurants and bars being built on the reclaimed waterfront land. With transport linking this area to the city, we now have a new perspective for our waterfront city. People reside, eat, drink and work in Docklands.

1. Bopha Devi

# RAKAIA WAY

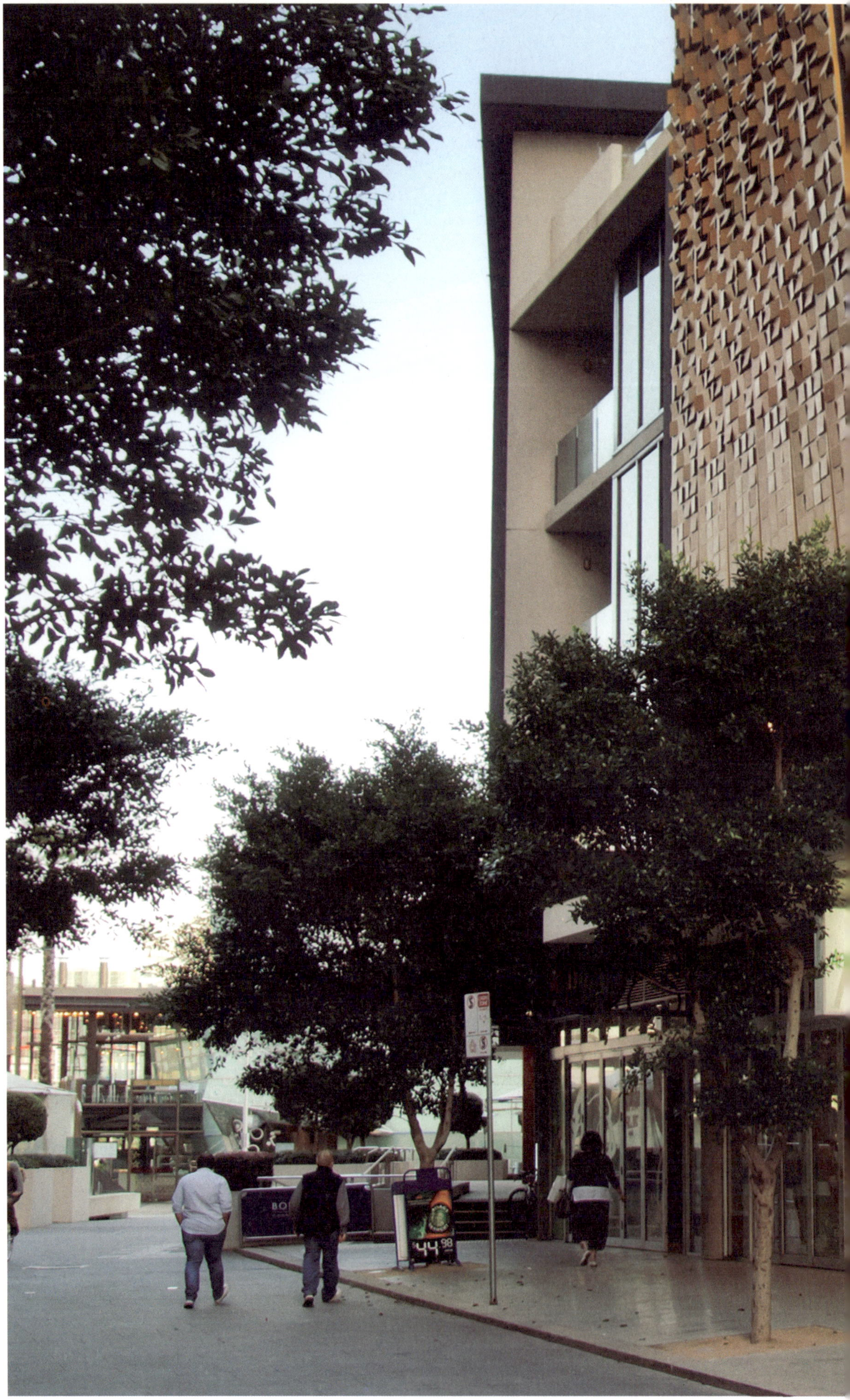

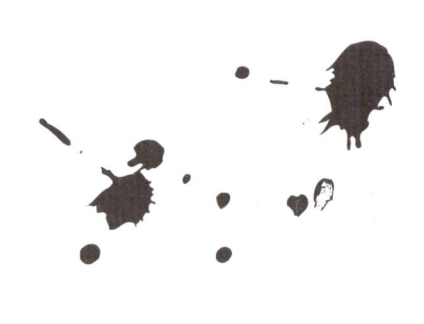

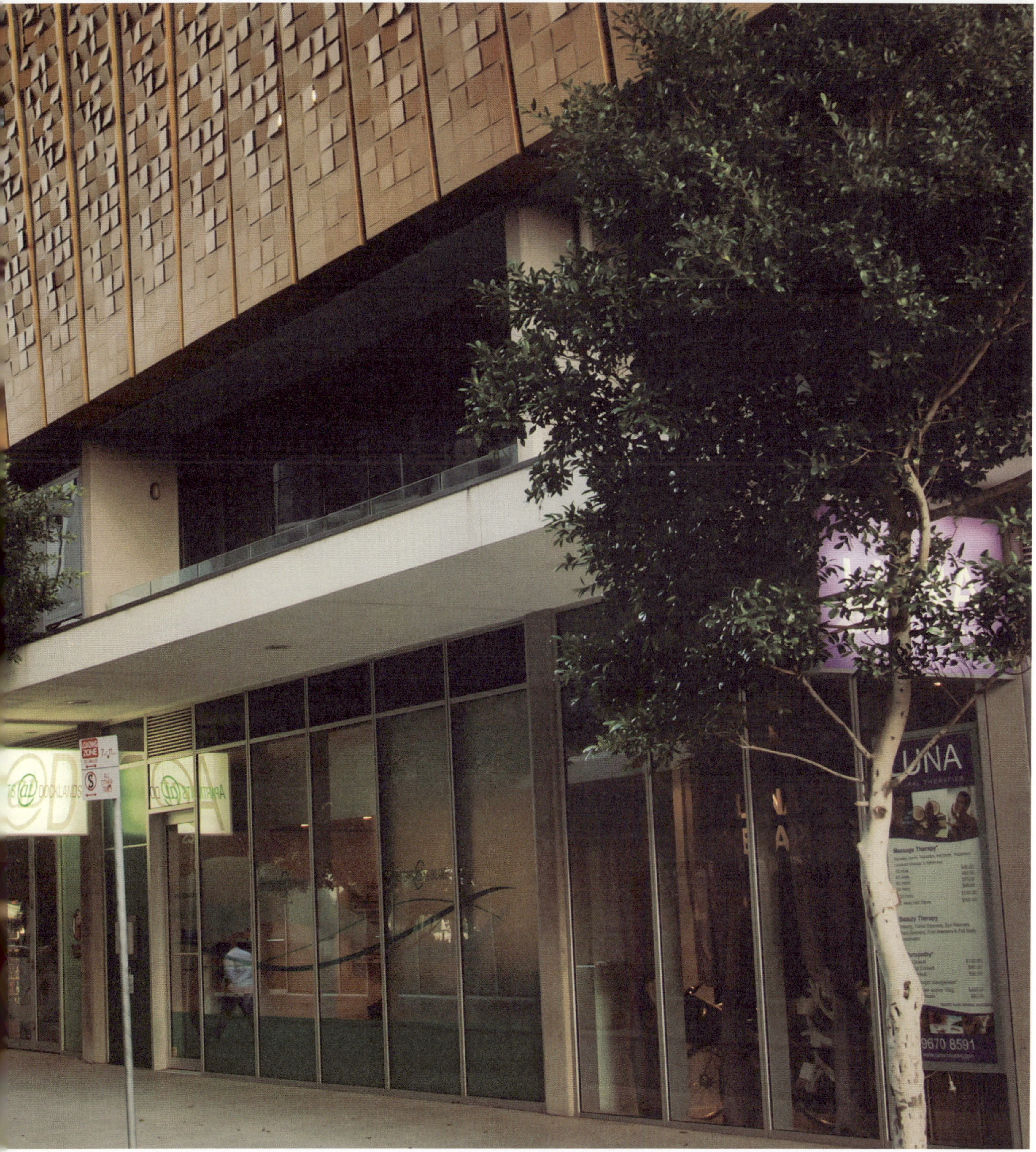
LUNA
9670 8591

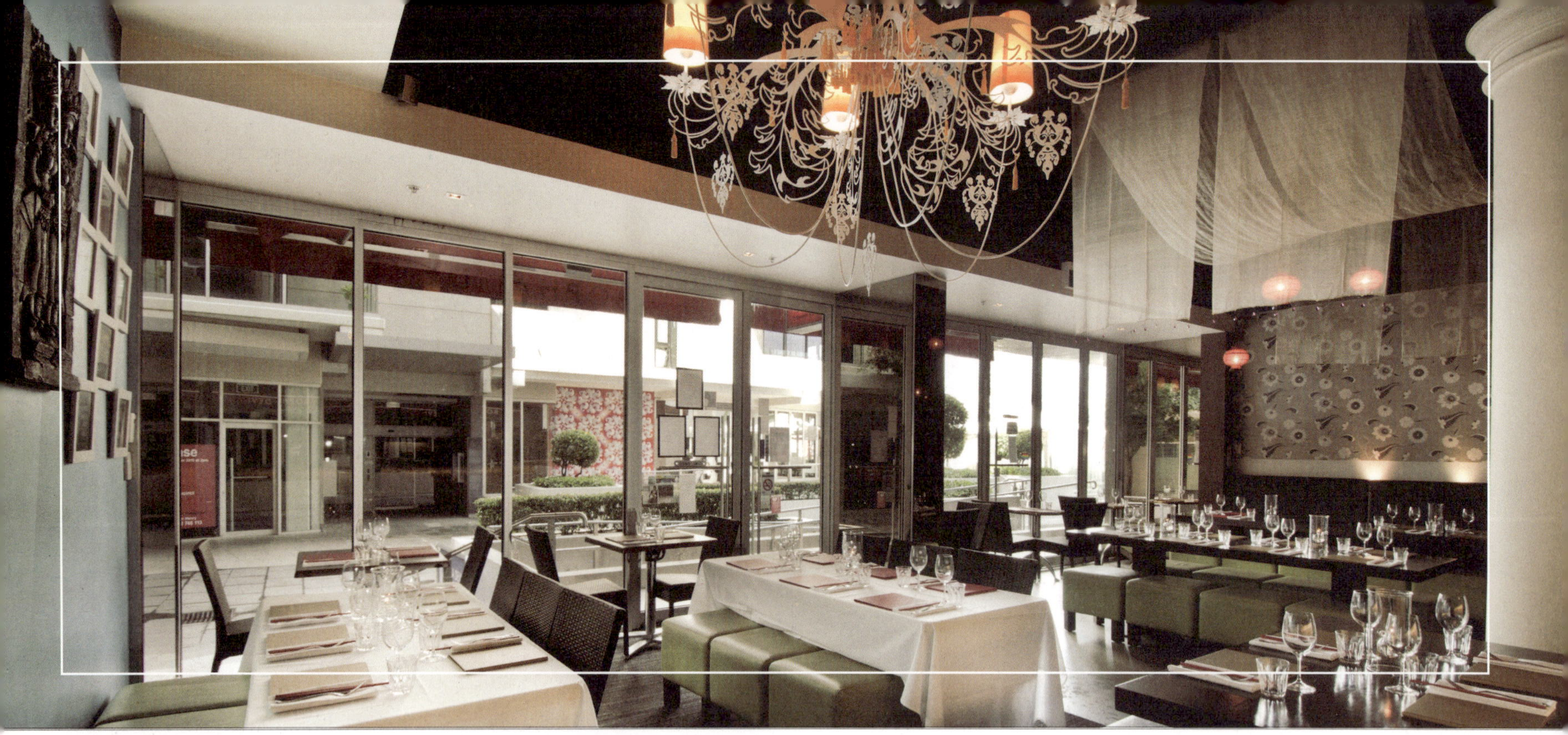

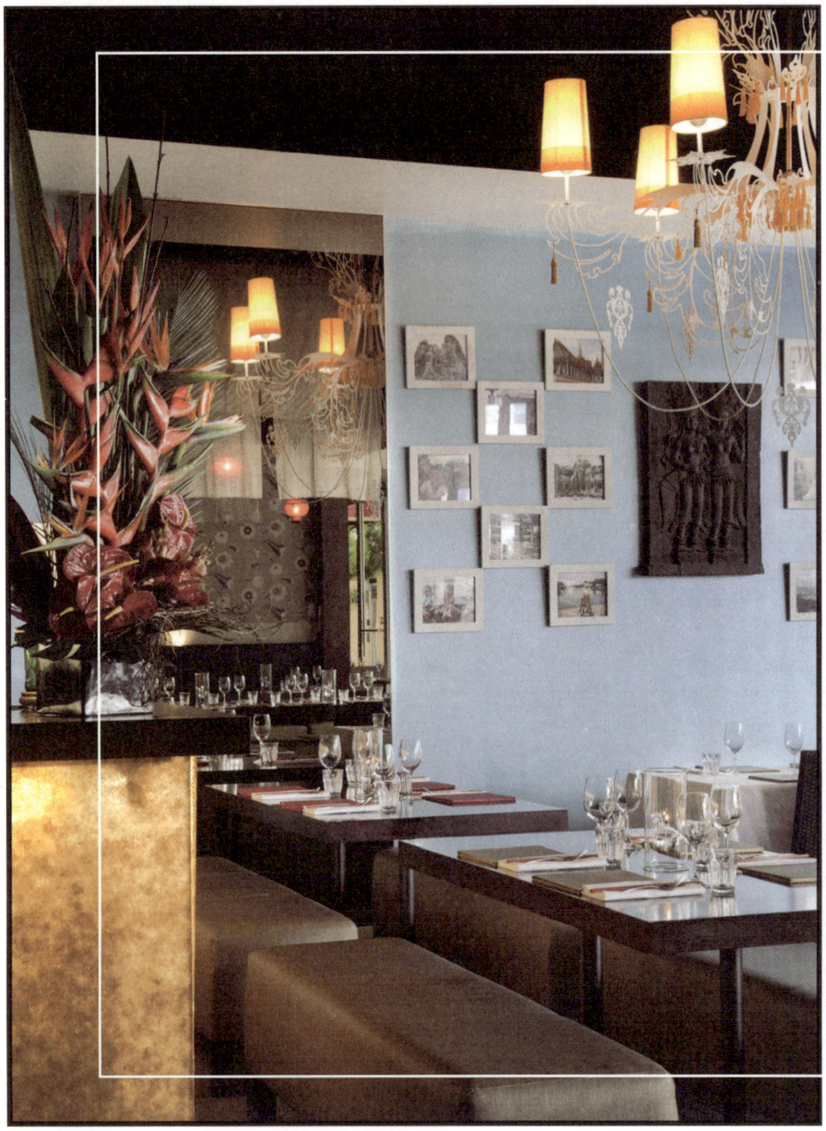

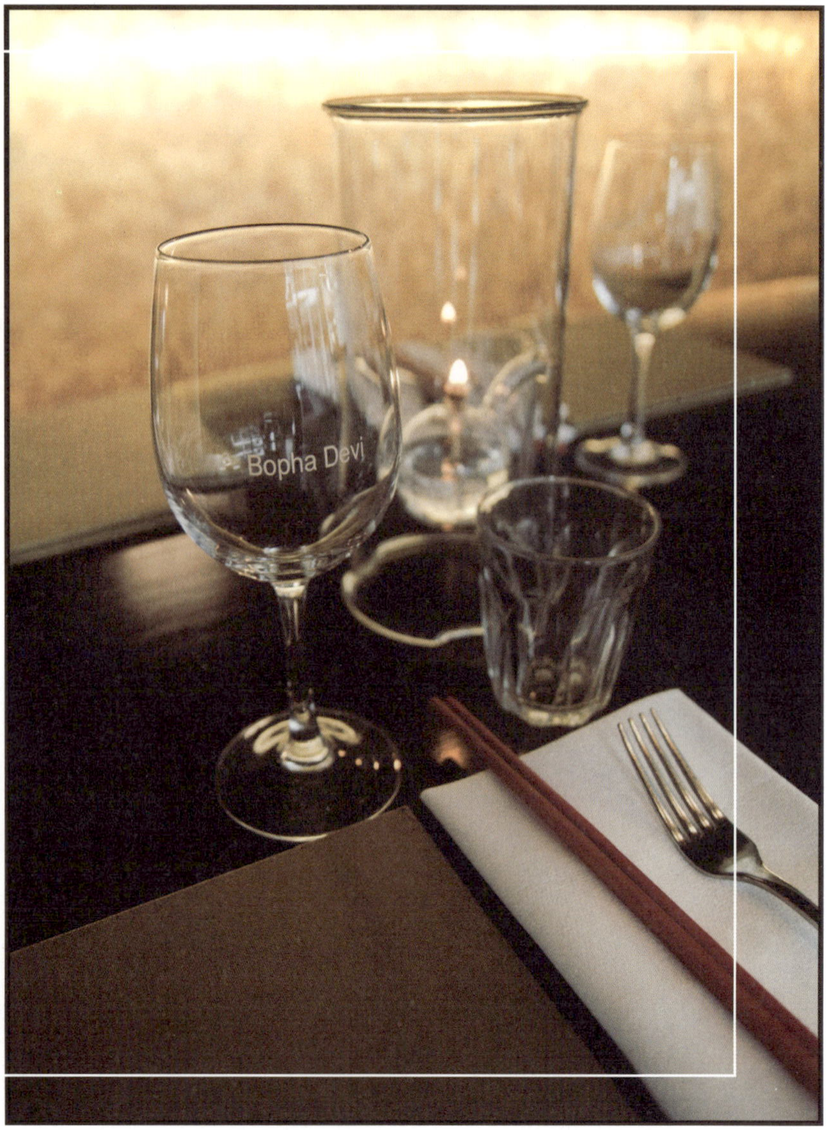
Bopha Devi

Rakaia Way, Located in the Docklands
03 9600 1887
www.bophadevi.com

# BOPHA DEVI

With bordering countries like Thailand, Laos and Vietnam, you would expect the food of Cambodia to have a blend of similar and familiar tastes. However the thrill of eating at the laneway restaurant in the docklands, Bopha Devi, is to discover that Cambodia might be close to these countries, yet the essence of its cooking style and taste is unique.

Chan Uoy and Sun Chung established Bopha Devi in Yarraville in 1999, and followed up its success by opening the larger restaurant in the Docklands in 2005 with Paul Thickett. "Fresh and piquant with crunch," only begins to describe the distinctive food you will find on the menu here. Coriander, mint and lemongrass rate very highly in fresh salads, while fish and nutty sauces combine with turmeric, galangal, lime leaves and coconut cream to form part and parcel of the national Cambodian fundamentals.

Chan was only a young boy when his family escaped the Pol Pot regime in 1975 and after six months in a refugee camp on the Thai/Cambodia border, he and his family arrived in Australia as refugees. One of Chan's earliest recollections was escaping from his home through jungle and over mountains to the border. He said, "I remember having bloodied feet from trekking barefoot through the jungle".

"One night when my father and I went to gather firewood, I remember my father suddenly standing dead still. We had stumbled across a Khmer Rouge camp, during the terrifying early days of the war that was to see 25% of the Cambodian population killed and any resemblance of culture or education was eradicated". Chan said, "If the Khmer Rouge had seen us we simply wouldn't be here today."

Growing up as a Cambodian living in Australia, Chan wanted to reveal to his new homeland his rich heritage, and what better way to start than through his national cuisine. The restaurant in Yarraville became the first Cambodian restaurant in Melbourne and he named it in honour of the Cambodian Princess, Bopha Devi, whose name is derived from the Hindu words Heavenly Flower Goddess. As a young princess, she was chosen by the Khmer Queen to become a dancer. By the age of 18 she was granted the title of Prima Ballerina and toured the world with the Cambodian Royal Ballet.

Chan said, "I chose this name for the restaurant because it encapsulated the art and heritage of Cambodia." He said that there was a void in Australia for Cambodian food and he believed that by opening of Bopha Devi, we would help enrich Melbourne's eating experience".

He said, "We revisited the cooking I grew up with and repackaged it to make it funky and cool."

Agus Putro, the head chef at Bopha Devi Docklands, has worked in various hotels in Indonesia and also in the wine industry in the Yarra Valley. He has learnt Cambodian cooking from Chan's Uncle, Sun Chung and now cooks a range of Cambodian cuisine.

Although this enchanting restaurant boasts character and style, it has not lost its original Cambodian roots. You will discover a diverse range of dishes on the menu, including traditional curries, vermicelli noodles and hearty-Cambodian style soups. Make sure you try a char-grilled sugar banana, coated in sticky rice and grated coconut to finish.

Bopha Devi is a restaurant with a social conscience, supporting a range of charities, including Cambodian orphans, street kids and community developments within Cambodia, which is still recovering from the trauma of war.

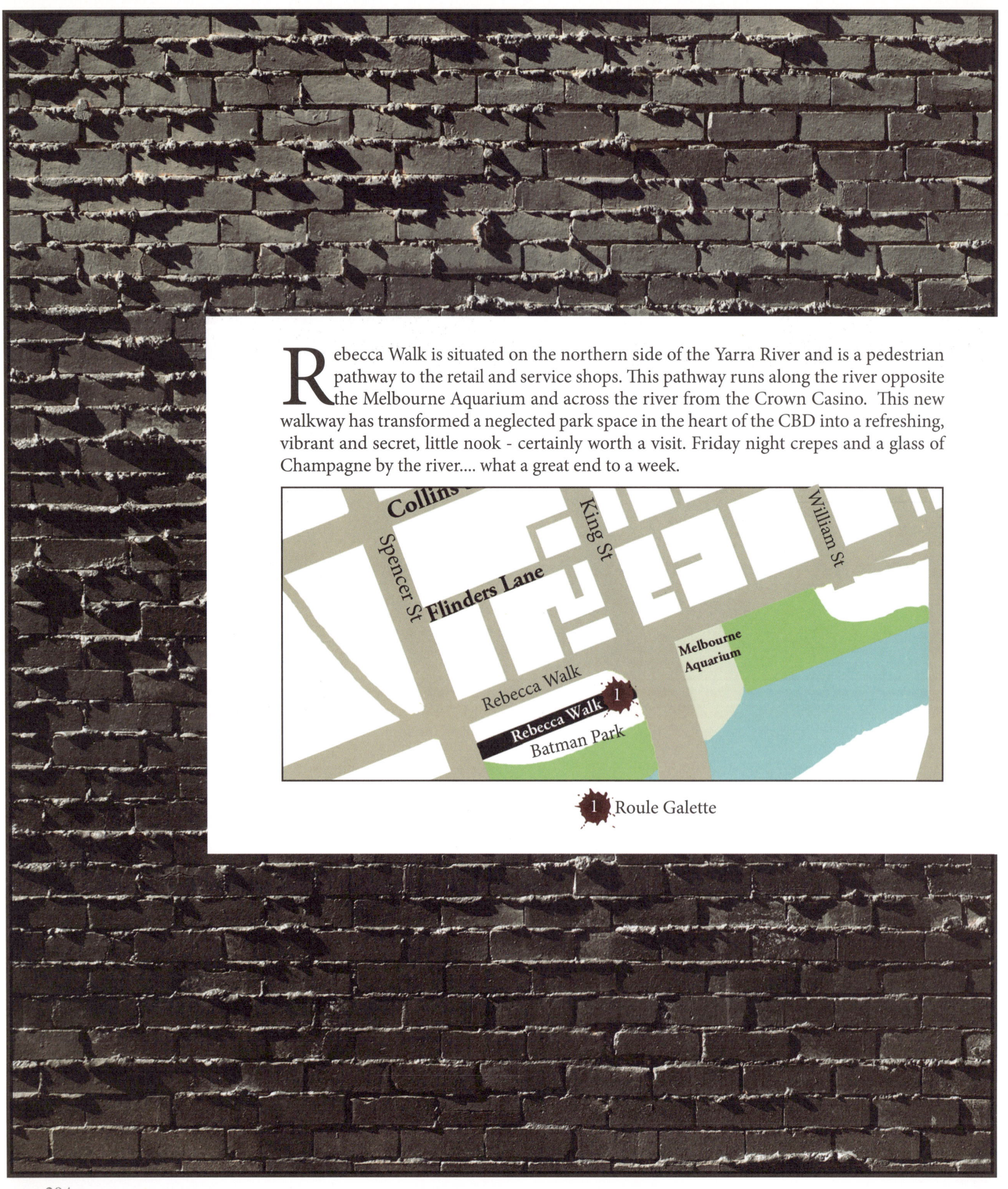

Rebecca Walk is situated on the northern side of the Yarra River and is a pedestrian pathway to the retail and service shops. This pathway runs along the river opposite the Melbourne Aquarium and across the river from the Crown Casino. This new walkway has transformed a neglected park space in the heart of the CBD into a refreshing, vibrant and secret, little nook - certainly worth a visit. Friday night crepes and a glass of Champagne by the river.... what a great end to a week.

1. Roule Galette

# REBECCA WALK

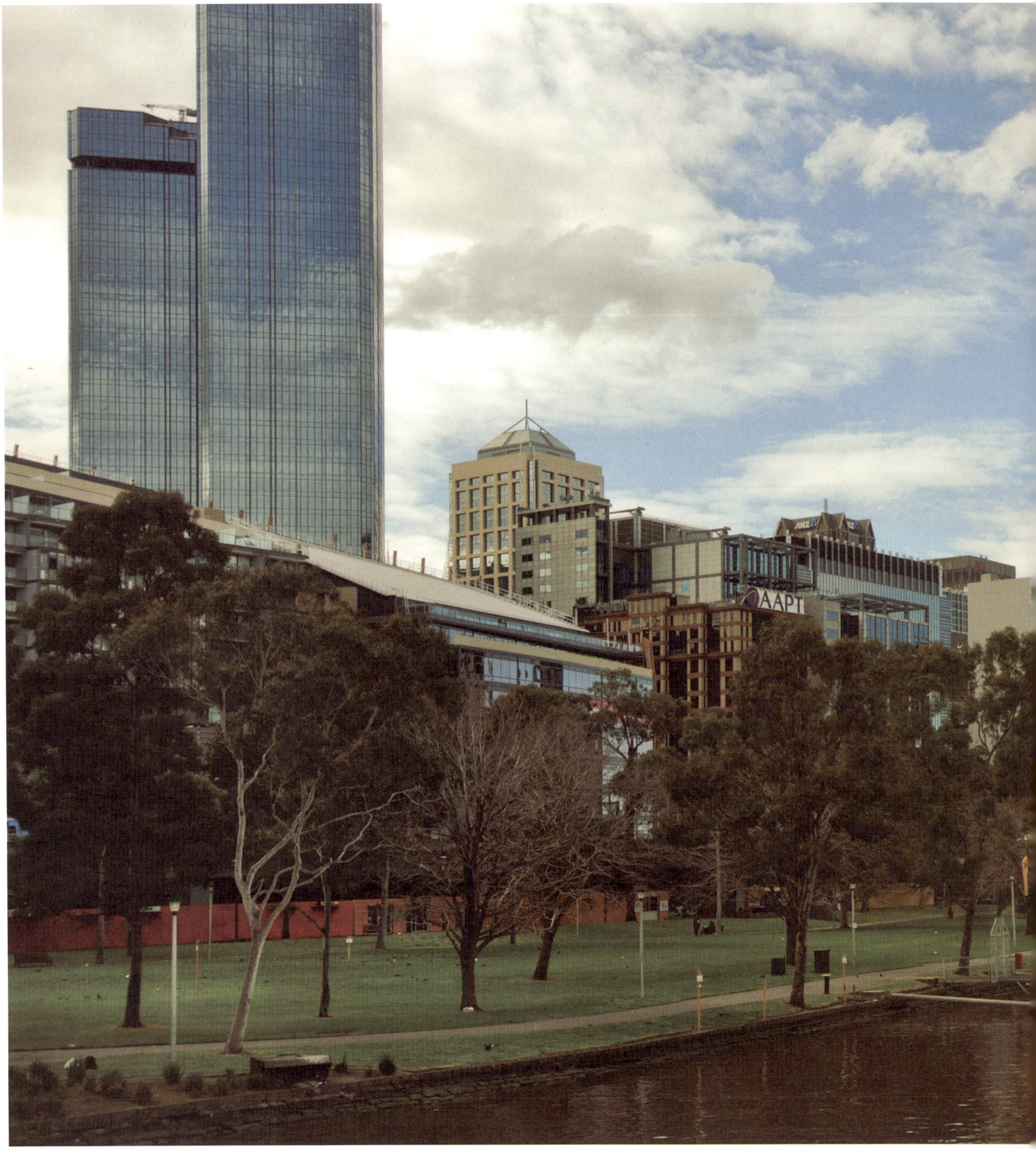
AAPT

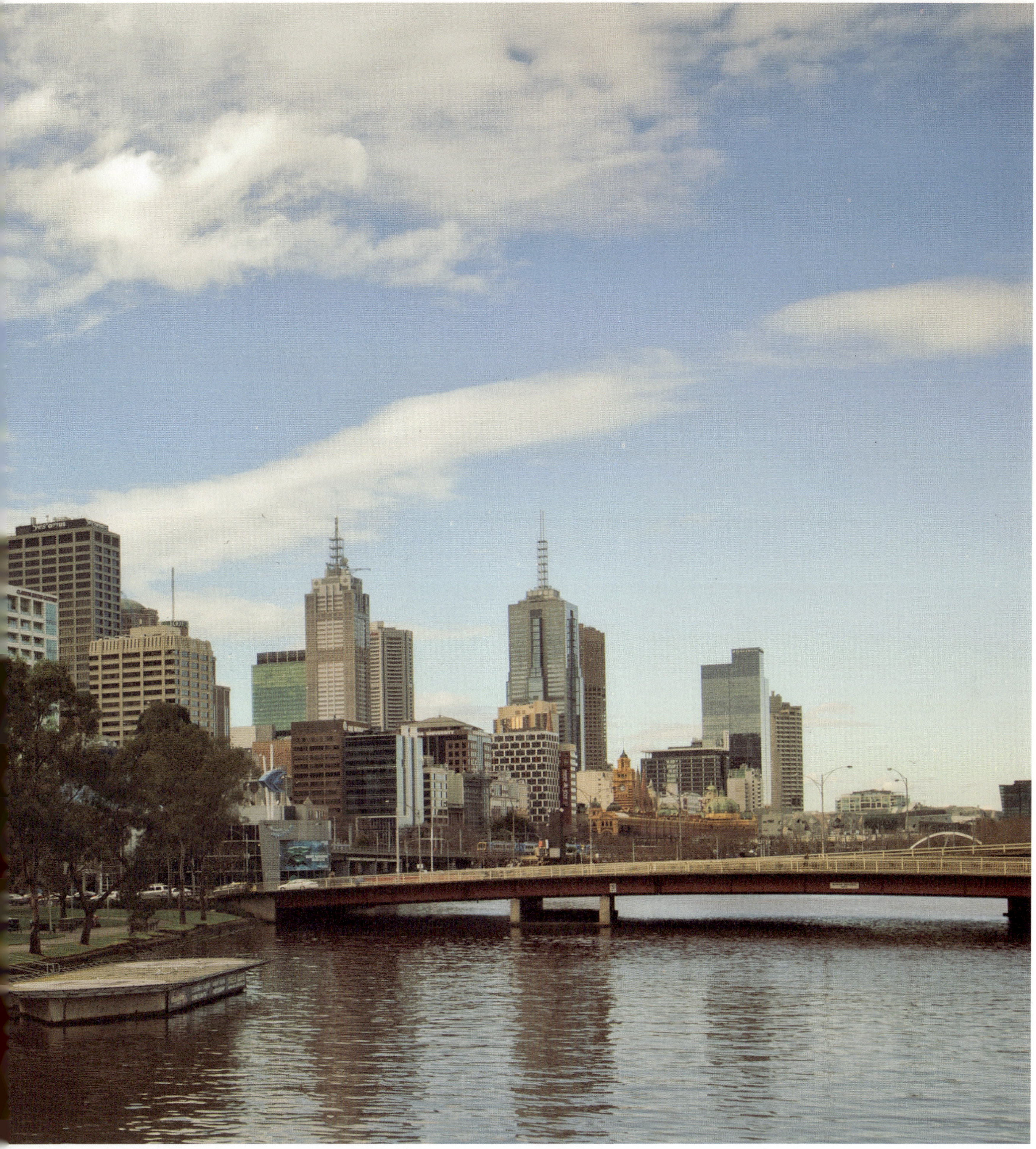

# ROULE GALETTE

26 Rebecca Walk
03 9614 3606
www.roulegalette.com.au

The famous French city crêperie, Roule Galette has opened a new restaurant in one of Melbourne's latest "laneways", Rebecca Walk. This walkway runs along the city side of the river between Kings Way and Spencer Street, and is opposite the Melbourne Aquarium and across the river from Southbank and Crown Casino.

This funky, new precinct has all the hallmarks of a futuristic laneway, complete with steel structures and colourfully constructed retail space. Street art looms on historic walls behind Roule Galette, while retro orange and green chairs deck the outdoor arena.

Michel felt there was a need for his customers to enjoy a larger version of Roule Galette, allowing them to take more time to sample the crepes and galettes and enjoy a drink or even organise a function. This location, on the bank of the Yarra River, is the perfect spot and you'll soon have the feeling you're sitting in a café on the Seine River in Paris.

Customers enjoy the same specialties as the Scott Alley crêperie, including a large range of crepes and galettes. They either choose their toppings or pick them up from the recipes inspired from Michel's childhood and family traditions. Just like in Scott Alley, crepes and galettes are made on the spot and you can watch the staff preparing your delicacy in front of you. All ingredients are carefully selected, with the cheese coming from France and the maple syrup from Canada. Michel insists he uses the same products at home and in his restaurants. It is so important for him to treat each customer individually, adjusting recipes when asked to and responding to allergies with delicious alternatives.

On a Friday night, weather permitting, you may find live music to help while away the evening as you dine on a galette, a savoury-style pancake or a dessert-style crepe. This is the perfect opportunity to taste a selection of French and Australian wines, or go for the traditional cider served in ceramic bowls, just like in the remote parts of Brittany. If you want to get home after work, you can simply order take away to go.

299

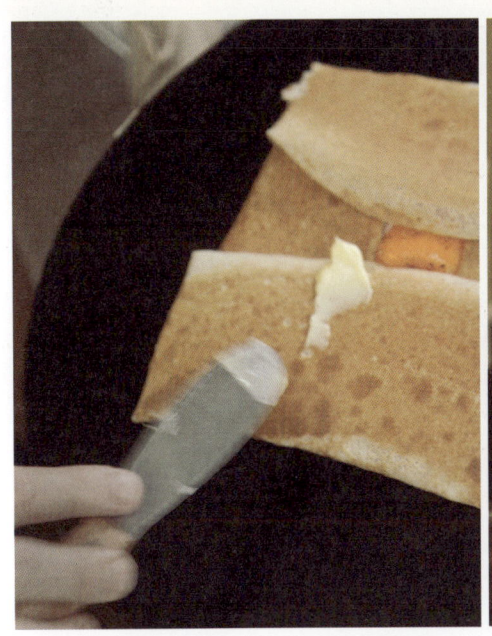

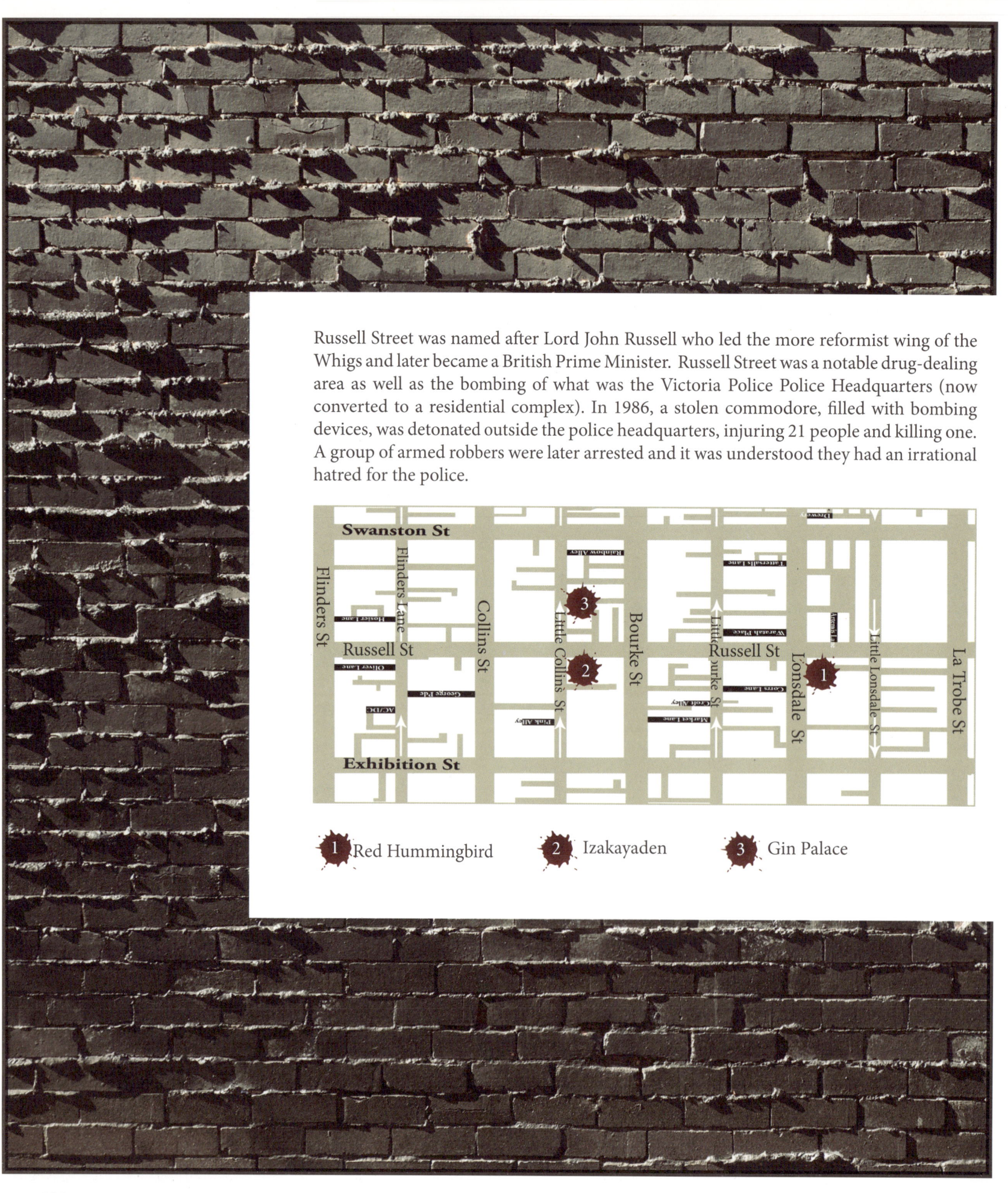

Russell Street was named after Lord John Russell who led the more reformist wing of the Whigs and later became a British Prime Minister. Russell Street was a notable drug-dealing area as well as the bombing of what was the Victoria Police Police Headquarters (now converted to a residential complex). In 1986, a stolen commodore, filled with bombing devices, was detonated outside the police headquarters, injuring 21 people and killing one. A group of armed robbers were later arrested and it was understood they had an irrational hatred for the police.

1. Red Hummingbird
2. Izakayaden
3. Gin Palace

# RUSSELL ST. & PLACE

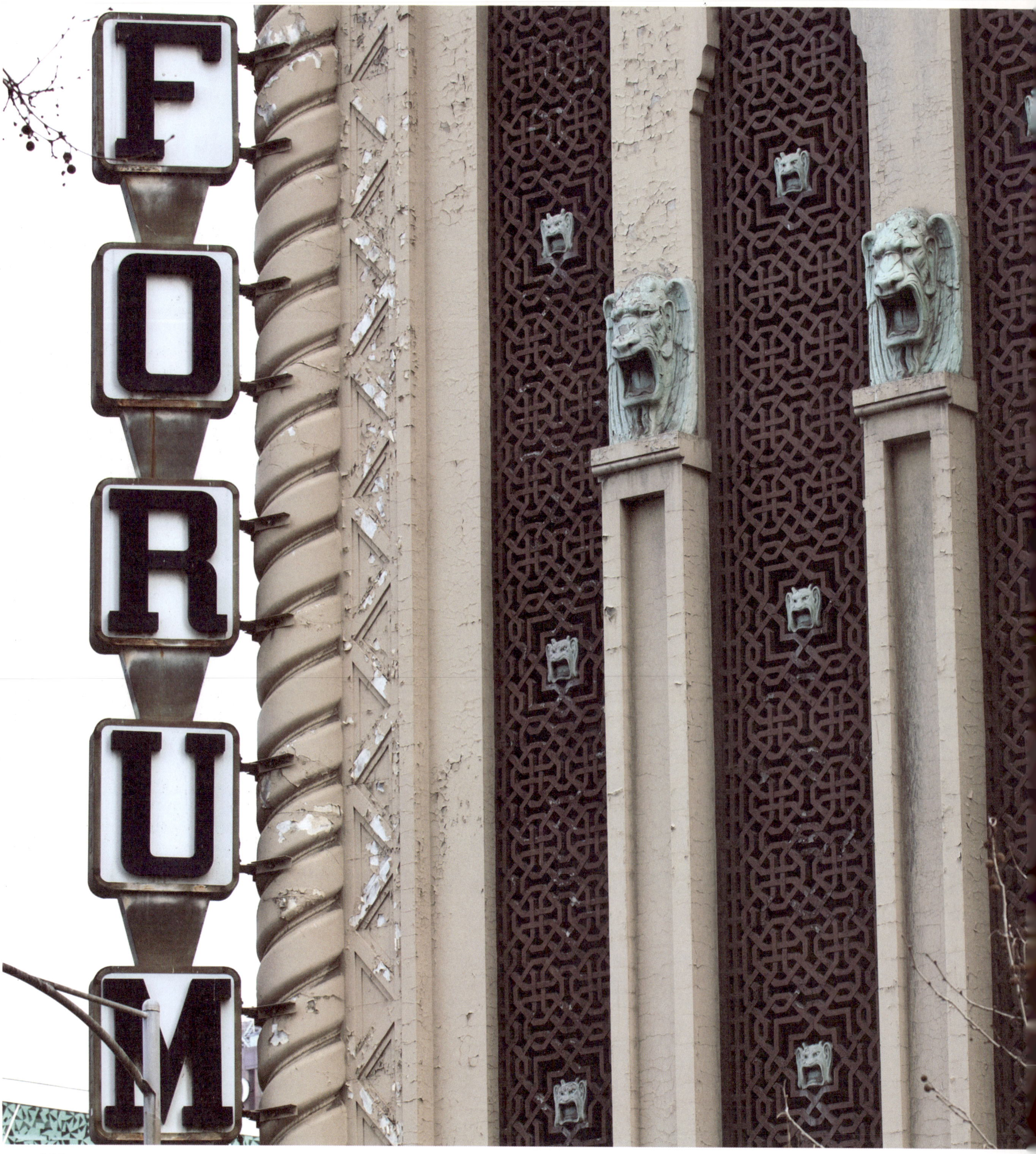
FORUM

303

# GIN PALACE

10 Russell Place
03 9654 0533
www.ginpalace.com.au

A late 19th century Budapest lounge bar, renovated during the fifties," was the brief for Gin Palace, which opened its doors in 1997. Irreverent, whimsical and a huge fan of the martini, the owner, Vernon Chalker said "I would rather serve a skateboarder a martini, than have a suit come in and ask for a bourbon and coke". Such is the reverence for gin and not much else in this plush palace of abundance and booze. Get the picture? Gin Palace is no European beer hall.

The name "Gin Palace", was used in the 19th Century to describe disreputable and socially undesirable drinking houses. By calling itself this Gin Palace sets itself up, very tongue in cheek, for a laugh and reveals it doesn't take itself too seriously.

Gin Palace currently stocks 55 different gins, many of which have been privately sourced. They are also keeping current with new cocktails and experimenting with their own. They are aging cocktails in oak casks and making their own syrups, cordials, vermouth, base spirits, liqueurs and bitters. With this cornucopia of ingredients to play with, no wonder the bartenders specialise in creating hot favourite cocktails, retaining the old feel and adding the trendy hue.

If martinis and cocktails aren't your thing, may I suggest you try something from the reserve wine menu, otherwise known as Vernon's Crusty Old Reds. You might also like to try one of their famous chicken sandwiches, a cheese platter to share or a chicken liver parfait.

The menu has changed little in its 12 year history and Vernon himself will tell you that Gin Palace martinis are made exactly the same today as they were when he opened. This fact, along with 'we never close' hours, have made Gin Palace the Melbourne institution it is today.

You will discover the table service cannot be faulted and Vernon says he requires his staff to serve professionally, happily, responsibly and, most of all, without attitude. You may get an odd look, though, if you order a chamomile tea!

With its hidden nooks and alcoves, you will feel the outside world slip away. You may even feel the need to enter the very secluded Harem – although what goes on in this dark, secluded corner, one can only guess. Vernon just says, "It's the naughtiest nook of all!"

---

IN THE LATE 1800'S, DOWN A DARK MELBOURNE ALLEY, THERE ONCE WAS AN INFAMOUS HOSPITALITY VENUE. HOW IT WAS FROWNED UPON DURING DAYLIGHT HOURS, YET SURPRISINGLY, OR MAYBE NOT SO SURPRISINGLY, HOW IT WAS FREQUENTED BY ALL KINDS AT NIGHT. WHETHER THROUGH POPULAR OPINION, A DESIRE FOR FRANKNESS, OR A SENSE OF IRONY, IT ADOPTED THE TITLE "GIN PALACE". HOWEVER TO THE DELIGHT OF THE LOCAL WOWSERS AND PRESS, THIS DRINKING HOUSE WAS ABRUPTLY SHUT DOWN BY COMMAND.

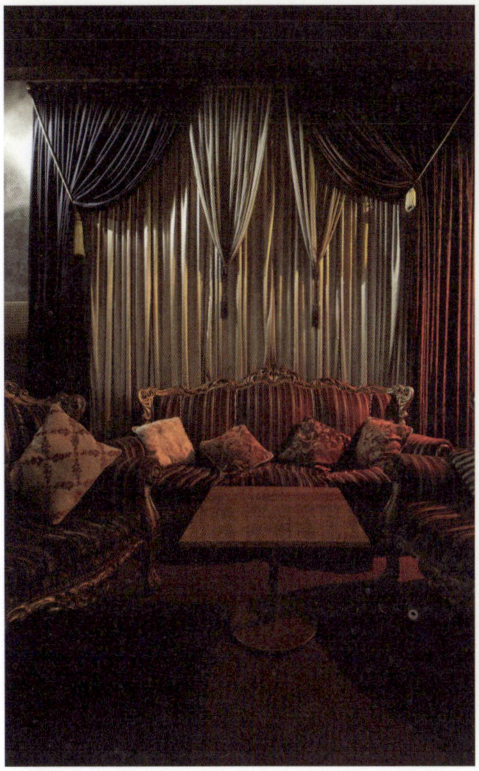
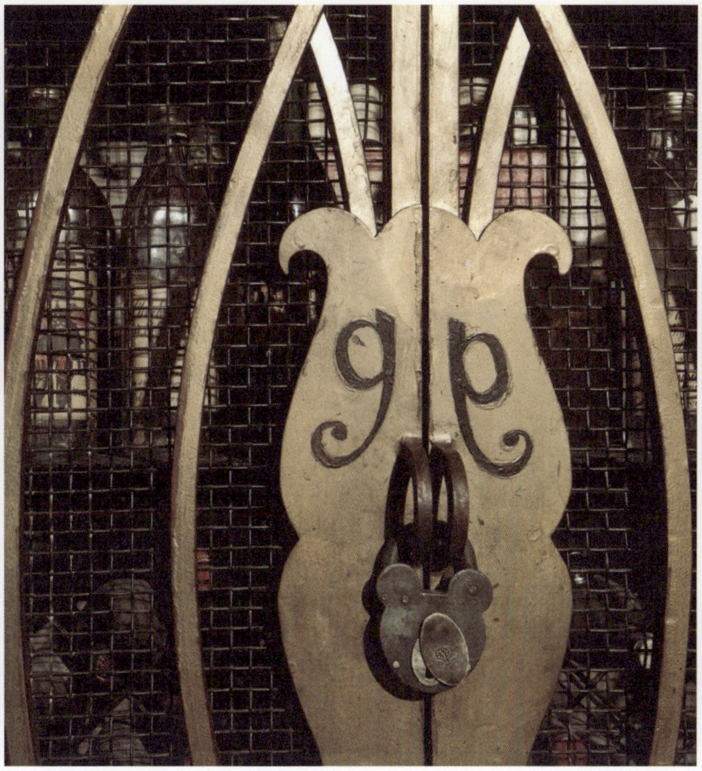
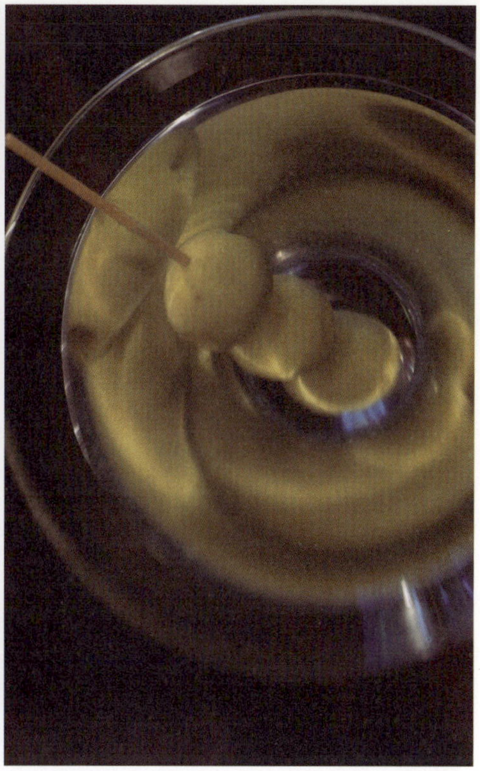
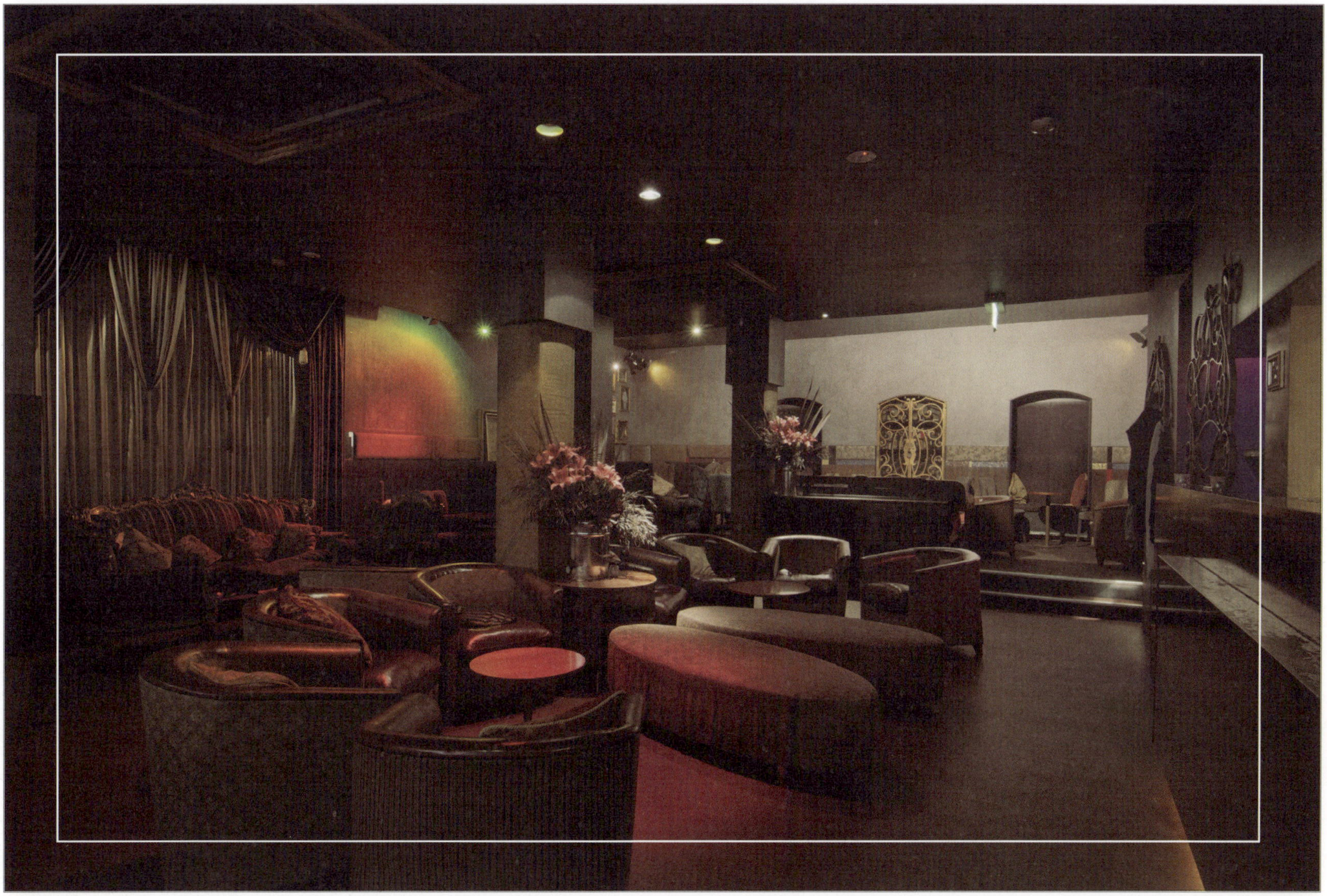

# IZAKAYA DEN

Basement, 114 Russell St
03 9654 2977
www.izakayaden.com.au

Let the adventure begin when you try to find this hidden Japanese den. You will have to look hard for the venue at 114 Russell Street, and that is just the beginning. You still have to find your way down two flights of stairs and be brave enough to poke your head through some dark curtains, to get to your destination. But it will be well worth it when you discover the sophisticated, Izakaya Den.

Its name, "izakaya", literally means a "sitting, sake shop", and izakayas are common throughout Japan. It is the Australian version of a pub or wine bar, where you can go to eat and drink in a relaxed atmosphere.

Owners of this underground, industrial-style restaurant are Simon Denton, Takashi Omi and Miyuki Nakahara, who have a serious obsession with all things Japanese. Right down to the urban-chic styling of Japanese waiters, dressed in all-black uniforms and red sneakers, menus written on wound up scrolls, and water served in glass cups with Japanese anime figures. Simon has made sure you are getting the authentic Japanese deal.

You may have to queue to get in, unless you make a booking for five or more, but you will be given an oshibori (wet towel) on arrival, invited to order a cocktail or drink from the bar, and enjoy the company of other excited customers waiting for their tables.

The restaurant design is very clever, with the open kitchen down one side, and the seating on the other. If the room looks extraordinarily long, there is a mirror at the end which makes it look double its size.

The menu is under the supervision of Yosuke Furukawa, the Japanese head chef. He oversees traditional izakaya fare with great precision. He produces a broad mix of Japanese izakaya classics, with some additions, utilising the best, local and seasonal produce.

The corn fritters are a specialty here, with fresh, plump and juicy corn kernels, lightly deep fried in batter. Try the tuna and the wagyu tataki which are full of flavour and finished off beautifully with micro-herbs.

The Den Fried Chicken is better than any Karaage you'll taste elsewhere. But the all-time favourite seems to be the Lamb Ribs with red miso – you will find groups of people chewing their bones as they swill sake, beer and a cocktail or two.

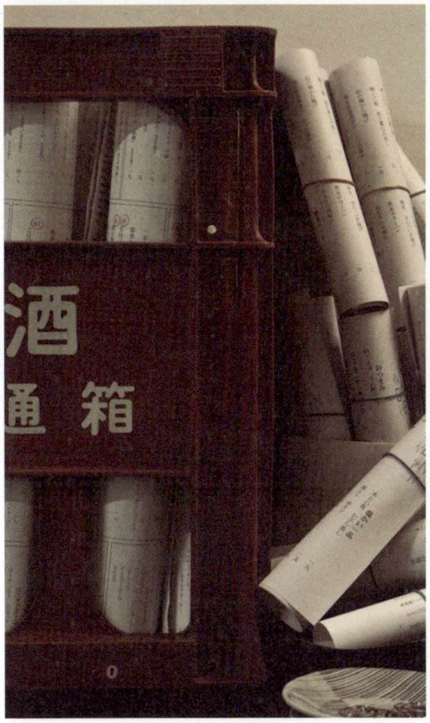
酒
通箱

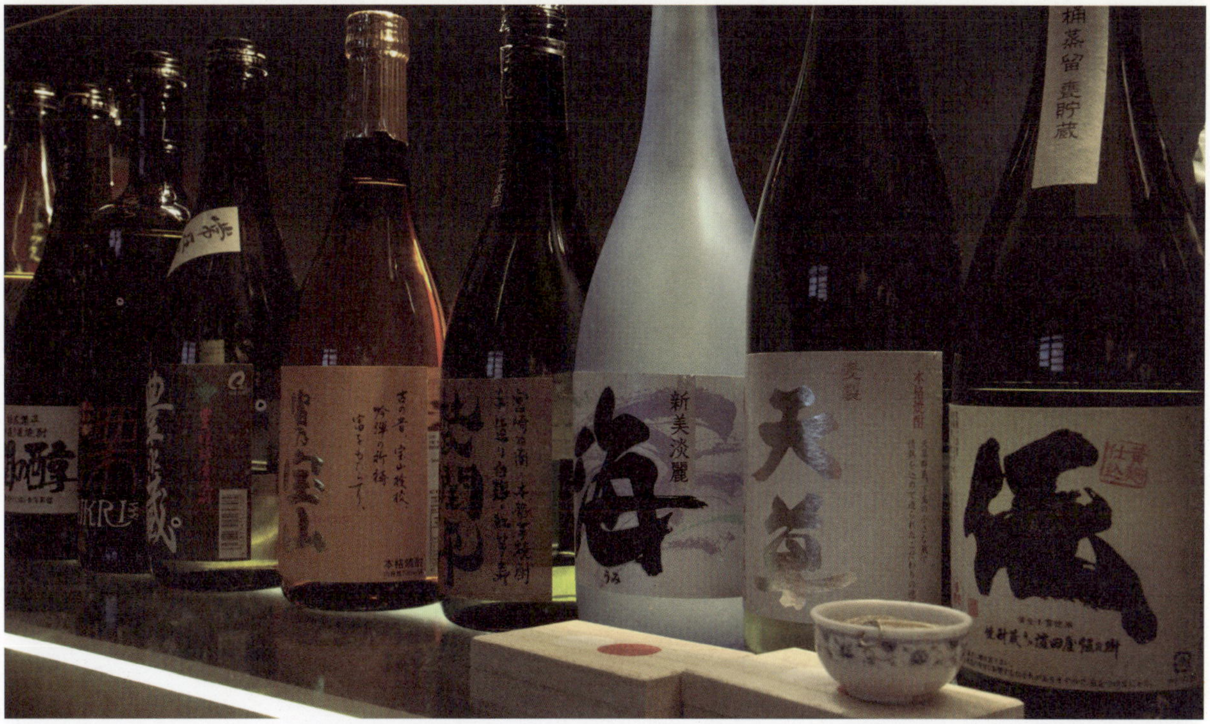
新美淡麗
海

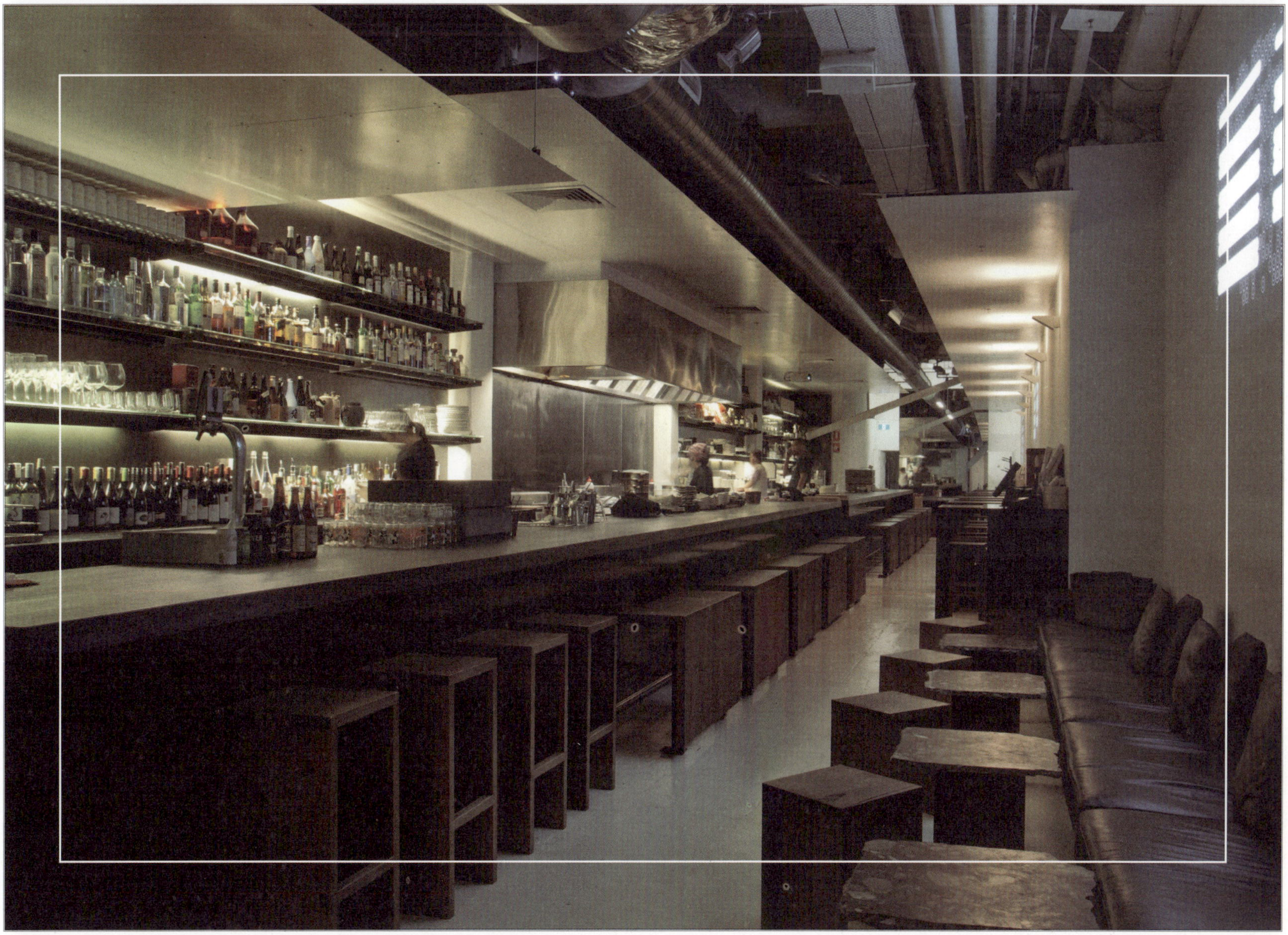

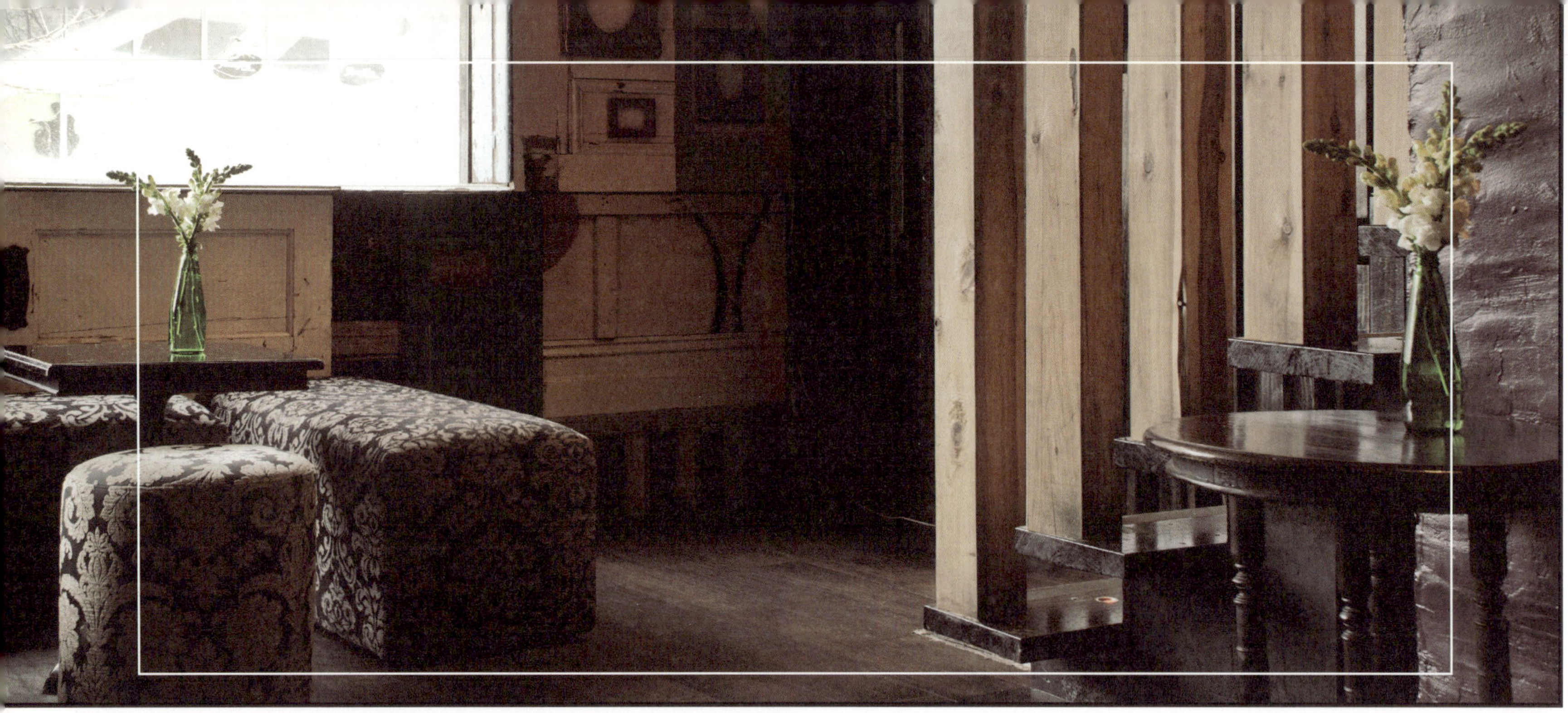

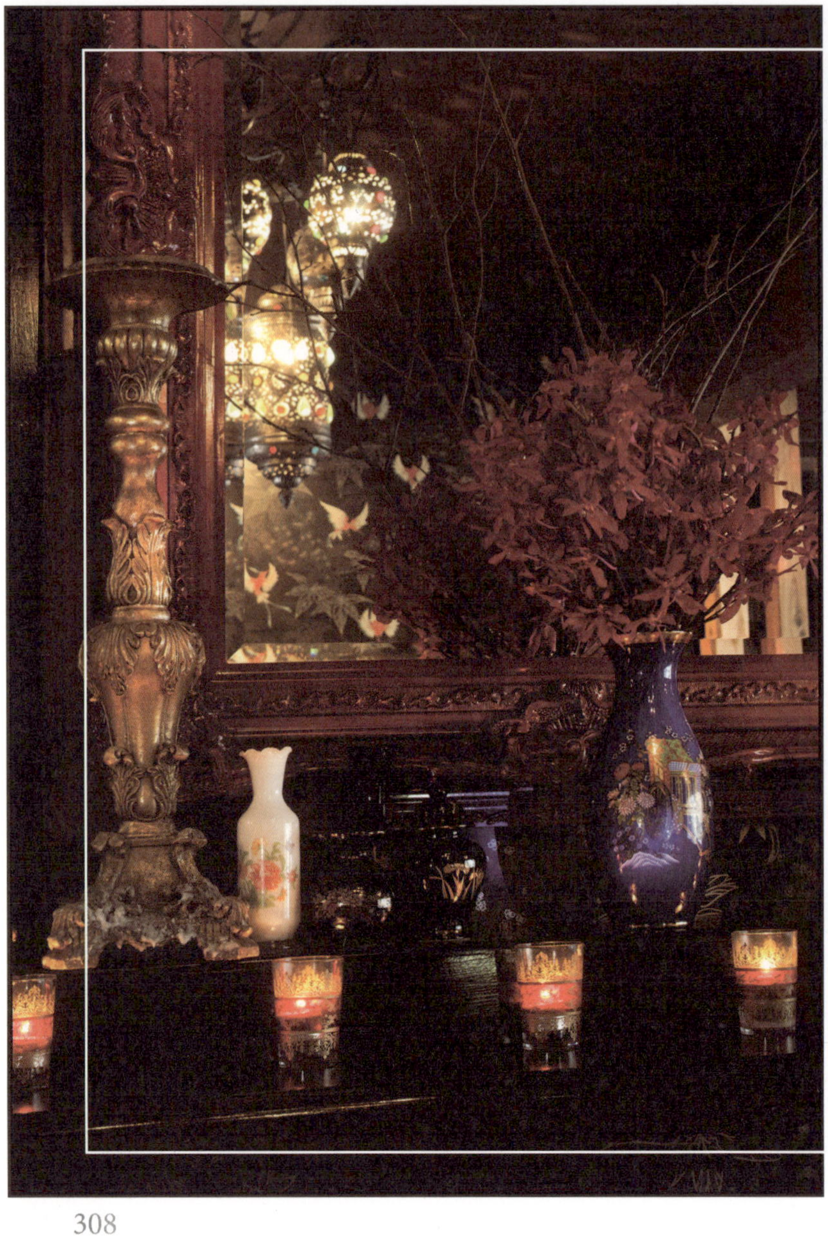

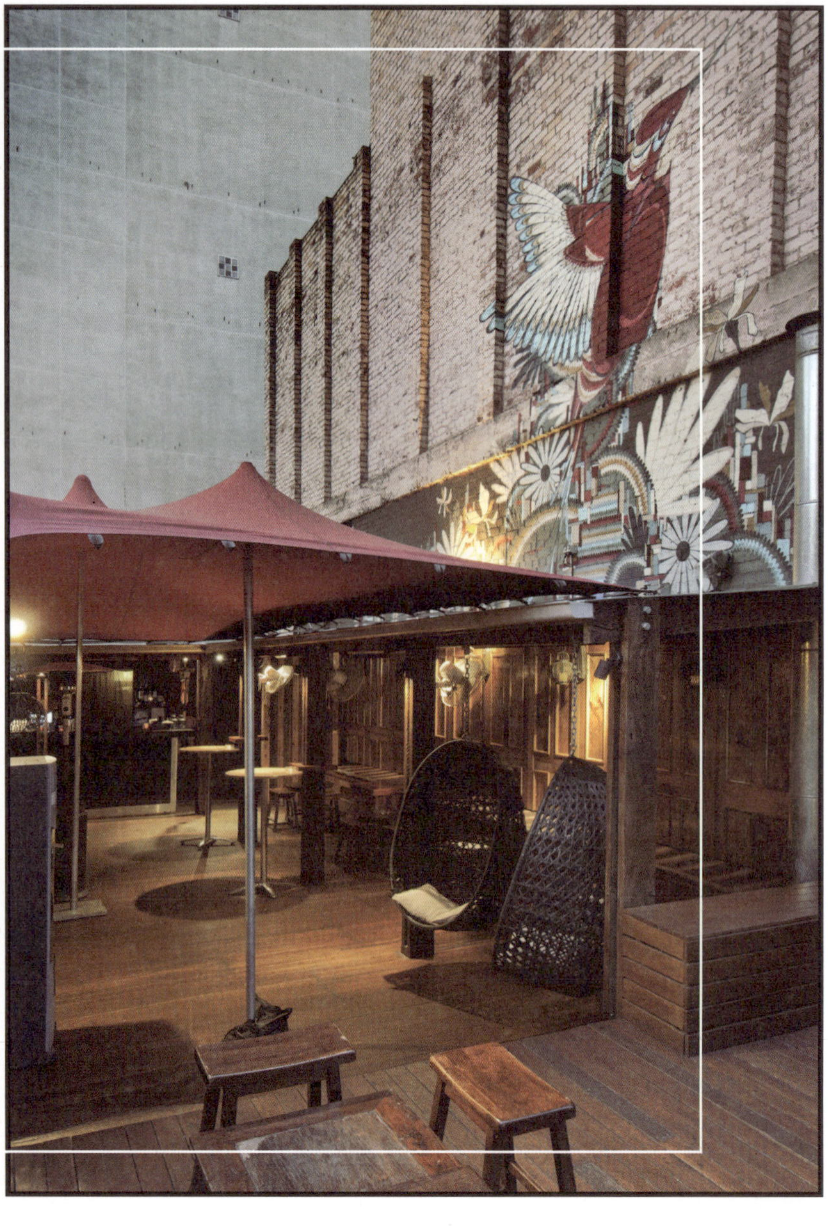

# THE RED HUMMINGBIRD

First Floor, 246 Russell St
03 96542266
www.theredhummingbird.com

Some true Melbournians may remember the five and dime karaoke bar that used to be on Russell Street near the corner of Lonsdale Street. If towards the end of its life you had crept inside, you would have found a decrepit and rundown space with an urban junkyard rooftop. After six months of elbow grease and a major revamp in January 2007, Taj Hospitality was able to give Melbourne a real gift.

Opened in a time when basement bars and minimalism were in full supremacy, The Red Hummingbird broke the mould, with its opulent classy art-house style, reminiscent of Paris or Prague. The bar comprises a first floor cocktail lounge, which is the essence of classic old world luxe with plush ottomans and a beautiful fireplace (perfect for winter). In the opulent corner, a large comfortably upholstered booth off the cocktail lounge, you can seek sanctuary surrounded by vintage trinkets and books. And of course the beautiful warm, wood-lined, Laurel Canyon-style rooftop holds its place as one of the most elite rooftops in Melbourne.

As we expect of any good bar, the beer and wine lists are sufficient, however Red Hummingbird's forte is its cocktails and these are taken very seriously.

This is truly the bar for a cocktail experience, with the old classics brought to life in a list of more elaborate and ingenious concoctions. Only premium spirits are used and when put in the hands of a professional like the Hummingbird crew, your taste-buds will be singing every time.

Designed around strawberries and guava juice, shaken with Bacardi Gold rum, lemon juice and homemade vanilla sugar, the signature cocktail, the Red Hummingbird, is a must. Topped off with an Old Skool toastie from the 'Bird Feed' menu your night is sure to take flight.

The crowd flowing through the unassuming birdcage-marked entrance is a flock of in-the-know, well dressed, social urbanites, generally within the age range of 20-35.

Across the board, Red Hummingbird has a very cosmopolitan customer base mixing professional with artsy and urban trend setters and can be counted on for a classy night out. Taj Hospitality Creative Director Kevin Singh said, "We took a risk and opened something totally opposite to the current trends...We love Melbourne, we love the urban landscape and we adore the fact there are many more rooftops still waiting to be discovered".

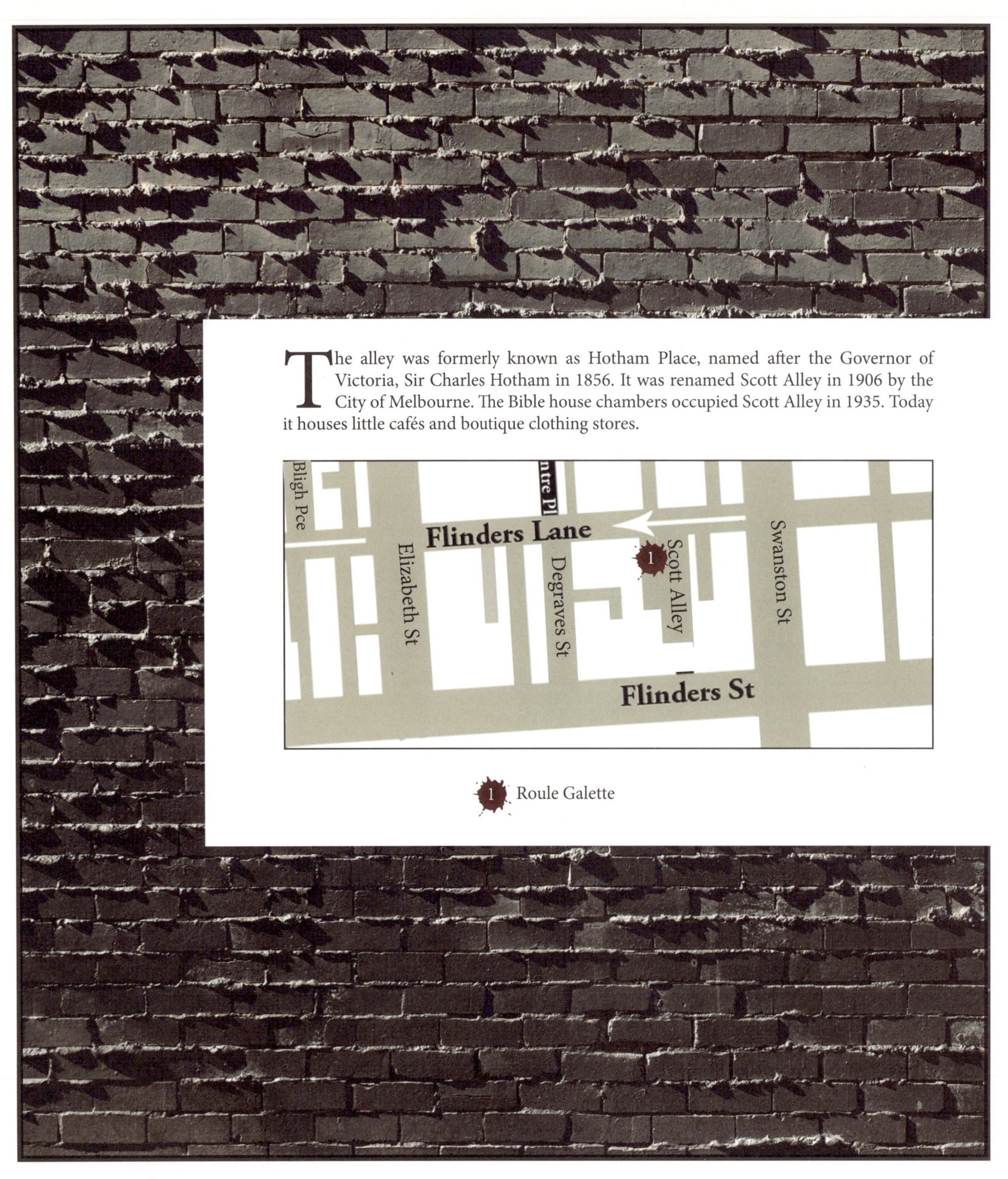

The alley was formerly known as Hotham Place, named after the Governor of Victoria, Sir Charles Hotham in 1856. It was renamed Scott Alley in 1906 by the City of Melbourne. The Bible house chambers occupied Scott Alley in 1935. Today it houses little cafés and boutique clothing stores.

1. Roule Galette

# SCOTT ALLEY

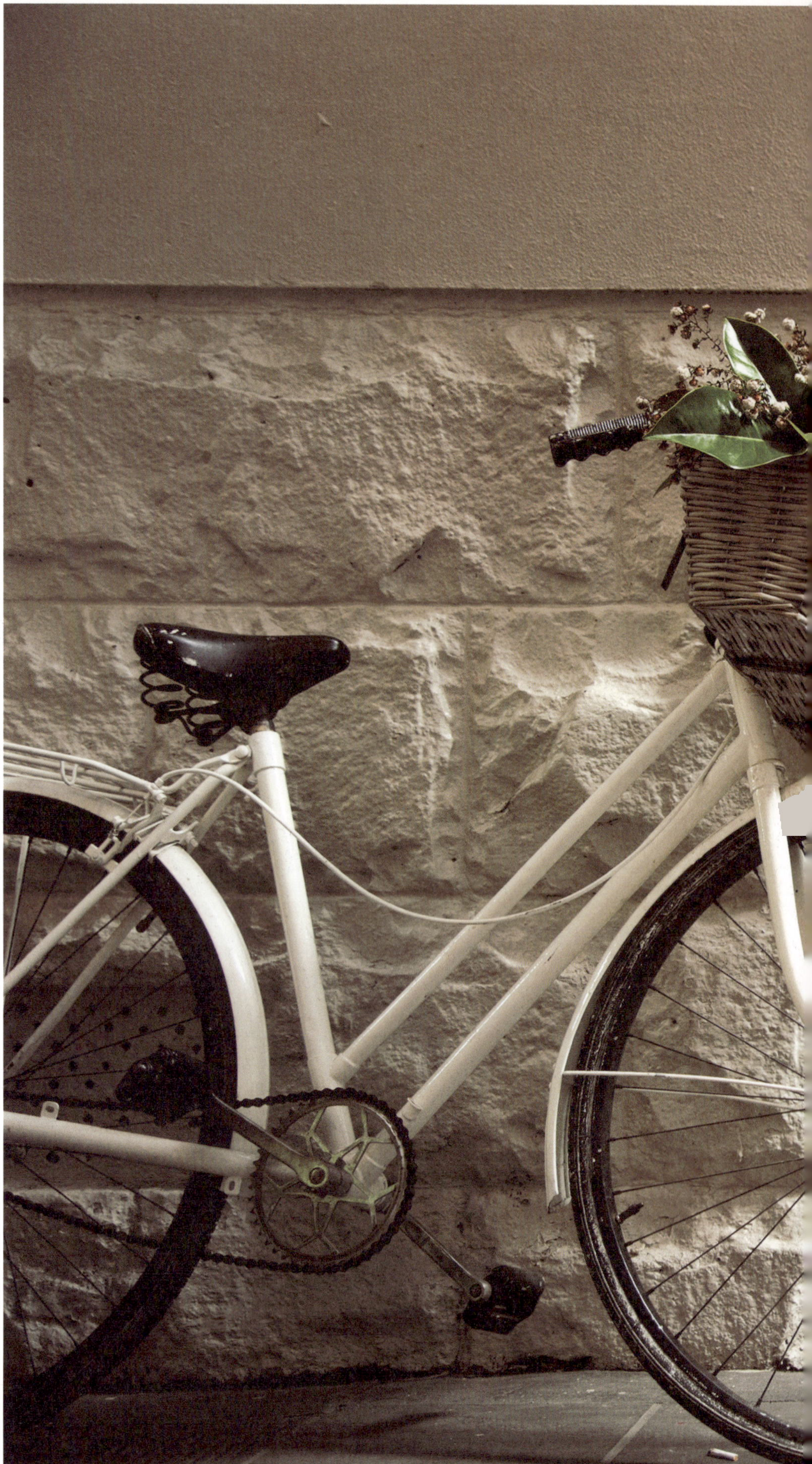

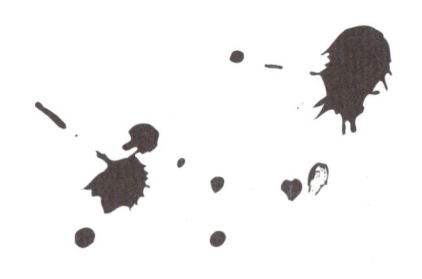

313

# ROULE GALETTE

Scott Alley
03 9639 0307
www.roulegalette.com.au

Possibly one of the tiniest laneway restaurants in Melbourne's CBD is the petite French crêperie, Roule Galette which is in Scott Alley, off Flinders Lane. Previously called Piccolo, a lot of guide books have quoted it as the smallest cafés in Melbourne.

Roule Galette's traditional crepes and galettes (savoury pancakes) have become a favourite amongst laneway explorers who have discovered the true meaning of this French cuisine.

Owner of the crêperie, Michel Dubois, opened the doors in 2007 following his move with his family from Paris. After working in IT for 20 years, he wanted to try something different in this new country he now calls home. Having fond memories of cooking a huge pile of crepes every Friday night for his 6 siblings since he was 10, Michel decided to introduce true French crepes and galettes to the people of Melbourne.

He explains that a true French "Crêpe" is a sweet pancake, served with a range of toppings including jam, sugar, lemon, Canadian maple syrup, melted chocolate, French chestnut purée, nutella and more. He said, "You will discover amazing desserts including the famous Crêpe Suzette".

"A Galette is an authentic, savoury pancake which comes from the French region of Bretagne," he said. "It is made from buckwheat flour and makes for a hearty breakfast or lunch. It is served with a range of fresh fillings including ham, cheese (from France of course, and with a wide selection depending on the recipe), smoked salmon, egg, spinach, béchamel and more."

Michel serves his galettes with a green salad and home-made dressing. Michel has always had a passion for cooking, inherited from his parents. He pays attention to selecting the best products, some imported and some local, while taking care to follow his family traditions. French music, French speaking waiters, French crêpes, French wine, Roule Galette is as close to what you would get if you were visiting France.

When Michel established his tiny crêperie he says it was a challenge and it was something new to him as a business. However the work has paid off and today the crêperie has built a reputation shaped by the people who worked there (most of the crepe and galette names on the menu are employee names) and by the clients who keep coming back.

Michel has now started a little sister, although bigger by size, Roule Galette on Rebecca walk. With a view of the river, the Casino and looking back towards the city, the new crêperie has all the hallmarks of becoming another French institution in Melbourne.

315

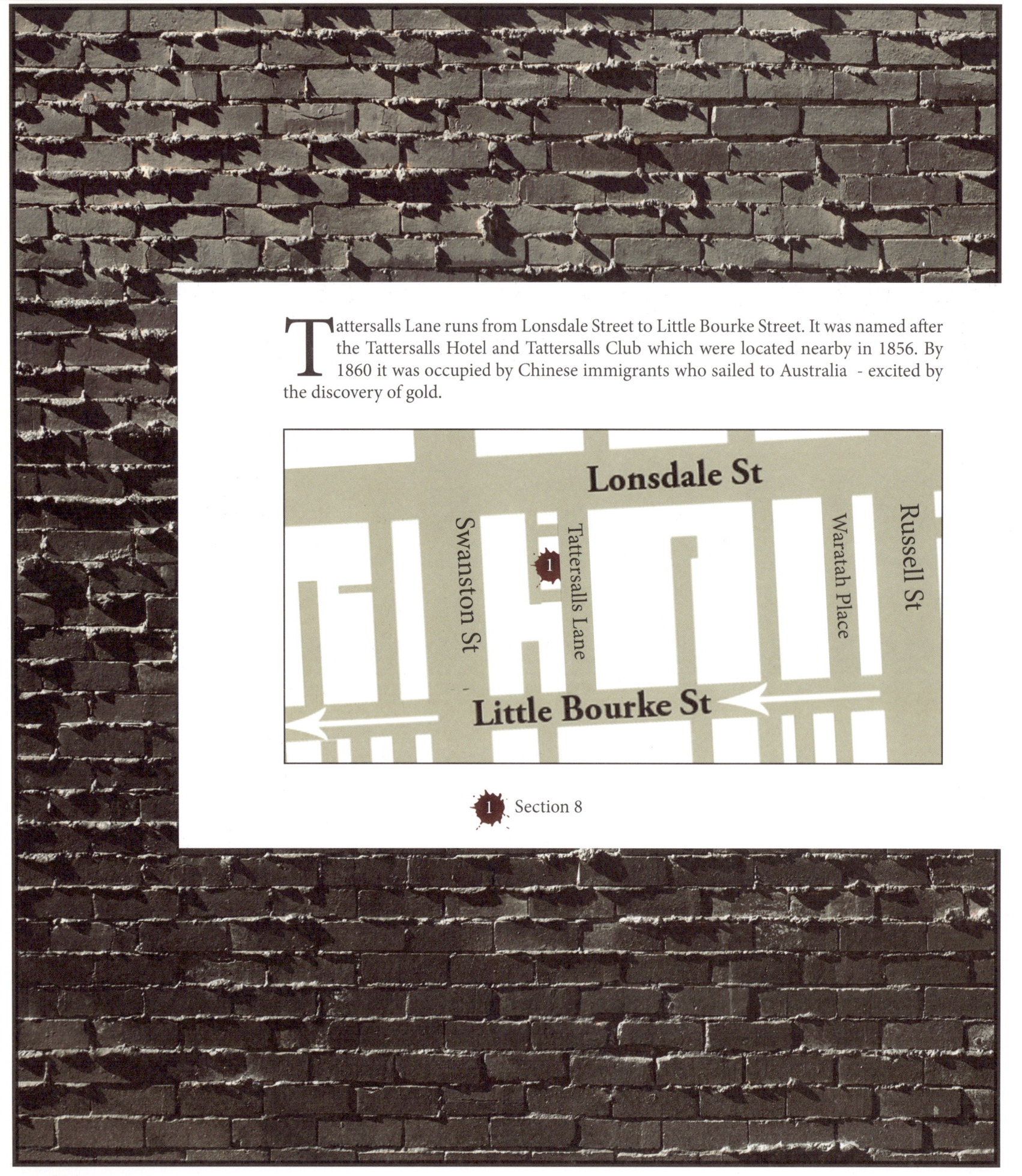

Tattersalls Lane runs from Lonsdale Street to Little Bourke Street. It was named after the Tattersalls Hotel and Tattersalls Club which were located nearby in 1856. By 1860 it was occupied by Chinese immigrants who sailed to Australia - excited by the discovery of gold.

**1** Section 8

# TATTERSALLS LANE

- ✳ MANAGEMENT RESERV...
- ✳ CAVITY SEARCH MAY...
- ✳ NO DICKHEADS
- ✳ AESTHETICALLY CHALL...
- ✳ MAYBE' MAYBE NOT
- ✳ POLITICALLY CHALLEN...
- ✳ LIES MAKE BABY JESU...
- ✳ FRIENDS ONLY

HOUSE RULES ✴

...ES THE RIGHT TO REFUSE EXIT

...APPLY

...ENGED MUST HAVE PROOF OF PERSONALITY

...GED MUST HAVE PROOF OF EMPATHY

...S CRY

**TATTERSALLS LANE TATTERSALLS LANE TATTERSALLS LANE TATTERSALLS LANE**

# SECTION 8

27-29 Tattersalls Lane
0430 291 588
www.section8.com.au

Transforming a car park into a bar took some creative, lateral thinking and when Section8 opened, it did it with style. Using an old shipping container as the bar and packing pallets for furniture, the austerity resonates perfectly with the backdrop of the laneway, street art and old, brick walls. The only rule here is "no ties", and you will be asked to remove it if you are wearing one. Such is the desire to keep this distinctive venue low-key, relaxed and anti-establishment. Outdoor heaters are an added luxury to keep the crowd warm while they choose from the wide range of drinks on offer including wine, spirits or one of Section 8's much loved cocktails. If your stomach starts to rumble you are safe with the café style menu of sandwiches and delicious sweet treats. Sharing a layered pallet creates a new sense of communal drinking and allows the conversation and joy to flow freely.

# TATTERSALLS LANE TATTERSALLS LANE TATTERSALLS LANE TATTERSALLS LANE

Previously known as Williams Lane, Waratah Place is mainly a grungy back entrance to many entrances, connecting Chinatown to the Greek quarter as well as the new QV shopping centre. Hidden bar, Manchuria, is a well-kept secret for lovers of a good drink and a social hide-out to meet good friends.

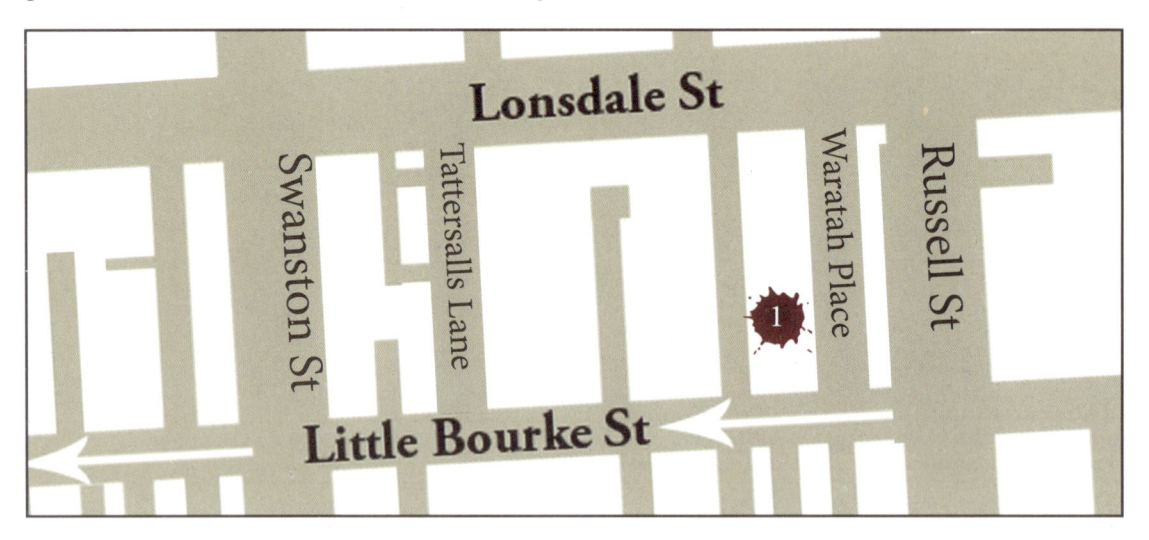

1. Manchuria

# WARATAH PLACE

324

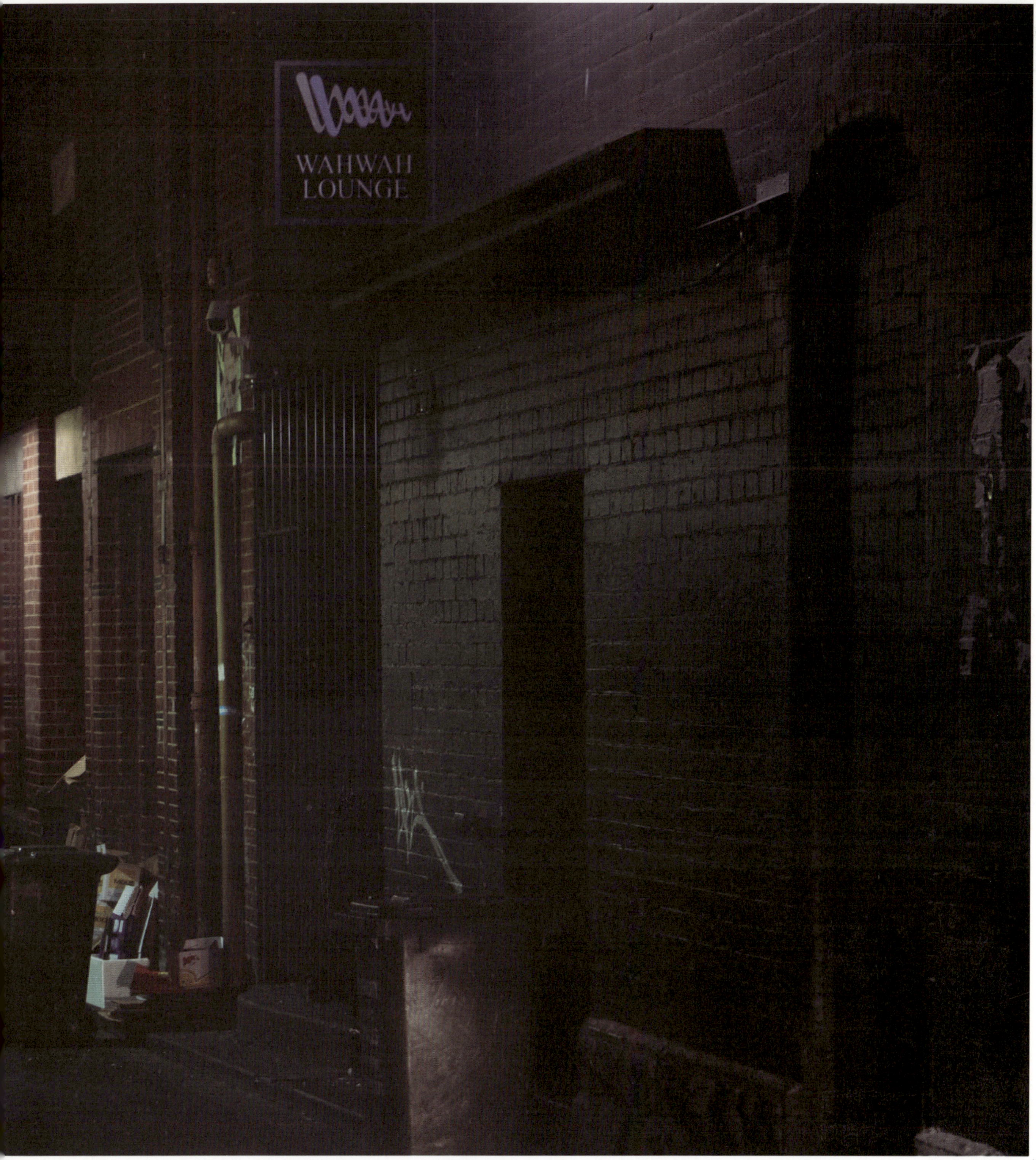
WAHWAH
LOUNGE

# MANCHURIA BAR

Level 1, 7 Waratah Place
03 9663 1997

Melbourne bars are like myths - everyone talks about them, but we are never sure if they were really there, according to Donnie Cornelis.

Travelling down a grimy back lane, Waratah Place, you will be surprised to discover the enchanting Manchuria Bar, owned by industry stalwart, Donnie Cornelis. Like the continent of Asia, Manchuria also has an immense mix of cultures on display.

Cornelis said he felt a need to come up with this mixed culture restaurant to cater for what he knew instinctively would ignite the taste buds of his fellow citizens.

"Whether your poison comes in the form of liquid, gold or silver, we're sure you'll find something to satiate those cravings. Just let us know: neat, on the rocks or in your favourite classic cocktail," are the lines written on the cocktail menu of the bar.

This cocktail bar serves small Asian style appetisers with a twist. Even the cocktails aren't served in the usual fashion. The traditional Bloody Mary, which is probably one of the most common cocktails in Australasia, has its own innovative surprise.

The purpose of visiting Manchuria Bar is to enjoy the drinks in a relaxed setting. It is one of those social places where friendships begin while sipping the cocktails. It is an excellent starter to get a relationship on the move or if you want to end it with a sweet note. The old-time music played inside the bar suits the wide and varied demographic which is as diverse as the city of Melbourne.

It comprises a blend of young and funky and late-night lovers of a good drink. The search for that ultimate euphoria of the classic opium ends here where the drug is replaced by great cocktails. The place has everything that makes it worthy of visiting it time and time again.

327

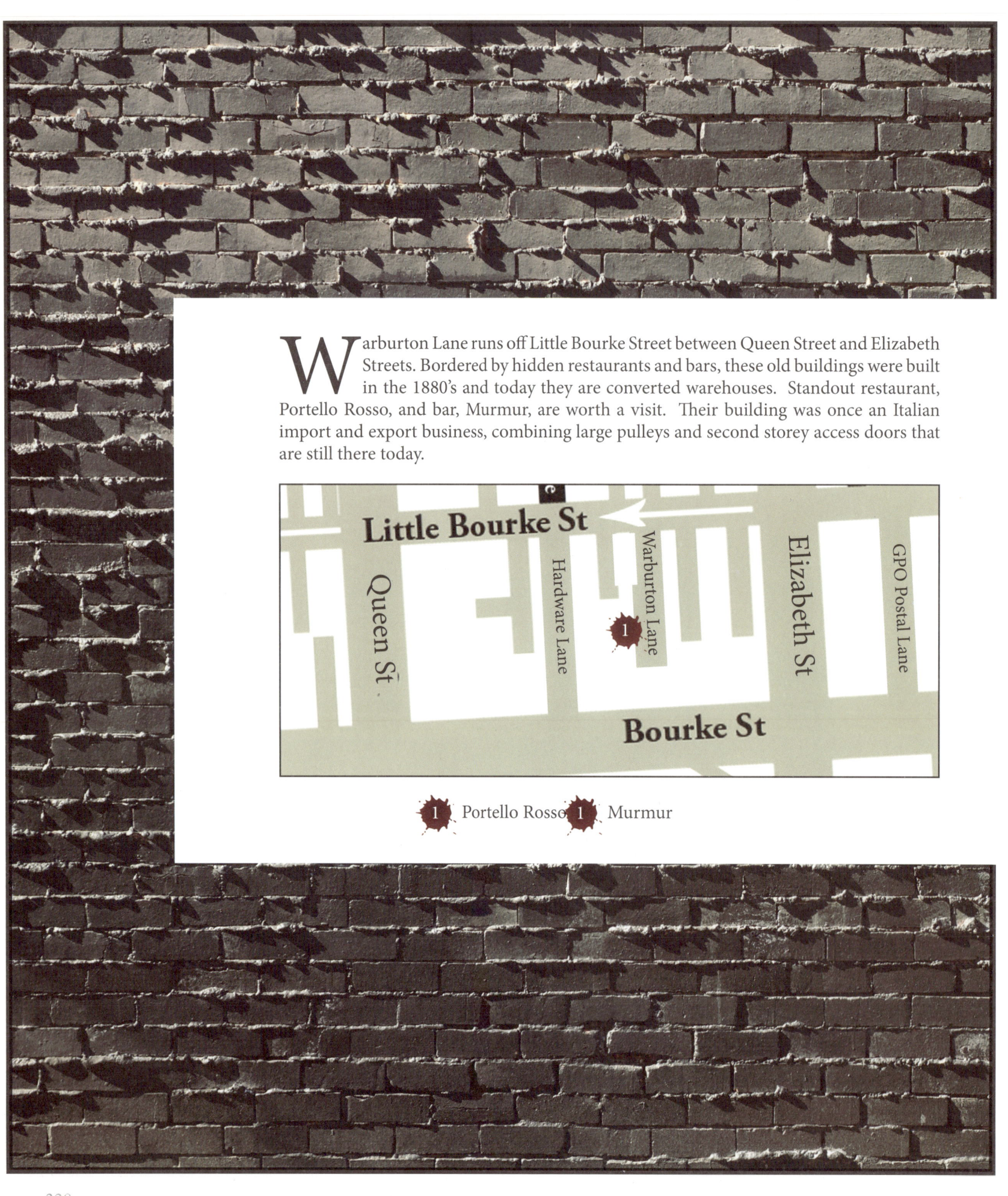

Warburton Lane runs off Little Bourke Street between Queen Street and Elizabeth Streets. Bordered by hidden restaurants and bars, these old buildings were built in the 1880's and today they are converted warehouses. Standout restaurant, Portello Rosso, and bar, Murmur, are worth a visit. Their building was once an Italian import and export business, combining large pulleys and second storey access doors that are still there today.

**1** Portello Rosso    **1** Murmur

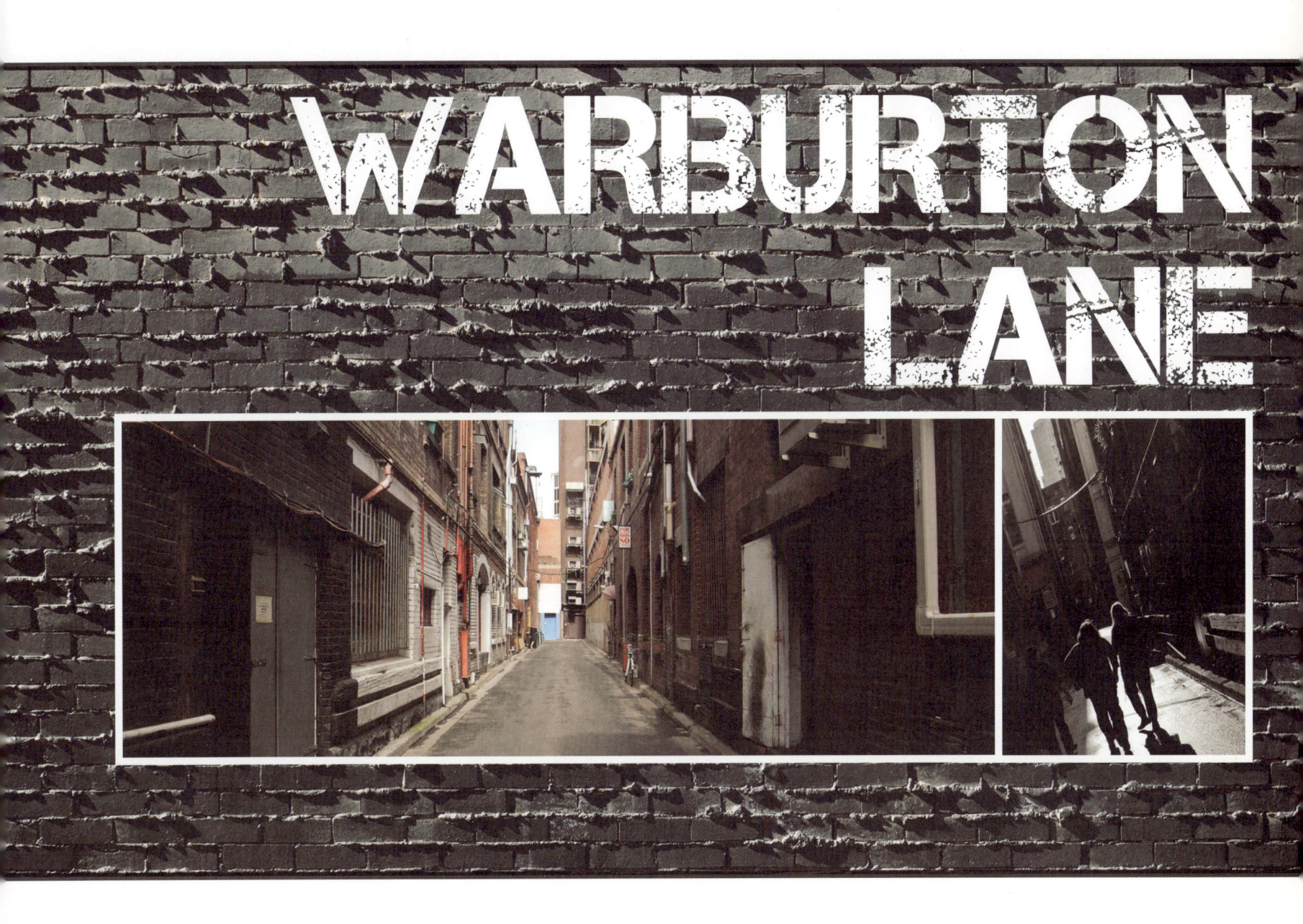

# WARBURTON LANE

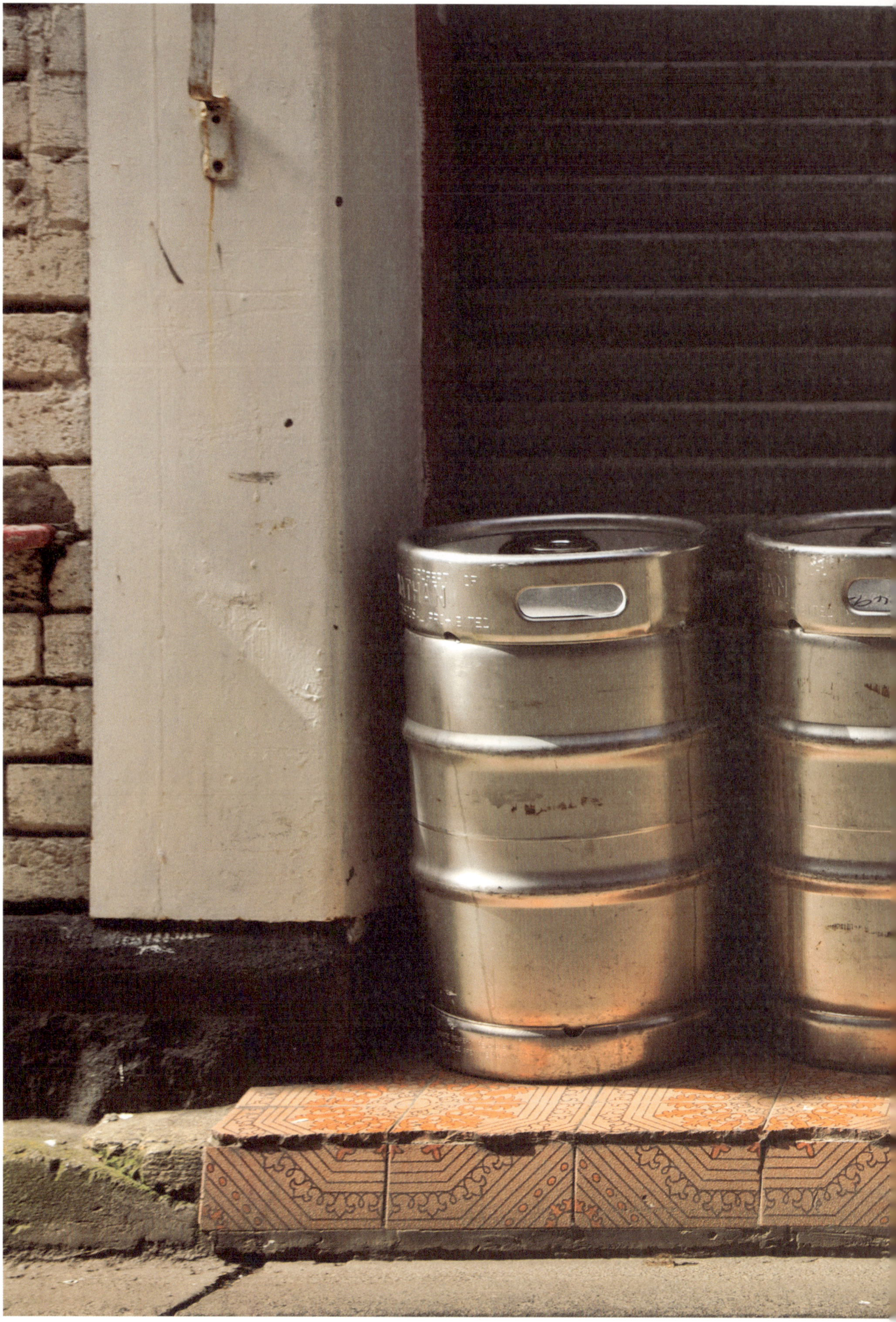

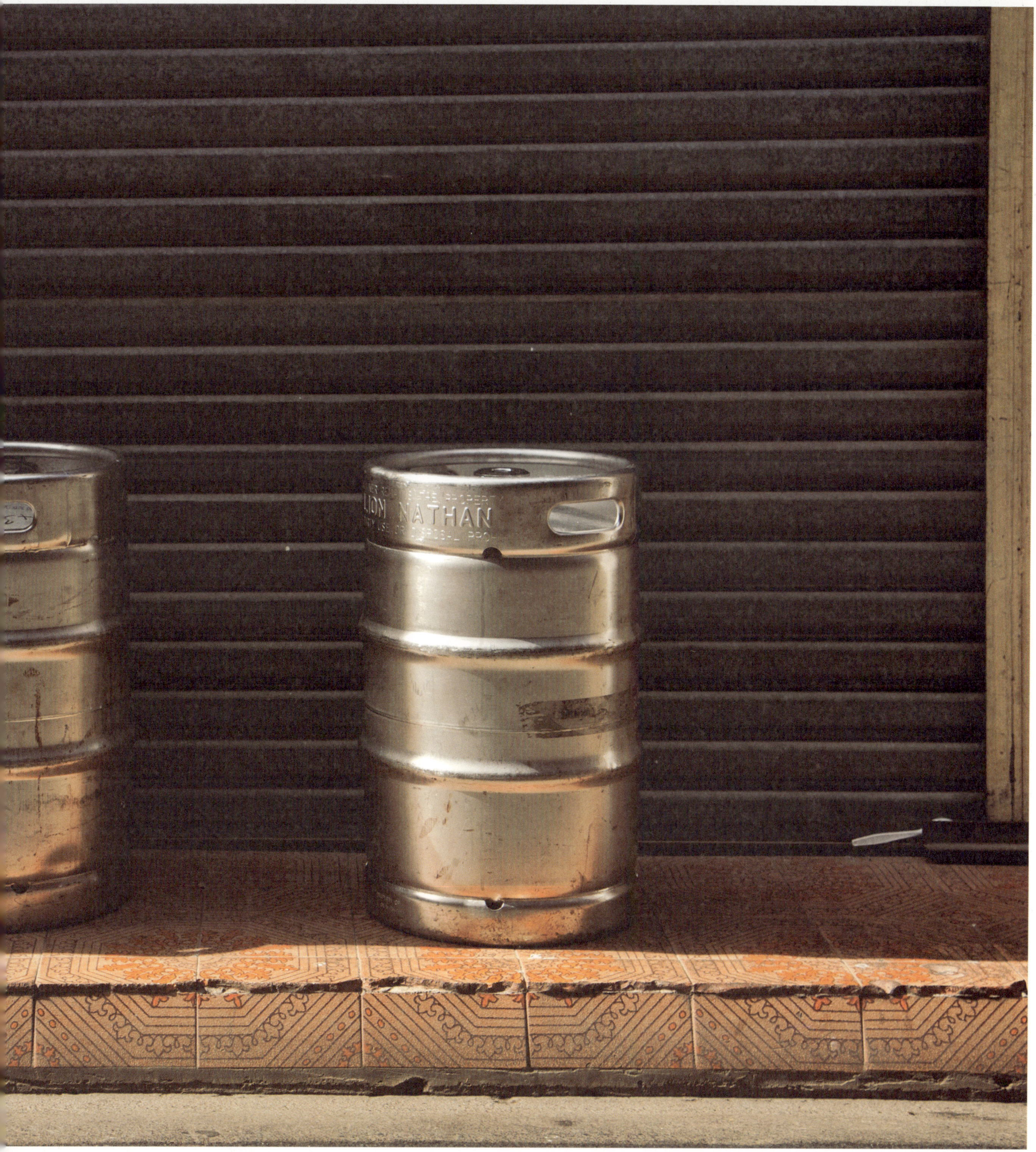
LION NATHAN

# PORTELLO ROSSO

15 Warburton Lane
03 9602 2273
www.portellorosso.com.au

**PORTELLO ROSSO IS LIKE VISITING SPAIN WITHOUT THE JETLAG**

Tucked down a laneway off the western end of Little Bourke Street, the authentic Spanish tapas and jamón restaurant, Portello Rosso, is named after the original, red warehouse doors that invite you to enter. The 1880's two-storey building down Warburton Lane is an old bastion of days gone by, complete with its antique gantry crane still in place. The transformed, warehouse space was once used as an Italian coffee import and export business, hence the pulleys and upstairs access doors.

The owners have furbished the warehouse space with an eclectic mix of Spanish ornaments and paintings. Large blackboards have been placed throughout the venue where daily specials and wines are scrawled. To add to the warehouse feel, you will be greeted with bare timber tables and a mix of old, Austrian-bent chairs and faux leather –covered benches. Steel reinforcing has been cleverly placed to house the restaurant's collection of wine.

Growing up in and around Byron Bay, Head Chef Aaron Whitney decided at a young age that he wanted to be in the hospitality industry. He dreamed of how he would run his own restaurant one day and became passionate about learning about food and wine. His rural upbringing taught him that fresh and seasonal produce not only tastes the best but also presents itself well on a dish. He has brought this experience to Portello Rosso and he says he prides himself on his honest and passionate interpretation of Spanish cooking and hospitality.

Plates are shared, produce is fresh, and wines come from Spain, Australia and around the world. Sherry, Sidra, Raciones and succulent slices of Jamón (cured, Spanish ham), are all tied together with relaxed yet professional service. Dishes such as croquettes de Jamón y queso, Galician octopus with black garlic aoili and Paella mixta, are all made with love.

You have a choice of dining upstairs or down. The upstairs, mezzanine level creates its own space while a large, communal table sits in the middle of the room downstairs for diners wanting to share their space. Of course, traditional tables for two, four or larger are also available, but it is advisable to book ahead. Group bookings are also welcome - there are three ample banquet menu options available to service larger parties.

Once inside the big, red doors, sit back, relax and soak in the Spanish and Latin soul while enjoying an authentic experience.

Estrella Galicia

PORTELLO ROSSO
e: contact@portellorosso.com.au
T: 03 9602 2273

# MURMUR

Upstairs Portello Rosso
15 Warburton Lane
03 96022273
www.portellorosso.com.au

It has taken more than a murmur to gain the reputation Melbourne bar, Murmur, has earned over the years. Hidden in the undergrowth of Melbourne's corporate jungle, this sophisticated, hideaway bar is tucked down a laneway and up a candle-lit stairwell.

Drawing a corporate and urban crowd of people "in the know", this boutique bar opened in Warburton Lane, off Little Bourke Street, in 2004. Today it is so well established, it has won "Cocktail Bar of the Year" at the Australian Bartender Awards.

Once climbing the stairs you will find this old brick storage space transformed into a hip, Cuban-style bar with one of Melbourne's finest spirits lists and an ever-changing range of premium local and international beers.

The 120 year-old building once housed a coffee import and export business, and today you will still find the upstairs trapdoor and steel gantry, once used for lifting and lowering the goods. Rough brick walls, timber floors, chesterfield lounges and the uber-stocked bar gives this warehouse space an atmosphere all of its own.

According to manager, bartender and part-owner, Andy Emans, "Since opening, we've developed a reputation for producing the highest quality cocktails in Melbourne. Our beer list, with over 34 local and international labels to choose from, is second to none".

Upstairs from Spanish tapas and jamón restaurant, Portello Rosso, Murmur takes its name from Rum rum backwards. And there is no shortage of rum to be found in this retro-urban bar. In fact the list of cocktails, wines, beers and other liquor potions could keep you drinking something new every day for years.

And drinking it is for the locals and corporate dwellers. Whether it's a cocktail after work, before dinner or after, an after-hours business meeting or a more romantic dalliance, you will find the long list of tempting drinks will satisfy the most fastidious of friends.

The beverage menu includes a serious list of cocktails, red and white wines, champagnes, home-grown and world beers, spirits and digestives.

Drop by for a drink and chat to Andy about any function you may have pending. You may find Murmur the answer to your next cocktail party, corporate function, product launch or wrap party. Whatever your occasion, intimate or large, you will leave Murmur relaxed and wondering if you have time to pop up the stairs for just one more.

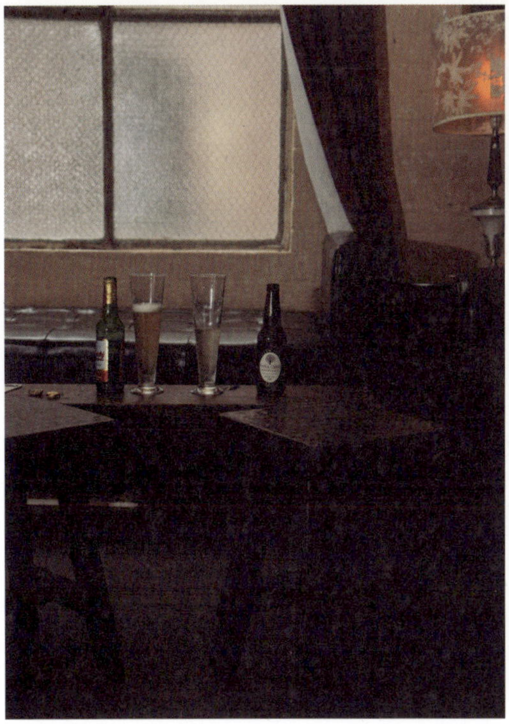

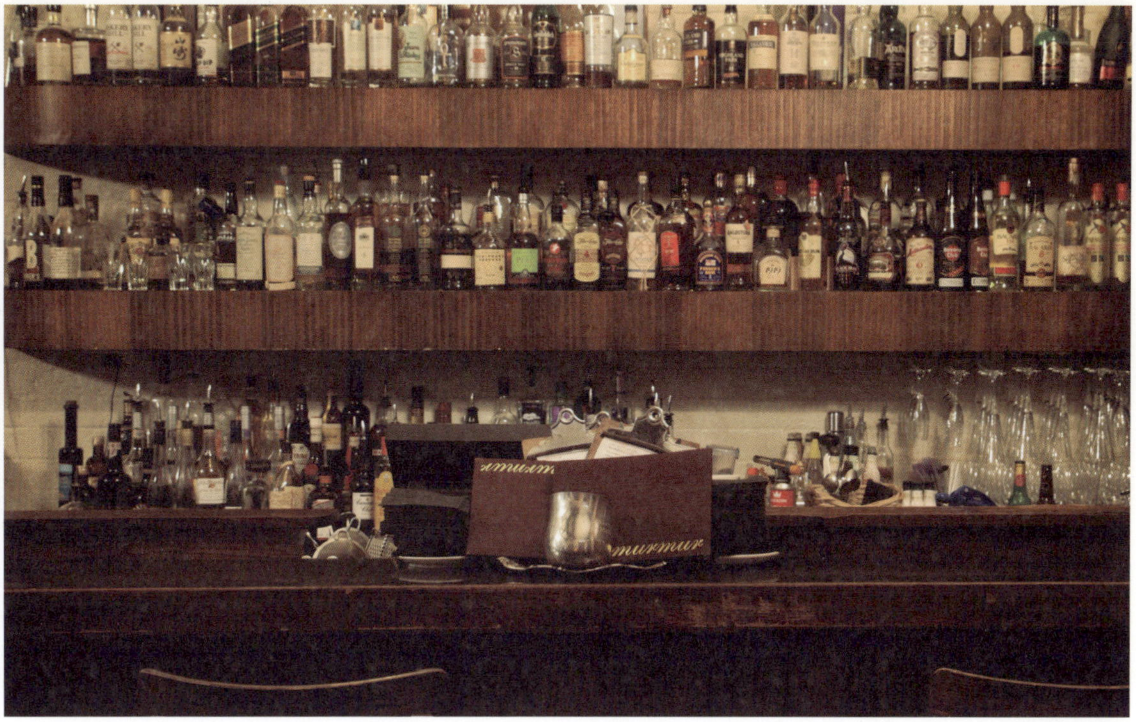
murmur

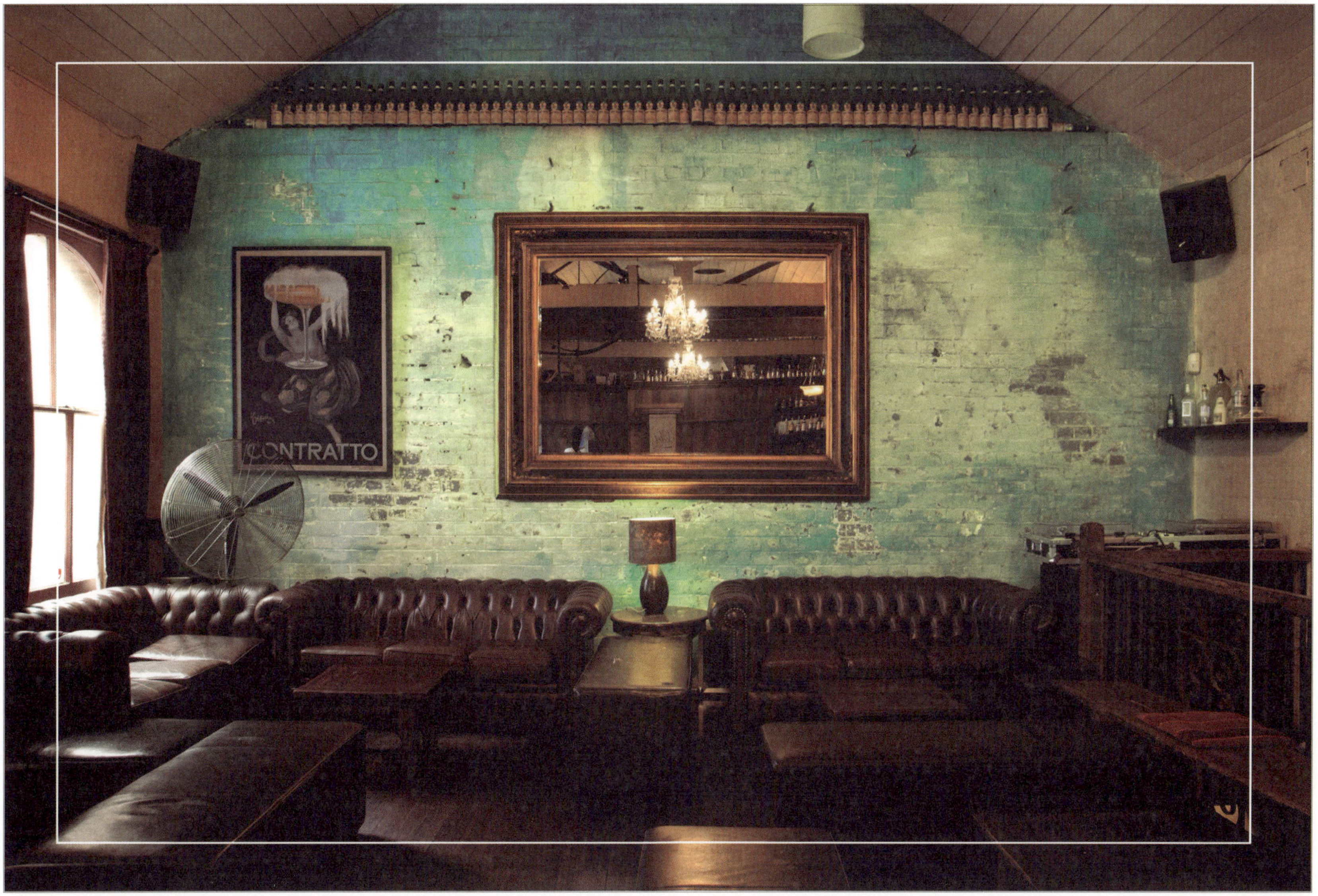
CONTRATTO

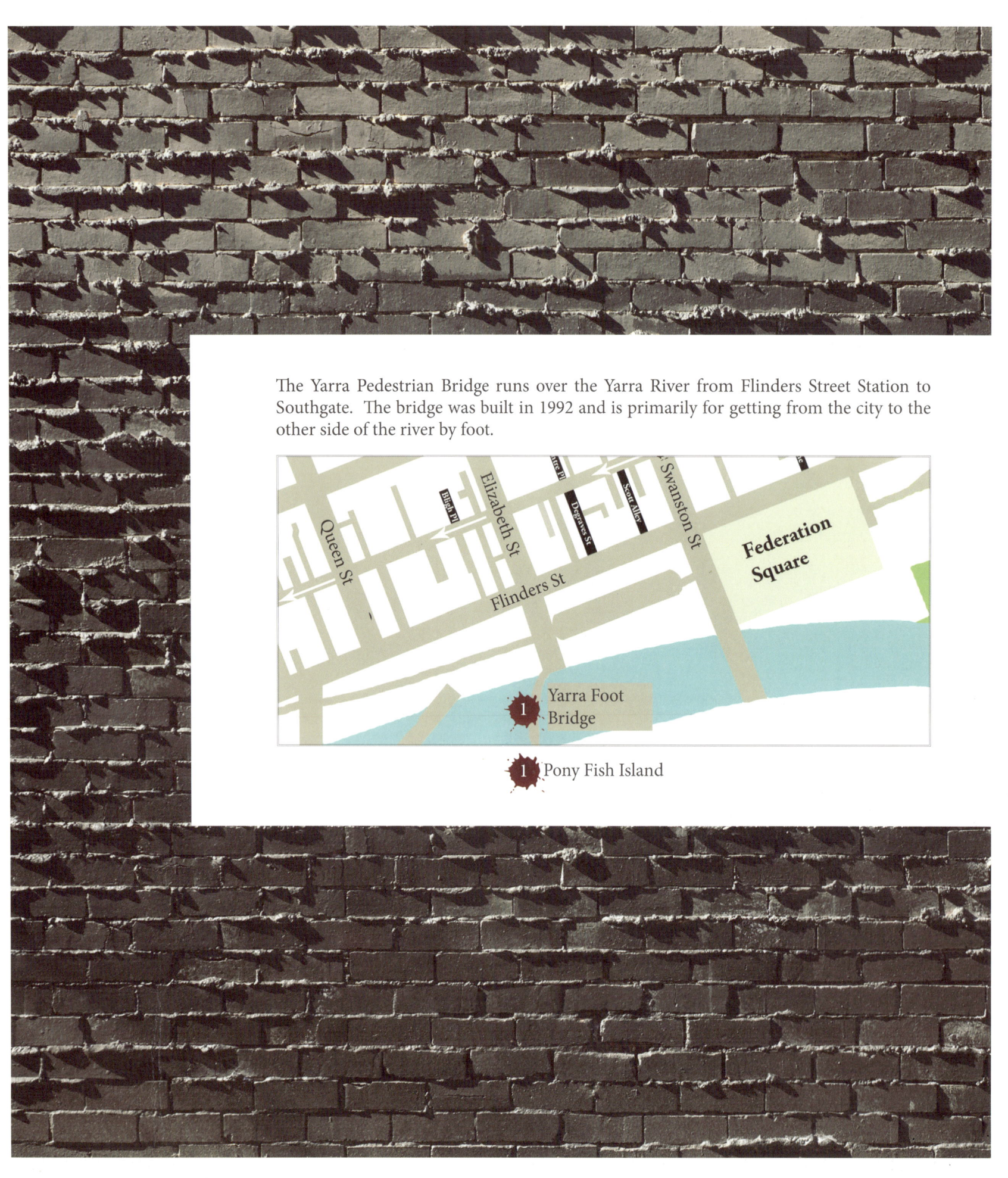

The Yarra Pedestrian Bridge runs over the Yarra River from Flinders Street Station to Southgate. The bridge was built in 1992 and is primarily for getting from the city to the other side of the river by foot.

1. Yarra Foot Bridge
1. Pony Fish Island

# YARRA FOOT BRIDGE

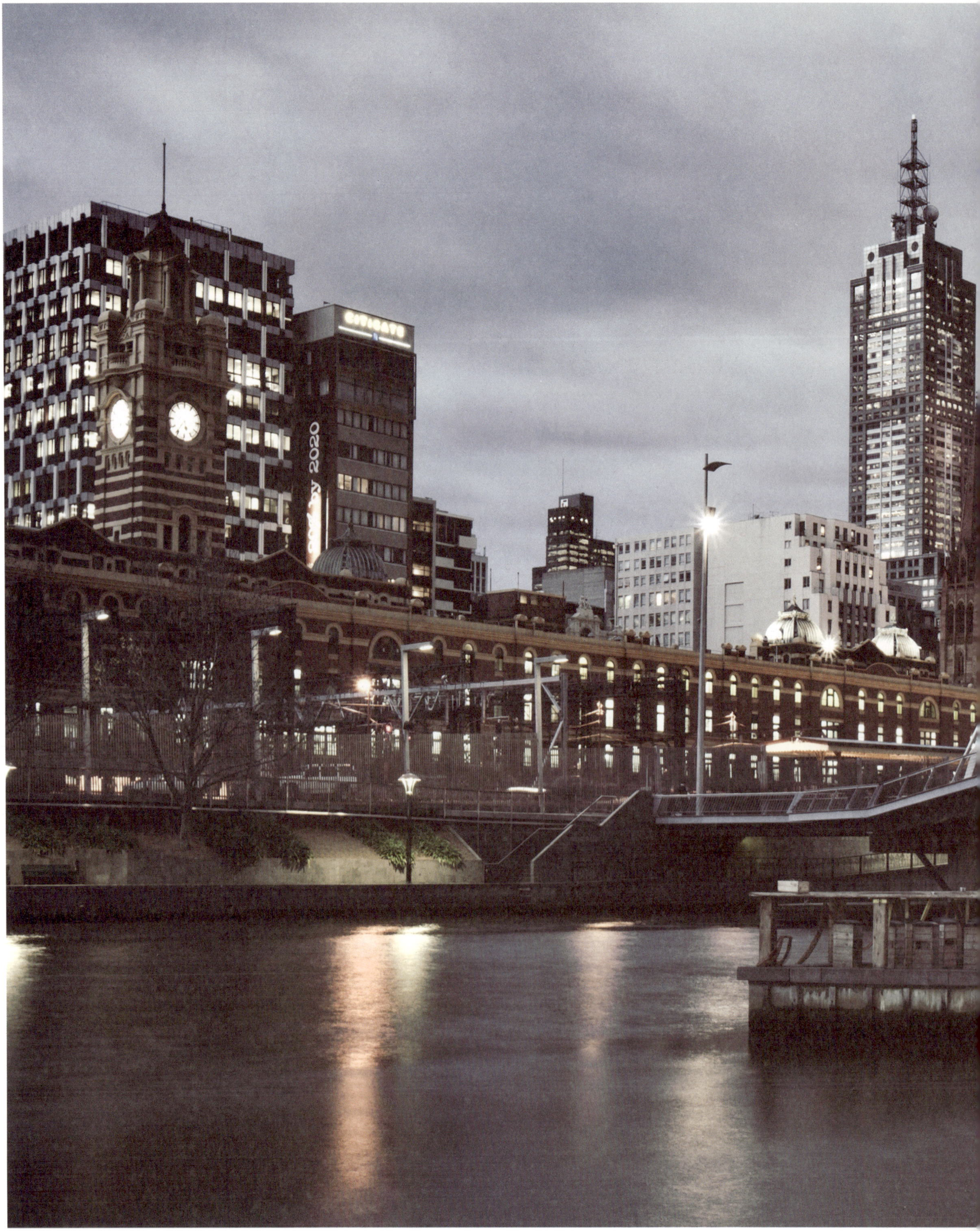

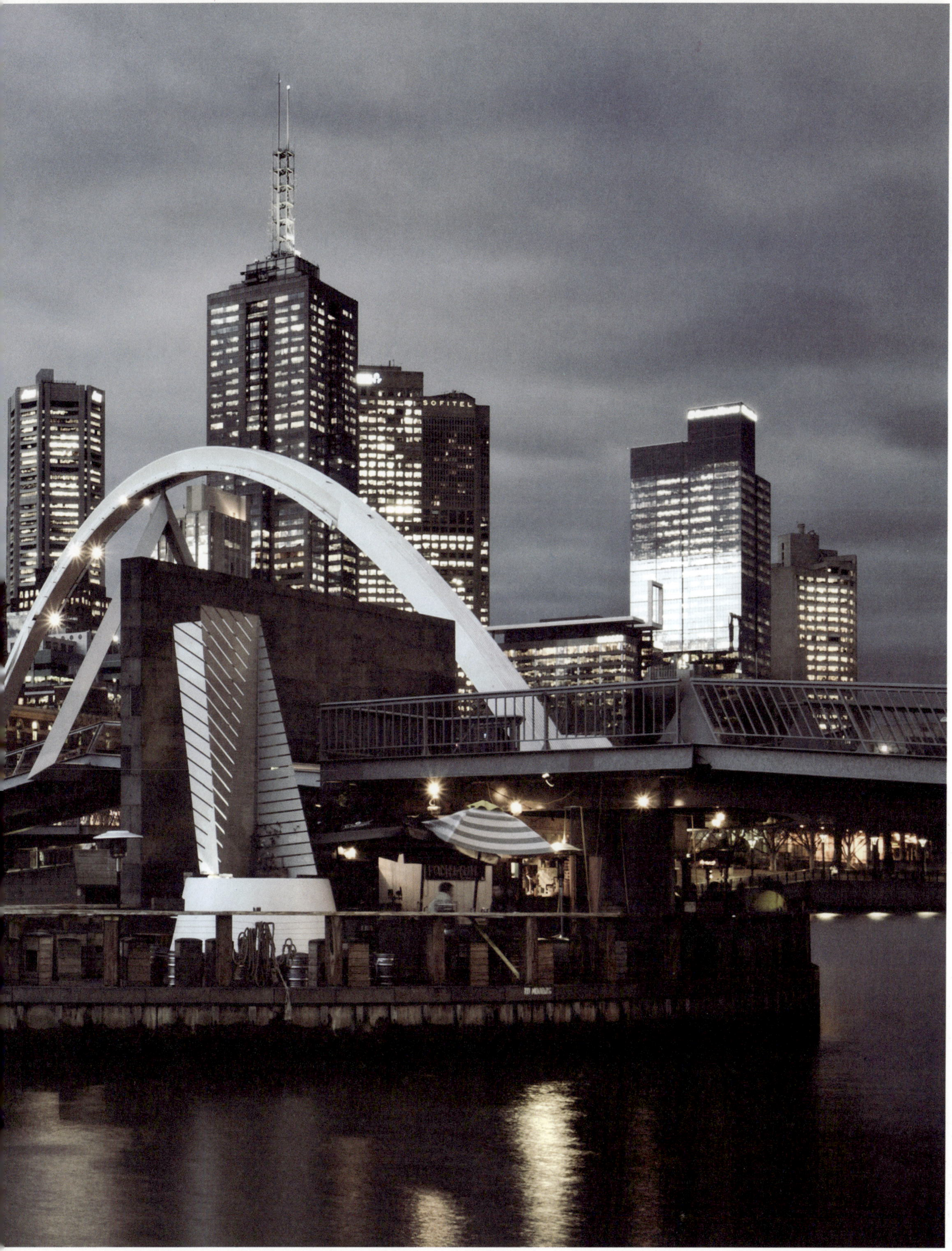
SOFITEL

# PONYFISH ISLAND

Underneath Southgate Pedestrian Bridge
0426 501 857
www.ponyfish.com.au

Jerome Borazio has become a legend in his own lifetime, when it comes to designing new, funky places for the "in-set" to wine and dine. Mix that with the influences of Grant Smile (from 360 Agency) and Andrew McKinnon (of the Taboo Group) and throw into the mixture one of the most interesting locations in Melbourne, and you have Ponyfish Island. If you can find your way to the only staircase you can descend on the underside of the Yarra Pedestrian Footbridge, you will find the little bar which is decked out in recycled timber and is literally floating on the Yarra. Try the simple menu for breakfast, lunch or dinner, going with old favourites like waffles, toasties or the hearty warmth of a good beef goulash. Have a steaming Niccolo coffee, or wet your whistle selecting from the bar's full drinks menu.

YARRA FOOT BRIDGE YARRA FOOT BRIDGE YARRA FOOT BRIDGE YARRA FOOT BRIDGE YARRA

RECIPE
INGREDIENTS
PREHEAT
CHOP   MIX
SAUTEE   BLEND
BAKE   ROAST
BOIL   BEAT
FRY   STEAM

# SIGNATURE RECIPES

Entrée

# CALAMARI WITH CHICKPEAS AND RADICCHIO

Chef, Guy Grossi and Matteo Tine. Grossi Grill.
Entrée, Serves 6

### Ingredients

Calamari
480g fresh calamari, cleaned and cut into 3cm pieces
Flour – for dusting
100ml Grossi extra virgin olive oil
2 cloves garlic, finely chopped
1 chilli, finely chopped
8 fresh basil leaves, torn
100g fresh peas, blanched
Juice of ½ a lemon
30g flat leaf parsley, chopped
Sea salt & freshly ground pepper
2 lemons cut into wedges for serving

Blanched chickpeas
Half a head of Radicchio washed and separated
Half clove of garlic finely chopped
Olive oil for frying

### Method

Calamari

Lightly dust the calamari in some flour (use a sieve if necessary). Heat olive oil in a pan and fry calamari golden brown, add the garlic, chilli and basil, and toss together, then add the peas, salt and pepper, lemon juice and some chopped parsley. Give a final toss.

Heat a small amount of olive oil in the pan and fry off finely chopped garlic. Add the chickpeas until lightly toasted and add the radicchio leaves just to wilt.

To serve

Combine the chickpeas and radicchio with the calamari in a bowl then place neatly in the centre of the plate.

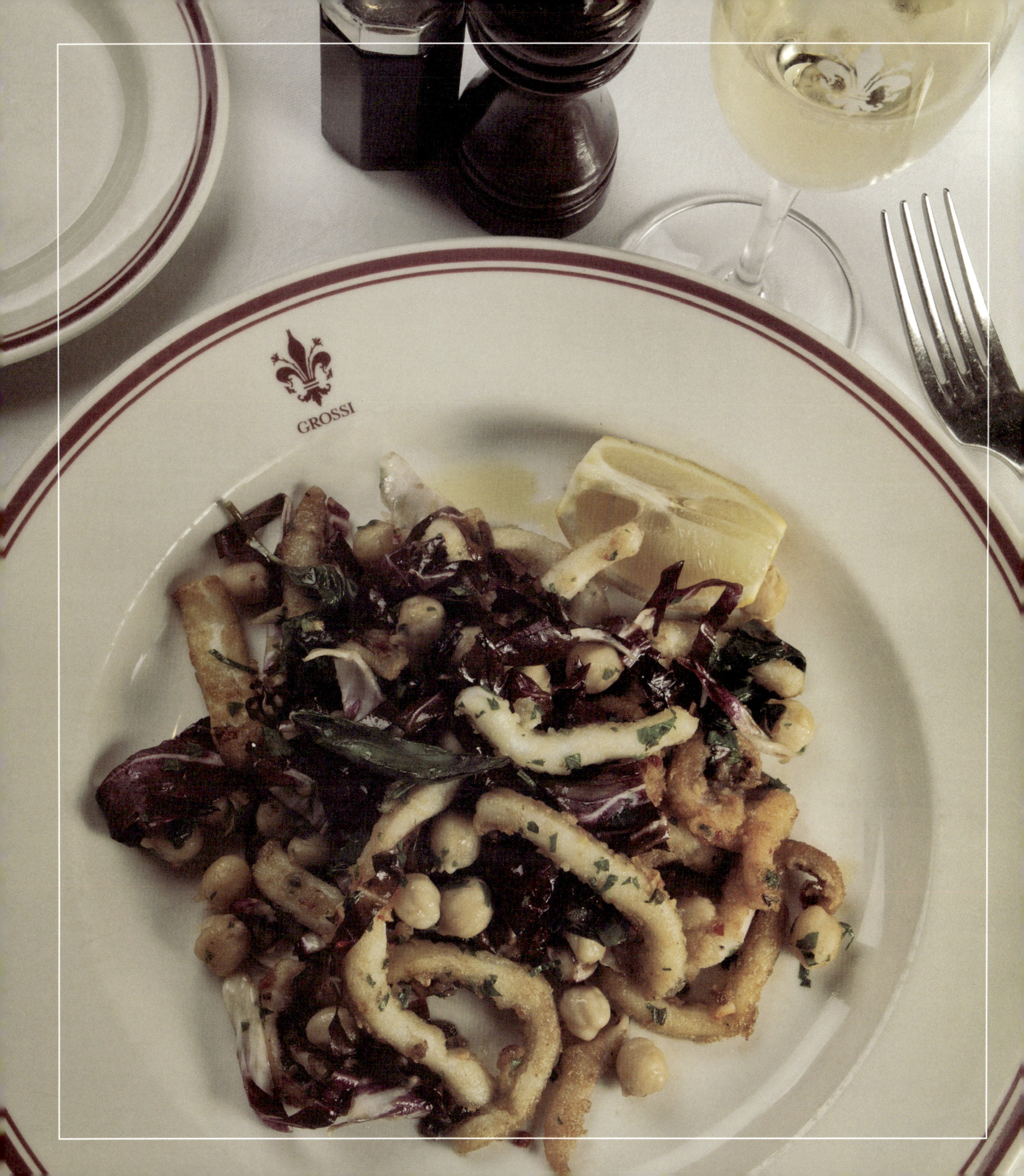
GROSSI

Entrée

# GALICIAN OCTOPUS WITH FRESH HERBS, SPANISH ONION & BLACK GARLIC

Chef, Aaron Whitney, Portello Rosso
Tapas Style, Serves 2

### Ingredients

- Octopus tenticles
- Sherry vin
- Kipfler potatoes
- Aioli
- Black garlic, sliced
- Sweet/smoked paprika
- Sea salt
- 1 garlic, sliced thinly
- 1 chilli, sliced thinly
- Oregano
- Bunch of parsley, chopped
- Bunch of mint
- 1 Spanish onion, sliced
- Sherry vin, to taste
- Extra virgin olive oil
- Sea salt & Pepper

### Method

Bring water, sherry vin and salt to the boil. Blanch octopus for 15 seconds, repeat four times. On the fourth time, leave simmering for 45 minutes. Leave to cool in liquid until just warm.

### Marinate

Remove suckers from tenticles and slice into pieces. In a marinating bowl, add tenticles, as well as chopped ingredients. Top with olive oil, refresh with vinegar and season with salt and pepper.

Pan boil the kipfler potatoes and cut into medalions. Lightly salt and dust with paprika. Top with octopus, herbs, and aioli into little stacks. Slice the garlic and place on top.

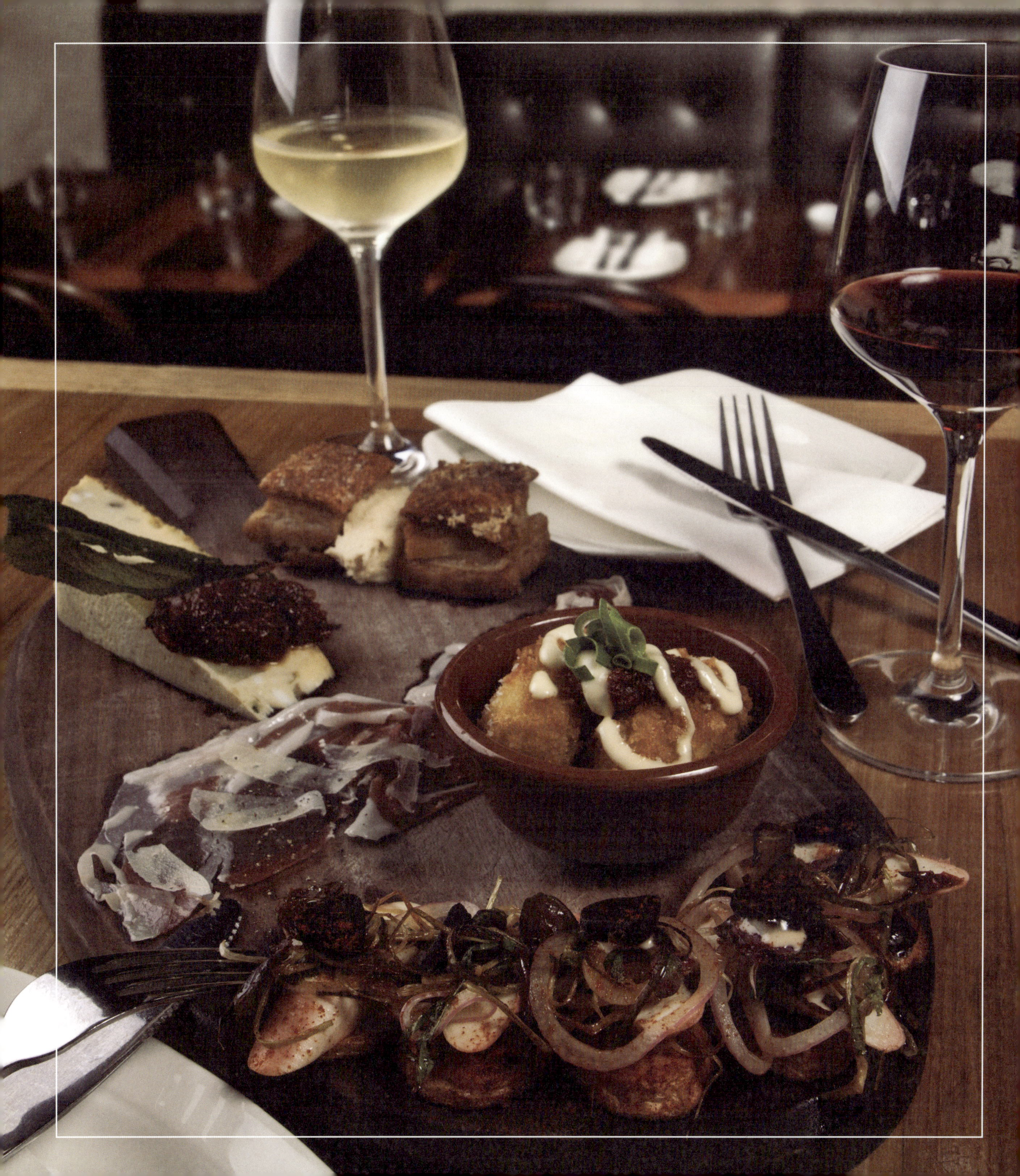

Entrée

# SPICY TUNA TATAKI WITH GARLIC SOY

Chef, Yosuke Furukawa, Izakaya Den
Entrée, Serves 4

### Ingredients

600g Yellow fin tuna (cut in square)
1/4 cup White sesame oil
1 cup Light soy sauce
1/2 cup Mirin (sweet sake)
1/2 cup Cooking sake
2 cloves garlic
10g Bonito flakes
5g Baby chives

Wasabi and chili bean tartar sauce
100g Japanese mayonnaise
2 eggs (boiled)
½ onions (diced)
10g dried parsley
8g wasabi
5g Chilli bean paste (to ban jan)

### Method

Marinated sauce

Put mirin and cooking sake into pot and heat until alcohol evaporates. Add soy sauce and bonito flakes. Keep it in the refrigerator for one night. Cut tuna into rectangular shaped rolls. Heat sesame oil in frypan and add garlic clove. When the garlic turns brown take it out and put it in the marinated sauce. Sear the tuna on all sides for 5 seconds each, then put tuna into marinated sauce and leave for 4 hours.

Wasabi and chilli bean tartar

Put diced onion and boiled eggs into food processor. Take it out and add mayonnaise and dried parsley and mix.

Separate for the two different types of tartar sauce. Put wasabi into one half and put chilli bean paste into other half.

To Serve

Place one dollop of tartar for each piece of sliced tuna, alternating the two sauces. Garnish with baby chive.

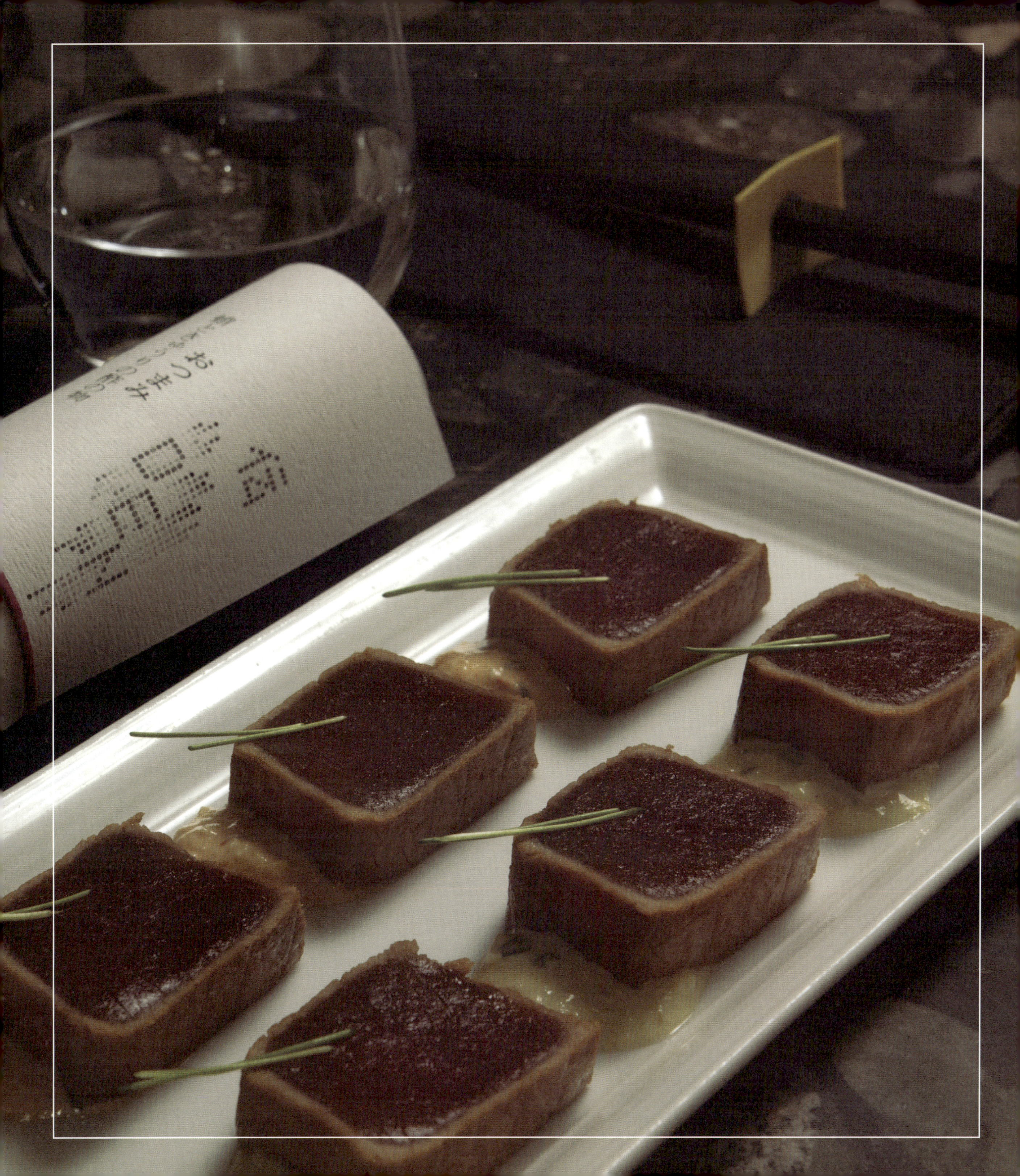
おつまみ

Entrée

# PORK BELLY WITH APPLE SLAW AND CHILLI CARAMEL

Chef, Gavin Van Staden, Red Spice Road

Entrée, Serves 4

Ingredients

800g piece pork belly
1 lt master stock
200ml chilli caramel
1 large red chilli, seeded and sliced
1 large pinch spring onions, chopped
2 cups tapioca starch
100ml light soy sauce
2 tablespoons five spice powder
1 lt vegetable oil
black vinegar

For the slaw
6 mint leaves, torn
1 pinch coriander leaves
6 Vietnamese mint leaves
6 shiso leaves, torn
50g cabbage, shredded finely
20g red cabbage, shredded finely
½ green apple, sliced finely
nuoc cham, enough to dress the slaw

Nuoc cham
2 garlic cloves
50ml fish sauce
50ml lime juice
50ml rice vinegar
2 red bullet chillies, sliced
70g castor sugar

Chilli caramel
500g castor sugar
500ml water
3 small red chillies, chopped
12 star anise
100ml fish sauce
100 ml light soy sauce

Method

Pre-heat oven to medium heat. Place the belly in a baking tray, add the master stock, cover with foil and place in oven.

Cook for around 4 hours, checking occasionally to make sure the master stock has not reduced too much. If it has, top up with a little more master stock or water.

Allow to cool slightly, remove the belly and place it on a tray and refrigerate. When chilled completely, cut the belly into 8 pieces. Put the pieces into a bowl, add the soy sauce, coat the belly then pour off the soy.

Add the tapioca starch and the five spice, making sure you coat the pork pieces evenly. Dust off any excess starch.

In a wok heat the oil to roughly 170ºC. Add the coated pork pieces to the wok being careful that the oil doesn't boil over. You may need to do this in 2 batches. Fry the pork for around 7 mins, then remove from the oil.

In a fry pan or wok heat up the chilli caramel, add the spring onions, chilli and the fried pork and cook for 30 seconds. Place the pork in a bowl, pour over the caramel and top with the apple slaw. Serve with a side dish of black vinegar.

To make the Nuoc cham

Mix all the ingredients in a bowl, stir until the sugar dissolves. Leave to stand for at least 30mins before using.

To make the Chilli caramel

In a saucepan add the sugar and the water and bring to the boil. Continue to boil until it starts to caramelise. Add the chillies, star anise, fish sauce and the soy, being careful that the caramel does not splash you. Turn down the heat and simmer for 5 minutes then turn off completely and leave for 5minutes.

Strain and set aside for later use.

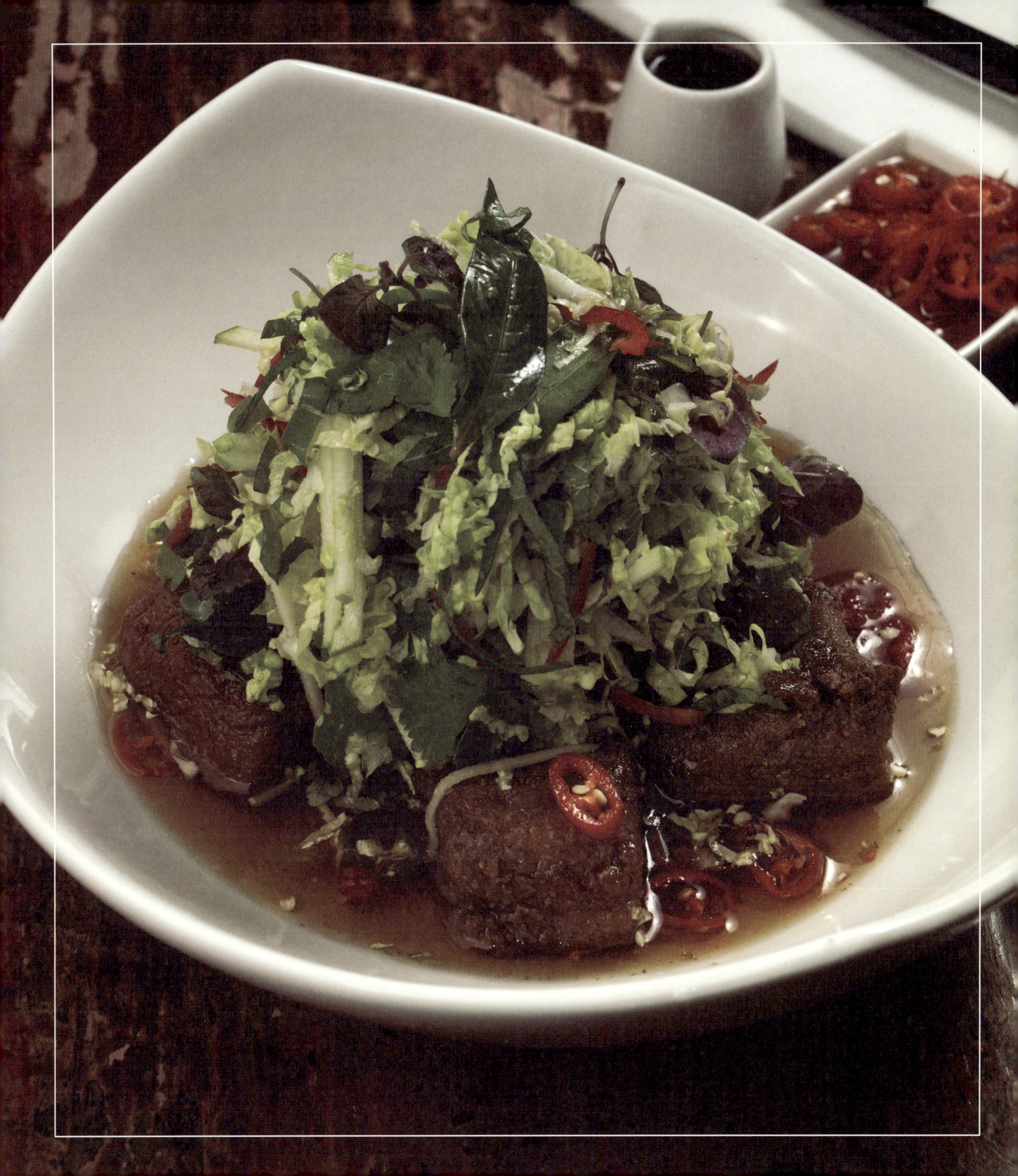

Entrée

# CHICKEN LIVER PARFAIT

Chef, Michael Nunn, Collins Quarter
Entrée, Serves 5

### Ingredients

200g chicken livers
200g melted butter
50ml port
50ml madeira
25ml brandy
75g diced shallots

1 clove diced garlic
1 sprig thyme
2 eggs (at room temperature)
pink salt
white pepper

### Method

Warm livers and eggs to blood temperature. Heat butter to 55°C.
Boil shallots, garlic, thyme and alcohol until almost dry. In a jug blender, blitz shallot mix, livers and salt. Add eggs one at a time.
Pass through fine strainer. With a stick blender, gradually add butter to liver mix.
Test for seasoning and pour into a cling film lined terrine mould in bain marie. Cover with tin foil and cook for 45 minutes at 160°C.
Chill until set.

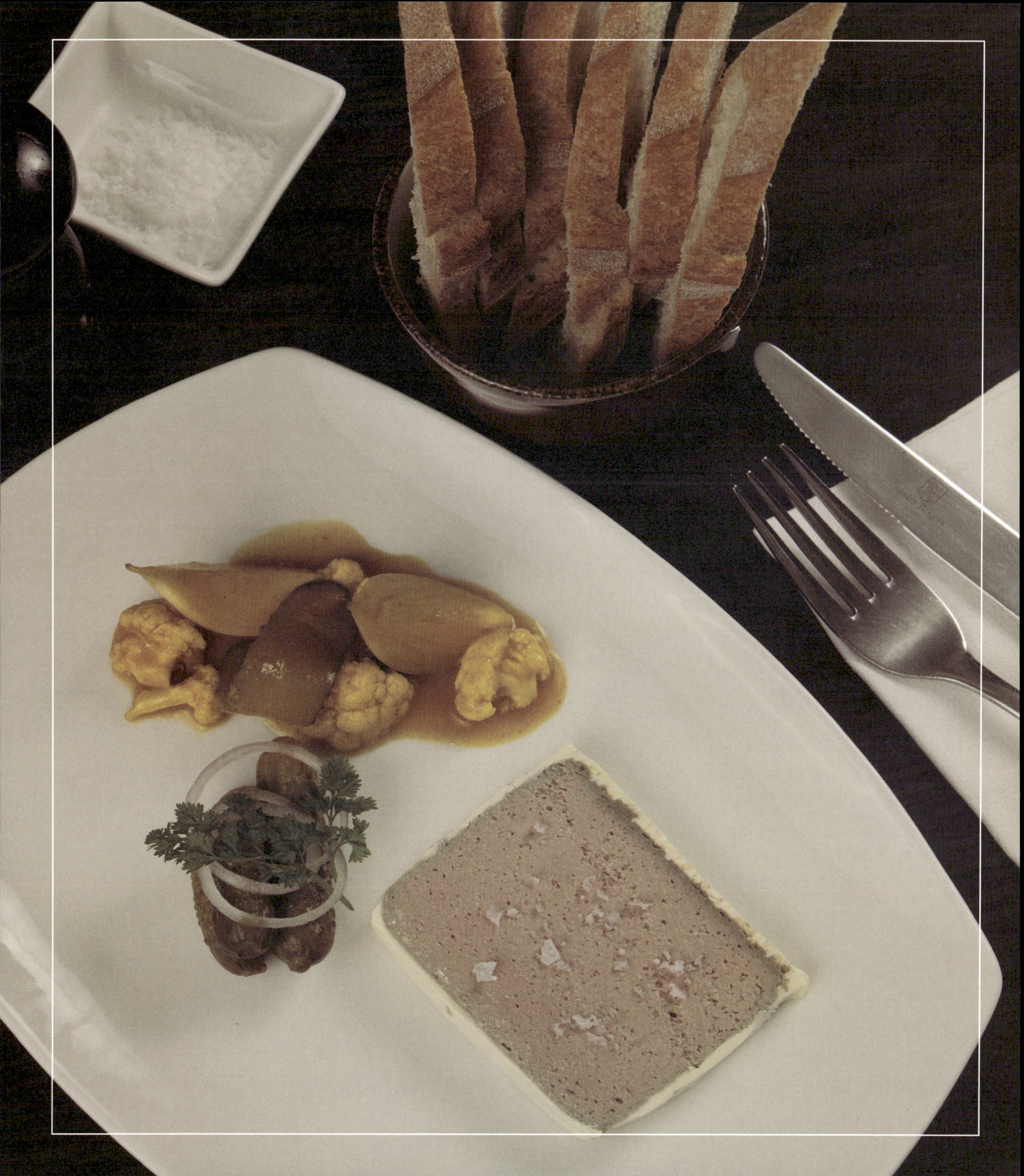

Entrée

# AMOK, A TRADITIONAL CAMBODIAN STEAMED FISH CURRY

Chef, Agus Putro. Bopha Devi
Main, Serves 4

## Ingredients

Kroeung
2 dried red chillies
3 cloves garlic
2 tbsp galangal, cut small
1 tbsp lemongrass stalk
Zest of 1/4 kaffir lime
1 tsp salt
300g silver beet leaves

1 tbsp fish sauce
3 tbsp kaffir lime leaves
1 red capsicum
Banana leaves to make cups
400g fish fillet
3/4 cup coconut cream
2 cups coconut milk
1 egg, beaten

## Method

Kroeung
First, make the kroeung in a mortar and pestle.
Fish
Slice the fish fillet thinly and set aside.
Remove the green of the silver beet from stalk; slice the kaffir lime leaves and red capsicum thinly. Stir the kroeung into one cup of coconut milk, and when it has dissolved add the egg, fish sauce and sliced fish. Then add the remaining coconut milk and mix well.
Banana leaf cups
First, clean the leaves with a wet cloth, then dip them into boiling water so they are soft and do not crack when being shaped. Cut circles 25cm in diameter and place two together. This is important, as one leaf is not strong enough to hold the mixture. Make a square in the middle of the circle, this will be the bottom of the cup. Then, put a thumb on one right angle of the square and pull up two sides, tucking in the fold, and pinning together with a tiny bamboo stick. Then move to the next right and repeat. Continue until all four sides of the cup are held together.
Make the banana leaf cups, and then put the silver beet leaves in first and top with the fish mixture. Steam for about 20 minutes or until the coconut milk is solid, but still moist. Before serving, top each cup with coconut cream and garnish with red capsicum.

Amok
This traditional Khmer curry comes from the region of Angkor Wat (North-West Cambodia). The ancient imperial gastronomy can be glimpsed in this dish which is steamed in a banana-leaf cup combining fish, coconut milk.

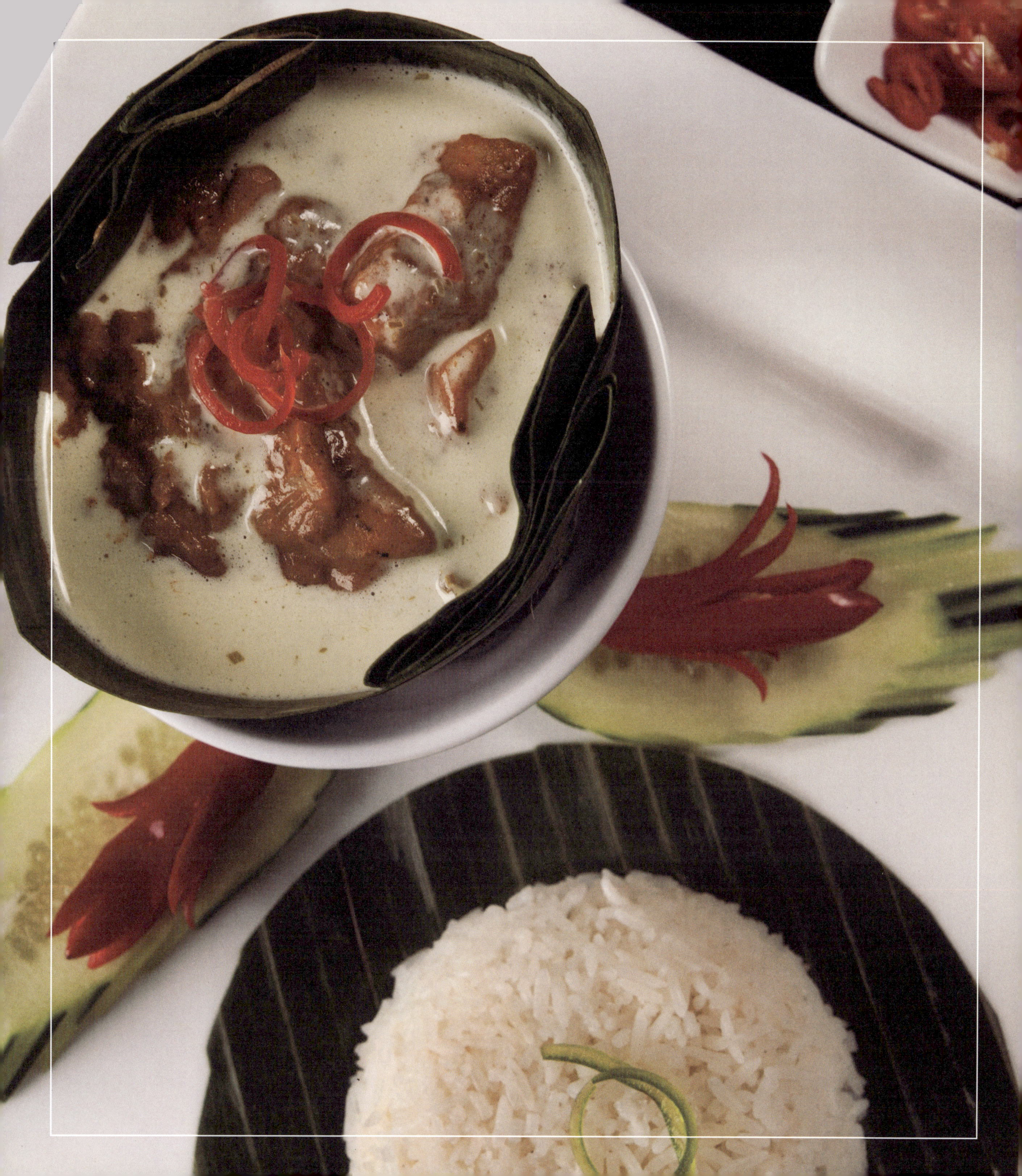

Entrée

# PORK & PEANUT TAPIOCA DUMPLINGS

Chef, Narlimol Chantrapen, Cookie
Entrée, Serves 6  (Makes approx. 30 dumplings)

Ingredients

400g tapioca / sago
Water
½ tsp ground white pepper
1 tbsp coriander root, chopped coarsely
1 tbsp garlic, chopped coarsely
400g pork mince
400g palm sugar
1 tbsp fish sauce

50g pickled turnip
1.5 cups roasted peanuts, crushed
Lettuce
Coriander
Chilli sliced
Garlic finely chopped & deep fried

Method

Place tapioca in a bowl and just cover with water. Let this stand for 2 hours. In a mortar and pestle, pound the pepper, coriander root and garlic to make a paste.

In a wok or pan, cook the pork, palm sugar and pepper paste over a low heat until sticky. This will take about 10 - 15 minutes. Add fish sauce, pickled turnip and peanuts.

Mix well. When cool to touch, take 1 teaspoon of mixture and roll into a marble. Pour a touch of hot water over the tapioca and squeeze with your hand to make a paste. Be careful not to add too much water.

Take a heaped teaspoon piece of tapioca dough and press between thumb and forefinger to make a disc about the size of a 50c piece. Place a pork marble on tapioca, roll with moist hands to form an even covering.

Steam for 8 minutes or until translucent.

Serve with lettuce, coriander, chilli and deep fried garlic.

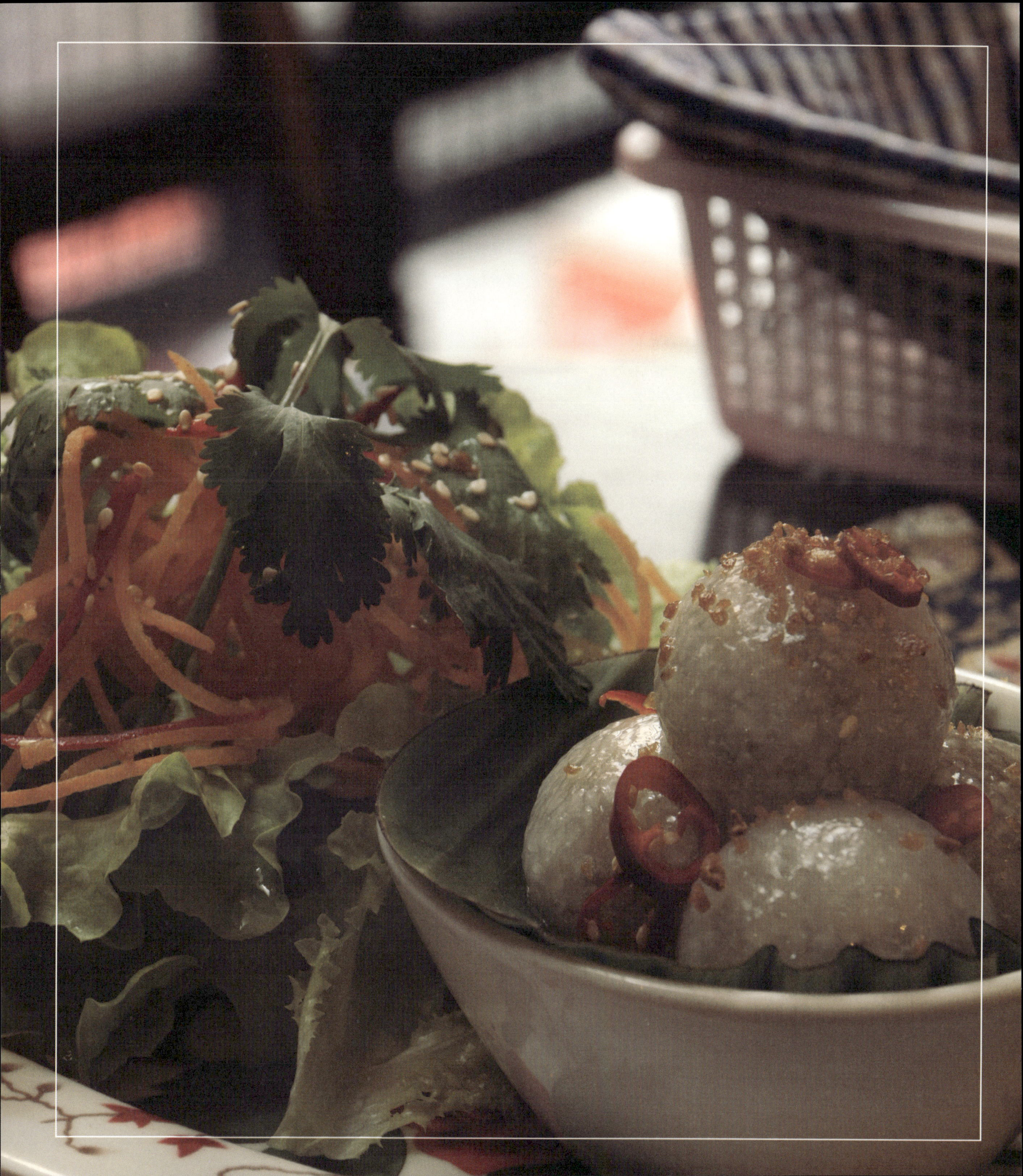

Entrée

# CURED OCEAN TROUT WITH FENNEL AND VANILLA CUSTARD, OYSTER, CANDIED OLIVE & PINENUT CRUMBLE

Chef, Michael Harrison. Syracuse Restaurant
Entrée, Serves 4

Ingredients

Custard
8 medium fennel
50g unsalted butter
2 vanilla beans
250ml water
3 whole eggs
Season - sea salt & white pepper

Ocean Trout
1 small pin boned ocean trout fillet
250g fine salt
250g castor sugar
1 handful toasted coriander seads

Candied Olives
Kalamata olives
Castor sugar

Pinenut Crumble
200g pinenuts

Kumomoto Oyster
Freshly shucked

Method

Custard
Chop fennel into slices and sweat down with butter over a low heat. Once softened add water and vanilla beans. Cook on medium heat until liquid is almost all gone and then purée. Let cool and then add in whisked whole eggs. Pass through a strainer.
Ocean Trout
Cover trout with salt and sugar mixture for two hours. Wash off and pat dry. Slice width ways to 5mm pieces.
Candied Olives
Coat in castor sugar and dry out overnight in a warm place. Finely chop before plating.

Pinenut Crumble
Roast pinenuts and crush in a mortar and pestal
Kumomoto Oyster
In a small oval ramekin place 250ml of custard and steam in a steamer for eight minutes. Take out of steamer and place three slices of trout on top.
Finish with the olive and pinenut crumble. Top with oyster. Garnish with edible flowers such as white or blue borage.

SYRACUSE

# RISOTTO VENERE WITH BUG TAILS

Chef, Guy Grossi and Chris Rodriguez. Grossi Florentino
Main, Serves 6

## Ingredients

360g riso venere (black risotto rice)
9 bug tails
60ml olive oil
4 shallots
120ml white wine
Chicken stock
30g unsalted butter
30g grated Parmesan
Salt and pepper

Parmesan zabaglione:
300ml cream
90g parmesan
1g agar
Sea salt
Cream siphon and charge

## Method

### Risotto

Cut the shallots into fine brunoise. On a moderate heat sweat shallots in the olive oil with no colour. Add the rice and toast until all the grains have reached a good temperature. Set timer for 20 minutes. Add the white wine, season with salt and pepper and reduce while stirring. Before the risotto becomes dry in the pan, add ladles of chicken stock as required. Stir frequently until rice has absorbed the liquid and the 18 minutes have elapsed. Spread out onto a flat tray to cool evenly.

### Parmesan zabaglione

Reduce the cream in a hot pan by half. Add the parmesan. Take off the heat, add 1gm of agar and blend with a stick blender. Pass through a fine strainer and season. Pour into a half litre siphon and charge with 1 charge. Keep in Bain Marie to keep warm before use. Shake vigorously before using.

### To serve

Cut 9 of the bug tails into small pieces and leave 6 for garnish.
Heat a stainless steel pot with some olive oil and sear the chopped bug tails quickly. Remove from the pot and set aside. In the same pot on a moderate heat, heat the semi cooked rice, then mixing continuously add a small amount of the hot stock as required so that the risotto is tender but al dente and wavey in consistency. This should take another 10 minutes.
To finish the risotto add the seared bug meat, unsalted butter and the grated parmesan, mixing in vigorously to creamy consistency [mantegato].
To serve, spoon the risotto into a bowl and siphon some parmesan zabaglione on top. Serve immediately.

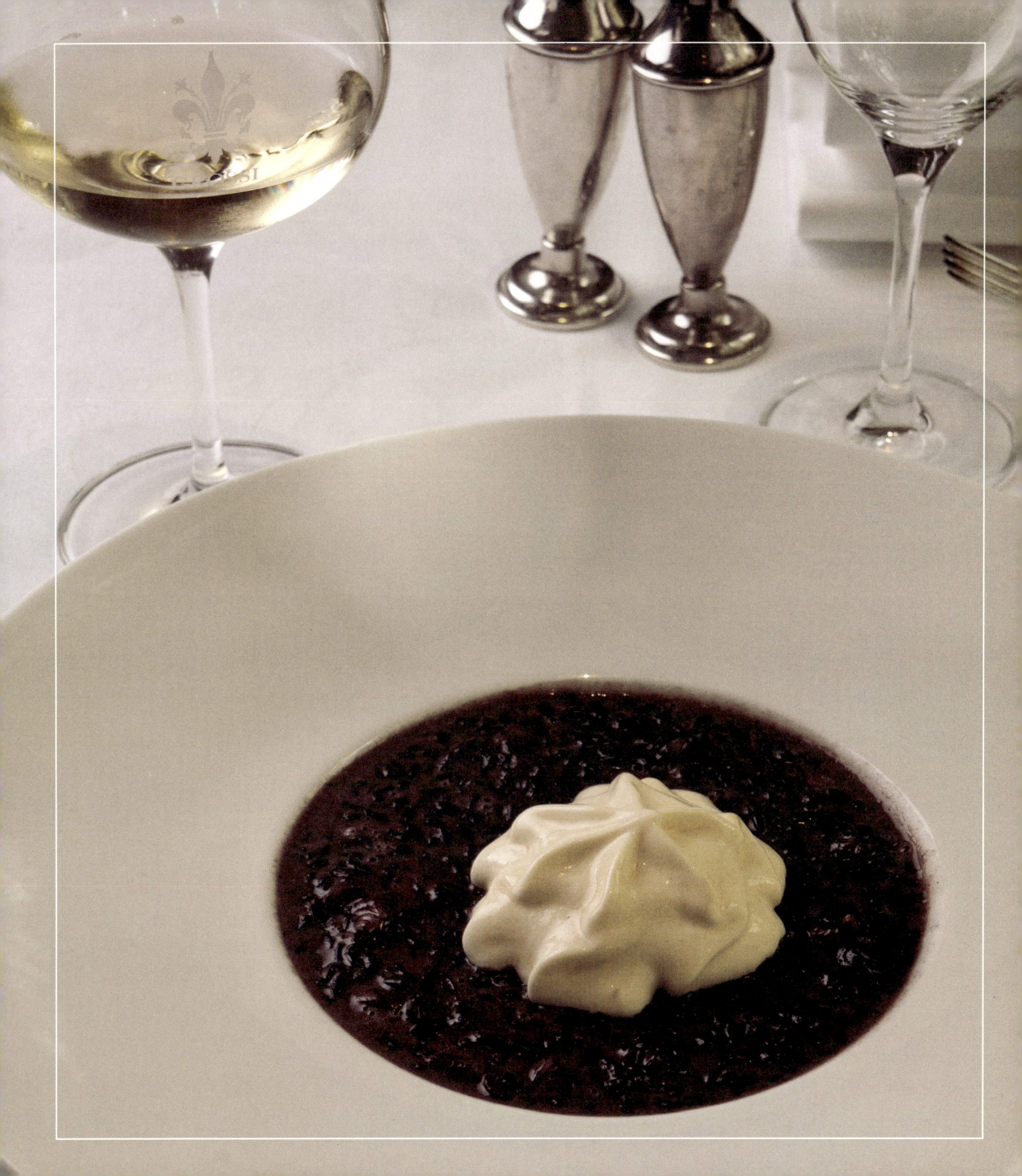

Main

# BRAISED PORK BELLY, DRUNKEN POTATOES, STEAMED BABY BOKCHOY & STAR ANISE CARAMEL

Chef, Anthony Humphries. Seamstress
Main, Serves 8

### Ingredients

Pork belly
2kg pork belly
1 tbsp black pepper corns
1 tbsp white pepper corns
1 tbsp Sichuan pepper corns
1 tbsp ground (whole) dried chilli
1 tbsp cumin seeds
1 star anise
2 bay leaves
1 tsp fennel seeds
1 cinnamon quill

Drunken Potatoes
4 whole Desirée potatoes
1 dried chilli
1 tsp cumin
1 knob ginger
1 clove garlic
2 sliced spring onions
2 tbsp brown sugar
Chinese Xiao Xing rice wine

Baby Bok Choy
½ baby bok choy
Sesame oil

Star Anise Caramel
100g brown sugar
50ml water
50ml cider vinegar
4 whole star anise
1 knob ginger (thickly sliced)

### Method

Pork belly
Lightly toast all spices in a pan, grind and mix with equal parts of salt. Rub a generous handful of spice into the skin as well as the flesh. Leave overnight.
Place pork on a wire rack on a baking tray. Roast at 140°C for 3 hours. At the 3 hour mark, brush with a mixture of honey and sesame oil and roast for further 30–45 minutes at 200°C.
Drunken Potatoes
Boil potatoes, chilli and cumin seeds until just under cooked. Drain off and allow to cool. When potatoes are cooled down, slice approximately 8mm thick. Pan fry a small amount of oil until starting to get brown, and add ginger, garlic and spring onions. Add brown sugar and allow to caramelise. Deglaze with rice wine and reduce down until syrupy.
Baby Bok Choy
Blanch bok choy in boiling water for about 45 seconds and add sesame oil for flavour.
Star Anise Caramel
Reduce all ingredients to a thick syrup. To test the consistency of the sauce, drop a small amount onto a cold plate.

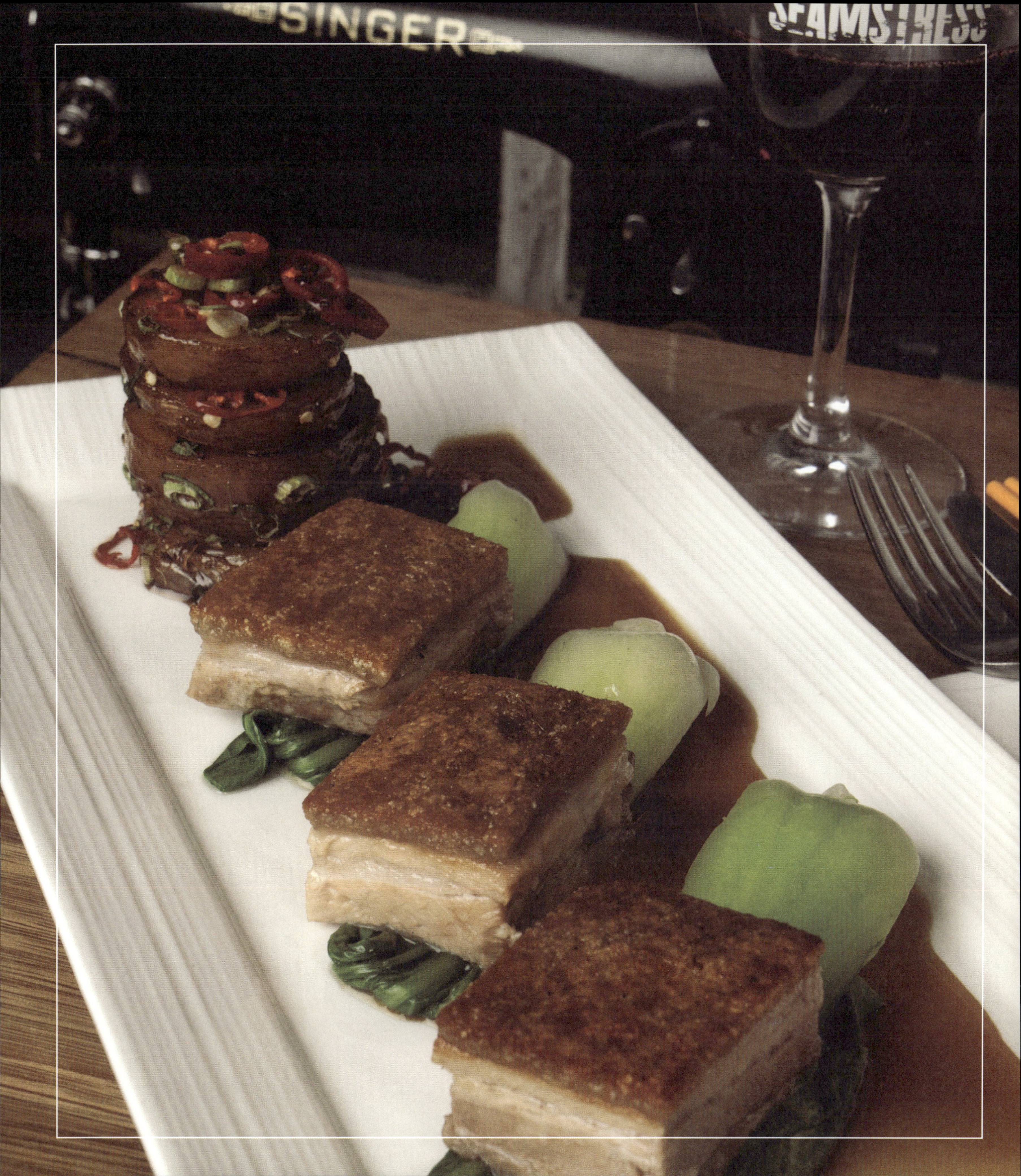
SINGER

Main

# CONIGLIO IN TRE MODI - TRIO OF RABBIT

Chef, Michelle Goldsmith. Caterina's Cucina e Bar.

Main, Serves 4

### Ingredients

Rabbit braise
1 1.5kg whole rabbit (farmed)
2 sprigs rosemary
4 sprigs thyme
4 garlic cloves
1 onion
1 carrot
1 celery stalk
4L chicken stock
Salt and pepper

Tagliolini (Pasta dough)
400g semolina
100g flour
5 eggs
2 tbsp truffle paste
Pinch salt
1 tbsp olive oil

Rotolo (Pasta dough)
300g semolina
100g chestnut flour
100g flour
5 eggs
Pinch salt
1 tbsp olive oil

Agnolotti (Pasta dough)
400g semolina
100g flour
5 eggs
Pinch salt
1 tbsp olive oil
1 tbsp chopped sage

### Method

Rabbit Braise
Remove legs from rabbit, place in large pot with remaining ingredients and gently simmer for several hours until the meat is falling off the bones. Remove meat from bones and place in two separate bowls. Remove loins from the saddle of the rabbit and set aside. Then place the remaining bones onto oven tray and roast at 180°C for 15 minutes. This will now be the base for the sauces. Add roasted bones to the braising liquid and simmer over low heat for two hours. Strain braising liquid (through a filter if possible), add one part reduced veal stock and allow to reduce over low heat for half an hour.

Tagliolini
Combine all ingredients, wrap in cling film and rest for half an hour. Roll out, using pasta machine at number 1, pass through tagliolini cutter.

Rotolo
Combine all ingredients, wrap in cling film and rest for half an hour. Roll lasagna sheets out to number 1 on pasta machine. Combine with two tablespoons of chopped and roasted chestnuts, large pinch of chopped Italian parsley, salt and pepper to taste and two tablespoons of reduced braising liquid.

Agnolotti
Combine all ingredients, wrap in cling film and rest for half an hour. Roll pasta sheets out to number 1 on pasta machine. Using the remaining picked meat from the above step, combine with two finely diced and fried shallots, one tablespoon of finely chopped rosemary, season with salt and pepper and finally add two tablespoons of reduced braising liquid.

To combine all steps
For the tagliolini: in a pot of boiling salted water, add 40g of pasta per person. Cook until al dente (to the tooth). In the mean time, add the remaining rabbit meat, one finely diced garlic clove, one tablespoon of truffle paste, four sage leaves finely chopped and one tablespoon olive oil to a saucepan. Add a small ladle of stock and large knob of unsalted butter and reduce over low heat. Toss tagliolini through this sauce.

Assembling the rotolo: prepare a square piece of lasagna sheet. Add a layer of the meat, and then the loin in the centre of the sheet. Roll up and place on a sheet of cling film. Roll tightly and tie ends so they are secured. Poach for 10 minutes, allow to cool and then cut into 3cm discs. Reheat to order. Serve on braised leek with thyme jus.

Lastly, for the Agnolotti: using a round cutter (10cm), cut out rounds from dough. Place a large tablespoon of mix on the top half of the circle, brush with water and fold into a half circle, making sure there is no air and then press edges with your fingers. Having the flat edge facing you, wet corners and fold them over each other. Cook in boiling salted water for five minutes. Serve on wilted spinach with a rosemary jus.

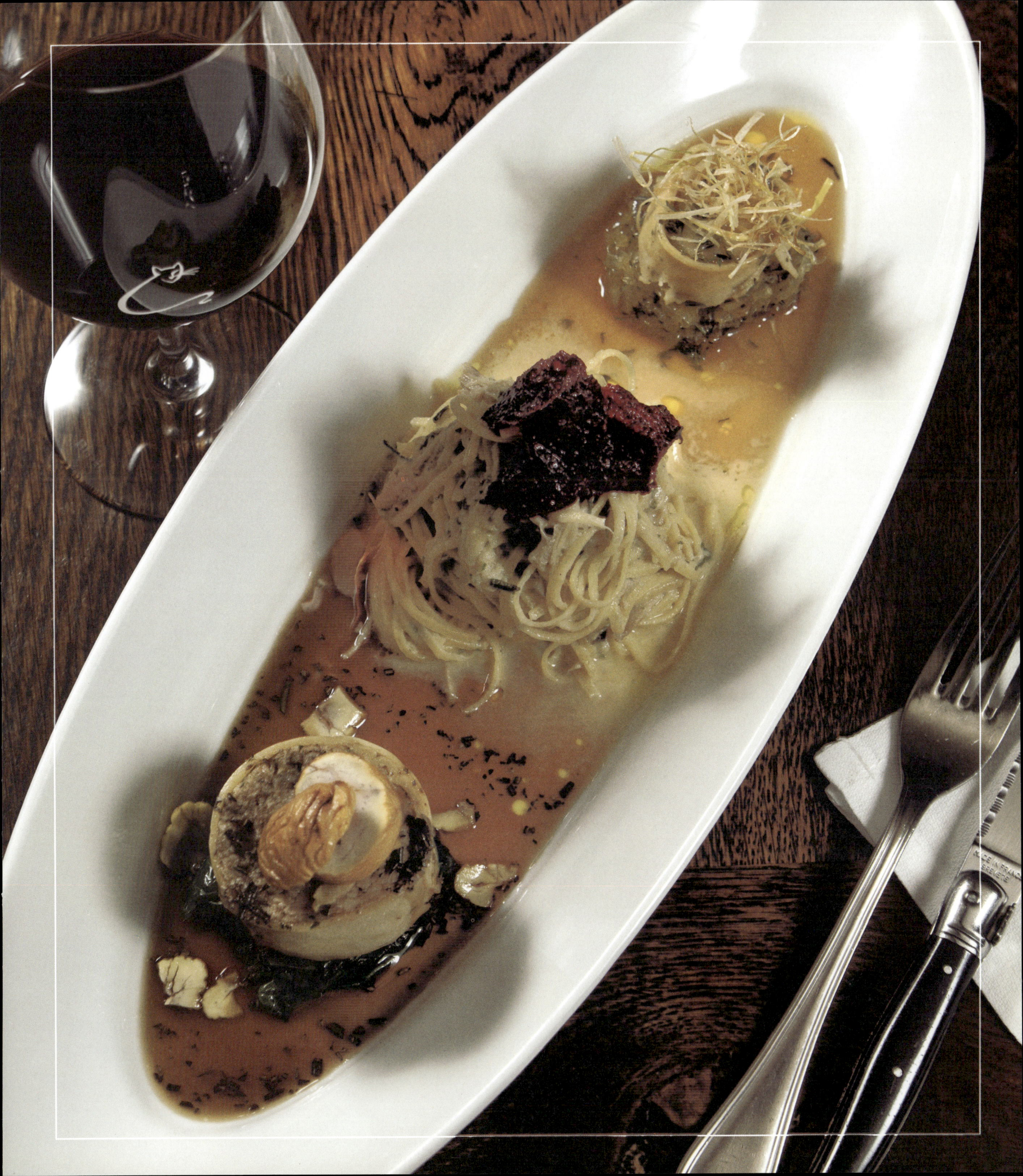

Main

# SHAKE OYAKO DON

Chocolate Buddha
Main, to share.

## Ingredients

120g Salmon fillet
Short grain rice
1 tsp white sesame seeds
1 Shiso leaf
1 tbsp salmon roe
Shredded nori
1 tblsp salt

2 tblsp sugar
Sushi vinegar
500ml Rice Wine vinegar
75g sugar
12.5g salt
1 piece kelp

## Method

Cover Salmon fillet thoroughly with sugar and salt and refrigerate uncovered for at least 4 hours. Wash Salmon and place in 190°c preheated oven on oiled backing tray – cook salmon approximately 4 minutes each side. Once Salmon is at room temperature it can be refrigerated once again.

Wash short grain rice until it becomes clear – cook rice. Fold through vinegar ensuring rice is covered thoroughly. Cover with wet cloth for 15 minutes. Place hot rice in deep bowl – place cured salmon on rice and garnish with salmon roe, shisho leaf, sesame seeds and shredded nori.

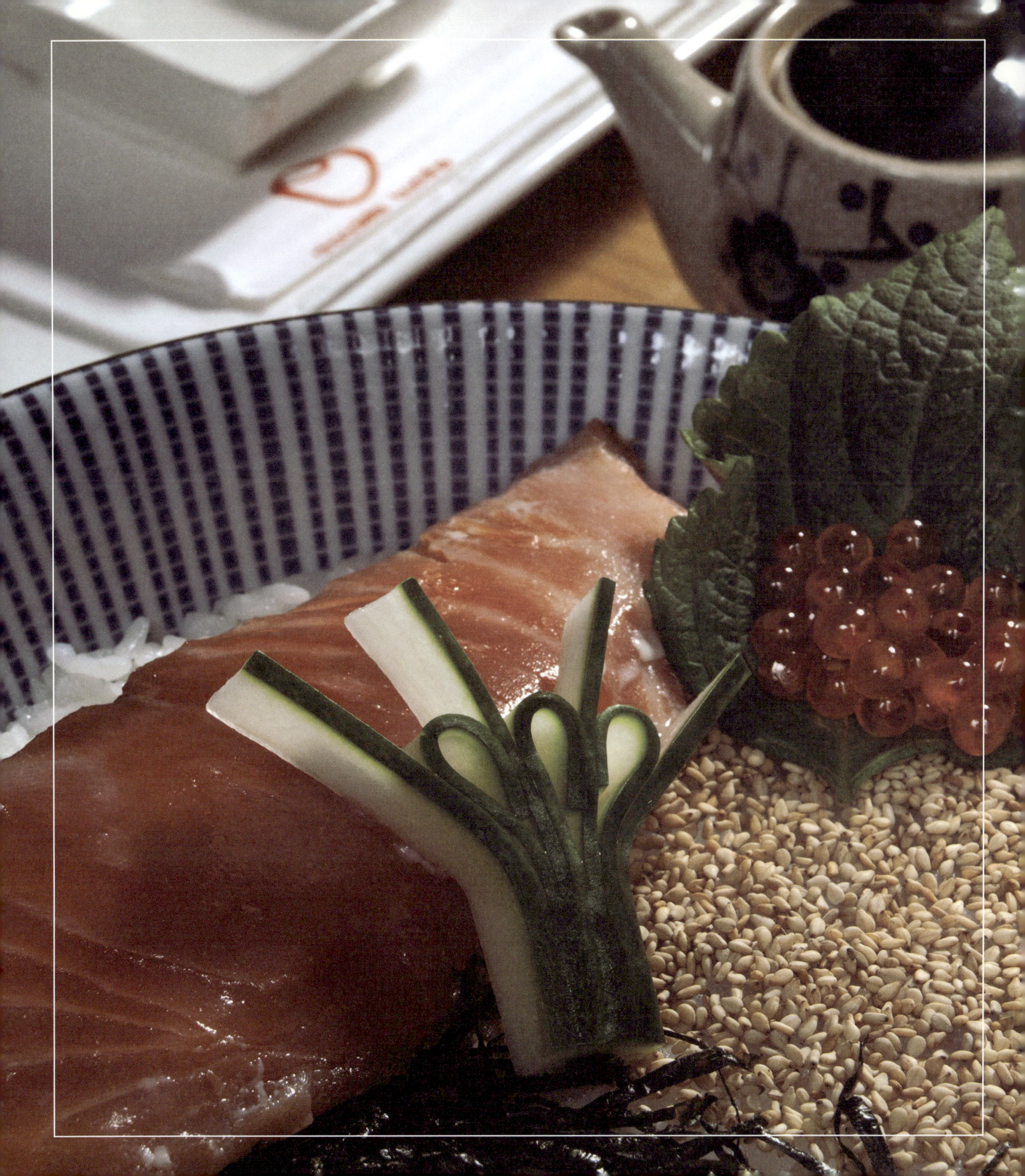

Main

# TORTELLINI DI ZUCCA

Chef, Guy Grossi and Domenico Marzano. Grossi Florentino Cellar
Main, Serves 6-8

### Ingredients

Pumpkin mix
1 butternut pumpkin
100g butter
50ml olive oil
2 cloves garlic chopped
1 chilli chopped
1 leek
½ bunch sage finely chopped
½ cup grated parmesan
100g grated gruyere cheese
½ cup bread crumbs
Salt and freshly ground pepper

Pasta
500g flour
3 large eggs
2 large egg yolks
Pinch of salt

For serving
100g unsalted butter
1tbsp sage chopped
2tbsp grated parmesan
A few leaves of sage

### Method

Pumpkin mix
Cut the pumpkin into even wedges and remove seeds. Roast pumpkin at 200°c for 40 min. Take out of oven and let cool slightly. Scoop the flesh away from the skin, discard the skin and leave the flesh in a colander so that any excess liquid is drained. Wash leek and dice into 1cm squares.
Heat the butter and olive oil in a large saucepan and sauté the garlic and chilli. Add the leeks, sauté until wilted and soft. In a bowl combine the pumpkin, parmesan, gruyere and the leek mixture together and mix in. Add breadcrumbs, making sure to keep the mixture not too moist and not too dry. Season to taste.

Pasta
Place the flour in a large bowl and make a well in the centre. Add the eggs, yolks and a pinch of salt and gently start to mix in the flour with a fork. Once the ingredients are mixed in, use your hands to knead the dough so it becomes smooth. Cling wrap and leave to rest for 1 hour. Cut the pasta into workable pieces and on the widest setting put through the pasta machine, folding into half and rolling through again repeating this process until pasta is smooth as silk. This is called "laminating". Roll out the dough to a thin sheet approximately 2mm thick and using a cutter, cut out 7cm diameter circles. Place 1 tsp pumpkin mixture into the centre of the circle, dip your finger into a glass of water and wet the pasta dough around the filling. This will make the pasta stick together. Fold the circle in half, pressing down. Then fold the straight edge of the semi circle forward half way to the top and taking the two points, curl the pasta forward and join the ends together by pressing the pasta together between the fingers. Place tortellini onto floured tray. Extra tortellini can be frozen on the tray then placed into a bag for later use.

To serve
Bring a large pot of water to the boil and add 1tbsp of salt, pour in the tortellini and gently stir the bottom of the pot with a wooden spoon so that tortellini doesn't stick to the bottom. Cook for about 3 minutes then drain into colander or remove with a sieve. Heat a pan with the butter and mix until butter turns nut brown. Add the sage, drained tortellini and a sprinkle of parmesan and toss through.

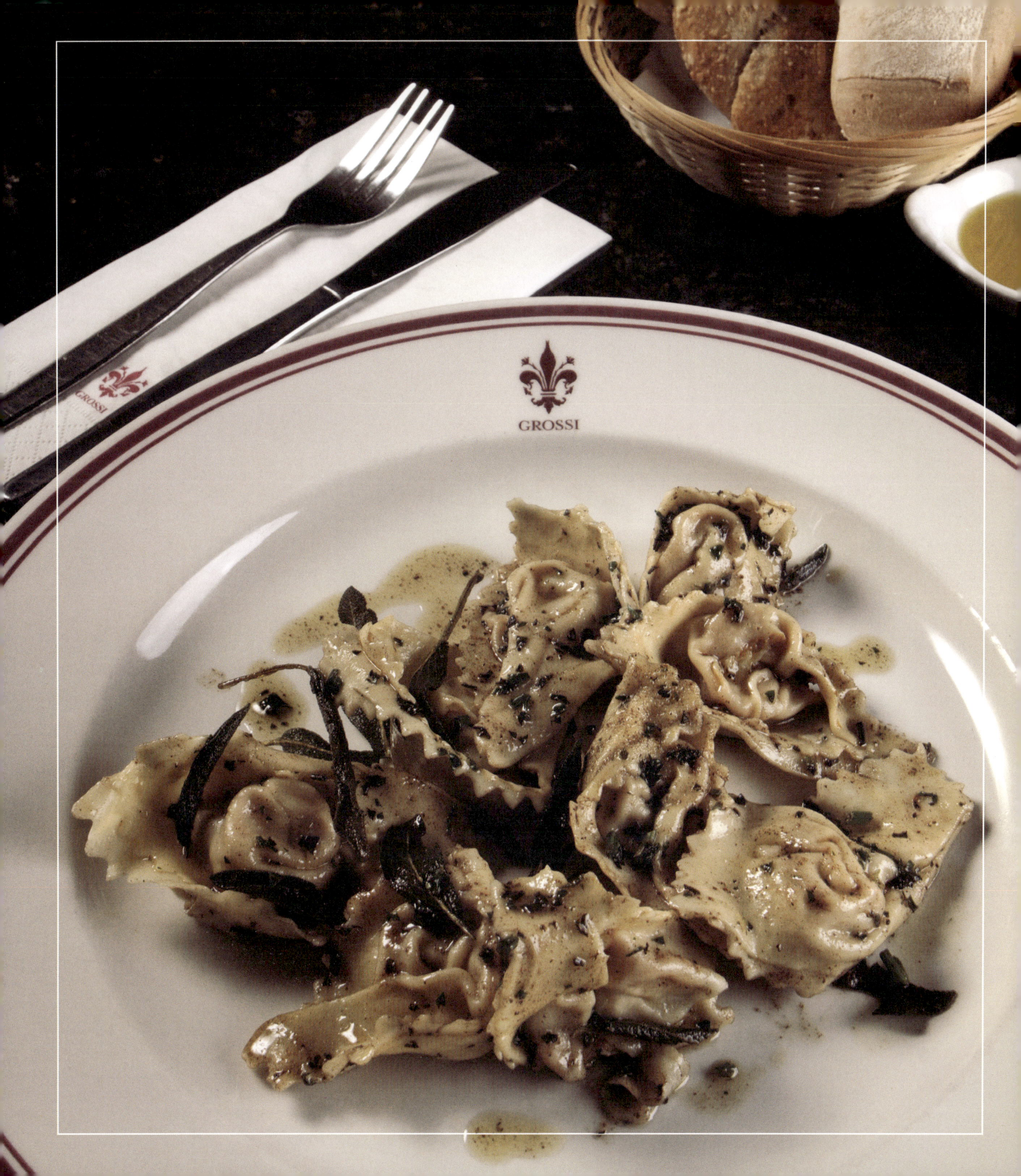
GROSSI

Main

# ROASTED RACK OF LAMB WITH BEETROOT RAVIOLI AND RED WINE REDUCTION

Chef, Christos Chalastras. Ca de Vin

Main, Serves 4

### Ingredients

| | | |
|---|---|---|
| 4 racks of lamb (4 joint each) | 2 whole eggs | 10 sprigs of thyme |
| Clove of garlic | 2 egg yolks | 10 sprigs of rosemary |
| Pinch of thyme | 1 egg beaten with fork (in small bowl set aside) | 400ml red wine (cabernet preferable) |
| 20g of butter | | 1 carrot |
| Salt for seasoning | Filling | 1 brown onion |
| Fresh cracked black peppercorn | 1 beetroot | 1 leek |
| 4 handfuls of baby spinach | 40g of feta cheese | 1 stick of celery |
| Ravioli | 5 sprigs of mint | 20g of plain flour |
| Fresh pasta | Red wine reduction | 30ml vegetable oil |
| 160g of 00 type flour | 2 kg of veal bone | 15g of sugar |
| 30ml of olive oil | 1 pig trotter | |
| 10g of fine salt | 2 cloves of garlic | |

### Method

Red wine reduction (demi glaze with wine)
Preheat oven to moderate. Place the veal bones on a tray and put in the oven for 2 hours at 170 C. Chop the vegetables as big chunks and sauté them in large saucepan with the vegetable oil. Add the rosemary and thyme. Sprinkle the flour on the bones and put back in the oven for 10 minutes. Add the bones to the saucepan, add the pig trotter and half the wine. Stir for 5 minutes and cover with water. Leave the pot on a slow fire for 3 hours to reduce in half. Strain and keep only the liquid. Add the other half wine and the sugar and leave on a slow fire again for 2 hours, add a clove of garlic and a few sprigs of thyme and rosemary.

Ravioli
Place the flour in to a mixing bowl. Add the eggs, the yolks and the salt and start mixing. Add slowly the olive oil. It comes up as tough yellow dough. Leave to rest for half an hour and meanwhile prepare the filling. Wrap the beetroot with foil and bake till soft. Mash it, add crumbled feta and finely chopped mint, stir in. Season to taste.

Clear large dry space and sprinkle flour. Tip out the dough and cut into two equal halves. Roll out each half into a long, narrow rectangle approx 10cm wide and 1.1/2 – 2mls thick. Cut the edges straight to complete the rectangle. Starting from the left, allowing 3cm, spoon out beetroot mixture in the centre. Place your palm flat on the pasta to measure the distance between the spoonfuls of mixture. Continue this pattern till the end of the pasta rectangle leaving again 3cms before the final edge. With a pastry brush cover the exposed edges of the pasta between the mixture with the beaten raw egg. Gently place the other trimmed pasta rectangle over the top and press down firmly.

Put a large pot of water on to boil add salt. Once boiling add a drop of olive oil, gently add ravioli and turn the heat down a little (so it is not boiling too furiously) for 6mins. Take out ravioli and place into large bowl of ice and water for 5mins.

Take the lamb and season with salt and pepper. Place frying pan on a high heat with olive oil. Seal the lamb on both sides (2mins each side) put pan aside. Place the lamb in the oven at 200C for 7mins. Place the frying pan back on medium heat. Add the butter, the smashed garlic clove and thyme just to melt and infuse flavor. Dip the lamb into the butter and remove lamb. Add the ravioli to the same pan to reheat and make the edges a little crispy. Remove ravioli and add spinach to wilt and glaze.

Assembly
Place spinach in the centre of the plate, put ravioli over spinach. Cut the lamb racks in half (2xpoints) and place 2 on each plate. Pour the red wine reduction over the lamb and ravioli.

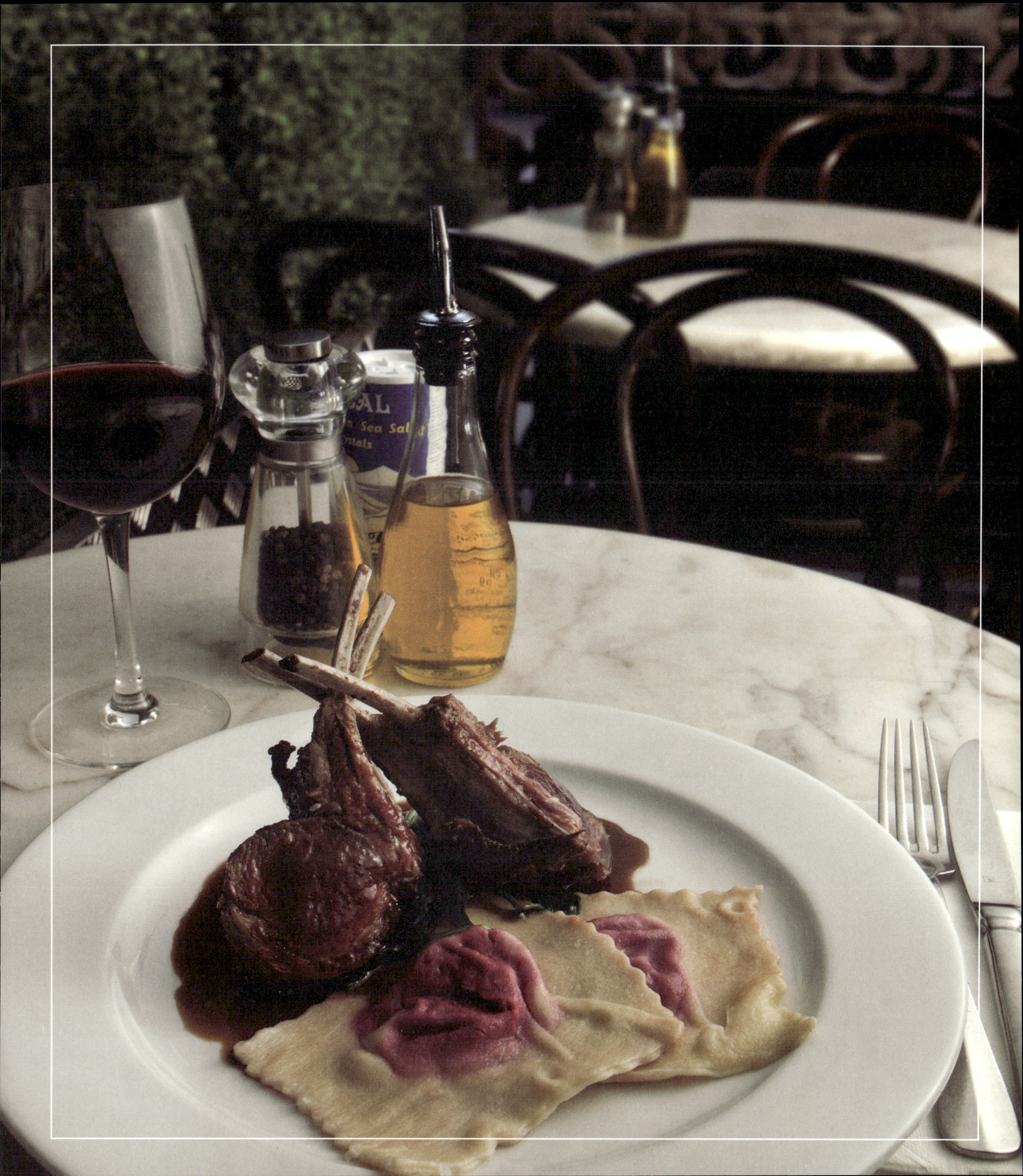

Main

# BACCALÀ ALLA LIVORNESE

Chef, Guy Grossi and Daniel Airo-Farulla, Merchant Restaurant
Main, Serves 6

### Ingredients

1 fillet of baccalà (salted cod)
2 large onions, finely sliced
1 clove garlic, finely chopped
2 cups of white wine
250g tomato paste
250ml cup olive oil
½ bunch continental parsley, roughly chopped
4 tsp capers
1L water
100g flour for dusting.

4 Spanish anchovies chopped
3 bay leaves
½ tsp of chopped chilli
1 tsp basil pesto

Polenta
8 cups water
2 cups polenta
1 tbsp salt
125gm grated parmesan

### Method

Place the fillet of baccalà in a large bowl and fill with fresh water. Allow to soak overnight, changing the water 3 or 4 times. Once the baccalà has undergone the soaking process, cut into serving size pieces.

Pre heat oven to 180°C. On moderate heat, heat half the olive oil in a large saucepan. Dust the baccalà pieces with flour and fry until golden, place in a braising tray.

In a large pot add the remaining half of the olive oil and heat. Add the onions, garlic and fry until translucent. Add the capers, chilli, bay leaves, pesto and the anchovies and mix together, then add the tomato paste and stir until the colour has darkened and the tomato paste has caramelised well.

Add the white wine and reduce slightly over the heat combining the wine with the tomato. Add the water and bring to the boil, turn down the heat and leave to simmer for 10 minutes. Cover the baccalà in the braising tray with the tomato sauce, sprinkle liberally with chopped parsley, cover with foil and place in the oven for 20-25 minutes.

Polenta

Bring the salted water to boil on the stove and rain in the polenta, stirring constantly. When all of the polenta has been added continue to stir for 2-3 minutes and reduce the heat and allow to cook for 15-20 minutes stirring occasionally. Once cooked add the parmesan and stir and serve

To serve

Spoon a large spoonful of polenta at the top of the plate, arrange some baccalà on the plate and spoon some sauce over the baccalà.

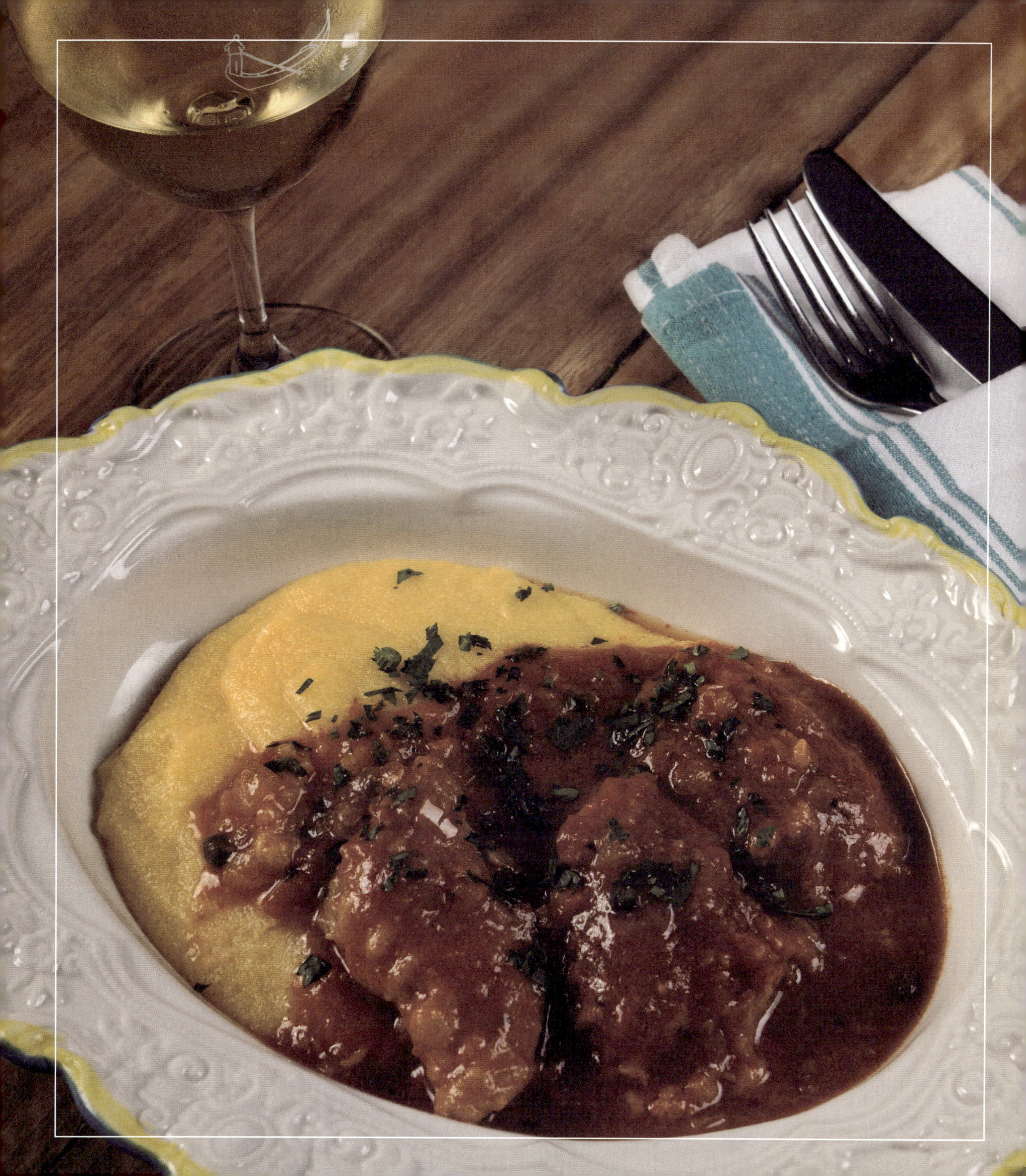

Main

# ALMOND PIMENTO CRUSTED LAMB RACK WITH SWEET TOMATO CINNAMON & SESAME SALSA & ROASTED GARLIC & POTATO PURÉE

Chef, Stan Delimitrou. Terra Rossa
Main, Serves 4

### Ingredients

**Lamb Racks**
¼ tsp sweet Paprika
80 grams flaked almonds
4 french cut lamb racks
2 tbsp olive oil
Sea Salt
Ground Black Pepper

**Salsa**
20 large ripe tomatoes
6 tbsp olive oil
6 tbsp warm honey
2 tsp ground cinnamon
2 tsp ground ginger
Pinch sea salt flakes
Ground black pepper
2 tbsp toasted sesame seeds

**Potato Purée**
8 large Desirée potatoes peeled
¼ tsp sweet paprika
80g butter
8 garlic cloves
2 tbsp olive oil
60mls thickened cream
salt
white pepper
cracked black pepper

### Method

**Lamb Racks**

Pre heat oven to 200ºC

Place the almonds and sweet paprika in a baking tray and toast in the oven till golden brown, set aside and allow to cool.

Trim fat off the lamb rack bones and wrap in foil, drizzle olive oil over the lamb and season with salt and pepper. Once the almonds have cooled enough to touch, place in bowl and gently crush by hand.

Place lamb in the same baking tray the almonds were roasted in and pat the paprika almonds onto the lamb, let it sit for 20 minutes.

Heat a heavy based pans or a cast iron pan, pour in some olive oil and seal the lamb racks till golden brown and return to the baking tray. Place the lamb in pre-heated oven and roast for 20 minutes.

Once cooked allow to rest for 4 minutes before serving.

**Salsa**

Pre heat oven to 200ºC  Wash and place tomatoes in baking tray, pour over olive oil and bake for 20 minutes, once cooked set aside to cool.

Peel skin from tomato, remove the seeds and finely dice. Place tomatoes in a heavy based sauce pan with 1 table spoon of olive oil, stir in warm honey, cinnamon and ginger and gently cook for 20 minutes stirring frequently until thick. Season with salt flakes and ground black pepper.

Toast sesame seeds and sprinkle on top

**Potato Purée**

Place peeled garlic cloves in a small saucepan with the olive oil and some cracked black pepper and slowly fry till soft and golden brown, place in a bowl and crush with a fork.

Peel potatoes and boil till soft, strain and put through a mouli or crush with a fork, preferably through a mouli as it will come out smooth.

Place potatoes back on the heat, add garlic (and olive oil it was cooked in), butter, cream, salt & pepper and gently stir till butter has melted.

Adjusted seasoning if required.

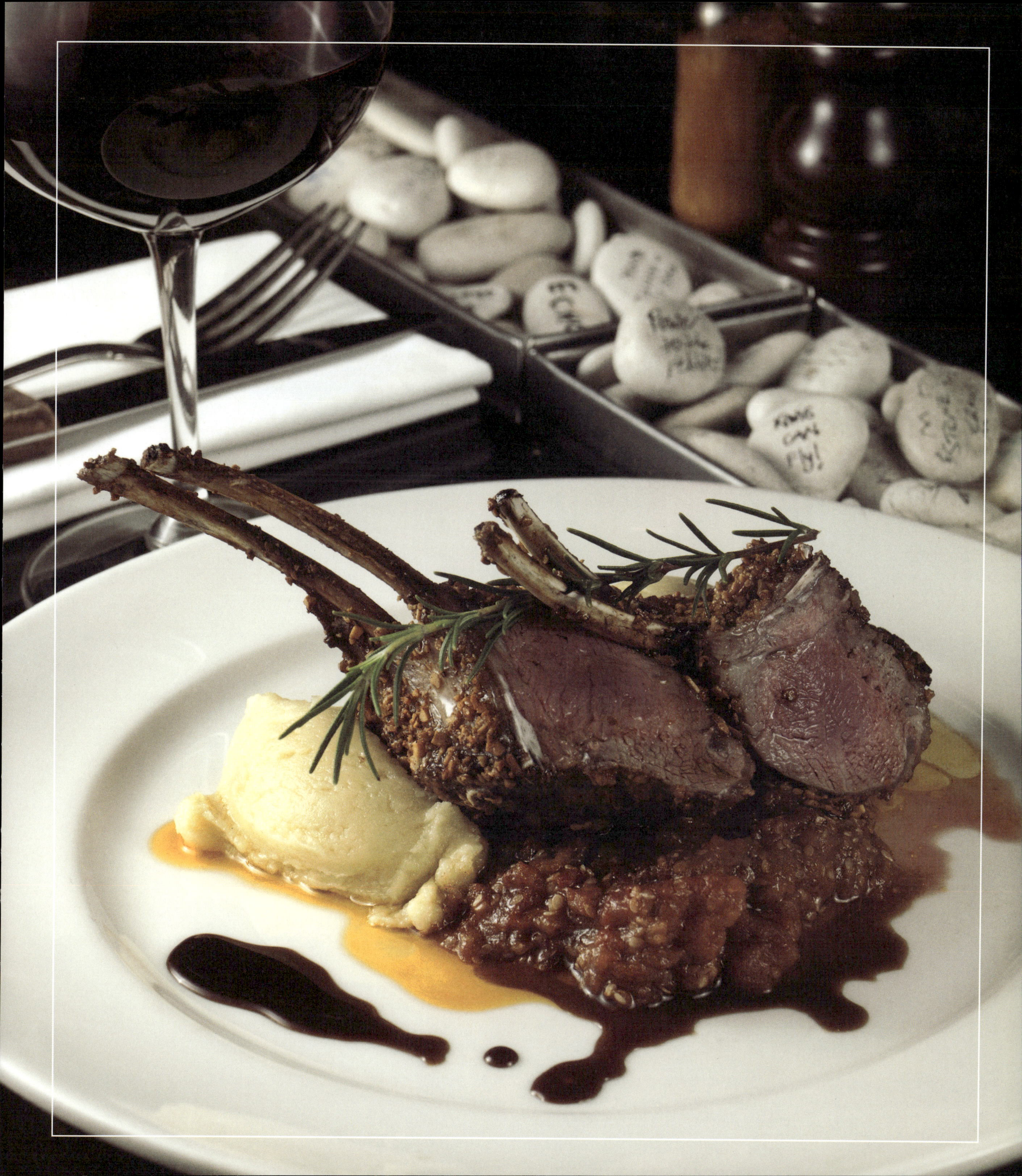

# Dessert

# RHUBARB & CUSTARD TART WITH GINGER ICE CREAM

Chef, Nikki Smith. Punch Lane
Dessert, Serves 6-8

### Ingredients

**Sweet paste**
120g castor sugar
240g plain flour
60g butter
1 egg
1 egg yolk
½ tsp mixed spice
1 tsp ground ginger

**Pastry cream**
4 egg yolks
75g castor sugar
25g corn flour
300ml milk
1 vanilla pod
35ml cream
30g butter unsalted
Pinch salt

**Rhubarb**
1 bunch rhubarb
Icing sugar
Stock syrup
250ml water
125g sugar
1 strip lemon zest

**Dried rhubarb**
1 stick rhubarb cut into 5cm pieces
Stock syrup

**Ginger ice cream**
450ml cream
450ml milk
260g sugar
180g fresh ginger sliced
1 tbsp ground ginger
9 egg yolks

### Method

**Sweet paste**

Place all ingredients into a food processor until it forms a ball, place in cling film and rest for 1 hour.

**Pastry cream**

Split the vanilla pod in half and scrape out the seeds place into the milk and bring to the boil. In a bowl mix the egg yolks, corn flour, sugar and salt until well combined once the milk is boiled pour over the egg mix then return the pan, stir all the time for 5-10mins until thickened and flour has cooked out, strain the pastry cream then add the cream and butter whisk through, place in a container and cover with cling film to prevent a skin from forming.

**Rhubarb**

Place water sugar and lemon zest into a pan bring to the boil and let the sugar dissolve boil for 3-4 minutes, then cool. Place a piece of parchment paper onto a tray, cut the rhubarb into 5cm pieces or the size to fit in your tart case. Wash the rhubarb and dry off. Place on baking sheet and sprinkle with icing sugar. Place into oven 200c for 5-10 min depending on the size of the rhubarb determinds cooking time. Check reguraly as the rhubarb can over cook very quickly. The rhubarb should be soft but hold its shape. When cooked place into the stock syrup until needed.

**Dried rhubarb**

Slice rhubarb on a mandolin, dip into stock syrup and place into a oven at 100ºC for 20-30 min or until crisp. Leave in a container until needed.

**Ginger Ice-cream**

Mix cream and milk with fresh and ground ginger bring to the boil. Whisk the eggs and sugar over a pan of hot water until light and doubled in size ribbon stage. Pour cream mix over eggs and sugar, stirring all the time. Return to the heat until custard coats the back of the spoon, chill in the fridge then pass through a sieve, once cool place in the ice cream machine for 50-60 mins.

Place a small drop of pastry cream onto plate then place the tart case on top, this stops it moving around on the plate. Spoon the pastry cream into the tart case then top with the rhubarb. Drizzle around a little strawberry sauce around the plate and 3 pieces of micro lemon balm. Scoop a ball of ice cream on top of the rhubarb then place a piece of dried rhubarb crisp on top.

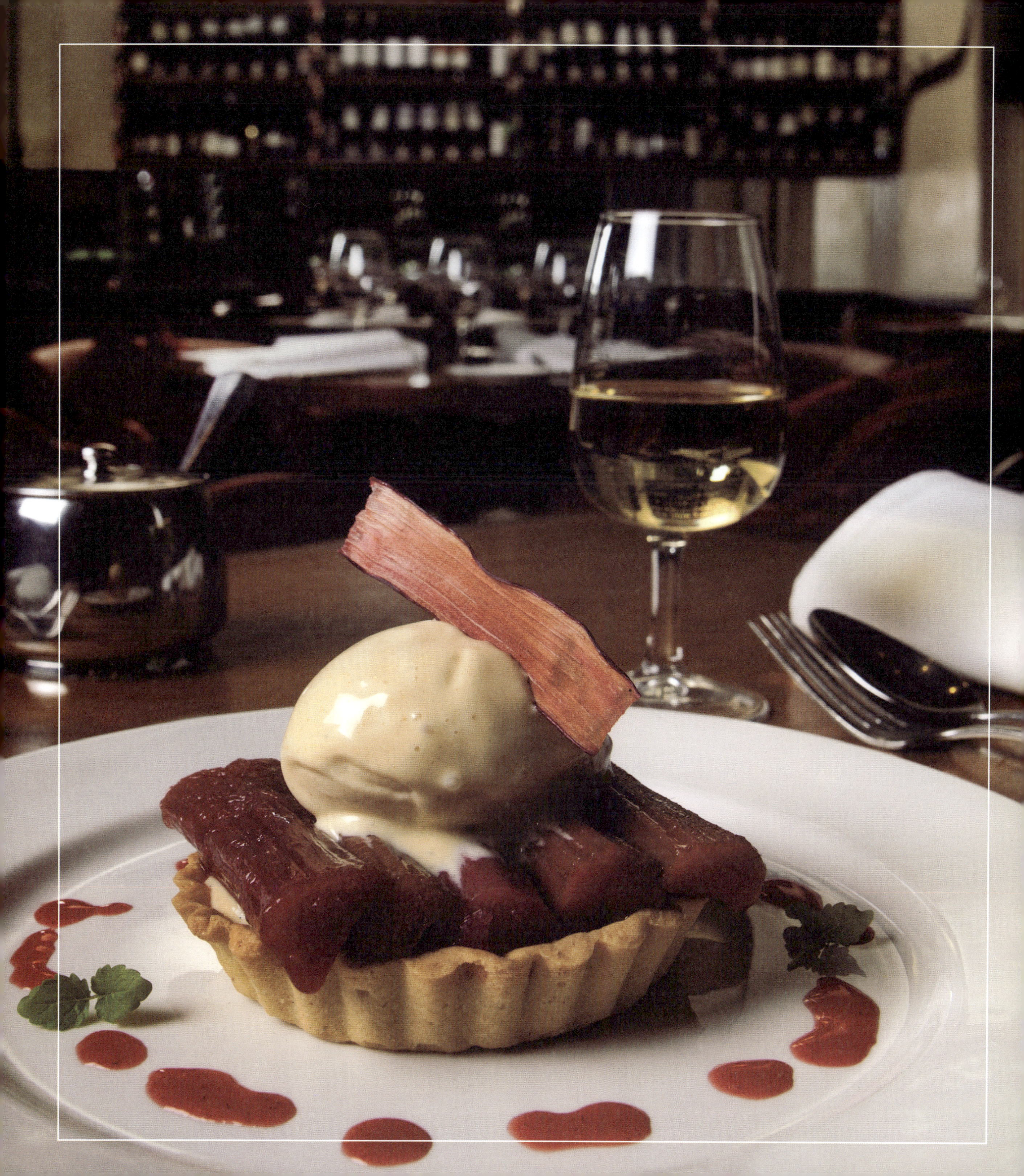

Dessert

# PAVLOVA

Chef, Harry Hajisava, Hopetoun Tea Rooms
Dessert, Serves 12

### Ingredients

French Meringue
8 egg whites
250g castor sugar
250g sifted icing sugar

To decorate Pavlova
100g strawberries
100g raspberries
100g blueberries
4 kiwi fruit, peeled and sliced to your liking
4 passionfruit, halved
½ -1 whole mango when in season, peeled and sliced to your liking
400ml double cream, fully whipped with a few drops of vanilla essence and sweetened with icing sugar to taste

### Method

French Meringue

In a bowl, beat the egg whites with a balloon whisk until soft peaks are formed. Still whisking continuously, shower in the castor sugar a little at a time and continue to whisk for about 10 minutes, until the mixture is smooth and shiny and holds firm peaks on the whisk, when you lift it out of the mixture. Shower in the icing sugar and fold it in with a spatula or alternatively you can continue to use the balloon whisk to mix it into the meringue.

To assemble and bake the Pavlova

Pre-heat oven to 150ºC. Line a baking tray with parchment (silicon paper) and spread the meringue into a disc approximately 25cm in diameter and 5cm in height. Bake in the oven for 30 minutes, then lower the setting to 120 degrees Celsius and cook for another 45 minutes. Switch off the oven and leave the pavlova inside to cool, for at least 6-8 hours, or preferably overnight.

It should then be half cooked on the inside middle, crisp on the outside and the edges should be slightly cracked

To serve

With a sharp bladed, serrated knife, dipped into very hot water and wiped dry between each use, with a perfectly clean tea towel or paper towel roll, carefully cut the pavlova into twelve (12) equal triangle portions.

Using a piping bag, with a star nozzle of 1.5cm attached, pipe the cream decoratively over the top of the pavlova starting from the outside edge working towards the centre in decreasing circles. Have fun placing all of the various fruits on top of the pavlova, ensuring each portion receives an even amount of all the fruits.

Drizzle the passionfruit seeds and juice over the pavlova using a teaspoon or the tip of a paring knife as the crowning 'glory'!

"With acknowledgement to and great respect for Mr and Mrs Michel and Robyn Roux 2011"

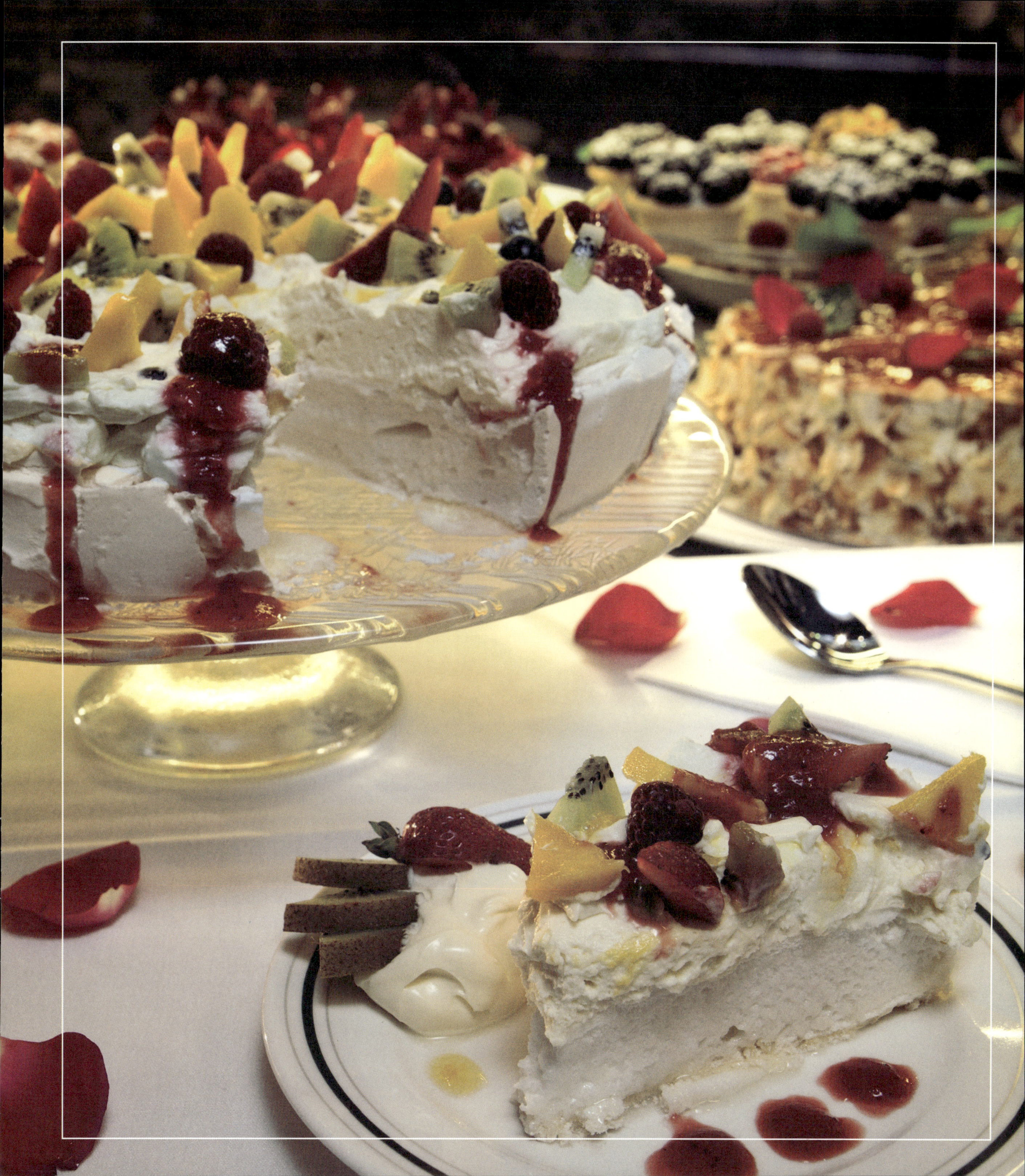

Dessert

# STRAWBERRY AND BERRY ALMOND TART

Chef, Pierrick Boyer, Le Petit Gateau.
Dessert, 1 large tart - 28cm

Ingredients

Shortcrust
200g butter
5g salt
80g castor sugar
25g plain flour
3 egg yolks

Almond cream
40g butter
40g castor sugar
40g almond meal
40g whole eggs
40g thicken cream

Raspberry jam
500g raspberries
150g castor sugar
1 lemon, juiced

Berry compôte
70ml lemon juice
2 oranges, made into zest
40g castor sugar
40g cornflour
450g assorted berries

Method

Shortcrust

Combine room temperature butter with salt and sugar in a mixer with a paddle.

Sift the flour, then pour in the mixture.

Then add the egg yolk last.

Reserve the mixture in the refrigerator for 1 hour, then roll the tart.

Almond cream

Mix the room temperature butter with the castor sugar. When mixed, add the almond meal, then the eggs and cream last.

Pour the almond cream on the raw tart, bake at 180°C

Raspberry jam

Bring the raspberry and sugar to 105°C then pour the lemon juice and cool down.

Berry compôte

In a cold pan, heat the juice, zest, sugar and corn flour.

Mix well and on a medium high, bring to a boil while stirring. Then add the fresh berries and place on the tart. Put a layer or two of fresh strawberries on the edge of the tart. Powder icing sugar over the tart for extra shine.

To Finish

Place, strawberries on the side and the berry compôte in the middle. Then add some fresh edible flowers to garnish.

le petit gâteau

Dessert

# CHOCOLATE BREAD & BUTTER PUDDING

Self Preservation.
Dessert, Serves 6

Ingredients

½ cup of castor sugar
370ml milk
250g of cream
1 vanilla bean
4 eggs
6 croissants
100g dark chocolate, sliced
40g pecan nuts, sliced

Method

Preheat oven to 180ºC.
Combine milk, cream and sugar in a saucepan. Scrape the vanilla bean seeds into the pan and add the bean. Stir until hot, but don't let it boil. Strain to remove the vanilla bean.

Whisk eggs in a bowl and pour the cream mixture over the eggs slowly while continuing to whisk. Grease 6 oven-proof ramekins then layer with croissants, chocolate, nuts, and pour the custard over.

Place ramekins on an oven tray and pour boiling water around the tray until it sits half way up each ramekin. Bake for 20-30 minutes or until set.
Serve with good quality vanilla ice cream.

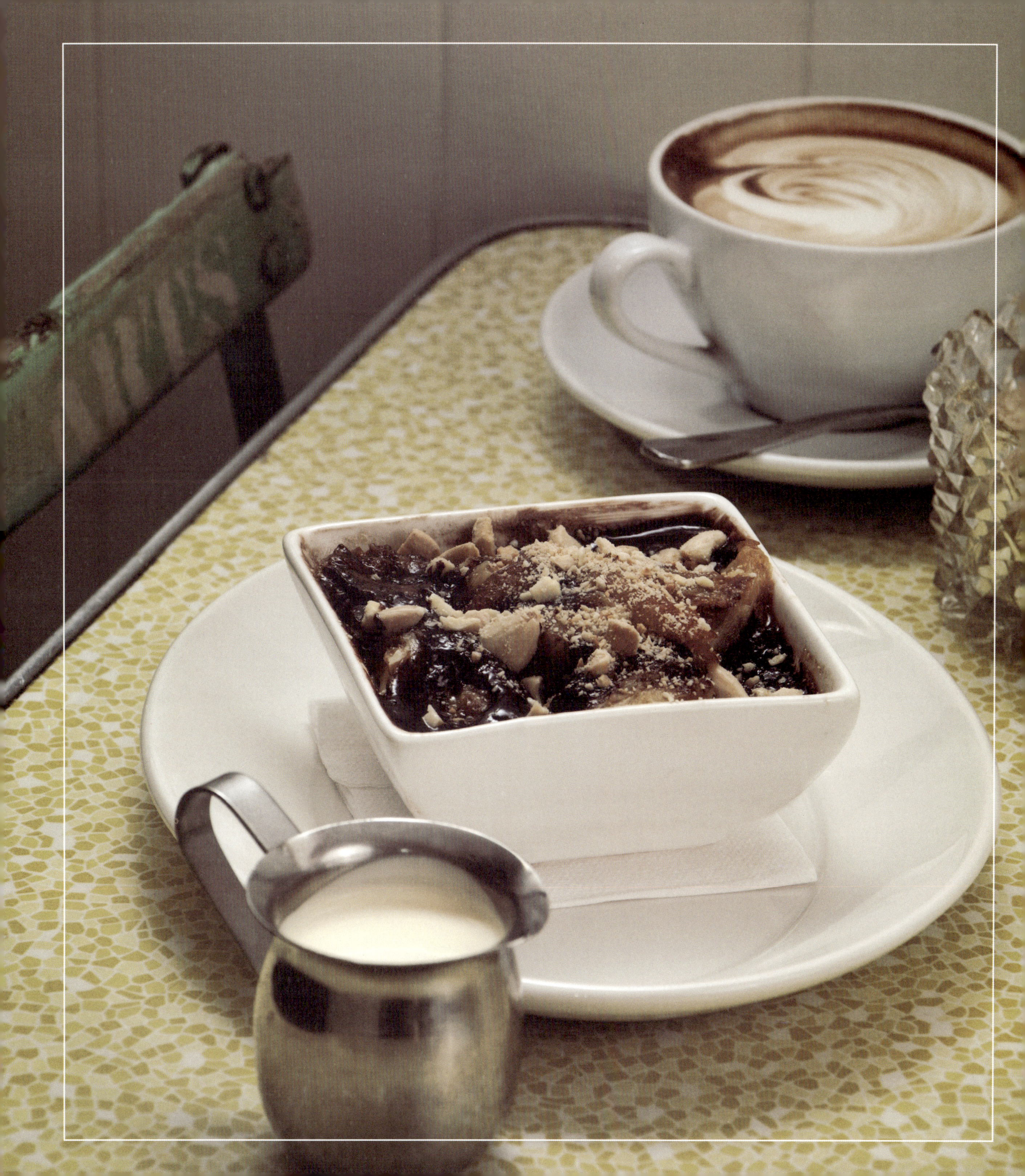

# ABOUT THE AUTHORS
## TWO LIVES LESS ORDINARY

The unique bond of mother and daughter has inspired a series of books showcasing regions of Australia. With a passion for food, wine and all things local, Jonette George and Daniele Wilton have explored the Mornington Peninsula and the Bellarine Peninsula & beyond, in an attempt to highlight the wonderful fruits to be found in our backyard.

They are currently working on an exciting project for inner Melbourne - focusing on restaurants, bars and cafes in hidden laneways, arcades, rooftops and through the urban jungle.

Jonette says she has not forgotten the original inhabitants of this place they called home and writes about our tribal ancestors and their 40,000+ years living along the Yarra River.

Today's urban explorers, she says, are the street artists who have explored every nook and cranny the city now provides. They have turned drab, backstreet laneways into vibrant streetscapes allowing the hidden gems of Melbourne to strut their stuff with tourists flocking to see this unique freestyle landscape.

Restaurants, bars and cafes are no longer hidden (though some may prefer their original understated presence) are now the new "chic" and are finding a new renaissance with customers enjoying this "new world".

Daniele and Jonette each hold a degree in Communications and are both avid writers, designers and publishers. They care for their local environment, and are very mindful that small achievements can have a universal impact.

Local, green and ethical are the 3 ingredients needed to repair a chaotic world. Compassion for our neighbours and caring for our local environment, can and will make important changes to the way we live our lives.

It comes back to a simple rule: "Love thy neighbour, and respect this earth".

The pair's empathy for shines through in their work and comes from travelling the hard, rocky road of life - with ups and downs less ordinary.

With the loss of son and brother, Clinton, in an Austrian avalanche in 2002 - life as they knew it changed. Jonette's brush with breast cancer reminded them of our fragile existence and short term footprint on this earth.

Jonette says they have learnt to hold their heads high and follow their passions with love and pride.

## LOVE

*Jonette George & Daniele Wilton*

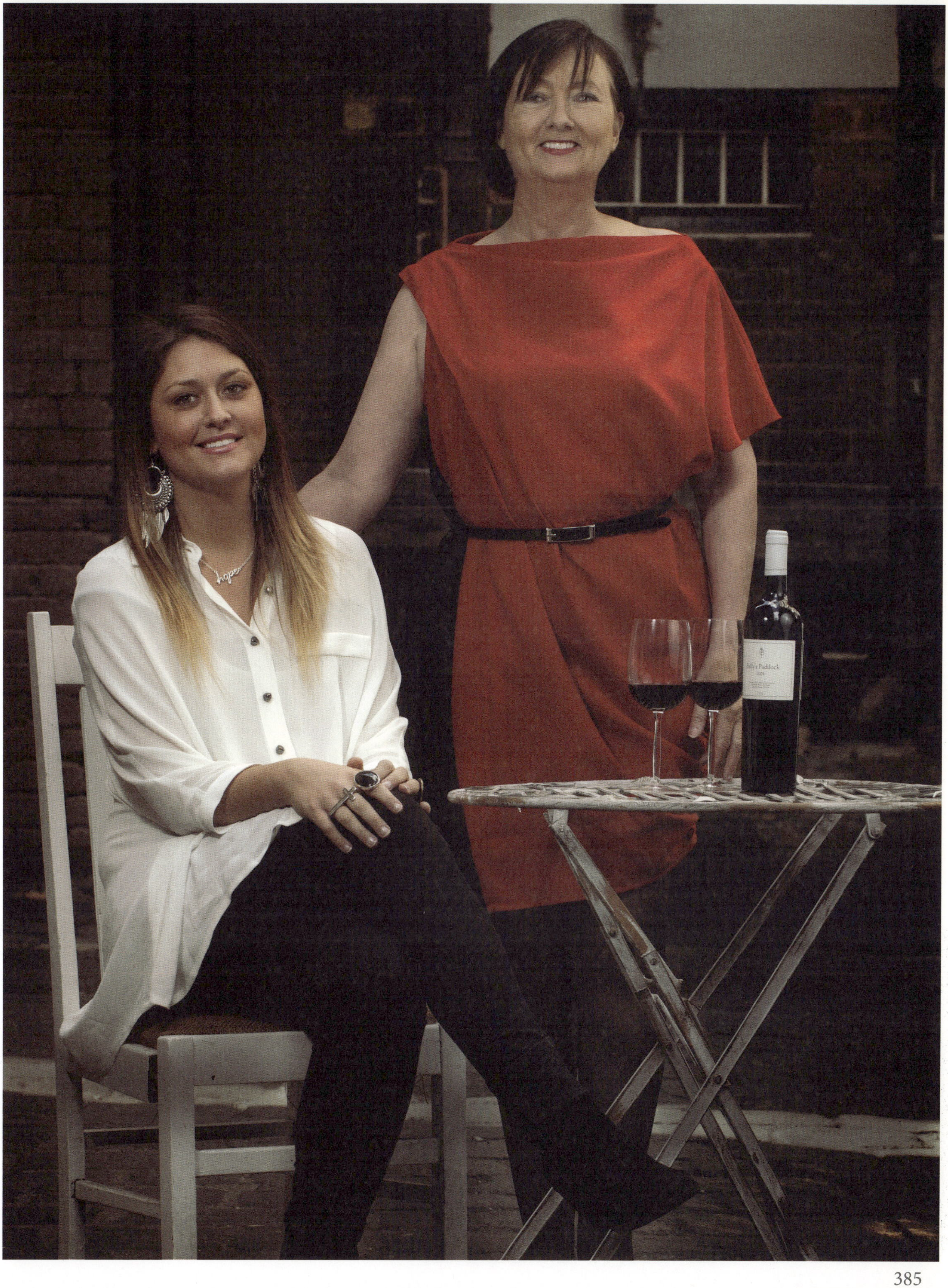

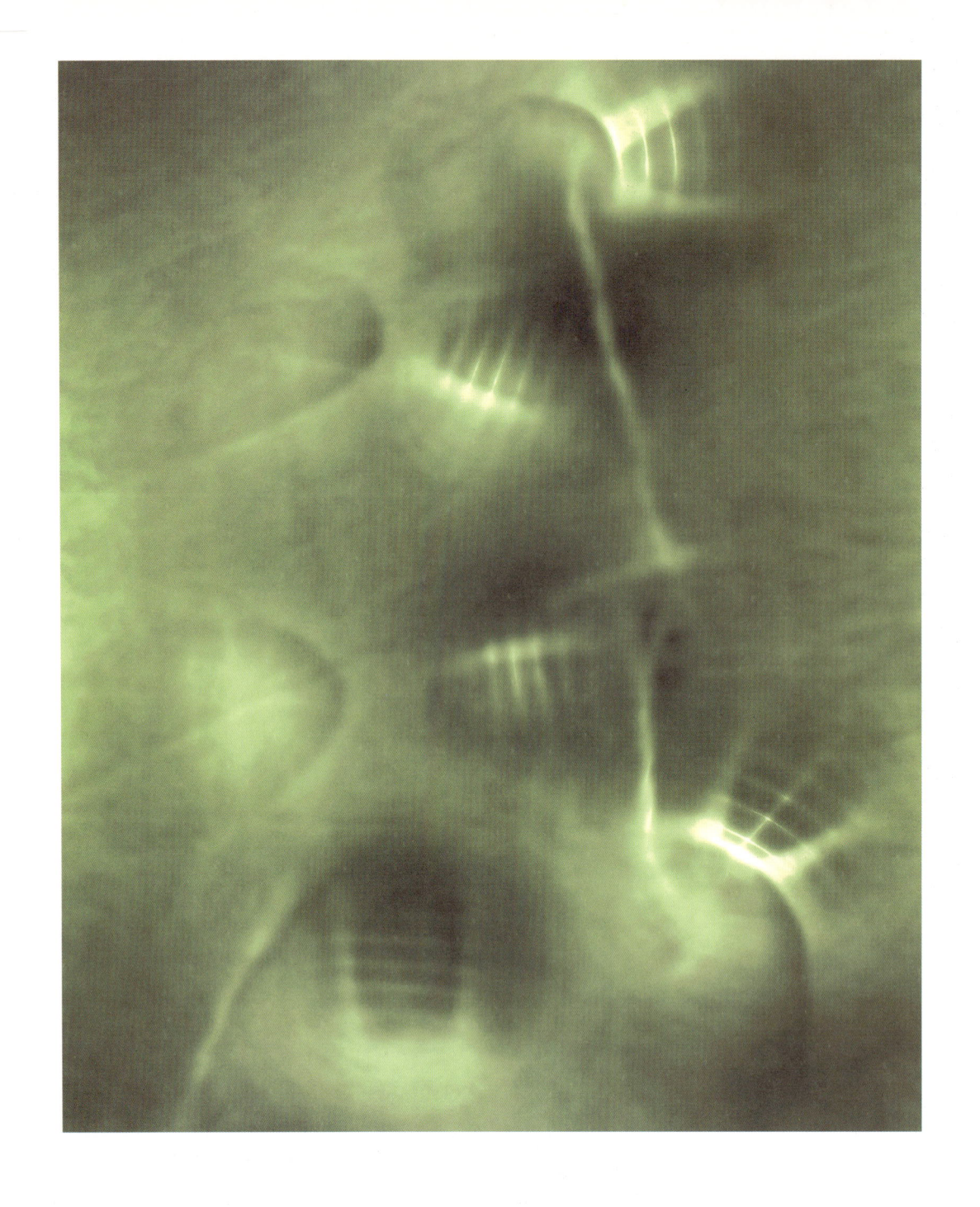

Brad Hill Imaging

# ABOUT THE PHOTOGRAPHER

Brad Hill is a Melbourne based commercial and architectural freelance photographer. This is the second book he has worked on with Jonette and Dani and being a resident of central Melbourne for more than 15 years, give or take a few years of travel, this project gave him the opportunity to highlight a side of Melbourne he knows and understands.

"This project emphasised to me how much the city has become a part of me slowly over time. You get to know its different moods and atmosphere instinctively as seasons change, as fashions evolve, as politics and economy ebb and flow... it does this both silently and with a bang as it continually renews and decays before your eyes."

"I'm not saying this is any different from a middle suburb or a country town but the concentration of humanity and urban form complicates or hides things and you really need to force yourself to stop and look around and really see what is really going on over time. If you do you will see a strong and deep identity, spirit or attitude that represents us as a people and I think it is something that all Victorians can be proud of."

Brad shoots for several magazines and private clients and more of his work can be found at -

# Index

## A

| | |
|---|---|
| 24 Moons | 70 |
| Aaron Whitney | 346 |
| About the Authors | 384 |
| About the Photographer | 386 |
| ACDC Lane | 66 |
| Agus Putro | 354 |
| Anthony Humphries | 362 |
| Artemis Lane | 72 |

## B

| | |
|---|---|
| Baccala Alla Livornese | 372 |
| Bank Place | 80 |
| Bar 1806 | 174 |
| Bar Mile | 194 |
| Baroq House | 169 |
| Berlin Bar | 146 |
| Bligh Place | 88 |
| Blind Alley | 266 |
| Block Arcade | 94 |
| Blue Diamond Club | 278 |
| Bluestone Restaurant | 193 |
| Bopha Devi | 292, 354 |
| Bourke St | 100 |
| Braised Pork Belly | 362 |
| Brother Baba Budan | 220 |
| Bunjil, The Eagle | 28 |

## C

| | |
|---|---|
| Ca de Vin | 272, 370 |
| Cabinet Bar | 286 |
| Café Frais | 93 |
| Calamari with Chickpeas & Radicchio | 344 |
| Cambodian Amok | 354 |
| Carlton Hotel | 104 |
| Caterina Borsato | 281 |
| Caterinas Cucina e Bar | 280, 364 |
| Centre Place | 122 |
| Chan Uoy | 293 |
| Chicken Liver Parfait | 352 |
| Chin Chin | 195 |
| Chinatown | 128 |
| Chocolate Bread & Butter Pudding | 382 |
| Chocolate Buddha | 180, 366 |
| Chris Rodriguez | 360 |
| Christos Chalastras | 370 |
| Collins Quarter | 138, 352 |
| Collins St | 134 |
| Cookie | 158, 356 |
| Corrs Lane | 142 |
| Croft Alley | 148 |
| Croft Institute | 152 |
| Crusted Lamb Rack | 374 |
| Cured Ocean Trout | 358 |
| Curtin House | 154 |

# Index

## D

| | |
|---|---|
| Daniel Airo-Farulla | 372 |
| Daniele Wilton | 384 |
| Dominico Marzano | 368 |
| Drewery Lane | 164 |
| Duck Duck Goose Bistro | 76 |
| Duck Duck Goose Restaurant | 78 |

## E

| | |
|---|---|
| Emerald Peacock | 246 |
| Exhibition St | 170 |

## F

| | |
|---|---|
| Fad Lounge & Bar | 147 |
| Federation Square | 176 |
| Flinders Lane | 184 |
| Foreword | 9 |

## G

| | |
|---|---|
| Galician Octopus | 346 |
| Gavin Van Staden | 350 |
| George Pde | 196 |
| Gills Diner | 228 |
| Gin Palace | 304 |
| Grossi Cellar | 368 |
| Grossi Florentino | 108, 360 |
| Grossi Grill | 344 |
| Grossi Grill & Cellar | 110 |
| Guy Grossi | 372, 368, 360, 344 |

## H

| | |
|---|---|
| Harry Hajisaba | 378 |
| Hells Kitchen | 126 |
| Highlander Bar | 206 |
| Highlander Lane | 202 |
| Historical Timeline | 31 |
| Hoddle's Grid | 34 |
| Hopetoun Tearooms | 98, 378 |
| Horse Bazaar | 234 |
| Hosier Lane | 208 |

## I

| | |
|---|---|
| Il Solito Posto | 200 |
| Introduction | 16 |
| Izakaya Den | 306, 348 |

## J

| | |
|---|---|
| Jerome Borazio | 340 |
| Jonette George | 384 |
| Journal Canteen | 190 |

## K

| | |
|---|---|
| Kitchen Cat | 201 |

## L

| | |
|---|---|
| Laneway Story | 37 |

# Index

| | |
|---|---|
| Laneways | 54 |
| Le Petit Gateau | 226, 280 |
| Lily Blacks | 260 |
| Little Bourke St | 214 |
| Little Collins St | 222 |
| Little Lonsdale St | 230 |
| Longrain | 221 |
| Lonsdale St | 236 |
| Loop | 258 |
| Lustre Lounge | 127 |

## M

| | |
|---|---|
| Madame Brussells | 114 |
| Manchura Bar | 326 |
| Matteo Tine | 344 |
| McKillop St | 248 |
| Melbourne Map | 40 |
| Melbourne Today | 38 |
| Merchant | 140, 372 |
| Meyers Place | 254 |
| Michael Harrisson | 358 |
| Michael Nunn | 352 |
| Michel Dubois | 314, 298 |
| Michelle Goldsmith | 364 |
| Mitre Tavern | 86 |
| Movida | 212 |
| Movida Next Door | 213 |
| Murmur | 334 |

## N

| | |
|---|---|
| Narlimol Chantrapen | 356 |
| Nikki Smith | 376 |

## P

| | |
|---|---|
| Palmz at the Carlton | 106 |
| Papa Goose | 192 |
| Pavlova | 378 |
| Pellegrini's | 120 |
| Pierrick Boyer | 380 |
| Pink Alley | 262 |
| Ponyfish Island | 340 |
| Pork & Peanut Dumplings | 356 |
| Pork Belly | 350 |
| Portello Rosso | 332, 346 |
| Postal Lane | 268 |
| Punch Lane | 218, 376 |

## Q

| | |
|---|---|
| Queen St | 274 |

## R

| | |
|---|---|
| Ra Bar | 266 |
| Rainbow Alley | 282 |
| Rakaia Way | 288 |
| Rebecca Walk | 294 |
| Recipes | 342 |

# Index

| | |
|---|---|
| Red Hummingbird | 308 |
| Red Spice Road | 252, 350 |
| Rhubarb & Custard Tart | 376 |
| Risotto Venere with Bug Tails | 360 |
| Riverland Bar | 182 |
| Roasted Rack of Lamb | 370 |
| Robot | 92 |
| Rooftop Bar & Cinema | 162 |
| Roule Galette - Rebecca Walk | 298 |
| Roule Galette Scott Alley | 314 |
| Russell St | 300 |

## S

| | |
|---|---|
| Savage Club | 87 |
| Scott Alley | 310 |
| Seamstress | 240, 362 |
| Seamstress Cocktail Bar | 242 |
| Section 8 | 320 |
| Self Preservation | 116, 382 |
| Sensory Lab | 229 |
| Shake Oyako Don | 366 |
| Sharkfin House | 132 |
| Sisterbella's | 168 |
| Society | 121 |
| Spicy Tuna Tataki | 348 |
| Stan Delimitrou | 374 |
| Strawberry & Berry Almond Tart | 380 |
| Streat | 46 |
| Street Art | 42 |
| Supper Inn | 133 |
| Sweatshop | 244 |
| Syracuse Restaurant | 84, 358 |

## T

| | |
|---|---|
| Tattersalls Lane | 316 |
| Terra Rossa | 188, 374 |
| The Toff | 160 |
| The Waiters Club | 261 |
| Thousand Pound Bend | 235 |
| Tortellini di Zuccha | 368 |
| Transit | 183 |
| Tribal Ancestors | 28 |
| Trio of Rabbit | 364 |
| Tuscan Rooftop Bar | 118 |

## W

| | |
|---|---|
| Waratah Place | 322 |
| Warburton Lane | 328 |
| William Buckley | 29 |

## Y

| | |
|---|---|
| Yarra Footbridge | 336 |
| Yosuke Furukawa | 348 |